THE ROUGH GUIDE TO
FIJI

ROUGH
GUIDES

This third edition
Ian Osborn a

Contents

Introduction to

Fiji

Sun-drenched beaches, turquoise lagoons, swaying palm trees – Fiji supplies all the classic images of paradise. No wonder, then, that every year thousands of travellers come to this South Pacific archipelago for the ultimate island escape. With over three hundred islands to choose from, Fiji is a versatile destination. Whether you're after a luxury honeymoon retreat, a lively backpacker island or a family-friendly resort, you won't be disappointed. You'll also find a warm, hospitable people, an intriguing blend of Melanesians, Polynesians and Indians.

With a reliable tropical climate, a good tourist infrastructure, English as its main language and no jabs or pills to worry about, travelling in Fiji is as easy as it gets. As the hub of South Pacific tourism, the country attracts almost a million visitors a year, mostly from Australia and New Zealand, its largest "neighbours" lying over 2000km southeast. Of the northern-hemisphere travellers, many are backpackers from Europe or surfers and scuba divers from North America.

While it can be tempting to spend your whole time in Fiji sunbathing and sipping cocktails from coconuts, there are plenty of **activities** to lure you away from the beach. Within a ten-minute boat ride of most resorts you can find yourself **snorkelling** over colourful reefs, sometimes amid dolphins and manta rays, or **scuba diving** at pristine drop-offs covered in soft corals and sea fans. In addition, at the exposed edges of the reefs are some of the world's finest and most consistent **surfing breaks**. **Nature lovers** are also spoilt for choice, both underwater and on dry land, and wildlife-spotting opportunities are plentiful, whether you're seeking turtles, exotic birds or 3m-long tiger sharks.

Away from the beach resorts is a land of stunning mountains, rainforests and **remote villages**. Here you'll find big-hearted and hospitable Fijians living a similar lifestyle to their tribal ancestors. Staying a night or two at a village homestay will give you an authentic insight into the ethnic culture as well as the chance to sample **yaqona** or *kava*,

ABOVE SURFING MALOLO BARRIER REEF

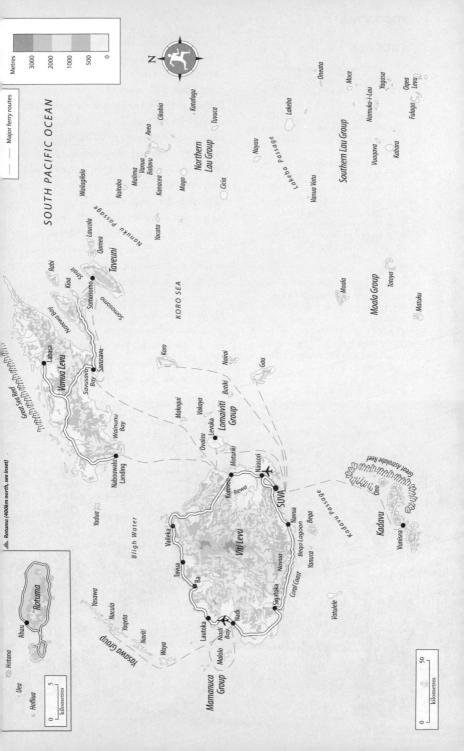

FACT FILE

- Fiji is made up of 333 **islands** and many tiny islets. Two thirds of Fiji's islands remain uninhabited.

- The **name** Fiji is an adaptation of the Tongan pronunciation of "Viti", originally written by Europeans as "Feejee".

- Of a total **population** of just over 900,000, roughly 500,000 are iTaukei (indigenous people) and 300,000 are Indo-Fijians (of Indian origin); the remainder are mostly Kailomas, meaning "in-between people" (of mixed Fijian-European blood), Rotumans (Polynesians) and Chinese.

- Some 87 percent of land in Fiji is tribally owned, with one in five of the population living a **subsistence lifestyle** in a communal village.

- English is one of three official **languages** in Fiji, and is spoken by almost all Fijians in addition to their mother-tongue.

the national drink. Fiji is also home to a large **Indian community** and their influence is seen in the delicious Indian food served in almost every town, Bollywood films showing in the cinema and vibrant Hindu festivals celebrated throughout the year. While Fiji is not renowned for its towns or **cities**, three are definitely worth exploring: quaint, colonial-era Levuka, yachting hotspot Savusavu, and Suva, the lively capital city and the best place to party in the South Pacific.

However long you spend in the country you'll notice an unhurried, good-humoured lifestyle. This is the essence of **Fiji Time** – an attitude that can be both inspiring and infuriating. Away from the organized upmarket resorts, life runs at a different pace; bus and ferry timetables serve more as guidelines and a simple meeting in a village can last for days. It's best to leave your inner control freak at home – you never know, you may come back a calmer person.

SEVEN OF THE BEST RESORTS

Fijian resorts range from simple beachside **bures** (traditional thatched huts) with cold-water showers to opulent **villas** with private spa pools. Out of almost a hundred resorts throughout the islands, we've picked our seven favourite.

Luxury *Jean-Michel Cousteau Resort*, Savusavu, Vanua Levu. See p.198
Budget *Barefoot Kuata*, Yasawa Islands. See p.95
Backpackers *Caqalai Island Resort*, Lomaiviti. See p.176
Romance *Matangi Island Resort*, off Taveuni. See p.208
Families *Volivoli Beach Resort*, north coast Viti Levu. See p.124
Divers *Taveuni Dive Resort*, Taveuni. See p.213
Eco-adventure *Colo-i-Suva Eco Lodge*, Suva, Viti Levu. See p.148

Where to go

The vast majority of travellers arrive at Nadi International Airport on **Viti Levu**, the archipelago's biggest island. Most stay around the suburban tourist hub of **Nadi** for a day or two to organize travel to other parts of the country, while some base themselves at **Denarau**'s international hotels and explore the surrounding country and offshore islands on day-trips. The most popular destination in Fiji lies visible off Nadi's coastline – a gorgeous collection of islands known as the **Mamanucas**. Here you'll find sublime beaches and tiny coral cays with suitably exotic names such as "Castaway" or "Treasure Island". Extending north of the Mamanucas are the palm-fringed volcanic **Yasawa Islands**, home to Fiji's most tantalizing snorkelling lagoons and a string of budget beach accommodation and secluded upmarket boutique resorts.

Almost as popular as the Mamanucas and Yasawa Islands, especially with families, are the beach resorts of the **Coral Coast** along the south coast of Viti Levu. Around an hour's

LEFT MUSKET COVE, MALOLO LAILAI IN THE MAMANUCAS

UNDERWATER FIJI

Dubbed "the soft coral capital of the world" by Jacques Cousteau, Fiji has ten thousand square kilometres of **coral reef** twisting and turning around every island, including the world's third longest barrier reef – the 200km-long Great Sea Reef, off the north coast of Vanua Levu. These amazing structures provide habitats for thousands of species of colourful fish, plants and animals, including sea fans, manta rays and reef sharks, and boast an astonishing biodiversity comparable to that found in rainforests. Throw in crystal-clear water and temperatures rarely below 25°C and you have one of the world's greatest snorkelling and diving destinations.

The three most common types of reef found in Fiji are **fringing reefs**, which are attached to an island and offer snorkelling direct from the shore; **patch reefs**, individual coral reefs found within a lagoon and usually attracting great numbers of reef fish; and **barrier reefs**, which are separated from the shore by a deep channel and feature steep drop-offs and strong currents.

FIJI'S TOP DIVE SITES

As well as reefs, divers will find big-shark encounters, exciting drift dives and plenty of wrecks to explore. The following are some of the islands' best dive sites:

Beqa Lagoon, Pacific Harbour The best open-water shark dive on Earth. See p.118.
Rainbow Reef, between Vanua Levu and Taveuni Gorgeous soft corals and fast drift dives. See p.206.
E-6, Bligh Water The photographer's favourite, accessed by live-aboard boat. See p.35.
Namena Marine Reserve, off Savusavu This protected reserve teems with fish and pelagics. See p.198.
Naiqoro Passage, Kadavu Beautiful drift dive on the Astrolabe Reef. See p.162.
The Salamander, Mamanucas A 40m wreck now home to puffer fish. See p.79.

Author picks

Our authors have island-hopped around Fiji in search of pristine beaches, vibrant markets and memorable sights. They share their personal highlights here.

Explore urban life on Viti Levu Towns such as Sigatoka (p.110), Korovou (p.121), Tavua (p.126) and Ba (p.128) receive few foreign visitors, but exploring these urban pockets provides an authentic window into Fijian life.

Travel like a local Hop on a local bus or carrier truck, or ride on a cargo boat (p.179) to the outer islands and really get to know the Fijians.

Party in Suva After a week or so in the wilds, Suva's restaurant, bar and club scene (p.146) can seem quite heady. The locals are known for their fondness for a night out.

Go to church Fijians are very musical as well as deeply religious: church services (p.67) give you the chance to hear them belt out harmonious hymns.

Eat like a local The superlative kokoda (p.29), made with raw fish and lime juice, is a little like ceviche, but the addition of coconut milk trumps anything you'll find in Latin America.

Smell the flowers Fiji's orchids (p.66) and hibiscus flowers (the latter tucked behind your right ear if you're single, the left if you're taken) are wonderfully exotic and colourful. Taveuni has its own rare flower, the tagimaucia (p.213).

Sample kava Downing the merry-making (but non-alcoholic) *kava* (p.31) is almost like a religion in Fiji: try it at a cheesy resort ceremony or, better still, hunt down a village "grog" hall, or a streetside group for the real local experience.

Discover ancient Fiji Petroglyphs at Vatulele (p.156), shards of Lapita pottery embedded in the sands at Sigatoka (p.111) and huge ocean-going canoes in the Fiji Museum in Suva (p.139) are just three reminders of the country's early culture.

> Our author recommendations don't end here. We've flagged up our favourite places – a perfectly sited hotel, an atmospheric café, a special restaurant – throughout the Guide, highlighted with the ★ symbol.

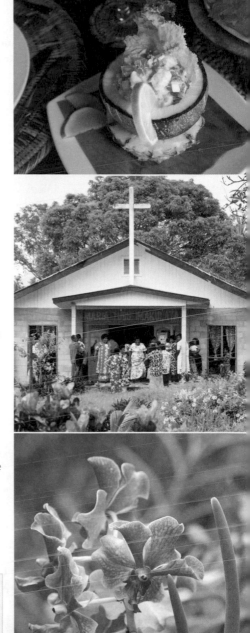

FROM TOP KOKODA; SUNDAY SERVICE IN NAVALA VILLAGE; ORCHID

drive from Nadi, these larger resorts offer good-value all-inclusive packages and a great choice of sightseeing tours. Inland is the rugged **rural interior of Viti Levu**. This region was once home to fierce, cannibalistic hill tribes and is crisscrossed with **hiking trails** including the route to Fiji's highest peak, **Mount Tomanivi**. Heading east along Viti Levu's south coast brings you to **Pacific Harbour**, Fiji's adventure-tour capital offering whitewater rafting, jet-ski safaris and world-renowned shark dives in the nearby **Beqa Lagoon**. Beyond is **Suva**, Fiji's cosmopolitan capital city and the hub for sea transport throughout the archipelago.

Of the outer islands, the most accessible are in the **Lomaiviti Group**, a short trip by boat from the east coast of Viti Levu. Here you'll find the quirky former capital of Levuka on the island of Ovalau and a good range of budget island resorts – a less commercial alternative to the Mamanucas and Yasawas. Spreading east for hundreds of kilometres is the vast **Lau Group**. Reached by small cruise ship or cargo boat from the mainland, these islands provide a true adventure for the intrepid traveller. South of Viti Levu is the snaking shape of **Kadavu**, a magnet for scuba divers thanks to the impressive Great Astrolabe Reef.

Fiji's second largest island, **Vanua Levu**, is in the northern part of the archipelago. On its south coast is the beautiful sailing anchorage of Savusavu while to the east is **Taveuni**, Fiji's lush "Garden Island". Half of Taveuni is protected as a national park and it's the best place in Fiji to hike through rainforest and encounter the country's rare, native birdlife. Offshore is the stunning Rainbow Reef, aptly named after its colourful soft corals. Far to the north of Vanua Levu, the tiny Polynesian island of **Rotuma** is politically part of Fiji but so isolated it feels like a different country, with its own language, culture and traditions.

When to go

The most comfortable time to visit is during the **dry season** between May and October when temperatures hover around 25°C by day and drop to a pleasant 19–20°C at night. At this time of year the almost constant southerly **trade winds** bring cool breezes off the sea and often quite blustery marine conditions favoured by sailors and windsurfers. Coinciding with the southern hemisphere winter, the dry season is also the **busiest** time to visit, with holiday-makers from New Zealand and Australia flocking to Fiji to escape the cold. Hotels in the popular resort areas are often booked months in advance, especially around the **school holidays** between June and July.

The summer months from November to April are known as the **wet season** when temperatures rise to a fairly constant 31°C but with greatly increased humidity. Rainfall during these months is substantially higher, although most of it falls in sudden torrential **tropical downpours**, usually in the mid-afternoon. Mornings and late afternoons generally remain sunny and the sea is often beautifully **calm** – a great time for scuba divers. During the wet season the islands are lush with vegetation and waterfalls are at their most impressive; however, walking trails can get slippery and dirt roads impassable. Low-pressure systems between December and April can bring a bout of cloud and rain lasting up to five days and, in extreme cases, **tropical cyclones** can develop. Direct hits on the islands are infrequent and damage is usually localized, although in 2016 the major cyclone Winston caused significant and substantial damage across the country (see box, p.26).

AVERAGE MONTHLY TEMPERATURES AND RAINFALL

	Jan	Feb	Mar	Apr	May	Jun	Jul	Aug	Sep	Oct	Nov	Dec
NADI												
Max/min (°C)	32/23	32/23	31/23	31/22	30/20	29/19	29/18	28/19	29/20	30/21	31/22	32/22
Max/min (°F)	90/73	90/73	88/73	88/72	86/68	84/66	84/64	82/66	84/68	86/70	88/72	90/72
Rainfall (mm)	343	292	341	160	89	65	45	65	70	102	132	178
SUVA												
Max/min (°C)	31/24	31/24	31/24	30/23	29/22	28/21	27/21	26/20	27/21	28/22	29/23	30/24
Max/min (°F)	88/75	88/75	88/75	86/73	84/72	82/70	81/70	79/68	81/70	82/72	84/73	86/75
Rainfall (mm)	371	265	374	366	270	163	136	158	177	221	245	277

15

things not to miss

It's not possible to see everything that Fiji has to offer in one trip – and we don't suggest you try. What follows is a selective and subjective taste of the islands' highlights: from lush rainforests and quaint villages to the best activities on and off the water. All entries have a page reference to take you straight into the Guide, where you can find out more. Coloured numbers refer to chapters in the Guide section.

1 NAVALA VILLAGE
Page 130

Fiji's most picturesque village, set deep in the highlands of Viti Levu and home to over two hundred traditional handcrafted bures.

2 LABASA
Page 190

Get off the tourist trail and visit this charming town, with its attractive river, surrounded by stunning and seldom explored countryside.

3 INDO-FIJIAN CULTURE
Page 53

Fiji's Hindu temples come alive throughout the year with exuberant festivals, the most spectacular being at Nadi's colourful Sri Siva Subrahmaniya Swami Temple.

4 SNORKELLING
Page 35

With colourful coral reefs found off almost every beach, Fiji is a fantastic place to slip on a pair of fins and dive in.

5 ISLAND-HOPPING THE MAMANUCAS AND YASAWA ISLANDS

Sample relaxed backpacker resorts or treat yourself to a luxury cruise.

6 RIVER RAFTING

Head deep into the mystical Namosi Highlands on a whitewater rafting trip.

7 MEKE DANCE NIGHT

The classic Fijian night out – traditional dancing accompanied by a feast of roast pig cooked in an underground oven.

8 SEA-KAYAKING

Paddle your way around the islands, stopping at fishing villages and camping under the stars.

9 FIJI MUSEUM

Killing stones, cannibal forks and the half-eaten shoe of the unfortunate Rev Thomas Baker are a few of the more gruesome exhibits at Fiji's best museum.

10 LEVUKA

Fiji's most beguiling town, a colonial museum piece full of stories and colourful locals.

11 HIKING IN THE YASAWAS
Page 94

Circumnavigate beautiful Waya Island, then hike to the summit of Vatuvula for stunning views, or explore the tropical vegetation of Tavewa.

12 MARKETS
Page 39

A slice of real Fiji – the bustling markets sell every imaginable type of exotic fruit, vegetable and seafood.

13 SPENDING A NIGHT IN A VILLAGE
Page 40

Sit cross-legged on the floor in one of Fiji's many rural villages and enjoy a local dinner, while Fijians perform a *kava* ceremony.

14 SWIMMING WITH SHARKS
Pages 118 & 93

Encounter mean-looking bull sharks and the odd tiger on shark-feeding dives at Beqa Lagoon or off Kuata; otherwise don your snorkel gear to spot reef sharks at Mouya Reef.

15 BIRDWATCHING IN BOUMA
Page 208

A huge tract of protected rainforest on Taveuni, Bouma National Heritage Park is littered with waterfalls and home to some fantastic birdlife, including pretty parrots, orange doves and the elusive silktail.

13

14

15

Itineraries

With 333 islands to choose from, you'll need a focus for your Fijian travels, though any itinerary should include at least one boat trip. Desert-island beaches are most people's image of the country, with good reason, but you'll also find densely forested mountain landscapes, lively towns and resolutely traditional villages. These itineraries will help you explore the highlights.

FIJI TASTER: BEACHES, VILLAGES AND ISLANDS

This popular backpacker route takes in the bustle of Nadi and the tranquil gardens of Viti Levu, then island-hops through the Mamanucas and Yasawa Islands, where you can lounge on beaches and snorkel in beautiful lagoons. You could do the trip in ten days, but once on the islands you'll surely want to linger longer.

❶ **Nadi** This tourist town is a great place to start your tour and plan your trip, with plenty of affordable accommodation around Wailoaloa Beach. **See p.50**

❷ **Sabeto Valley** Most tours include a free pick-up from Nadi hotels to the spectacular orchid gardens, therapeutic mud pools and exhilarating zip wires of the Sabeto Valley. **See p.65**

❸ **Mana Island** Head to Mana Island in the Mamanucas, with its beautiful beaches and coral reefs right off the shoreline – you can visit on a day-trip from Nadi, or stay longer for excellent diving and snorkelling. **See p.86**

❹ **Waya** Scenic Waya and Wayasewa are highlights of the Yasawas, with rocky peaks, walking tracks and white sand beaches, plus shark dives and snorkelling trips. **See p.94**

❺ **Naviti** The largest of the Yasawas, Naviti features some great snorkelling opportunities, particularly the blue depths and manta rays of the Drawaqa Lagoon. **See p.95**

❻ **The northern Yasawas** With a good range of accommodation from locally owned backpacker resorts to fantastic village stays, these low-lying islands boast breathtaking beaches, turquoise lagoons and the limestone caves of Sawa-i-Lau. **See p.97**

❼ **Beachcomber** Last stop before heading back to Nadi is the party island of Beachcomber, a tiny coral speck in the Mamanucas. **See p.80**

EXPLORING VITI LEVU

Fiji's largest island has a bit of everything: townscapes, ancient sites and gorgeous beaches. This route takes you on a full circuit of the island, with a detour to Ovalau. Allow at least ten days.

❶ **Nadi** Starting out at Nadi, take the coastal bus southeast around the island along the Queens Road. **See p.50**

❷ **The Coral Coast** One of Fiji's most attractive stretches of coastline to drive along, the Coral Coast passes by pretty bays and through verdant rainforest. **See p.115**

❸ **Pacific Harbour** Fiji's adrenalin capital is a great place for backpackers to jet-ski, go on rafting expeditions and shark dives. **See p.116**

❹ **Suva** The only real city in Fiji, Suva has plenty of metropolitan charm: colonial architecture, some excellent Indo-Fijian restaurants, bars and clubs and a fine museum. **See p.134**

ABOVE FIJI'S CORAL COAST

⑤ Ovalau This volcanic island with mountain rainforest is a fascinating diversion from the main island. Its highpoint is laidback Levuka, Fiji's former capital and a World Heritage Site. **See p.168**

⑥ Kings Road Once you are back on the main island of Viti Levu, head over to Nadi via the northern Kings Road. If you have time to dawdle, stop off at some of the quaint towns along the way. **See p.121**

VANUA LEVU AND TAVEUNI: THE FRIENDLY NORTH

Small planes, ferries, speedboats and buses provide the transport for this itinerary through northern Vanua Levu, and east to the garden island of Taveuni. Allow ten days to explore the highlights – Savusavu and Taveuni – with as much leisure as possible.

❶ Labasa From Nadi, fly to Labasa and mingle with the locals in Fiji's most absorbing market, then take a boat trip upriver past sleepy villages. **See p.190**

❷ Labasa hills and villages Ride with the locals in an open-sided bus stopping at pretty settlements, such as Vunivau. **See p.193**

❸ Savusavu Stay a day or two in Savusavu, a small town with hot springs, mountain walks and some decent restaurants and bars overlooking the glorious bay. **See p.194**

❹ Buca Bay dive resorts From Natuvu, a couple of dive resorts can send a speedboat to collect you, and you can enjoy a few days of utter seclusion. **See p.202**

❺ Kioa Island Spend time in the tightly-knit fishing community on this unusual island, settled by Tuvaluans – it's a hidden gem between Vanua Levu and Taveuni. **See p.202**

❻ Taveuni There are some great activities on verdant Taveuni, including natural rock slides, birdwatching, hikes, snorkelling tours, dives and famous surf breaks. **See p.203**

❼ Suva Take a passenger ferry back to Fiji's lively capital for some intrepid urban exploration. **See p.134**

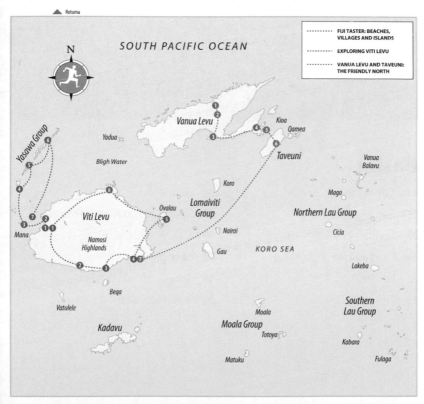

SEA-KAYAKING

Basics

Getting there

Fiji is the travel hub for the South Pacific, and a popular stopover on round-the-world tickets. The majority of direct flights arrive from New Zealand, Australia or Los Angeles, and travellers from North America or Europe must usually connect through one of these. Arriving by boat is only possible on a private yacht or on one of the cruise ships calling in at Denarau or Suva.

From Australia or New Zealand, Fiji's main tourism market, there are heaps of **package deals** available that include flights. Most travel agents focus on the ever-popular resorts in the Mamanucas, international hotels on Denarau and the large resorts along the Coral Coast on the main island. Many offer discounts and deals, particularly in the low season months of November, February and March. From North America, the UK or continental Europe, package options are more limited, although you should find Fiji as a stopover on many round-the-world tickets.

Most packages tend to be based in a single resort for one or two weeks, so if you want to head to the outer islands or explore several different islands or regions you'll have to book your flights independently, then reserve your accommodation direct with the hotels or through a hotel booking site.

Flights from the US and Canada

The only airline that flies direct to Fiji from **North America** is Fiji Airways, which code shares with Qantas and American Airlines. It has daily direct flights from **Los Angeles**, twice weekly flights **from San Francisco**, plus three flights a week from **Honolulu**. Nonstop flights from Los Angeles (11hr 20min) and San Francisco (11hr 10min) cost from US$1600 return, while flights from Honolulu (6hr 40min) start at US$1100.

There are no direct flights to Fiji **from Canada**, so the easiest route is to travel via San Francisco or Los Angeles. You may find lower fares, however, by flying on the more popular routes to Auckland, Brisbane or Sydney, then getting onwards flights from there (see below).

Flights from the UK and Europe

From the **UK**, you have the choice of travelling west via North America or east via Asia – it's 16,000km and takes around 24 hours either way. Fares follow the high and low seasons between Europe and North America or Europe and Australia, with June to August and the Christmas holidays being particularly busy, with fewer discounted deals available.

The most popular routes tend to be through Asia, with return flights from the UK starting at £1100: Korean Air flies **via Seoul**, while Fiji Airways (code shares with Qantas and Cathay Pacific) flies **via Hong Kong** or **Singapore**. Flights via North America transit through **Los Angeles** or **San Francisco** (see above), with fares starting at £1300.

The cheapest option is to fly to Fiji from the UK with Qantas or Virgin **via Australia** (see below), where you can opt for a stopover: flights on this route start at £970, but take upwards of 30hr.

Flights from Australia, New Zealand and South Africa

There are frequent daily flights to Fiji from **Australia and New Zealand,** with the best deals and accommodation packages available direct from the airlines.

Three airlines fly direct from **Australia**: Virgin Australia and Fiji Airways depart daily from **Brisbane** (3hr 30min; A$700) and **Sydney** (4hr; A$700), while Fiji Airways also offer direct daily flights from **Melbourne** (4hr 50min; A$800), and twice weekly flights from Adelaide (5hr; A$800); JetStar flies four times a week from Sydney (4hr; A$700).

You can fly from **New Zealand** to Fiji with Fiji Airways or Air New Zealand; both have daily flights from **Auckland** (3hr; NZ$800), while Fiji Airways also has two weekly flights from **Wellington** (3hr 45min; NZ$800) and three weekly flights from **Christchurch** (4hr; NZ$850).

The most direct route from **South Africa** is to fly to Sydney or Auckland and from there on to Fiji.

A BETTER KIND OF TRAVEL

At Rough Guides we are passionately committed to travel. We believe it helps us understand the world we live in and the people we share it with – and of course tourism is vital to many developing economies. But the scale of modern tourism has also damaged some places irreparably, and climate change is accelerated by most forms of transport, especially flying. All Rough Guides' flights are carbon-offset, and every year we donate money to a variety of environmental charities.

Flights from elsewhere in the Pacific

Flying to Fiji from elsewhere in the South Pacific is generally easy, although often quite expensive. Fiji Airways flies direct to Nadi from Nuku'alofa, **Tonga** (4 weekly, plus 1 flight weekly to Suva; 1hr 20min; F$670 one way); Vava'u, Tonga (2 weekly; 2hr 10min; F$830 one way); Funafuti, **Tuvalu** (2 weekly to Suva; 2hr 35min; F$1020 one way); Port Vila, **Vanuatu** (4 weekly; 2hr 35min; F$690 one way); Apia, **Samoa** (6 weekly; 2hr 50min; F$750 one way); Tarawa, **Kiribati** (2 weekly; 3hr; F$2030 one way); Christmas Island, Kiribati (1 weekly; 4hr 40min; F$2030 one way); and Honolulu, **Hawaii** (3 weekly; 6hr 30min; F$1960 one way).

Other regional airlines serving Nadi include Aircalin from Noumea, **New Caledonia** (1 weekly; 2hr; F$950 one way); Air Vanuatu from Port Vila, **Vanuatu** (1 weekly; 1hr 40min; F$690 one way); Solomon Airlines from Honiara, **Solomon Islands** (1 weekly; 3hr 15min; F$870 one way); Nauru Airlines from **Nauru** (1 weekly; 3hr 10min; F$1570 one way); and Air Nuigini from Port Moresby, **Papua New Guinea** (2 weekly; 4hr 10min; F$1060 one way). There are no direct flights between Fiji and the Cook Islands, Tahiti or Easter Island – the easiest way to get to Fiji from these eastern Polynesian destinations is via Auckland or Los Angeles.

AIRLINES

Aircalin Ⓦ aircalin.com
Air Nuigini Ⓦ airniugini.com.pg
Air New Zealand Ⓦ airnz.co.nz
Air Vanuatu Ⓦ airvanuatu.com
American Ⓦ aa.com
Cathay Pacific Ⓦ cathaypacific.com
Fiji Airways Ⓦ fijiairways.com
JetStar Ⓦ jetstar.com
Korean Air Ⓦ koreanair.com
Nauru Airlines Ⓦ nauruairlines.com.au
Qantas Ⓦ qantas.com
Solomon Airlines Ⓦ flysolomons.com
Virgin Australia Ⓦ virginaustralia.com

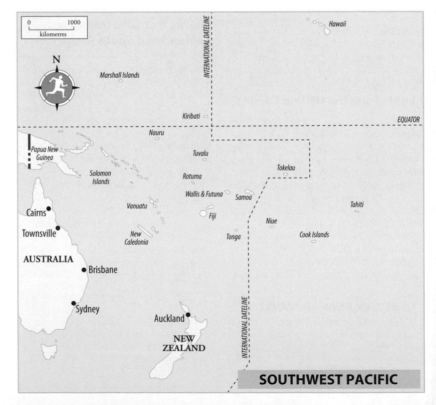

SOUTHWEST PACIFIC

ONLINE BOOKING

🔱 ebookers.com
🔱 expedia.com
🔱 lastminute.com
🔱 travelocity.com
🔱 travelonline.com
🔱 zuji.com

AGENTS AND OPERATORS

All Ways UK ☎ 01628 526 585, 🔱 awtm.co.uk. Long-established independent travel agent offering tailor-made trips to Fiji and the South Pacific.

Beautiful Pacific Fiji ☎ 672 2600, 🔱 beautifulpacific.com. South Pacific travel specialist offering discounted room-only deals at the smaller, boutique-style resorts in Fiji.

Rosie Holidays Fiji ☎ 672 2755, 🔱 rosiefiji.com. Locally owned and the oldest and largest inbound operator in Fiji with a competitive and very knowledgeable travel agency.

Spacifica Travel Australia ☎ 1800 800 722, 🔱 spacificatravel.com. Travel company offering package deals around Fiji and the South Pacific.

STA Travel US ☎ 1 800 781 4040, UK ☎ 0333 321 0099, Australia ☎ 134 782, New Zealand ☎ 0800 474 400, SA ☎ 0861 781 781; 🔱 statravel.com. Worldwide specialists in independent travel; also student IDs, travel insurance, car rental and more. Good discounts for students and under-26s.

Trailfinders UK ☎ 020 7368 1200, Republic of Ireland ☎ 01 677 7888; 🔱 trailfinders.com. One of the best-informed and most efficient agents for independent travellers.

Getting to Fiji by boat

Although a romantic proposition, arriving in Fiji **by boat** is tricky unless you're on a private yacht – it's a five- to ten-day journey up from New Zealand depending on the weather, or at least a month's sailing across the Pacific from the US west coast. Several large **cruise liners** visit Fiji but usually spend only a few days in Nadi Bay before visiting one of the port towns of Lautoka, Suva or Savusavu and then cruising around the islands for snorkelling trips, and then heading back to the open seas.

If you're arriving **by yacht**, Fiji has four main **ports of entry**, Suva, Lautoka, Levuka and Malau, all overseen by Fiji Ports (🔱 www.fijiports.com.fj, ☎ 331 2700, ☎ 330 0064). Clearance must be requested via Customs (☎ 330 2864, ✉ yachtsreport@frca .org.fj, 🔱 www.frca.org.fj/yachts-arrival/) at least 48 hours before arrival. For detailed sailing info, Yacht Help (☎ 675 0911, 🔱 yachthelp.com), based at Port Denarau on Viti Levu publishes the extremely useful and free *Fiji Marine Guide*; they'll also try and find a yacht charter if you don't have your own boat. Otherwise, you may find **crew work** at one of the marinas and possibly passage on to New Zealand,

Australia or California. Most yachts depart Fiji by September or October before the start of the hurricane season and start to arrive again, often having sailed via Tonga or Tahiti, from May to August.

Finding passage on a **container ship** is no longer possible, due to heightened security concerns.

CRUISES

P&O Cruises Australia ☎ 1300 159 454, New Zealand ☎ 0800 780 716; 🔱 pocruises.com.au. Large passenger cruise ships departing Sydney, Brisbane and Auckland and visiting various ports including Denarau, Suva, Lautoka and Savusavu as well as Beqa and the Yasawas, usually on twelve-day itineraries.

Getting around

Fiji is spread over a huge area of the southwest Pacific, covering almost 1.3 million square kilometres. On a map, the islands may look close enough together to hop between, but with limited infrastructure this can be a time-consuming process, often involving back-tracking to either Nadi or Suva. Viti Levu, the main island, is extremely well connected by public transport and easy to explore, as are the popular beach destinations of the Mamanucas and Yasawa Islands, connected by fast catamaran. Exploring further afield, though, requires patience and a sense of adventure, with cumbersome passenger ferries and cargo boats visiting the outer islands, sometimes only on a monthly basis, and flights in small propeller planes landing on gravel or grass airstrips.

Nadi, on the main island of Viti Levu, is the nation's tourist hub, home to the international and main domestic airport and with sea access to the Mamanucas. **Suva**, 120km away on the opposite side of the mainland, is the transport hub for all outer-island shipping, as well as having air access to twelve outer-island airstrips.

On the two largest islands of **Viti Levu** and **Vanua Levu**, as well as on **Taveuni**, exceptionally cheap buses travel around the coast and countryside on a fairly regular basis and carrier vans or taxis can be hired for private tours. On all other islands, though, getting around usually involves a boat journey, often in a small, ten-passenger fibreglass boat with a 60HP single engine, and these, when chartered, are expensive. Hitching a ride with the locals is much cheaper but more often than not boats are filled to the brim, sometimes with as many as twenty large Fijians plus their luggage.

By air

Fiji's **domestic flight network** is dominated by **Fiji Link**, the domestic arm of the government-owned Fiji Airways (☎672 0888, ⓦ fijiairways.com), and served by small twin-propeller planes only. While flying in such aircraft may cause a little nervousness, it is by far the quickest way to get around. Flights are far from cheap, however, with standard fares F$235 one-way from Nadi to Suva and up to F$685 from Nadi to far-flung Rotuma, though if you plan ahead, online specials are usually half the price. Availability is seldom a problem, except at Christmas when flights can be booked out months in advance. The **baggage allowance** on internal flights is a meagre 15kg per person: if you plan on travelling with your own scuba diving equipment or surfboard, check with the airline in advance. Alternatively, **Northern Air** (☎992 2449, ⓦ www .northernairfiji.com.fj), operates from Nausori Airport (Suva) only and flies to Levuka, Labasa, Savusavu, Taveuni, Gau and Moala.

Two **seaplane** companies operate in Fiji: Turtle Airways (☎672 1888, ⓦ turtleairways.com) based at Wailoaloa Beach in Nadi, and Pacific Island Air (☎672 5644, ⓦ pacificislandair.com) based at Nadi Airport. Turtle Airways offers a daily flight to Turtle Island in the northern part of the Yasawas for F$380 one way, with a minimum of two passengers, but you must pre-arrange a boat transfer on to your intended destination – departure times vary and can only be advised the day before based on sea conditions. There are also two **helicopter** companies shuttling guests to upmarket resorts: Island Hoppers (☎672 0410, ⓦ helicopters.com.fj) based at Nadi Airport, and Heli-Tours Fiji (☎675 0255, ⓦ helitoursfiji.com) based at Denarau. The baggage allowance on seaplanes and helicopters is also 15kg per person, with excess charges thereafter.

For an overview of air routes see the map below; details of individual flights are given throughout the Guide.

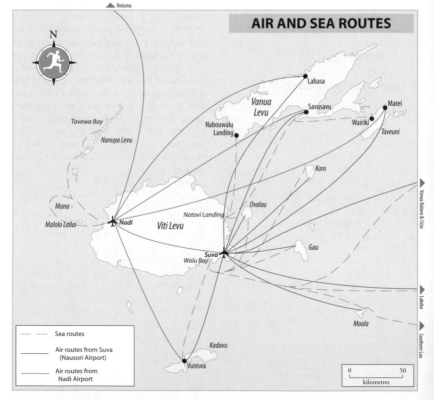

AIR AND SEA ROUTES

By passenger ferry and cargo boat

The busy tourist destinations of the Mamanucas are served by fast **passenger catamarans** offering fabulous views from their upper decks and enclosed air-conditioned seating on the lower levels. By contrast, the bulky and ageing **vehicle and passenger ferries** visiting Kadavu, Vanua Levu, Taveuni and the Lomaiviti Group suffer particularly from sea swell, and often meander around an erratic schedule. Christmas is especially hectic, with overladen boats common during the summer school break from early December to late January, while rough seas often disrupt schedules between December and April. While the daily fast ferry service to the Yasawas is fairly pricey (F$180 one way, or F$420 for 5 days' travel), it only costs around F$55 for the long trip from Lautoka to Savusavu.

Cargo boats (see box, p.179) have been plying Fiji's waters since the pioneering days of the late nineteenth century, bringing in trade, exporting copra and connecting the islanders with the outside world. It is still common practice for passengers to join cargo boats supplying the outer islands, usually sitting and sleeping on deck amidst barrels of oil, boxes of tinned meat and bunches of bananas. For those with a little time and a spirit of adventure, it's a chance to rub shoulders with Fijians from all walks of life, and it's cheap and cheerful, too: the route from Suva to Kadavu, for example, will set you back just F$45 one way.

For an overview of sea routes see the map opposite; details of individual ferries and cargo ships are given throughout the Guide.

By bus

With no rail service and few people owning cars, **buses** are the only practical way to affordably get around the large islands of Viti Levu and Vanua Levu. Both islands have reliable, frequent and exceptionally cheap bus services operating out of all town centres.

Express buses between towns on Viti Levu and Vanua Levu are modern, comfortable a/c vehicles, often with free wi-fi; the five-hour journey between Nadi and Suva costs around F$20. **Local buses**, however, are a lot more fun: usually with open-sided windows, they visit pretty much every rural location imaginable, travelling along dirt roads, up steep mountains and across narrow wooden plank bridges over rivers, stopping on request. If you prefer something more organized, an a/c tourist bus run by Feejee Experience (☎672 5950, ⓦfeejeeexperience.com) circumnavigates Viti Levu on a seven-day adventure journey (from F$910 including dorm accommodation). A very limited bus schedule operates on **Ovalau** and **Taveuni**, mostly for shuttling kids back and forth from school, but on all other islands buses are non-existent.

Minivans and carrier vans

Also running in urban centres and speeding along the main roads are ten-seater **minivans**, which stop by the roadside to pick up waiting passengers for the same fare as a bus. Many operate illegally and drive carelessly but if your only consideration is to get from A to B quickly and cheaply, they're a good option. More basic **carrier vans**, with an open back usually covered by tarpaulin and with a wooden bench along each side, travel along the rural dirt roads carrying people and their produce between the villages and town markets.

By car

On the main island of Viti Levu **a car** is without doubt the best way to explore the countryside. Although buses and carrier vans travel to most regions, the freedom to stop at will for photos, to chat with locals along the way and simply to travel at your own convenience is both pleasurable and time saving. **Renting a car** is straightforward using your home licence, but you must be aged 21 or older. Rates are relatively cheap, starting at F$100 per day including insurance (twenty percent more on Vanua Levu and Taveuni due to less competition and poor road conditions), but the relatively high cost of fuel (presently around F$1.90 per litre), which is fixed by the government, makes longer trips quite expensive.

It's a good idea to rent a **4WD**, or, at the very least, a car with high clearance – most roads off the coastal highway are unsealed, of compacted dirt and often littered with crater-sized potholes; with rain (and it often rains in the mountains) these roads become very slippery and sometimes impassable without a 4WD. Rental companies tend to void insurance for breakdowns or accidents on dirt roads so check in detail beforehand.

The same applies to Vanua Levu, though renting is not so straightforward, with only a couple of rental firms in Savusavu and Labasa, and these have only a few cars available, so pre-booking is advisable. The only other island where you can rent a car is Taveuni.

Driving tips

Driving between towns along the sealed coastal road of Viti Levu is very straightforward, but turning off the main road can be intimidating, with absolutely no **signposts** and roads splitting and veering in every direction. Keep an eye open for the tiny white roadside markers which indicate distance from set points, usually from major towns or turn-offs and the main connecting roads. There are no decent maps available to help navigation in the countryside – the only option is to ask for directions along the way.

The most common **hazards** apart from the potholes are mindless pedestrians and stray animals. Driving is on the left, with the **speed limit** generally set at 40kmph through towns, 60kmph in the suburbs and 80kmph elsewhere. If you **break down**, call your car rental company which should provide you with a 24hr service number – but be warned there are few telephones along the roadside and mobile phone coverage is pretty sporadic in rural areas.

Car rental

The following major **car rental** companies have offices at Nadi Airport, where you can arrange a rental before your trip. Independent local companies are listed throughout the Guide.

CAR RENTAL AGENCIES

Avis US and Canada ☎ 1 800 633 3469, UK ☎ 0845 581 8181, Republic of Ireland ☎ 021 428 1111, Australia ☎ 13 63 33, New Zealand 0800 655 111; ⓦ avis.com.
Budget US ☎ 1 800 218 7992, Canada ☎ 1 800 268 8900, UK ☎ 0845 544 3455, Australia ☎ 1300 362 848, New Zealand ☎ 0800 283 438; ⓦ budget.com.

Hertz US & Canada ☎ 1 800 654 3131, UK ☎ 020 7026 0077, Republic of Ireland ☎ 01 676 7476, Australia ☎ 133 039, New Zealand ☎ 0800 654 321; ⓦ hertz.com.
Thrifty US and Canada ☎ 1 800 847 4389, UK ☎ 0333 332 1222 , Republic of Ireland ☎ 0207 365 3384, Australia ☎ 1300 367 227, New Zealand ☎ 03 359 2721; ⓦ www.thrifty.com.

Taxis

Getting about **by taxi** in Nadi and Suva is cheap and practical, regulated by the government with flag-fall set at F$1.50 between 6am and 10pm (F$2 outside these hours), plus 10¢ for every 100m travelled, all calculated by meter. Competition is fierce, with unlicensed minivans scouring the streets and picking up passengers along the way, charging F$2 for an inter-urban journey.

Hiring a taxi for rural **sightseeing** or travel between towns is a good option if you don't want to drive yourself, and works out as a cheap alternative if travelling with three or more people. Negotiate a rate beforehand and expect to pay around F$100 for half a day depending on how far you want to travel.

By bicycle and motor scooter

There are few **cyclists** to be found on Fiji's shoulderless, potholed roads, and good reason for it – cyclists are shown little courtesy from motorists. However, exploring rural Viti Levu or Vanua Levu by bicycle will certainly draw attention and conversation when passing through villages and should be a great adventure for those confident enough to try. Unless you bring your own bike though, you'll have to buy one in Nadi, Suva or Labasa, but don't expect quality.

TROPICAL CYCLONE WINSTON

The most intense tropical cyclone ever recorded in the Southern Hemisphere bounced around Fiji's islands on 20–21 February 2016. Entering the country from the east, **Cyclone Winston** hit the northern Lau islands first with gusts of over 300km/h, then passed between Taveuni and Koro, with ten-minute sustained winds of 230km/h. It then travelled west between Vanua Levu and Viti Levu, causing Savusavu Bay to bubble like a cauldron and Rakiraki Town to flood, before it twisted around the southern Yasawas and over the small resorts of the Mamanucas Islands.

The devastation throughout Fiji was widespread: 40,000 homes were either destroyed or damaged; 130,000 people were left homeless; 44 lives were lost; and the country's food plantations suffered significant losses. In all, the storm did some F$3 billion-worth of damage, equating to 40 percent of the country's GDP. Many of the coral reefs in the path of the storm suffered significant damage too, though these are slowly recovering.

The majority of the resorts that bore the brunt of the storm have now reopened, and most travellers will see little sign of the devastation wrought by the cyclone. However, in the villages most impacted by the wind and sea-surges on southern Taveuni, Koro and north Ovalau, things are slower to recover and, at the time of going to press, many villagers are still living in makeshift tents.

The only places that **rent bicycles** are Stinger Bikes in Nadi (☎ 992 2301, ⓦ stingerbikes.com), and Bula Bikes, based at Port Denarau and Maloalo Lai Lai in the Mamanucas Islands (☎ 779 8888, ⓦ bulabikes .com), although the later only rent single-gear cruisers. A few resorts provide mountain bikes for guests to use, such as *Naveria Heights Lodge* (see p.198) and *Fiji Lodge* (see p.200), near Savusavu.

Motor scooters are rare except in Nadi, where they are something of a novelty. Travelling along the busy town roads is practical, though not particularly safe and you should certainly expect the unexpected with motorists who seem to be blind to anything on two wheels. Travel beyond the town area is not recommended.

Accommodation

For a developing country, Fiji is a fairly expensive place to visit, with room prices and standards closer to those in Australia than Southeast Asia. However, at many budget island resorts and some of the more remote, upmarket boutique resorts, meals and some activities are included, making the price more reasonable than it may seem at first sight. On the outer islands there's usually nowhere else to eat other than the resort restaurant, which can inflate the cost of staying. Nevertheless, you'll find a great variety of accommodation around the islands, with some resorts dedicated to scuba diving, surfing or ecotours while others specialize in spa services and fine dining.

Outside of the main towns, almost every place to stay is on a beach or overlooking the sea and called a **resort**, regardless of its amenities. The highest concentration of accommodation is in Nadi and along the south coast of Viti Levu, which are the **best-value** places to stay, and in the Mamanucas, with delightful beach resorts ranging from budget to upmarket. There's less, but still adequate, choice of hostels, retreats and boutique resorts around rural Viti Levu and on the outer islands of Kadavu, Ovalau, Vanua Levu and Taveuni, the last of these also being popular for longer stays and holiday homes. Beyond, in the remote Lomaiviti Group, Lau Group and Rotuma, accommodation is scarce and provisions and general infrastructure are basic.

For those travelling on a **budget**, there are plenty of affordable beach resorts all around the islands, with cheap hotel rooms and dorm beds in most towns. Obtaining **discounts** direct from the resorts is difficult, although the large international hotels usually run tempting website promotions. The best bet is to seek out online accommodation-only deals.

Several companies specialize in diving, kayaking and ecotour holidays in Fiji. See "Sports and outdoor activities", p.35, for information on these niche operators.

Rates

The majority of resorts quote rates in the **local currency** of Fijian dollars (F$), although a few of the upmarket resorts, particularly those focusing on the US market, quote in US$.

All rates in Fiji are quoted **per room** and not per person, except for dorm beds. Only a few places, mostly urban hotels and hostels, offer single-person room rates. Almost all published prices include local **taxes** which are currently nine percent VAT, ten percent Service Turnover Tax and six percent Environment Levy – the last two are aimed specifically at tourists and, together with the VAT, add a whopping 25 percent to what the hotel itself charges. If you haven't booked in advance, you may be able to get a favourable **walk-in rate** at large hotels, though seldom at backpacker hostels. To encourage longer stays, many resorts offer a "stay six/pay five" incentive or similar. Rooms overlooking the beach and ocean are sold at a premium but note that terminology is often ambiguous – a "beachfront" bure may not be right on the beach and an "ocean view" room may only have a partial glimpse of the sea through trees or other buildings.

For the most part, everything from food to activities within a hotel or resort is charged to your room and paid for at the end of your stay by **credit or debit card**, though usually only Visa and Master-Card are accepted, and often with a four percent surcharge added, so check beforehand. Paying **tips** to individuals is not encouraged, but communal staff fund boxes are usually left on reception counters and distributed to staff as a Christmas bonus or used for community projects.

ACCOMMODATION PRICES

Unless noted otherwise, the prices for all accommodation reviewed in this guide refer to the least expensive double or twin room in high season, including all taxes.

BURES

The most common style of accommodation in Fiji is a **bure**, an open-plan, traditionally styled building with high ceilings and thatch roofing ensuring natural ventilation. At the upmarket resorts, bures are exquisite handcrafted palaces, usually with king-sized beds, walk-in showers and wooden floors, while at a backpacker resort you can expect thin bamboo walls, a simple foam mattress, no electricity and a communal bathroom. At some of the mid-range and larger resorts, a bure is often an A-frame wooden structure split into two or four rooms and referred to as a duplex or quad bure.

Hotels and inns

On the main island of Viti Levu, particularly on Denarau Island and along the Coral Coast, you'll find a dozen or so large **hotel complexes**. Their facilities usually include air-conditioned rooms with flat-screen TVs, huge swimming pools with swim-up bars, multiple restaurants serving international cuisine, souvenir shops, spas, gyms, tennis courts, kids' clubs and jet-ski rental. Unlike the huge US all-inclusive resorts, the majority are "pay as you go", giving you the freedom to eat where you want and to do as little or as much as you wish. You'll also find smaller, cheaper **hotels and inns** around the Coral Coast, some offering self-catering air-conditioned rooms, others with small restaurants; these usually have few watersports or amenities available except for a swimming pool. Apart from two large beach hotels in the Mamanucas, the majority of places to stay in the outer islands are small, intimate boutique resorts.

Boutique resorts

A small **boutique resort** spanning a secluded beach on a remote island is Fiji's speciality. Some have as few as three bures, others up to fifty, but all focus on providing exceptional service. A few of the more upmarket boutique resorts are all-inclusive affairs, some even including alcoholic drinks in the price. The majority have 24hr reception, small shops, room service, nightly turndown, restaurants and sunset bars as well as scuba diving and spa/massage facilities. The downside is the lack of freedom to sightsee or choose where to eat, although for most people this simply makes the experience more relaxing.

Guesthouses, homestays and village stays

Guesthouses in Fiji tend to be colonial-style wooden buildings with simple rooms, communal lounges and shared bathrooms. They are usually cheap, with rooms costing less than F$60, and make convenient bases for travellers wanting to explore off the tourist trail; note that guesthouses are often used by government contract workers in the outer islands or remote settlements.

More appealing to tourists are the handful of **bed and breakfasts** around the country. Those in Nadi and Suva on the main island attract business travellers, while several charming bed and breakfasts and self-contained cottages in the small towns on Vanua Levu, Ovalau and Taveuni are mostly operated by expatriates and charge from F$100 per night and up.

In more than a dozen villages around the islands you can stay in a **village homestay**, whereby local families open up their homes to travellers. They cost around F$60 per person per night including meals, which are sometimes served with the family and laid out on the floor, Fijian style. **Village stays** are similar but are run by the community instead of individuals and travellers stay in community-owned guest bures, as opposed to

TYING THE KNOT

Many Fijian resorts offer **wedding packages** with ceremonies held on the beachfront. For those with large groups in attendance, getting married on the main island of Viti Levu is more convenient, but the atmosphere on the offshore islands is far more intimate and a better option for smaller parties. Among the best options are *Paradise Cove Resort* (see p.97) in the Yasawas; *Matamanoa Island Resort* (see p.88) and *Treasure Island Resort* (see p.81), in the Mamanucas Islands; and *Matangi Private Island Resort* (see p.208) off Taveuni. If you're getting married on the **beach**, find out about the tides and sun direction before fixing a time. Early-morning weddings are worth considering as it's not only cooler and less windy, but also less likely to rain.

The practicalities of obtaining a **marriage licence** are very straightforward and all resorts will help with the paperwork. For more information contact ⓦ iwasmarriedinfiji.com.

private homes, giving both parties a little more privacy. They generally cost the same as homestays, but the profits go towards community projects within the village: see box, p.40 for more details.

Hostels and backpacker resorts

There's a huge amount of **budget accommodation** in Fiji, although those expecting Southeast Asian prices are likely to be disappointed. Standards are variable, but members of the Fiji Backpacker Association (W fijitravel.deals) are usually reliable, as are those places promoted by Awesome Adventures (W awesomefiji.com). By staying at these established hostels, however, you'll miss out on the less polished places which offer a real insight into Fiji – spending a few days in Nadi and meeting other travellers is a sure way to get on the grapevine and suss out where's new and happening.

The term "hostel" usually refers to a town boarding house aimed specifically at locals. A more common name is "**backpacker resort**", and these can be found throughout the islands and even in Nadi. Most have rooms or lodges crammed with dorm beds, but often the price of a simple double room or bure is the same as two dorm beds.

Student discount cards are not widely accepted – if you've travelled around Australia or New Zealand and already have one you may be able to save yourself around ten percent at certain places. The Australian-operated Nomads (W nomadsworld .com) and VIP Backpackers (W vipbackpackers.com) both have affiliates in Nadi but there's no YHA.

Camping

Wild camping is not encouraged in Fiji – it's perceived by Fijians as an insult, as if you're saying the local village is not good enough to sleep in. However, several backpacker resorts permit the pitching of tents within their grounds and several organized tours, with the consent of village landowners, make temporary camp on secluded beaches.

Food and drink

When eating out, most Fijians opt for international fast-food chains or the cheap, locally-owned Indian and Chinese canteens that dominate the country's high streets. However, both Nadi and Suva have a few fine-dining restaurants and healthy cafés, as well as a good variety of reasonably priced restaurants serving everything from Italian to Japanese food: a growing number of places also serve well-presented traditional Fijian cuisine. Most of the beach resorts offer a mix of casual fine-dining, sometimes cooked by internationally acclaimed chefs, and buffet-style themed dinners.

Fijian cuisine

Every-day **Fijian cuisine** in rural areas includes plenty of locally caught, bony reef fish cooked in rich coconut cream, and sometimes *kai* mussels, mud crabs and even lobster, but little meat except for slow-cooked pig (*taro*) on a special occasion. When the seas are rough or the season's pickings are slender, Fijians resort to imported fatty mutton and tinned corned beef, the latter perceived as something of a delicacy and often served up by the carton at ceremonial functions.

Appearing at every mealtime is a hefty portion of starchy **root crop**, either cassava (a bland and extremely dry tuber), *dalo* (known as *taro* in Polynesia, a large corn) or yams (huge tubers, sometimes two metres long, and the most flavoursome of the three root crops). **Vegetables** are less common, with the most popular being *bele*, a green, sometimes slimy leaf, and *rourou*, the leaf of the *dalo* crop, which is both tasty and has a higher nutritional benefit – if it's cooked too quickly, however, it can cause an itchy sensation in the throat. The availability of **fruit** is dependent on the season (see p.30).

Traditional Fijian dishes include: **kokoda**, made from a large fish, usually tuna or wahoo, diced, marinated overnight in lime juice and chillies, seasoned with coconut cream and served cold; **palusami**, coconut cream wrapped up in the leaf of *dalo* and slow cooked; and the kids' favourite **vakalolo**, a sticky pudding made from cassava mixed with sugar and thick coconut cream and best served with ice cream and bananas. Fish in *lolo* (coconut cream) with cassava or *dalo* is served as counter food in most high-street restaurants, but finding the more delicate dishes of kokoda, palusami, *vakalolo* or lovo suckling pig is more challenging: *Nadina* in Nadi (see p.62) is one of the few restaurants serving traditional Fijian cuisine.

Indo-Fijians tend to be more adventurous in taste, relying on home-cooked curries, often made of freshly picked vegetables seasoned with hot chillies and other spices, accompanied by home-made dhal soup and chutney that's usually drowned in oil or ghee.

THE LOVO

In pre-European times, the Fijian islanders cooked food in bamboo strips on an open fire but, with increased trade with the Tongans, the underground oven or **lovo** was adopted. To make a lovo, a hole is dug in the soil, laid with wood over which black volcanic stones are placed. A fire is lit, the stones are heated and the food, wrapped carefully in banana leaves or tin foil, is placed on top. The main constituents are usually a whole pig at the bottom with *dalo*, yam, chicken, fish and palusami laid on top in order to give each the correct amount of cooking. The hole is covered with coconut leaves with soil spread on top sealing in the heat and cooking the food slowly (anything from an hour to five hours depending on size). Most Fijian families prepare a lovo early Sunday morning before heading to church so it is ready for eating at lunch. Lovos also form the heart of ceremonial feasting at weddings, funerals and any other communal gathering.

Seasonal fruit and vegetables

While it is available in supermarkets, **imported food** is often too expensive for Fijians and the resorts have been encouraged by successive governments to source more produce locally. The results are slowly being realized, giving Fijians a new source of income.

The availability of **fruit** and some vegetables is determined by the seasons, with local produce extremely cheap when in abundance – **bananas**, **pawpaw** (also known as papaya) and **coconuts** are available year-round, while expensive imports such as apples, oranges and melons bolster lows in productivity. The following is a list of fruits grown extensively in Fiji:

January Watermelon, pineapple, *vi* (Tahitian apple), avocado, *vutu* (small nut, similar to almond), guava, lemon.

February Pineapple, *vi*, avocado, guava, lemon, *lvi* (Tahitian chestnut).

March Pineapple, guava, lemon, *lvi*, mandarin, orange.

April Guava, lemon, *lvi*, mandarin, orange, *daruka* (Fijian asparagus).

May Lemon, mandarin, orange, *daruka*.

June Mandarin, orange, passionfruit, *tarawao* (small, round and crunchy with a hard seed), *dawa* (Fijian lychee), watermelon, soursop (large, spiky looking fruit with lots of hard seeds, creamy in texture).

July Passionfruit, *tarawao* (tiny hard, sour fruit), *dawa*, watermelon, soursop.

August *Kavika* (wax apple), soursop.

September Mango, pineapple, *kavika*, soursop.

October Mango, pineapple, *kavika*, jackfruit.

November Mango, pineapple, jackfruit, *vi* (Tahitian apple), breadfruit, *vutu*.

December Watermelon, pineapple, *vi* (Tahitian apple), breadfruit, avocado, *vutu*.

Breakfast and lunch

Breakfast at resorts inevitably includes fresh fruit and a continental-style buffet with freshly baked breads and cereals. In the Fijian home it's often a much heartier affair, with a large plate of boiled rice or cassava, fish if caught the night before, coconut-flavoured pancakes, plain biscuits and lemon tea.

Lunch is the most commonly overlooked meal in Fiji, and many tourists often find it too hot to consider eating anything substantial, with salads and quick snacks most popular.

Dinner and eating out

Dinner is usually eaten early, and you'll find all restaurants open by 6pm and often winding down by 9pm, or 10pm on busy nights. At independent restaurants mains start from F$9 and seldom rise above F$40 even in Nadi and Suva.

Dinner at **resort restaurants** is always more expensive, and at most island resorts it's your only option, with mains starting around F$15 and often reaching F$50 or more. **Buffet dinners** are popular at the large resorts, particularly the weekly Fijian lovo night (costing from F$50–80 a person), when a suckling pig and root crops are cooked in an underground oven and usually preceded by a traditional dance.

Drinks

Fijians have a reputation for enjoying a **drink**, always in company and often to excess, be it the national drink, **yaqona** (known as *kava* in Polynesian countries; see box opposite), beer or local dark rum. Drinking sessions are invariably all-male affairs with a single glass or cup passed around in rotation and the contents swallowed in one gulp – a sure way of ending up drunk quickly. In bars and nightclubs, **closing time** is usually 2am, although it can be late as 5am at weekends.

Beer

The local **beers** are passable. The most common lagers, Fiji Gold and Fiji Bitter, are brewed in Suva by the Australian Fosters Group and come in two sizes, 375ml "stubbies" and the larger 750ml "long necks", popular with the locals, as well as in cans. Fiji Premium is a slightly smoother lager, as is Vonu, made by an independent brewery based in Nadi – both come in 355ml bottles only. In the shops a stubby costs around F$3, in the local bars it's anything from F$4 to F$6 and in the resorts it starts at F$6. Draft Fiji Bitter can be found at the more upmarket bars and resorts and tastes infinitely better. Imported bottled beer, mostly lagers from Australia, cost a few dollars more.

Rum and other spirits

Rum, brewed from local sugar in Lautoka, is popularly referred to as "wash down", drunk neat after a *yaqona* session to sweeten the palate. The smooth, mellow Bounty Dark Rum has won several international awards and costs around F$60 for a 750ml bottle. The Fiji Rum Company has a tasting cellar on Denarau Island in Nadi, located between the Golf & Racquet Club and the *Sheraton Resort* (W fijirumco.com; daily 1pm–9pm), where you can sample seven exotically flavoured infusions. Both dark and white rum are regular ingredients in the gorgeous **cocktails** concocted by resort barmen – these usually cost from F$20 to F$30 although happy-hour prices are substantially discounted. Locally brewed gin, whisky and vodka are less appealing.

It's worth noting that you can buy up to 2.25 litres of **duty-free liquor** on arrival at Nadi Airport beside the luggage carousel before clearing customs.

Wine

Wine is usually imported from Australia and New Zealand – a reasonable bottle will cost F$20 in a bottle shop, and perhaps double that in a restaurant. BYO is not a common practice but some restaurants do permit this, with a corkage fee around F$10. In the villages, **home-made wine** made from pineapples, watermelon or oranges is worth trying if offered.

Soft drinks

Despite the abundance of fruit, freshly squeezed **fruit juices** and smoothies can be hard to come by in towns or even resort bars. However, you will find that Fijians are amazingly adept at shinning up tall palm trees, felling a **coconut**, slicing off its top and offering the milky contents as a refreshing drink. Trying one is something of a must-do in Fiji – you'll see them being sold along the roadside for $3, or try the Queens Road around Saunaka in Nadi.

Tap water in towns is filtered and chlorinated and on the whole safe to drink, although it's best avoided after heavy rains when sediment often appears. Chilled, sweetened tap water mixed with fresh limes is sold from glass tanks at all town markets. At rural and outer-island resorts, water is sourced from natural springs or wells, although for drinking purposes **rainwater** collected in tanks is preferable. Brackish well water is sometimes a problem, and in places of scarcity, especially in the Mamanucas, desalination plants have been

---

YAQONA

Also known as *kava* or more simply "grog", **yaqona** is Fiji's national drink. Made from the pounded roots of the pepper plant (*piper methysticum*), it has an earthy, rather bitter taste and resembles muddy water. Although it takes some getting used to, *yaqona* (pronounced "yan-gon-a") is refreshing and has a relaxing effect upon the body. Drunk socially by Fijians and Indo-Fijians, it is also used in formal situations and will be offered as part of a **ceremony** to welcome you to a village.

The ritual begins with the presentation of your *sevusevu*, or introductory gift (see box, p.40), accompanied by a speech of introduction by the bearer and a reciprocal speech of thanks by the village herald. After this, the *yaqona* roots are mixed with water in a carved bowl (*tanoa*) while all participants sit in a circle on the floor. Once ready, the drink is served in a half coconut shell known as a *bilo*. It is presented first to the chief and then to any guests. When it's your turn to drink, cup your hands, clap once and say "**bula**" (cheers); you then take the cup and down the contents in one go. Return the cup to the bearer and clap your hands again three times, proclaiming "**maca**", a signal of gratification. The formal ceremony ends when the bowl is empty, indicated by a round of clapping. Throughout the ceremony it's considered bad manners to talk, turn your back on the chief or to point your feet towards the *tanoa* bowl.

After a few cups of *yaqona* your tongue and lips may become numb, a temporary effect caused by the active ingredients in the root. Consuming *yaqona* in large quantities can cause **drowsiness**, so avoid driving or going swimming immediately after drinking it.

For something rather less potent, try **Taki Mai**, a *kava* extract drink mixed with coconut and pineapple flavours: you can buy a bottle at the ubiquitous Jacks stores.

installed which often give a slightly saline taste to the water and anything made from it.

Bottled water, for which Fiji is globally renowned, costs from F$2 for a large 1.5-litre bottle in the shops, depending on the brand, and at least triple that in the resorts. Fiji Water, owned by a private American company and hugely popular in the US, is sourced from a deep well beneath the Nakauvadra Range in northern Viti Levu, with a multimillion-dollar bottling plant at Yaqara. Other local brands include Island Chill and Aqua Pacific, both sourced on Viti Levu.

Health

Fiji presents few major health issues for visitors. The most common problems are sunburn and/or heat stroke caused by overexposure to the tropical sun; fungal ear infections from swimming, which are easily cured with ear drops; mosquito or sandfly bites; and on rare occasions, fish poisoning.

No **vaccinations** are required to enter Fiji unless you are coming from a yellow fever area, in which case you need an International Health Certificate indicating that you have been immunized against yellow fever sometime in the past ten years. Vaccination against Hepatitis A is often recommended by independent medical advisories. Isolated outbreaks of typhoid have occurred on Vanua Levu in recent years during the wet season.

Heat stroke

Heat stroke is a serious and sometimes fatal condition that can result from long periods of exposure to high temperatures and high humidity. The wisest approach is to always wear a high SPF **sunscreen** (over 35), even in cloudy weather, not forgetting your lips, ears, feet and back; wear a wide-brimmed hat and sunglasses; **drink plenty of water**, generally a litre every two hours, bearing in mind that room-temperature water is better for you in the tropics and that drinking alcohol is going to add to your dehydration; and **cover up** when snorkelling by wearing a T-shirt to protect your back, still with sun cream on, and wear a long-sleeve shirt with a collar when out walking. Better still, stay in the shade.

Symptoms of heat stroke include nausea, fatigue, a high body temperature, severe headache, disorientation and/or little or no perspiration despite the heat. Eventually the sufferer can become delirious and fall into convulsions, and rapid medical treatment is essential. First aid is to seek shade, remove the victim's clothing, wrap them in a cool, wet sheet or towels, and fan around them.

Drinking water

Although urban **tap water** is filtered, chlorinated and safe to drink, travellers with sensitive stomachs should consider boiling it first or buying bottled water, especially after heavy rains when tap water can appear murky. In rural Viti Levu and the outer islands water is mostly sourced from natural springs which may appear extremely pure but can cause upset stomachs – most travellers are encouraged to buy bottled water or drink rain water which is usually supplied to guests free of charge from large tanks and which is less likely to be contaminated. Drinking from a pristine stream while out walking in the forests might be tempting but it's not recommended as water-borne diseases such as bilharzia and leptospirosis can be present.

DENGUE FEVER

Although there is no malaria in Fiji, occasionally **dengue fever** outbreaks occur. The mosquito-borne disease has similar symptons to malaria, but it's not nearly as threatening. Outbreaks usually occur in urban areas after heavy rains and are acted upon swiftly by the authorities who spray and kill the dengue-spreading mosquitoes – it's only the black and white striped day-biting mosquito that causes dengue.

Signs of infection include aching joints, intense headaches, a sudden high fever, chills, nausea and sometimes a red rash which usually first appears on the lower limbs or chest. The symptoms will last from five to fifteen days. Although the recommended cure is simple – stay in bed, drink plenty of water and wait it out – it's advisable to consult a doctor. In more severe cases, a doctor will administer intravenous fluids to prevent dehydration and acetaminophen to reduce fever. Avoid aspirin as this can often cause complications. While the fever is rarely life-threatening in fit adults, the elderly and children are prone to complications and death can result – if an outbreak is present, take extra precautions against being bitten by mosquitoes.

Bites and stings

Mosquitoes are most widespread during the **wet season** from December to April. Most resorts spray gardens to keep mosquitoes at bay, but in less-developed parts of the islands they can be voracious, almost unbearable at dusk and dawn when it may be wise to stay indoors or sit by the sea, preferably facing a stiff wind. Most resorts have well-screened windows, but if not, a **mosquito net** and/or mosquito repellent should be used. The best type of **repellent** is the Good Knight electric mat heaters which cost around F$8 from supermarkets, plus F$1.70 for a packet of ten mats, one mat being sufficient per night. You'll need constant electricity to use them and when this isn't available, you may have to resort to mosquito coils, which can be slightly noxious on inhalation. **Roll-on mosquito repellent** works for both mosquitoes and sandflies on a temporary basis: environmentally sensitive brands that are safer on your skin, such as Australian products Rid or Aerogard, cost around F$9 a bottle and are available from most supermarkets or pharmacies.

Sandflies can cause irritating rashes through their bites, usually spreading over a larger area than a mosquito bite, and are found not surprisingly along sandy beaches, appearing at dusk and dawn.

Ciguatera fish poisoning

Ciguatera fish poisoning is a fairly common ailment among rural Fijians and can be caught by **consuming reef fish** which have been feeding on toxic algae. Although seldom life-threatening, the poisoning causes nausea, diarrhoea, vomiting and a numbness or tingling sensation often in the fingers; it usually commences within 24 hours of consumption. If you believe you have the symptoms of ciguatera, head straight to a doctor or local hospital where you can receive treatment via an injection. Although not confined to any particular fish, it is most common in older and larger reef fish, typically grouper, red snapper, Spanish mackerel and barracuda. Most villagers know which fish to avoid at certain times of the year.

MEDICAL RESOURCES FOR TRAVELLERS
US AND CANADA
CDC ☎ 1 800 232 4636, ⓦ cdc.gov/travel. Official US government travel health site.
International Society for Travel Medicine ☎ 1 404 373 8282, ⓦ istm.org. Has a full list of travel health clinics.
Canadian Society for International Health ☎ 613 241 5785, ⓦ csih.org. Extensive list of travel health centres.

AUSTRALIA, NEW ZEALAND AND SOUTH AFRICA
Travellers' Medical and Vaccination Centre ☎ 1300 658 844, ⓦ traveldoctor.com.au. Lists travel clinics in Australia, New Zealand and South Africa.

UK AND IRELAND
Hospital for Tropical Diseases Travel Clinic ☎ 0157 322 6901, ⓦ thehtd.org.
MASTA (Medical Advisory Service for Travellers Abroad) ⓦ masta.org or ☎ 0330 100 4200 for the nearest clinic.
Tropical Medical Bureau Republic of Ireland ☎ 1 2715 200, ⓦ tmb.ie.

The media

Fiji's media has often been suppressed under military rule, and tends towards the bland and parochial. When conventional media has been censored, the internet has proven invaluable in distributing the views of Fijians, notably through blogs often written by critical emigrants living outside of Fiji.

Newspapers and magazines

Of the English-language daily **newspapers**, the *Fiji Times* (ⓦ fijitimes.com), once owned by Murdoch's News Corporation but now published by a local Indo-Fijian businessman, is the most dominant, with the broadest international coverage. Its closest rival is the locally owned *Fiji Sun* (ⓦ fijisun.com.fj), a slightly more tabloid-style publication.

Radio

The part-government-owned Fiji Broadcasting Corporation (ⓦ fbc.com.fj) operates six **radio stations**, two each in Fijian, Fiji-Hindi and English; of these, one focuses on news and community issues, the other music and chat. For Fijian music, try Bula FM (FM102.4 in Nadi) – all stations have varying FM frequencies depending on location. The independent Communications Fiji Limited (ⓦ www.cfl.com.fj) broadcasts five mostly music stations, two Fiji-Hindi, one Fijian and the popular English music and gossip stations – FM96 and Legend FM (FM106.8).

Television

Fiji has three free-to-air **television** channels. Fiji One's programming is almost exclusively in English, with only a few locally produced shows, the rest being sourced from the US. The one-hour *Fiji News* is shown daily at 6pm, with mostly local content and a smattering of international headlines. Mai TV is sports orientated, and FBC TV has attempted to raise the standard of local news broadcasting.

Festivals

Ethnic Fijians tend to express their culture in day-to-day life rather than through specific festivals. By contrast, Indo-Fijians celebrate most events with gusto, whether it's a local wedding, religious festival or one of the many fascinating firewalking ceremonies held around the country. The country enjoys eleven public holidays; the most likely of these to feature traditional dance and other public displays is Constitutional Day on September 7 and Fiji Day on October 10.

The main **towns** of Nadi, Lautoka and Suva each have a commercially driven week-long **festival** (see calendar below) with fairground rides, food stalls, parades, beauty-queen crowning and an alternative Priscilla night when gays and transvestites take centre stage. The town festivals held in Levuka and Savusavu are more culturally inclined.

Indian festivals are commonly celebrated in public and with great fanfare, with Diwali the biggest and loudest for Hindus and Eid a serious affair for Muslims – towns with a large Indo-Fijian population are naturally the best, especially Lautoka and Tavua on Viti Levu or Labasa on Vanua Levu. There are over forty Indian **firewalking** ceremonies held around the country between April and September. These are fascinating and spiritual experiences – ask around at local temples to find out where one is being held. The two largest are listed below.

JANUARY

Thaipusam Festival End Jan/early Feb with main day being the last Sat of the festival. This ten-day Hindu festival at the Nadi temple (see box, p.54) has devotees piercing their bodies and dragging chariots using meat hooks.

MARCH

Holi One day after full moon, usually early March. Hindu festival celebrated with throwing of coloured turmeric powder, feasting and the singing of religious poems.

APRIL

Indian firewalking First Sun after the full moon. Held at the Malolo Temple south of Nadi, with devotees walking across a pit of burning wood embers.

MAY

Rotuma Day 13 May. Dance and feasting among Rotumans throughout Fiji to celebrate Rotuma's cession to Fiji and Britain.

JULY

Bula Festival Mid to end of the month (ⓦ bulafestival.com.fj). Nadi's annual week-long celebrations at Koroivoli Park.

AUGUST

Indian firewalking First Sun after the full moon. The largest of the Indo-Fijian firewalking events is held at the Sangham Temple on Howell Rd, Suva.

Hibiscus Festival Mid-Aug, coinciding with school holidays (ⓦ hibiscusfiji.com). Suva's yearly week-long celebrations at Albert Park.

Friendly North Festival End Aug (ⓣ 995 4281). Labasa's annual week-long celebrations at Subrail Park.

SEPTEMBER

Fiji Regatta Week Usually second week of Sept. Musket Cove Marina, Mamanucas (ⓦ musketcovefiji.com). Pirate trips, races (in small Hobie-Cat boats) and general yachty hoo-ra.

Sugar Festival Usually the first week of Sept (ⓣ 666 8010). Lautoka's yearly week-long celebrations at Churchill Park.

OCTOBER

Bilibili Race 10 Oct. Sigatoka-based competition for Fiji's hotel workers with a tug-of-war and bamboo rafting along the Sigatoka River.

Fiji Day 10 Oct. Public holiday celebrating the day when Fiji was both ceded to Britain (1874) and given independence (1970). Dance performances are sometimes held in Albert Park, Suva.

Back to Levuka Week 10 Oct. Traditional re-enactments of cession, art displays and agricultural shows.

Diwali Late Oct to mid-Nov, depending on lunar calendar. Fireworks and lights are the star attractions of this Hindu celebration.

Rising of the Balolo Mid-Oct to mid-Nov, depending on moon. Naturally occurring event at a dozen or more coral reefs around the islands – the tail of a mysterious worm rises to the surface, is collected and eaten as a delicacy (see box, p.234).

NOVEMBER

Savusavu Music Festival ⓦ fiji-savusavu.com. Local musicians and dance troupes perform throughout this week-long event.

DECEMBER

Fara 1 Dec to mid-Jan. Door-to-door dancing and merry-making on the outer island of Rotuma, known as *fara* (see box, p.214). Sometimes indulged in by Rotumans living in urban centres, particularly Suva.

Sports and outdoor activities

With endless beaches, teeming coral reefs and water temperatures averaging 27°C, Fiji is renowned for its scuba diving, snorkelling, surfing and other watersports. But adventure also awaits in the sultry tropical rainforests with fabulous hiking, river rafting and ecotours on offer.

Scuba diving and snorkelling

Fiji offers superb **scuba diving** and **snorkelling**, with exceptionally colourful and easily accessible reefs as well as plenty of diverse fish species including sharks. Diving is excellent year-round, with visibility usually at least 30m – the very best months are October and November, after the trade winds have subsided and before the tropical wet season begins.

Almost all resorts offer scuba diving, with dive sites normally between five and forty minutes by boat. Many resorts offer **dive training**, with PADI Open Water courses the most popular, costing F$650–900 for a three- to four-day package. For the more tentative, introductory scuba lessons offer a few hours learning the basics in a swimming pool – these cost around F$200. Advanced Courses (F$650) and Rescue Diver (F$850) are also widely available. Options for diving using Nitrox include Jean-Michel Cousteau Diving in Savusavu (see box, p.198), *Garden Island Resort* on Taveuni (see p.213), and *Lalati Resort* on Beqa (see p.154), as well as on the live-aboard cruises (see opposite).

For scuba divers, the **soft corals** for which Fiji renowned are most prolific in the nutrient-rich channels between the larger islands: the Great Astrolabe Reef, which twists its way around Kadavu;

Beqa Lagoon, off southern Viti Levu; the isolated Bligh Waters between northern Viti Levu and Vanua Levu; and the Rainbow Reef, between Vanua Levu and Taveuni. These passages are often flushed with strong currents, making them only suitable for experienced divers. The more protected lagoons in the Mamanucas offer fun and easy dives for **beginners** as well as some more challenging dives including wrecks, caves and reef shark dives. The Beqa Lagoon off Pacific Harbour is renowned for its pelagics, particularly **sharks**, including two of the three most dangerous sharks in the world, bulls and tigers, while pilot **whales** and minke whales can be seen off Ovalau. For exploratory diving, **live-aboards** ply the remote reefs around the Koro Sea to the north of Ovalau.

DIVING CONTACTS

CWM Hyperbaric Chamber ☎ 331 3444 or ☎ 903 4093. Based at the Colonial War Memorial Hospital in Suva, Fiji's only recompression centre offers a 24hr service.

Dive Worldwide UK ☎ 01962 302 087, ⓦ diveworldwide.com. Specialist dive holidays from the UK, with an extensive selection of Fiji itineraries.

PADI Australia ☎ 02 9454 2888, ⓦ padi.com. The Professional Association of Diving Instructors provides basic information on diving, courses and certification, as well as a list of all PADI-registered companies in Fiji.

LIVE-ABOARDS

Fiji Aggressor US ☎ 1 800 348 2628, ⓦ aggressor.com. US-based company with a sleek 10-passenger vessel based in Fiji, visiting the Koro Sea including E-6, Hi-8 and Namena Marine Reserve. From US$3195 per person for a one-week charter.

Nai'a US ☎ 1 888 510 1593, Fiji ☎ 345 0382; ⓦ naia.com.fj. Seven- and ten-day charters on a serene 40m sailing yacht for 18 passengers. Visits the Koro Sea, E-6, Mount Mutiny and Namena Marine Reserve. From US$3875 per person for a one-week charter.

Snorkelling

For **snorkellers**, the great beauty is that most reefs start just a few metres from the shoreline. Some of

---

RESPECTING THE REEF

Lying at the crossroads of the Pacific, Fiji's reefs are recognized as a globally important area of **biodiversity** and make up four percent of the world's total area of coral reefs. As well as attracting thousands of tourists, they protect the islands from hurricanes and provide an income for fishermen. Despite their often vast size, coral reefs are fragile and complex ecosystems that require care and respect from snorkellers and scuba divers. It's imperative you **do not touch** the reef, or try to stand or tread water close to coral heads. Even a brief contact is likely to destroy the delicate coral polyps which can take years to grow back. Although they make tempting souvenirs, **shells** should not be removed from the reef as they play a vital role in providing homes for invertebrates. Avoid buying shells from the village markets, especially tritons, or trumpet shells, the only natural predators of the coral-destroying crown of thorns starfish.

the best **shore sites** are off the rocky west coast of Taveuni where the waters drop off dramatically, along Lesiaceva Point in Savusavu, in the Mamanuca-i-Cake Group and along the entire Yasawa chain of islands. Resorts which don't have good shore snorkelling provide **boat trips** to bommies, passages and outer reefs where marine life and corals are prolific. Of these, Vesi and Naiqoro passages in Kadavu, the Namena Marine Reserve off Savusavu and the Rainbow Reef between Taveuni and Vanua Levu are particularly outstanding.

Manta rays congregate at Galoa and Vuro islands off Kadavu and around Drawaqa in the Yasawas between May and October. The best places to swim or snorkel with **spinner dolphins** are at the slightly remote regions of Natewa Bay in Vanua Levu or at Moon Reef off east Viti Levu.

Snorkel gear provided by resorts may not fit and masks often leak, so it's worth investing in your own mask, snorkel and fins.

Surfing

Fiji is a regular venue for international **surfing** competitions, with over a dozen extremely challenging but reliable reef breaks. For the casual surfer, perhaps an even greater attraction is uncrowded waves. The only **beach breaks** for novices are at Sigatoka (see p.110); otherwise all surfing breaks are **reef breaks** usually over shallow razor-sharp coral with a wipeout bound to graze, or more likely cause serious injuries – this is for experienced surfers only. The dozen or so breaks along the Malolo Barrier Reef (see box, p.85) are the most accessible, although several of the biggest breaks are reserved under exclusive agreements with upmarket surf resorts that sell only via the US. More isolated surfing destinations include Maqai off Qamea, Wilkes in Beqa Lagoon and Kia off northern Vanua Levu.

Windsurfing and kitesurfing

The best place for **windsurfing** is from *Safari Lodge* (see p.124), facing the trade winds on the exposed east beach of Nananu-i-Ra island off north Viti Levu; you can take week-long courses here or rent equipment by the hour. Other good locations include Matamanoa Island (see p.87) where winds can sometimes be stiff, or Plantation Island which features a sandy-bottomed shallow lagoon ideal for beginners, both in the Mamanucas. The optimum time for windsurfing is when the trade winds are blowing strongest between June and September.

Kitesurfing is also offered at *Safari Lodge*, but the best place to learn is at *Fiji Lodge: Vosa Ni Ua* (see p.200) outside Savusavu, which runs certified courses. If you have your own equipment, the flat lagoon between Malolo and Malolo Lailai in the Mamanucas is another good kitesurfing spot; the winds funnelled through the channel create ideal conditions.

Sailing

Although Fiji is a paradise of stunning islands and bays, treacherous reefs make **sailing** a challenging experience. Unless you have your own yacht, it's unlikely you'll find anyone prepared to offer boats for hire, with the few **sailing charters** operating from the marinas below on a skipper-and-crew basis only. The country's six **marinas** with full facilities are Port Denarau, Vuda Marina and the Royal Suva Yacht Club, all on Viti Levu; Musket Cove in the Mamanucas; Levuka on Ovalau; and Savusavu on Vanua Levu.

Yachties arrive in Fiji between May and August, usually sailing with the trade winds from California via Tonga and heading onwards to Australia or New Zealand, via Vanuatu or New Caledonia, no later than October when the trade winds subside and dangerous storms can occur. Popular regions for exploring include Vanua Balavu in the Lau Group, the islands off Taveuni and the idyllic lagoons and bays of the Mamanucas. See the section "Getting to Fiji by boat" for more information about immigration and customs.

Most resorts in the Mamanucas have small **sailing catamarans** for mucking around in the lagoons, while the best facilities for casual sailing are at Vuda Marina or Musket Cove..

Sea-kayaking

Every resort seems to have **sea-kayaks** for guest use, usually as a complimentary activity; note that it's always wise to wear a life jacket and inform somebody of your intended journey in case you get caught in a dangerous current or a squally storm suddenly descends. Two companies (see below) offer week-long **kayaking expeditions** between May and October, snorkelling in the lagoons and camping on beaches or overnighting in remote fishing villages. Another good option is the half-day trip along the Lavena Coastline (see box, p.210) within the Bouma National Heritage Park on Taveuni.

WATER SAFETY

Swimming and snorkelling in Fiji's waters is pretty safe but there are a few precautions to be aware of. Wave action on the beaches is generally very sedate – the only places you may face danger are around river passages on the larger islands where **riptides** can pull you out to sea. In the event of this happening, never fight it – go with the rip and try swimming sidewards to get out of the current, then swim parallel with the beach for 100m before trying to swim back to land.

When snorkelling, avoid contact with coral – apart from killing the delicate polyps you're likely to cut or graze yourself, which can cause painful infection. Avoid snorkelling at low tide – with less water between you and the reef, collisions can be common. If you do get a **coral cut**, clean it immediately, preferably using iodine, and apply an antibacterial cream regularly.

Reef sharks are present in the lagoons – if you're lucky enough to see one it's very unlikely to stir unless you aggravate it, when it might swipe a bite in protest. Stinging jellyfish and crocodiles are not present in Fiji, although fire coral and sea-lice can be irritating, particularly between December and April. Perhaps the greatest danger is the **sun** and without the protection of a UV swimming vest, or at the very least a high-factor sunscreen, sunburn is inevitable, even on a gloomy overcast day.

KAYAKING OPERATORS

South Sea Ventures ☏ 02 8901 3287 in Australia, **ⓦ southernseaventures.com.** Australian-run group trips exploring the northern Yasawas in either single or twin sea-kayaks. Eight-day packages from A$2370.

Tamarillo Tropical Expeditions ☏ 04 239 9885 in New Zealand, **ⓦ tamarillo.co.nz/fiji.** New Zealand-based company exploring the rugged and remote coastline of Kadavu with support boats. Seven-day packages from NZ$2595 per person.

Fishing

Fishing is a way of life for many Fijians, using nets, spear guns and fish traps in the shallow lagoons and simple hand lines along the riverbanks as a matter of subsistence. Commercial fishermen with small wooden fishing boats head to the deeper waters for tuna, mahi-mahi and wahoo. For tourists, **game fishing** is an exciting prospect, particularly in pursuit of **billfish** in the deep waters off Taveuni and Savusavu in the north and in the rich fast-flowing currents between Beqa and Kadavu in the south. Fishing licences aren't required but you'll need to find a reputable fishing charter with a proper game-fishing boat, good equipment and most importantly, a knowledgeable skipper – charters are usually available at Savusavu on Vanua Levu and at Pacific Harbour on Viti Levu, with more casual game fishing from Port Denarau in Nadi; otherwise, recommended resorts include *Matangi Private Island Resort* (see p.208) off Taveuni; *Makaira* (see p.206) on Taveuni; or *Matava* (see p.162) on Kadavu; rates start from F$750 for half a day.

Casting into the fringing reefs from small boats is usually excellent, with snapper, barracuda and trevally the prize catches; fly fishing in the shallow lagoons is good in places although there are few opportunities to land the highly prized bonefish, prolific in other parts of the South Pacific, and you'll definitely need to bring your own gear. Fishing in the **rivers** is seldom practised as a sport, although a couple of lodges along the south coast of Vanua Levu are idyllically set up for this.

Hiking and horseriding

Compared to its South Pacific neighbours, Fiji stands out as a great **hiking** destination. There are fine tropical rainforest walks in the Namosi Highlands, mountain treks on Viti Levu, Taveuni and Kadavu and stunning coastal walks on Waya Island. Of the national parks, Koroyanitu and Bouma on Taveuni are the best for hiking. For less avid walkers, there are usually short trails leading to hilltop lookouts overlooking islands and lagoons. Resorts offering excellent local hikes include *Castaway Island Resort* (see p.85), *Botaira Beach Resort* (see p.96), *Naveria Heights Lodge* (see p.198) and *Matangi Island Resort* (see p.208).

Horseriding hasn't really developed as an attraction, although the potential is excellent. You can hire saddled horses at Wailoaloa Beach in Nadi and along the wild beachfront at the Sigatoka Sand Dunes (see p.110).

River rafting and adrenaline sports

River rafting is a fun way of exploring the remote regions of Viti Levu, with the Grade III rapids of the upper Navua River on the south coast of Viti Levu the only place with established operators (see p.119).

NATIONAL PARKS AND HERITAGE PARKS

Fiji's first official national park, protected by law, is the fascinating **Sigatoka Sand Dunes National Park** (see p.110) on the southwest coast of Viti Levu. The fragile sand-dune ecosystem, scattered with ancient bones and pottery, has an informative visitor centre and two trails for exploring.

Otherwise, the lush **Bouma National Heritage Park** (see p.208) encompasses almost half of Taveuni, while **Koroyanitu National Heritage Park** (see p.70) sits inland from Lautoka on Viti Levu. Both offer walking trails to waterfalls, village interaction and community-run accommodation.

Other projects managed by the **National Trust of Fiji** (☎330 1807) include Momi Guns (see p.65), south of Nadi; Levuka Town (see p.169) on Ovalau; Yadua Taba Island (see p.194); and Waisali Reserve in Vanua Levu (see p.194).

For adrenaline seekers there's **skydiving** available from Nadi Airport (see p.58), **jet-skiing** from Port Denarau (see p.58), **canopy zip wires** in the rainforest at Pacific Harbour (see p.119) and just north of Nadi at the Sleeping Giant (see p.66), and **paddleboarding** in the Mamanucas and off Ovalau (see p.176).

Golf

Fiji is beginning to establish itself as a major **golfing** holiday destination, thanks to its great year-round weather and affordable green fees. Fiji's stand-out golf course is the Natadola Bay Golf Course (see p.109), home to the Fiji International, with outstanding sea views. There also are championship golf courses at Denarau (see p.58) and Pacific Harbour (see p.119), with simpler resort courses for families at *Koro Sun* (see p.200) and *Plantation Island Resort* (see p.83).

Ecotours and village visits

Fiji is well positioned as an ecotour destination, with **village-based cultural visits** and **marine biology** the main focus. There are no specific ecotour holiday packages but most resorts, especially those in the outer islands, can organize village visits, plantation tours and guided hikes.

Visiting a village is more often than not an overwhelmingly positive experience. Apart from relishing the tourist-orientated *yaqona* ceremony (see box, p.31), travellers can usually visit people's homes, sample foods, learn to weave, go fishing and generally immerse themselves in daily Fijian life. Several villages have set up **community resorts**, usually located at the parameters of the village so as not to disrupt village affairs. For more background on village visits see box, p.40. For a more thorough introduction into Fijian life, consider joining one of the internationally organized gap-year education programmes where you assist in teaching at a remote village school and live with the people (see below for details).

Boasting numerous diverse and unchartered coral reefs, Fiji is also the focus for several global institutions conducting scientific **marine research**. It's possible to join one of these groups on a working holiday, volunteering in research and gathering information, often on remote islands. Make sure you research your trip thoroughly though, since there have been reports that some for-profit organizations fail to feed and house volunteers adequately, turning what should be a rewarding break into an ordeal.

ORGANIZATIONS FOR WORKING HOLIDAYS AND VOLUNTEERS

Frontier UK ☎ 020 7613 2422, 🖰 frontier.ac.uk. English-teaching project based in Suva costs £1195 for four weeks including a weekend of TEFL training. They also run medical, marine, journalism and animal welfare projects.

Gapforce UK ☎ 020 736 2796, US and Canada ☎ 1 888 249 4533, 🖰 gapforce.org. Six- to ten-week programme assisting in the survey of coral reefs on behalf of the World Conservation Society. From £2000 per person. No dive experience required.

Lattitude Australia ☎ 03 9826 6266, 🖰 lattitude.org.au. Six-month teacher placements in Nadi, Suva and Levuka from A$6585.

Loloma Foundation US 🖰 lolomafoundation.org. Medical and dental missions by volunteer doctors, nurses and consultants visiting remote villages in Taveuni and the Yasawas.

Peace Corps US ☎ 855 855 1961, 🖰 peacecorps.gov. Over eighty volunteers work all around Fiji assisting in a wide range of community projects, from environmental and health awareness to teaching information technology.

Think Pacific UK ☎ 0113 335 9919, 🖰 thinkpacific.com. Sports coaching and teacher placements in Levuka and Suva from £1100 for four weeks.

Vinaka Fiji Fiji ☎ 999 5512, 🖰 vinakafiji.org.fj.com. Mixing holiday and volunteering, visitors stay at backpacker resorts in the Yasawas and help with village community projects or marine conservation. From F$1659 for a week.

Culture and etiquette

Any discussion of Fijian culture must take account of the split between ethnic Fijians, popularly known as iTaukei, and their Indo-Fijian adopted neighbours. Over the years, racial tensions between the two groups have plagued the country and, although at street level iTaukei and Indo-Fijians get on well enough, they have vastly different cultures and aspirations and tend not to mix socially. Considering them as a whole is thus difficult, although you'll find the Fijian people generally extremely hospitable, generous and community-orientated. As a nation, they tend also to be deeply religious with church, temple and mosque well attended.

In **rural areas**, both among iTaukei and Indo-Fijians, men and women have distinct roles and seldom mix in social settings. Macho behaviour is common and women travellers may find they experience unwanted attention. Among iTaukei a strong heritage of tribal customs influences day-to-day life. For more information on these traditional customs, see box, p.40.

As for **dress codes**, local women dress modestly. Shorts, sleeveless tops and short skirts are acceptable in town centres although they may draw unwanted attention. Bikinis are fine at the pool or the beach, but not out and about, and bathing topless is strictly forbidden. Most restaurants and resorts have a pretty casual, relaxed dress code. The most conservative environment for dress is in the villages where it's expected that women cover their shoulders and that both men and women wear *sulus* or at least shorts covering the knees: see box, p.40 for more on village etiquette.

Fijians tend to go to bed early and wake up early so don't expect much to be going on after 9pm. When meeting, locals are eager to shake hands and ask you where you're from, and usually exchange pleasantries when passing – a hearty "**bula**" being almost mandatory in rural areas, although in town centres this greeting is usually a ruse for selling you something. Fijians do not, as a rule, shout at each other or demand service. Visitors often become frustrated at how slowly things move and the detached attitude when a problem arises – **sega na leqa** rules, a mix of the Latin American *mañana* and the Australian "no worries mate". There is little you can do about it and the more anxious or frustrated you get the less sympathy or assistance you'll be shown. Slow down, relax and take it Fiji time.

Shopping

Fiji is not a great shopping destination, hindered by its isolation and heavy import duties and starved by lack of individual creativity in design and fashion. With a dearth of boutique shops and art galleries, your best bet is to head to the urban municipal markets, which ooze character, overflow with local produce and have the most authentic collection of handicrafts.

Both Nadi and Suva have **handicraft markets**, although both suffer from pushy sales people – try to pick out the artisan traders who are often busy weaving, polishing or sewing their wares. Woodcarving items include beautifully polished and patterned rimmed *tanoa* bowls, war clubs, cannibal forks and totemic items such as turtles and face masks. Bags woven from pandanus leaves and styled with tapa cloth are often eye-catching, as is jewellery made from coconut shells. Hand-woven mats costing from F$80, depending on the fineness of the weave, make practical souvenirs.

The best places to buy **local crafts** direct from the artisans are from the Flea Market in Suva (see p.147) or, if your timing is right, at one of the craft fairs in Nadi organized by the Western Arts & Craft Society every few months. Otherwise, there are several Jacks stores on Viti Levu which sell quality crafts, a variety of scented **coconut oils**, creams and soaps, locally harvested **black pearls**, colourful ranges of clothing and other knick-knacks often sourced from overseas – they also provide a shipping service.

The shopping experience can be hampered by shopkeepers standing in their doorways pestering tourists to come in and look, particularly in Nadi. You'll need to **haggle** at all souvenir and clothes shops, particularly the smaller Indo-Fijian shops and market stalls. Hard bargaining, though, is not an iTaukei custom so if buying at market from an indigenous Fijian, the asking price will invariably be realistic. You should avoid buying any type of **shell**, especially giant clam, turtle and triton shells which are all banned as export items, as is the *tabua* **whale's tooth**.

Shops are few and far between on the outer islands so it's wise to **stock up** on provisions before

VISITING A FIJIAN VILLAGE

Visiting a traditional village provides a unique insight into Fijian culture. As soon as you arrive at a village, excitable kids call out "bula!", elders take the time to shake your hand and you'll invariably receive offers to stay for a meal or longer.

TOURS AND VILLAGE STAYS

Most resorts offer **village tours**, often including a trip to a craft market and a simple *yaqona* ceremony (see box, p.31). While these can be a good option for those short on time, you may end up visiting nearby villages which have become over-commercialized. The best tours visit the more remote, traditional villages and are often combined with adventure activities such as rafting or kayaking.

There's nothing to stop you visiting a village **unaccompanied**, providing you follow the tips below. For a full immersion into Fijian life consider staying overnight in a Fijian **village** either with a family or in a purpose-built community-owned guest bure. Kadavu (see p.157) is an excellent place to experience traditional culture, as are the Yasawa Islands (see p.90), which come with the added bonus of beautiful beaches.

VILLAGE ETIQUETTE

When visiting a village there is a certain amount of **etiquette** to follow – the government is currently in the process of introducing a somewhat controversial bylaw outlining the expectations of traditional village etiquette and its enforcement. As a foreigner, locals won't expect you to follow all the rules but the more you pick up the more you'll be respected. The following are a few useful pointers:

- Dress conservatively – men and particularly women should cover shoulders and knees, and preferably wear a **sulu** (Fijian sarong) around the waist, even if over trousers.
- Avoid visiting a village on a **Sunday**, which is a special day for religion, family, rest and attending church.
- Before entering a village, remove anything covering your head, such as hats or sunglasses, and carry any backpacks in front of you – don't hide them as this arouses suspicion. These rules don't apply on beaches, which are outside village jurisdiction.
- On arrival, you should present a **sevusevu** or introductory gift to the **turaga-ni-koro** (village headman). *Yaqona* is the most appropriate form of *sevusevu* and can be bought at all town markets, preferably in root form or otherwise prepared as *waqa* (powder) – the minimum per group should be 300g of roots or powder to a value of around $30. A small gift of around F$20 for the village chief is sometimes requested as well.
- Other appreciated **gifts** include books and magazines; food, such as a cake or pudding (if staying overnight); school stationery for children or toys such as balloons or balls.
- When first entering a house or hall, always use the front door; remove your shoes beforehand, crouch when passing through the door and sit cross-legged with your head a little stooped as a sign of respect. It is polite to shake hands with anyone you meet in the village and introduce yourself simply by name, town and country.
- As part of the ceremony to welcome you to the village, you may be invited to drink **yaqona**, Fiji's national drink, with the chief. For more details on this ceremony, see box, p.31.
- Taking **photos** is acceptable except during the initial *yaqona* ceremony. Fijians take pride in being photographed and will often ask you to take their picture and to see it afterwards. Sending printed photographs, preferably with you in it as well, is a nice follow-up gesture.
- If invited to **eat**, sit cross-legged and wait until everybody has sat down. The head of the house will say grace (*masu*) after which you can start eating, normally using your hands. You may find yourself the only person eating, with someone fanning the food for you – don't be put off, this is a common gesture reserved for guests.

TOP 5 VILLAGES TO VISIT

Malakati, Nacula, Yasawa Islands (see p.99)
Navala, inland Viti Levu (see p.130)
Natale-i-Ra, east coast Viti Levu (see p.122)
Arovudi, Ovalau (see p.174)
Lavena, Taveuni (see p.209)

you depart Viti Levu. In an emergency, most outer-island resorts have small shops selling sun cream and other essentials at greatly inflated prices.

Travelling with children

Often viewed as a romantic escape for couples, Fiji is in fact a popular family holiday destination, especially among Australians and New Zealanders. With enormous empathy and affection for children, Fijians make fabulous hosts and those with infants will find the locals eager to entertain your children at every opportunity. Most resorts have complimentary kids' clubs and plenty of family-orientated water activities.

Soft sand and gentle waves are a great formula for family holidays, with the beach resorts along the **Mamanucas** a particular favourite, notably *Treasure Island* (see p.80), *Plantation Island* (see p.83) and *Castaway Island* (see p.85). In the Yasawas, try *Paradise Cove* (see p.97), *Oarsman's Bay* (see p.100) or the more budget-orientated *Barefoot Kuata* (see p.95). The large resorts along the **Coral Coast** (see p.115) are also popular, with several good family attractions including the Kula Eco Park as well as adventure activities around **Pacific Harbour** for older children.

Most resorts allow kids under a certain age to **stay for free** if sharing a room with their parents – some even offer free meals too. The upmarket boutique resorts, however, often have a strict **no-child policy** to ensure a romantic atmosphere for their guests, or may allow kids only during dedicated holiday periods. The *Jean-Michel Cousteau Resort* (see p.198) on Vanua Levu is one of the few luxury resorts that welcomes families: other outer-island resorts which actively encourage families are *Tides Reach* (see p.207) on Taveuni and *Papageno Resort* (see p.162) on Kadavu. For those on a budget, many of the backpacker resorts have family rooms, especially in Nadi.

Rural **villages** are a fascinating environment for children of all ages and they'll most likely be enthusiastically welcomed by the village kids, encouraged to play and generally well looked after.

Minor **health issues** are the greatest concern for parents travelling with young children, especially from the adverse effects of high humidity, intense sun and mosquito bites. Medicated baby powder for the prevention of rashes and sores is an essential item to carry. In the main towns, high-quality baby formula, nappies and children's medications imported from Australia are readily available. **Breast feeding** in public is fairly commonplace, especially so in rural environments, although baby-changing facilities are rarely offered. Note that **public toilets** are few and far between.

If travelling by car or taxi, seat belts, let alone dedicated infant **car seats**, are difficult to find, although the major car rental companies do provide them. **Prams** in general are not that practical to travel with: pathways are sandy at many of the resorts, and even around towns pavements are seldom pram friendly.

Travel essentials

Costs

For travellers most items will appear very affordable, especially public transport, dining out and buying local food. If frugal, you can survive on F$70 (£26/€31/US$33) per day, staying in dorms, preparing your own meals and travelling on public transport. Stay in private rooms and eat out regularly and you'll need around F$150 (£57/€67/US$72), although extras such as alcohol, car rental, scuba diving and sightseeing tours will all add to your costs. Travelling around the two largest islands of Viti Levu and Vanua Levu offers the best value, with prices on the outer islands usually inflated by at least 20 percent. Note that **tipping** is not expected and in traditional Fijian society causes embarrassment.

Hostel **accommodation** will set you back around F$30 a person for a basic dorm bed, or F$120 per person including meals at the popular Yasawa backpacker resorts. Town hotel rooms start from around F$90, with double or twin rooms often the same price as a single. A moderate beach resort bure starts from F$300, the more popular holiday resorts cost from F$450 and a luxury boutique resort will set you back anything from F$800 to over F$2000 per night.

Food on the whole is reasonably cheap, with local produce offering by far the best value, especially when purchased from the roadside or at municipal markets. Supermarket shelves tend to be dominated by more expensive imported food items, mostly canned and restricted in variety. Dining out is affordable, with cheap restaurant counter food costing from F$7 a serving, and main dishes ordered from a menu from F$10 to F$25; resort restaurants are invariably more expensive.

Travelling around Viti Levu by public transport is especially cheap, with the five-hour journey from Nadi to Suva costing just F$20, and local journeys starting from 80¢. Visiting the offshore or outer islands is going to eat up a larger chunk of your budget. For example, the hop-on, hop-off boat pass along the Yasawas costs F$530 for seven days, and a domestic flight from Nadi to Taveuni can cost up to F$390 one way, although discounted fares are often available via airline websites. The cheapest fare on a passenger ferry from Suva to Taveuni costs from F$67 one way.

Every traveller over twelve years of age leaving Fiji pays a **departure tax** of F$200, although this is always included in the cost of your airline ticket.

Crime and personal safety

As in any society, **crime** exists in Fiji but it's certainly not rife and not nearly as common as in most European or North American cities. **Petty theft** stems from a cultural trait where the individual owns few possessions, shares everything freely and is bound by the beliefs of *kerekere*, a form of asking for something with the owner being obliged to give. It's especially common among hotel workers and you may find clothes or small change frequently going missing from bures and communal resort areas. Bring in clothes and shoes at night and certainly don't leave money or jewellery lying about as an invitation.

With machismo entrenched in Fijian culture, **sexual harassment** can be an issue for female travellers – a firm "not interested" should ward off any unwanted attention while all the usual precautions apply, such as avoiding walking alone at night. If in need of assistance contact the Fiji Women's Crisis Centre (ⓦfijiwomen.com) in Nadi (ⓣ670 7558), Ba (ⓣ667 0466), Suva (ⓣ331 3300), Rakiraki (ⓣ669 4012), or Labasa (ⓣ881 4609). Domestic violence, or *buturaki*, "**the beating**" as it's rather crudely known in Fiji, is also disturbingly prevalent, and a bruised eye is seldom concealed or reported to the authorities. At the same time Fijians are a respectful society and treat each other and

especially visitors with kindness.

Although commonly smoked by young urban Fijians, **marijuana** possession is strictly illegal and is strongly discouraged in more traditional rural areas where it is perceived as a dangerous evil – if a village youth is caught smoking more than once, public floggings may result. The official penalty for marijuana possession is three months in jail, so think carefully before indulging.

The **Fijian police** are for the most part helpful, with police stations in all towns and major settlements. Larger towns have additional posts in busy areas.

Electricity

Fiji's electrical current is 220–240 volts (50Hz) with a **three-pin plug** common with Australia and New Zealand. Fluctuation in current and surges are common, especially in the outer islands where electricity is run by diesel generator, so it's advisable to have a **surge protector** if using electrical equipment. In many resorts, 110 volt outlets for shavers and hairdryers are provided.

Entry requirements

All visitors to Fiji must hold a valid passport for at least six months beyond the intended period of stay, and proof of onward travel to another country. Adhering to the above, a four-month **tourist visa** is issued on arrival to most nationals including those of Australia, New Zealand, South Africa, the US, Canada and EU member states. For a complete list, check the Tourism Fiji website (ⓦfiji.travel).

A maximum **two-month visa extension** may be issued on application to the Immigration Department at Nadi Airport or Suva, but there are no provisions for stays beyond six months for any overseas nationals unless obtaining resident status or work/student visas.

All visitors are required to fill out standard immigration cards upon arrival; the retained perforated section must be surrendered to Fiji immigration authorities upon departure.

FIJIAN EMBASSIES ABROAD

Australia Fiji High Commission, 19 Beale Crescent, Deakin, ACT 2600 ⓣ06 260 5115.

Belgium Fiji Embassy, 92–94 Square Plasky, 1030 Bruxelles ⓣ32 2 736 9050.

New Zealand Fiji High Commission, 31 Pipitea St, Thorndon, Wellington 6011 ⓣ04 473 5401.

UK and Ireland Fiji High Commission, 34 Hyde Park Gate, London SW7 5DN ⓣ020 7584 3661.

EMERGENCIES

ⓣ917 is the free **emergency** telephone number to summon the police. Call either ⓣ910 or 911 for ambulance or fire service.

US Fiji Embassy, 1707 L St, Suite 200, Washington DC 20036 ☎ 202 466 8320.

EMBASSIES AND CONSULATES IN FIJI

Australia High Commission, 37 Princes Rd, Tamavua, Suva ☎ 338 2211.
European Union Commission, 6th floor, Tappoo City Complex, Victoria Parade, Suva ☎ 331 3633.
Federated States of Micronesia 37 Loftus Rd, Suva ☎ 330 4566.
Kiribati 36 McGregor Rd, Suva ☎ 330 2512.
New Zealand 10th floor, Reserve Bank Building, Pratt St, Suva ☎ 331 1422.
South Africa 16 Kimberley St, Suva ☎ 331 1087.
Tuvalu 16 Gorrie St, Suva ☎ 330 1355.
UK High Commission, 47 Gladstone Rd, Suva ☎ 322 9100.
US Embassy, 158 Princes Rd, Tamavua ☎ 330 0081.

Gay and lesbian travellers

Gay and lesbian travellers shouldn't feel any sort of discrimination in Fiji, especially within resort environments where many openly homosexual staff work. However, gay behaviour is far more evident than lesbian and open affection between women may generate curiosity. In urban areas, homosexuality and cross-dressing are quite open, although it's frowned upon in the conservative Christian-dominated village environment where discretion is advisable.

Insurance

You should always have **travel insurance** that covers you against theft, illness and injury. Most policies exclude so-called dangerous sports unless an additional premium is paid: in Fiji this can mean snorkelling, surfing or scuba diving. If you need to make a claim, you should keep all receipts for medicines and treatment as well as transport and any additional accommodation bills while recuperating. In the event of having anything stolen, you must obtain an official statement from the police confirming this.

Internet

Almost all large hotels and boutique resorts offer **internet access** – a few of the larger hotels around Viti Levu also have wi-fi or broadband sockets in rooms. On the outer islands, internet access is not always available, especially at the budget resorts in the Yasawas; when it is available it's generally slower and more expensive than elsewhere. Throughout this guide, we have included the symbol ☞ in accommodation reviews where free wi-fi is available and ☞($), where wi-fi is available but at an extra charge. Prices are typically at least F$25 an hour at the luxury hotels and outer-island resorts, F$5 to F$10 an hour at the backpacker hostels and around F$1 to F$2 an hour at private **internet cafés**. Internet cafés can be found in most town centres – especially in Nadi, Lautoka and Suva – where competition is fierce and prices sometimes fall below F$1 an hour.

Laundry

Most hotels and resorts provide a **laundry service** for guests, although self-service machines are seldom available. Independent laundries, which tend to be better value, can be found in the larger towns, or at Vuda, Port Denarau and Savusavu marinas.

Living in Fiji

Due to high levels of unemployment, it is difficult to obtain a **work permit** for Fiji. Many expatriates work in the hospitality industry and if you have relevant work experience or **specific skills** such as languages or scuba diving qualifications, you may find resort work. However, prospective employers in any field must demonstrate that they have conducted an exhaustive but unsuccessful search for a qualified Fijian candidate and must post a bond to cover the costs of shipping you home if

---

ROUGH GUIDES TRAVEL INSURANCE

Rough Guides has teamed up with WorldNomads.com to offer great travel insurance deals. Policies are available to residents of over 150 countries, with cover for a wide range of adventure sports, 24hr emergency assistance, high levels of medical and evacuation cover and a stream of travel safety information. Roughguides.com users can take advantage of their policies online 24/7, from anywhere in the world – even if you're already travelling. And since plans often change when you're on the road, you can extend your policy and even claim online. Roughguides.com users who buy travel insurance with WorldNomads.com can also leave a positive footprint and donate to a community development project. For more information, go to ⓦ roughguides.com/travel-insurance.

you become incapacitated. Few are willing to go through this process unless your skills are particularly desirable.

International students may apply for enrolment at the University of the South Pacific (ⓦusp.com.fj, ☎323 1000) on either a cross-credit semester or a full-time course, providing you have attained a High School certificate pass or similar from your home country. There's no age limit for enrolment and a student visa is granted to all successful applicants providing a clean police record and clear medical including a negative HIV test.

Alternatively, a variety of marine conservation organizations offer unpaid or even you-pay **internships** for periods lasting a week to several months (see p.38).

Alternatively, if you have a large chunk of money you're willing to invest and you can find a local partner who must hold at least a fifty-percent shareholding, you can set up or purchase a **business**. Specific questions should be addressed to Investment Fiji (☎331 5988, ⓦinvestmentfiji.org .fj), at Civic Tower on Victoria Parade in Suva, with another office at 21 Tui Street in Lautoka.

Mail

Run by Post Fiji, all **post offices** (Mon–Fri 8am–5pm, Sat 8am–noon) have telephones and sell phone cards for international and local calls; larger branches sell stationery and postcards.

Post can be slow, especially **posting items to Fiji** and it's not uncommon for letters to take three weeks from North America or Europe, with delivery to the outer islands often taking an additional week. **Posting items from Fiji** is cheap and somewhat quicker, with letters to Europe commonly taking less than ten days. All letters and postcards should be labelled with an airmail sticker otherwise they may go by boat, taking months to arrive. UPS, DHL and Federal Express all have offices in Suva and Nadi, although Post Fiji's in-house **courier service**, EMS, is considerably cheaper.

Stamps are available from most hotels and gift shops, as well as some bookstores. Public mail boxes are very rare, and you should always find the nearest post office to mail important items; most resorts, especially those on the outer islands, will post letters for you.

Poste restante is available at all post offices. Letters should be marked "General Delivery, Poste Restante", followed by the location of the post office and your name. Letters will be held for two months – for post sent to Nadi, be sure to specify either Nadi Town or Nadi Airport. To receive a parcel in Fiji, you must clear it through the post office's customs counter (Mon–Fri 9am–1pm & 2pm–4pm), and pay a service charge plus any customs or import duty.

Maps

Navigating between towns is very straightforward, with just one or two main roads on each island. General-purpose town or island **maps** are hard to come by, the most useful being the free Jason's Travel Media map available from most hotel tour desks. A slightly more detailed folded sheet map is published by Hema and available in bookstores and large chain stores around Nadi and Suva for F$12.95.

For 1:250,000 **topographical maps** of the individual islands and 1:15,000 town maps (around F$8–9 each), contact the Lands and Survey Department (☎331 8631, ⓦlands.gov.fj) or visit the Map Shop at 94 Raojibhai Patel St in Downtown Suva.

Money

Fiji's currency is the **Fiji dollar** (F$) divided into 100¢. Notes come in F$2, F$5, F$10, F$20, F$50 and F$100 denominations; F$100 notes are hard

---

ADDRESSES

Fijian **addresses** are something of an enigma. There is no door-to-door postal service so anybody wanting to receive mail uses a PO Box number; consequently few people know their residential address or display a house number. In towns, the majority of shops and businesses don't have a shop number, although street addresses are mostly signposted. On Viti Levu, the main road around the island – called the Queens Road along the south coast and the Kings Road along the north coast – passes through most towns where it more commonly reverts to "Main Street" or "High Street". On outer islands, addresses are a complete unknown except identifying a village or settlement. Directions are equally vague and you shouldn't necessarily take someone's earnest advice as fact.

PUBLIC HOLIDAYS

The following are **public holidays** in Fiji, when government offices, banks, schools and most shops are closed. Note some public holiday dates vary from year to year – see ⓦfiji.gov.fj for official dates.

New Year's Day January 1
Good Friday
Easter Saturday
Easter Monday
National Sports and Wellness Day June 30
Constitution Day September 7
Fiji Day October 10
Diwali Late October/early November
Prophet Mohammed's Birthday November – date varies each year
Christmas December 25
Boxing Day December 26

to trade at small shops or in villages. All notes proudly feature Queen Elizabeth II along with other traditional and iconic symbols. Any foreign currency should be exchanged at one of the five bank chains, including ANZ and Westpac, or with one of the many currency exchange outlets found in the main towns and at Nadi Airport. The current **exchange rate** at the time of going to press is F$1=US$0.49; £0.39; €0.45; AUS$0.63; and NZ$0.69

Travellers' cheques tend only to be accepted by hotels or cashed at banks, but **credit and debit cards** are widely accepted, although only Visa and MasterCard, and very occasionally AMEX; all usually incur a service charge of around 4 percent. Almost all hotels operate a room-billing system paid on check-out rather than pay-as-you-go. If visiting the Yasawas, bear in mind some of the budget resorts and village stays are cash-only; check with the resort beforehand.

ATM machines are available in all towns on Viti Levu except Tavua and Korovou, in Levuka on Ovalau, at Savusavu and Labasa on Vanua Levu and at Naqara on Taveuni, as well as at Nadi Airport, RB Jetpoint in Martintar, Midwest Superette at Wailoaloa, the shopping mall in Port Denarau and several of the large hotel chains in Nadi and along the Coral Coast. If you plan on using your debit card or credit card at an ATM, make sure you have a PIN number that works overseas.

Having **money wired** from home is never convenient or cheap and should only be considered as a last resort. The post office and NewWorld Supermarket act as agents for Western Union (ⓦwesternunion.com), which also has branches at Nadi Airport, Nadi Town, Lautoka and Suva; MoneyGram (ⓦmoneygram.com) operates

via Westpac Bank and most Morris Hedstrom supermarkets. Direct bank transfers are also possible but you'll need the address and swift code of the bank branch where you want to pick up the money and the address and swift code of the bank's Suva head office which will act as the clearing house; money wired this way usually takes two working days to arrive and costs around £25/US$40 per transaction.

Opening hours

Business hours at government and private offices are Monday to Friday 8am to 5pm, with offices generally closed for at least an hour for lunch, sometimes two. Regular **banking hours** are Monday to Friday 9am to 4pm, although banks have slightly shorter hours on Mondays and Fridays; specific bank details are listed throughout the Guide. Most **high street shops** are open Monday to Friday 8.30am to 5pm and Saturday 8am–noon, while bakeries tend to open at 6am and some **supermarkets** and local grocery shops don't close until 8pm. The majority of **restaurants** are open seven days a week, the most likely time of closure being Sunday lunch and for a couple of hours from 3pm to 5pm.

Phones

Before travelling, contact your mobile network provider to ensure you can use your phone in Fiji. It will almost certainly work out cheaper buying a **local SIM card** for your phone along with pre-paid calling time: these are available from many retail outlets around the islands. Alterternatively, you can buy a simple mobile phone with SIM card in Nadi for under F$100. Mobile phone **coverage** around

CALLING HOME FROM FIJI

Note that the initial zero is omitted from the area code when dialling the UK, Ireland, Australia and New Zealand from abroad.

Australia 00 + 61 + city code.
New Zealand 00 + 64 + city code.
Republic of Ireland 00 + 353 + city code.
South Africa 00 + 27 + city code.
UK 00 + 44 + city code.
US & Canada 00 + 1 + area code.

the main islands of Viti Levu and Vanua Levu is poor outside the main urban areas and certainly in the highlands; reception in the Mamanucas and Yasawa islands is pretty good throughout, although in some places you might have to climb a hill to get reception.

The cheapest option of all though, is **VoIP** (Voice over Internet Protocol), calls (for example ⓦ skype .com) from an internet café.

Public phones and phone cards

Public phones remain a good option for calling, with over 1500 distinctly styled *drua* phone booths around the country operated by **TeleCard**. Cards, available in F$3 and F$5 denominations only, can be purchased from all post offices and many retail outlets, and can be used from private landlines, although they are often barred from being used in hotel rooms.

Local calls have become substantially cheaper in recent years: they cost 10¢ a minute from landlines, and 40¢ per minute from a Fiji SIM mobile phone. **Overseas calls** to major destinations cost 20¢ per minute from a Fiji SIM mobile phone and 30–40¢ per minute from a landline. Calling from hotel rooms usually involves a hefty surcharge. Consider buying a **telephone charge card** from your phone company back home. Using a PIN number, you can make calls from most hotel, public and private phones that will be charged to your account, but check to see Fiji is covered and bear in mind that rates aren't necessarily cheaper than calling from a mobile phone.

Photography

Fiji is a photographer's paradise, with wonderful scenery and vivid colours. If in a village, it's polite to ask before taking photographs. As Fijians tend to pose for the camera it can be difficult to get natural and spontaneous expressions – after snapping a few posed pictures, wait until the

scene becomes more natural before shooting again. The most dramatic **light** is experienced early in the morning and late in the afternoon, although taking pictures of beaches and lagoons is good when the sun is high in the sky and the blues are pronounced. **Memory cards** are available in Nadi, Lautoka and Suva, although at higher prices than in the US or Europe.

Smoking

Smoking is socially acceptable in public places, although it has been officially banned on public transport. Some restaurants and a few bars have self-imposed smoke-free zones.

Time

Fiji has a single **time zone**, being twelve hours ahead of Greenwich Mean Time (GMT), an hour ahead of Sydney and twenty hours ahead of Los Angeles. The sun has a minimal variation from summer to winter, rising between 5am and 6am and setting from 6pm to 7pm, always with only a brief period of twilight. **Daylight saving** occurs over the Christmas holiday period, with the clocks going forward an hour in late November and back an hour at the end of January.

Tourist information

Almost every hotel, resort and hostel in Fiji has its own tour desk offering brochures and a booking service.

The government-funded **Tourism Fiji** provides basic tourist information through its website ⓦ fiji .travel. Its head office is sited in an obscure location at the Colonial Plaza in Namaka, Nadi (Mon–Thurs 8am–4.30pm, Fri 8am–4pm; ☏ 672 2433) where you can pick up tourist brochures but not much else.

Three of the outer-island regions have their own privately funded tourism organizations: the Savusavu Tourism Association (ⓦ fiji-savusavu.com); the Taveuni Tourism Association (ⓦ pure-taveuni .com); and Tourism Kadavu (ⓦ kadavufiji.org).

TOURISM FIJI OFFICES OVERSEAS

Australia Level 12, St Martin's Tower, 31 Market St, Sydney ☏ 02 9264 3399.
New Zealand 177 Parnell Rd, Parnell, Auckland ☏ 09 376 2533.
UK Lion House, 111 Hare Lane, Claygate, Surrey KT10 0QY ☏ 0800 652 2158.
US 5777 West Century Boulevard, Suite 220, Los Angeles, CA 90045 ☏ 310 568 1616.

USEFUL WEBSITES

Ⓦ **fiji.travel** The official Tourism Fiji website.

Ⓦ **islandsbusiness.com** Current events and issues affecting Fiji and its Pacific Island neighbours.

Ⓦ **spto.org** Useful website for sourcing hotels, tours, travel agents and cultural events throughout the South Pacific.

Ⓦ **www.met.gov.fj** Daily weather forecasts and 7-day outlooks: it's particularly handy in times of weather warnings.

GOVERNMENT SITES

Australian Department of Foreign Affairs Ⓦ dfat.gov.au, Ⓦ smartraveller.gov.au.

British Foreign & Commonwealth Office Ⓦ fco.gov.uk.

Canadian Department of Foreign Affairs Ⓦ dfait-maeci.gc.ca.

Irish Department of Foreign Affairs Ⓦ foreignaffairs.gov.ie.

New Zealand Ministry of Foreign Affairs Ⓦ mft.govt.nz.

US State Department Ⓦ travel.state.gov.

Travellers with disabilities

Fiji has a poor infrastructure for **travellers with disabilities**. There's no provision for wheelchairs on public transport and pavements are rarely in a fit state for wheelchairs or the visually impaired – holes, ledges and cracks are all too common and there are few ramps at street corners. Moreover, many resort pathways are made of sand, making mobility extremely difficult. Fortunately, Fijians will go out of their way to make your travels comfortable, assisting whenever possible and even building temporary ramps for disabled guests at resorts. The Fiji National Council for Disabled Persons, at Qarase House on Brown Street in Suva (☎ 331 9045, Ⓦ fncdp.org), can offer general advice and information.

Nadi and around

NADI MUNICIPAL MARKET

1

Nadi and around

Almost all of Fiji's 800,000 annual visitors get their first glimpse of the country descending towards Nadi International Airport. Tiny tropical islands glint in the ocean off Nadi Bay while Viti Levu's spectacular mountains loom inland. Given this introduction, Nadi (pronounced *Nan-dee*) itself can come as an anticlimax. Despite boasting Fiji's third largest population, it's not really a city, rather a collective of three rather chaotic commercial precincts, two tourist-orientated beach suburbs and a handful of Fijian villages all interspersed by sugarcane fields. Where Nadi is useful is in its extensive choice of accommodation and abundance of excellent restaurants: with almost half the country's tourist beds, from five-star resorts to beach hostels dotted along the coastline, it makes a popular base for exploring the inland valleys, forests and villages and for day-cruises to the islands. Its nightlife, however, is tame and for most backpackers it is merely the starting-point to plan an onward journey around the islands.

Nadi Airport, 10km north of the Downtown area, is a low-key and verdant arrival point, with a small cluster of hotels and surrounded by farmland. Heading south along the two-lane Queens Road you arrive first at **Namaka**, a frenetic shopping parade, while further south the suburb of **Martintar** is home to Nadi's best nightlife, plus an abundance of ethnic and international restaurants and half a dozen affordable hotels. South again, beyond the villages of Navoci and Namotomoto, scruffy **Downtown Nadi** is the lively terminal for buses, and home to the municipal market, internet cafés, boutique shops and cheap Chinese restaurants, but little accommodation. The southern point of town, where sugarcane fields take over, is guarded by Nadi's sole attraction, the colourful, iconic **Sri Siva Subrahmaniya Swami Temple**. A few kilometres west off the Queens Road lie the beaches of **Nadi Bay**, with the budget hotspot of **Wailoaloa** and upmarket **Denarau Island** in the centre, and **Vuda** and **Momi** at its northern and southern tips respectively.

Inland, there are tropical waterfalls, traditional villages and some breathtaking hiking trails in the serene valleys and mountain ranges of **Sabeto**, **Nausori Highlands** and **Koroyanitu National Park** – the latter accessed via the utilitarian port of **Lautoka**, home to the region's best shops.

Brief history

Before the 1870s, Nadi was a wild, uncharted land feared by the tyrants of eastern Viti and rarely visited by European explorers or missionaries. In 1870, a small British community, known as the **Nadi Swells** for their broad-brimmed hats and affluent demeanour, set up cotton and cattle farms along the Nadi River. Soon after, with the establishment of **sugarcane** as a viable crop and with indentured labourers arriving from India, the region began its transformation to an Indian-dominated market centre. During World War II, the US military constructed a major **airbase** here and two large British gun batteries were erected at either end of Nadi Bay to protect the two navigable

SUNSET AT WAILOALOA BEACH

Highlights

❶ Sri Siva Subrahmaniya Swami Temple The largest Hindu edifice in the Southern Hemisphere is a riot of colours and beautiful carvings. **See p.53**

❷ Newtown Beach, Wailoaloa Take a sunset stroll along the beach at this travellers' hotspot and grab a cool beer at the *Bamboo Travellers* bar. **See p.54**

❸ Zip Fiji Momi Enjoy a day whizzing between ancient trees in the rainforest. **See p.65**

❹ Tifajek Mud Pools and Hot Springs Cake yourself in mud then clean off in the volcanically heated water – both fun and therapeutic. **See p.66**

❺ Lautoka market This provincial town hosts one of the country's most dramatic markets – a huge concrete dome overhanging stalls crammed with colourful fresh produce. **See p.68**

❻ Koroyanitu National Heritage Park Make an overnight trek to this stunning region and sleep in a small hut on the top of Mount Batilamu. **See p.70**

HIGHLIGHTS ARE MARKED ON THE MAP ON P.52

1

passages. The Japanese invasion never came, but the paved runway was big enough to receive the first jet planes and, with a slight expansion in the 1960s, Nadi established itself as Fiji's **tourist hub**. In 2017, the town was granted official status as Fiji's third city.

Downtown Nadi

With a population of around fifty thousand, split almost evenly between iTaukei (indigenous Fijians) and Indo-Fijians (of Indian origin), **NADI** has a friendly, rural charm, enhanced by an almost constantly sunny climate. The muddy, flood-prone Nadi River separates **Downtown Nadi** from its northern suburbs. South of the Nadi Bridge, the congested Queens Road, commonly called **Main Street**, is lined with fashion and accessory shops and has a lively market square off to one side. East of the

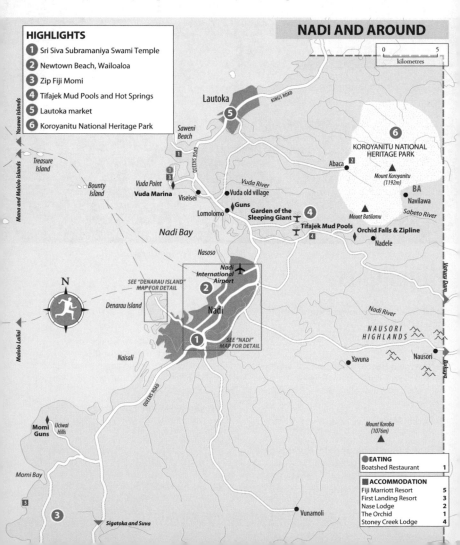

NADI AND AROUND

HIGHLIGHTS
1. Sri Siva Subramaniya Swami Temple
2. Newtown Beach, Wailoaloa
3. Zip Fiji Momi
4. Tifajek Mud Pools and Hot Springs
5. Lautoka market
6. Koroyanitu National Heritage Park

0   5
kilometres

KINGS ROAD

Lautoka **5**

Saweni Beach

Koroyanitu National Heritage Park **6**

Abaca **2**

Mount Koroyanitu (1192m)

BA

Navilawa

Sabeto River

Vuda Point
Vuda Marina
Viseisei
Vuda old village
Lomolomo
Guns

Vuda River

Garden of the Sleeping Giant
Tifajek Mud Pools **4**
Mount Batilamu
Orchid Falls & Zipline
Nadele

Nadi Bay

Nasoso

Nadi International Airport **2**

Denarau Island
SEE "DENARAU ISLAND" MAP FOR DETAIL

Nadi

1
SEE "NADI" MAP FOR DETAIL

Nadi River

NAUSORI HIGHLANDS

Naisali

Yavuna

Nausori

Mount Koroba (1076m)

Yasawa Islands

Mana and Malolo Islands

Treasure Island

Bounty Island

Malolo Lailai

Momi **Guns**
Uciwai Hills

Momi Bay

5

3

Sigatoka and Suva

Vunamoli

Yanuya Dam

EATING
Boatshed Restaurant	1

ACCOMMODATION
Fiji Marriott Resort	5
First Landing Resort	3
Nase Lodge	2
The Orchid	1
Stoney Creek Lodge	4

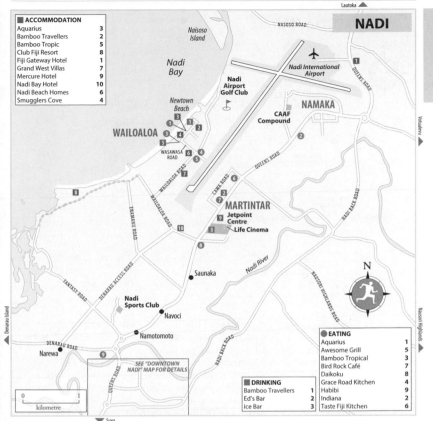

ACCOMMODATION	
Aquarius	3
Bamboo Travellers	2
Bamboo Tropic	5
Club Fiji Resort	8
Fiji Gateway Hotel	1
Grand West Villas	7
Mercure Hotel	9
Nadi Bay Hotel	10
Nadi Beach Homes	6
Smugglers Cove	4

EATING	
Aquarius	1
Awesome Grill	5
Bamboo Tropical	3
Bird Rock Café	7
Daikoku	8
Grace Road Kitchen	4
Habibi	9
Indiana	2
Taste Fiji Kitchen	6

DRINKING	
Bamboo Travellers	1
Ed's Bar	2
Ice Bar	3

market and beyond the **bus stand** is a tiny grandstand overlooking Prince Charles Park, venue for Nadi's rugby and football games.

The **northern half of town**, closest to the river, is by far the most pleasant, with several excellent restaurants serving Indian dishes and some interesting boutique handicraft stores. South of Hospital Road and the **Westpoint Arcade**, however, the sidewalk touts take over, hassling tourists with "Bula mate!" or "Best prices in my shop!", and the area degenerates into cheap canteens and poky convenience shops.

The markets

The liveliest part of Nadi is off Main Street, down Clay Street and into Market Road towards the covered **Nadi Municipal Market** (see p.64), an attractive place to escape the sun, pick up local produce and *yaqona* roots and mingle with the locals.

A few hundred metres south in the Children's Park, 25 wooden stalls make up the **Nadi Handicraft Market** (see p.63), where you'll need to negotiate on prices.

Sri Siva Subrahmaniya Temple

Queens Rd · ☏ 675 1111 · Daily 6am–7pm · F$5 · Remove your shoes before entering

The largest in the Southern Hemisphere, the impressive **Sri Siva Subrahmaniya Swami Temple** (also known as Nadi Temple) dominates the southern end of downtown.

Opened in 1994, this evocative three-tower Hindu temple was built by eight specialist craftsmen brought in from India and took ten years to construct. A leaflet for visitors details the stories behind the vividly coloured murals. The Dravidian temple is dedicated to the deity Murugan, whose statue, specially carved in India, is housed within the 12m-high main pyramidal *vimanam* with a rectangular toped roof. The two towers at the rear of the temple with colourful dome-shaped roofs are dedicated to Ganesh and Shiva. The best time of year to visit is during one of its festivals, the most striking of which is the **Thaipusam Festival** (see box below), held in January/February.

Wailoaloa and Newtown Beach

Although the 3km-long beach fronting **Wailoaloa** has neither gleaming white sands nor an aquamarine lagoon, it does have a tranquil ocean outlook and stunning views towards the mountains. The centrepiece of Wailoaloa is the laidback resort enclave of **Newtown Beach**, Nadi's liveliest spot to spend a few nights and meet fellow travellers.

THAIPUSAM FESTIVAL

The bizarre **Thaipusam Festival** at Nadi's Sri Siva Subrahmaniya Swami Temple calls together thousands of Hindu worshippers to celebrate the birthday of Subrahmaniya, or Lord Murugan, the god of war worshipped among South Indians. During the ten-day festival held over the full moon between January and February, devotees arrive at the temple to pray and cleanse their spirits. Some prove their faith with multiple **body piercings** on the chest, arms, face and tongue while others drag **chariots**, or *kavadris*, attached by sharpened meat hooks pierced into their backs. It's a fascinating and absorbing festival with trance-like parades around the temple buildings led by hypnotic musicians. Be sure to observe common courtesies such as removing shoes before entering the temple grounds and not attending if you have recently drunk alcohol.

1

DAY-TRIPS TO THE MAMANUCAS ISLANDS

If you want to visit the Mamanucas Islands but can't afford to stay at one of the pricey island resorts, Nadi makes an affordable alternative base. Heaps of sightseeing cruises, day-trips to the islands, scuba diving, snorkelling, surfing and game-fishing charters depart from Port Denarau, with most tour companies including complimentary road transfers to and from Nadi hotels.

Around Wasawasa Road, you can enjoy a quiet beer, grab a meal, indulge in *kava* sessions or watch Polynesian dancing (see p.63), with the beach community well connected to Nadi Town by local bus: otherwise it's a 30-minute walk to the shops and restaurants at Martintar.

The sea at Newtown Beach is decent enough for **swimming**, although the murky lagoon can be rather off-putting, blackened from the surrounding mangrove estuaries.

Denarau Island

Denarau Island was once a swampy mangrove forest but with substantial landfill, reclamation and landscaping and, more recently, hotel and residential development, it is now a picturesque but heavily manicured environment. The island boasts nine large resorts – including global giants *Hilton*, *Sofitel*, *Westin*, *Sheraton* and *Radisson* – standing in a line along a sombre grey beach. The beachfront is divided by a rocky point: narrow **west beach**, facing Malolo Island, has the *Sheraton* and *Radisson* resorts and is good for beachcombing, with stronger waves and often littered with driftwood; the wider **north beach** faces Nadi Bay, with tranquil views overlooking the Sleeping Giant, a shapely mountain feature separating Nadi and Lautoka. An eighteen-hole championship **golf course** (see p.58) with meandering canals connecting man-made lakes carpets much of the island, with several holes hemmed in either side by hotel apartments and premium residential properties. Adjacent to the golf clubhouse is a large inflatable **water park** (daily 10am–5pm; F$99), plus a mini-golf course (daily 8.30am–5pm; F$25) and bungee swings (F$17).

Port Denarau

The commercial centre of Denarau and terminal for ferries and day-cruises to the islands is **Port Denarau**. Its modern and sterile shopping centre boasts a dozen **restaurants**, most of which double as bars with views overlooking the marina. You'll also find tour operators, car rental outlets, bicycles, beauty and massage outlets, a bank with ATM and some **shops**, including a newsagent with post office counter, deli and liquor store.

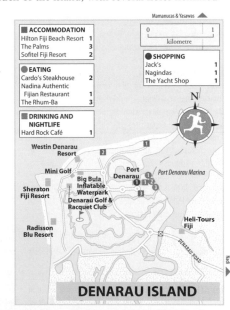

Mamanucas & Yasawas

■ ACCOMMODATION	
Hilton Fiji Beach Resort	1
The Palms	3
Sofitel Fiji Resort	2

0		1
kilometre		

● SHOPPING	
Jack's	1
Nagindas	1
The Yacht Shop	1

● EATING	
Cardo's Steakhouse	2
Nadina Authentic Fijian Restaurant	1
The Rhum-Ba	3

■ DRINKING AND NIGHTLIFE	
Hard Rock Café	

N

Westin Denarau Resort

Mini Golf

Port Denarau

Port Denarau Marina

Sheraton Fiji Resort

Big Bula Inflatable Waterpark

Denarau Golf & Racquet Club

Heli-Tours Fiji

Radisson Blu Resort

DENARAU ROAD

Nadi

DENARAU ISLAND

1

As a tourist hub, Nadi is a major centre for travel, with the international airport, plus the ferry terminal for the Mamanucas and Yasawa Islands at Port Denarau. The easiest way of moving on from Nadi is by bus, with frequent services heading north to Lautoka and south to Suva from both Nadi Airport and Downtown Nadi.

BY PLANE

Nadi International Airport (☎672 5777, ⊛afl.com .fj) handles all international flights into Fiji. International airlines, including Fiji Airways (☎672 0888, ⊛fijiairways .com), Air New Zealand (☎672 2955, ⊛airnewzealand.com) and Aircalin (☎672 2145, ⊛fj.aircalin.com), are based at the arrivals concourse. The domestic flights terminal is in the adjacent building, with Fiji Link (☎672 0888, ⊛fijiairways .com) and Pacific Island Air (☎672 5644, ⊛pacificislandair .com), the latter flying only to the Mamanucas.

Destinations Kadavu (5 weekly; 50min); Labasa (daily; 45min); Malolo Lailai (2 daily; 10min); Mana (2 daily; 15min); Matei, Taveuni (2 daily; 1hr 25min); Nausori, Suva (6 daily; 30min); Savusavu (2 daily; 1hr 10min).

INFORMATION

Tourist information There's no official tourist information at the airport. Once through customs, a help desk manned by Airports Fiji Limited can point you in the right direction for taxis, buses, tour operators and travel agents. For booking assistance, call at the reliable Pacific Destinationz (☎672 3894; daily 5am–9pm) on the far right of the arrivals concourse.

Facilities The airport has free basic showers at both the domestic and arrival concourse toilets and you can leave luggage in a secure storage room (daily 5am–10pm) on the left as you enter the general public area of the arrivals concourse (F$9.50 per item, per day). Tourist SIM cards can also be bought here at Digicel or Vodafone outlets.

GETTING INTO TOWN

Most accommodation includes complimentary pick-ups from international flights; check when you book your room.

By bus Express buses running between Lautoka and Suva call at the departures concourse and will drop you Downtown (F$1.70; 20min). Regular local Downtown buses, stopping at all suburbs along the Queens Rd, leave from opposite *Fiji Gateway Hotel*, a 2min walk from the arrivals concourse (daily 6am–6pm; F$1.10).

By taxi Taxis wait directly outside arrivals (F$11 to Martintar; F$15 to Wailoaloa and Downtown; F$25 to Denarau Island and Vuda).

BY BUS

The main bus station in Nadi is Downtown. For express buses, you buy tickets from the booths run by the individual companies; local buses tickets are purchased on-board.

Express buses At least one express bus departs from Nadi Airport hourly (daily 6.30am–8.30pm) travelling along the Nadi Back Rd to the Downtown bus station (15min) and on to Suva (4hr 30min) with a/c and free wi-fi: the most comfortable is Sunbeam Transport (☎666 2822, ⊛sunbeamfiji.com; F$15.50), with large cushioned seats and big windows. Other options include Pacific Transport (☎670 0044, ⊛pacifictransport.com .fj; F$14.50) and Sunset Express (☎354 3697; F$16.50). There's also roughly one express bus every hour from the Downtown bus station to Lautoka (daily 6am–6pm; 30min; F$2.80) from where you connect to the towns of Ba, Tavua and Rakiraki along the northern Kings Rd.

Destinations Lautoka (40 daily; 45min–1hr 45min); Sigatoka (18 daily; 1hr–1hr 45min); Suva via Pacific Harbour (13 daily; 4–5hr).

Minivans Minivans can be substantially quicker than buses but are often hair-raising experiences and you won't get to see much of the scenery along the way. They leave from Raniga St east of the bus stand in Downtown (F$17 to Suva, or F$10 along the Coral Coast).

BY BOAT

Arriving by sea on the fast catamarans from the Yasawas or Mamanucas you will most likely come into Port Denarau (see p.55). Small boats arrive at Newton Beach, Wailoaloa.

Destinations from Port Denarau Beachcomber (4 daily; 45min); Bounty (4 daily; 35min); Castaway (3 daily; 1hr 50min); Malolo (3 daily; 2hr); Malolo Lailai (3 daily; 55min); Mana (3 daily; 1hr 25min); Matamanoa (2 daily; 1hr 30min); South Sea (5 daily; 30min); Tokoriki (2 daily; 1hr 45min); Treasure (4 daily; 45min); Yasawa Islands, Kuata to Nacula (daily; 2–5hr).

Destinations from Wailoaloa Beachcomber, Bounty, Malolo, Malolo Lailai, Mana (all 1 daily; 50min–1hr 30min).

BY TAXI

A taxi costs around F$40 to Lautoka, F$70 to Sigatoka or F$180 to Suva; negotiate in advance. The cheapest taxis are privately owned and leave from beside the main Downtown bus terminal.

INFORMATION

Tourist information There's no formal tourist office in town, but the official Tourism Fiji, on the first floor at Colonial Plaza off the Queens Rd between Namaka and Martintar, offers moderate advice and maps, though not

1

bookings (Mon–Fri 8am–5pm; ☎ 672 2433).

The best source of information is your accommodation. Beware of the shops on Main St disguised as "tourist information centres" – these are manned by pushy sales agents trying to sell private tours which are neither registered nor insured.

Touts Nadi is a magnet for touts trying to steer you into tacky handicraft shops where you'll be offered a bowl of *kava* then asked to pay for it if you don't buy a woodcarving. While they can feel intimidating, a firm "No thanks" should stop you being followed around.

Services You'll find ATMs dotted along Main St in Nadi, and the Queens Rd. There's a useful Westpac Bank with ATM machine at Port Denarau and on Palm Rd at Newtown Beach in Wailoaloa.

GETTING AROUND

A constant stream of cars, minivans and buses dart along the main Queens Rd between Nadi Airport and Downtown, and picking up public transport here is easy. There are also regular bus services from Downtown to the busy tourist areas of Wailoaloa and Denarau, though travelling off the main road usually involves taking a taxi. The suburban layout of Nadi, with farmland between attractions, makes exploring by foot impractical. You can bypass the whole of suburban Nadi by taking the Nadi Back Road from the roundabout south of Nadi Airport to the southern end of Downtown, a journey that takes less than 10min; the new Denarau Access Road connects Martintar and Denarau Road cutting out the traffic jams leading up to the Downtown area.

BY BUS

Downtown Local buses run every 10min or so along the Queens Rd between Downtown and Nadi Airport (daily 6am–6pm; F$1.10): half continue on to Lautoka, with the other half diverting off the Queens Rd to rural settlements. Ten buses daily run from Downtown to Wailoaloa (7.10am–5pm; F$1.10).

Denarau Island Westbus runs from Downtown to Denarau Island every 20min (daily 8am–5pm; F$1.10). Once on the island, the hotels, the Golf and Racquet Club and Port Denarau are connected every 15min by the Bula Bus (daily 6am–11pm; F$9.40 for an all-day pass, no single ticket fares).

BY MINIVAN

Minivans run constantly along the Queens Rd picking up passengers by the roadside for a standard F$2 rate.

BY TAXI

Hire taxis (with a registration starting "LH") are based at most hotels, but cost more than the local taxis ("LT") which you hail on the street. Nadi International Airport taxis are painted yellow and wait outside the international and domestic arrivals concourses.

Taxi firms Airport Taxi (☎ 670 3249) at Nadi Airport; Taxi 2000 (☎ 2000) in Martintar and covering Downtown.

Fares Agree a fixed rate beforehand with hire taxis ("LH") to avoid dispute, and feel free to bargain if you feel you are being overcharged. Local taxis (LT) are supposed to charge by the meter, with a flat fee of F$1.50 (F$5 from the airport) plus 10¢ for every 100m travelled, although not all will switch on their meter unless asked: Downtown to Denarau or the airport should cost F$15, to Wailoaloa F$10, or to Martintar F$7.

BY CAR

If you're planning to explore Nadi and Viti Levu, renting a car is more economical than hiring a taxi and a lot more convenient than taking the bus. Rates range from F$100 to F$170 per day (plus F$15–20 a day for insurance); all agencies offer free drop-off at any hotel in the Nadi area.

Rental firms Avis (☎ 672 2233, ⓦ avis.com.fj) at Nadi Airport and Port Denarau; Budget (ⓦ budget.com.fj), Nadi Airport (☎ 672 2735), Port Denarau (☎ 675 0888) and Downtown (☎ 672 4679); BulaCar Rentals, Nadi Airport (☎ 670 1209; ⓦ bulacarrentals.com.fj); Hertz, Nadi Airport (☎ 672 3466, ⓦ hertz.com.fj); Satellite, Queens Rd, Martintar (☎ 670 2109, ⓦ satelliterentacar .com.fj); Thrifty (ⓦ thriftyfiji.com) Nadi Airport (☎ 672 2935) and at *Westin* Denarau (☎ 675 0948); Viable, Queens Rd, Martintar (☎ 672 2202; ⓦ viablerentals .com.fj).

BY SCOOTER AND MOTORBIKE

Westside Motorbikes, in Namaka Industrial Estate (☎ 672 6402; F$99/24hr), rents out scooters for buzzing around town, though they not safe on the main highways, and larger motorbikes including Pango 125cc (F$99/24hr) and Harley Davidsons (F$500/24hr).

BY BIKE

The highly enthusiastic Stinger Bicycles (☎ 992 2301, ⓦ stingerbikes.com) offers excellent off-road cycling day-tours (mountain tour including pick-up, fruit, juice and helmet from F$190) plus good quality bike rental (F$60 per 24hr plus $30 for return bike delivery to Nadi hotels).

TOURS AND ACTIVITIES

Nadi offers a huge range of tours and activities, including full- and half-day cruises to the nearby Mamanucas (see p.77), day-trips to Navala village (see p.130), or to explore the Sigatoka region (see p.110), plus half-day excursions

1

exploring Nadi's rural hills and valleys. You can book all tours and activities via your accommodation, though almost all tour desks at the larger hotels are run by Rosie Holidays collaborating with their preferred operators only. If in doubt, contact the operators listed below direct or try Pacific Destinationz at Nadi Airport (☎672 3894; daily 5am–9pm), or Fiji's Finest Tours at Port Denarau (☎675 0046; daily 8am–8pm). Most tour operators include free pick-up and drop-off from Nadi hotels.

ADRENALINE SPORTS

Go Dirty Tours Nadi Airport ☎672 6402, ⓦgodirtytoursfiji.com. Guided quad-bike tours along muddy tracks with river crossings to the Nausori Highlands (F$249/2hr 30min) or the Sabeto River Valley with a stop at the Tifajek Mud Pools (F$299/4hr). Alternatively, ride your quad bike deep into the Nausori Highlands stopping for lunch in a remote Fijian village and then return by helicopter (F$699/4hr).

Tandem Skydive Nadi Airport ☎672 8166, ⓦskydivefiji.com.fj. Tandem freefall from over 4000m with a pro skydiver, landing on the beach at either Denarau or on Mana or Malolo Lailai islands. F$525–780 depending on the height.

GOLF AND TENNIS

Denarau Golf & Racquet Club Opposite the *Sheraton*, Denarau Island ☎675 9711, ⓦdenarau .com/golf. A long, flat course, well manicured with virtually no rough but lots of bunkers, canals and large fast greens. Book ahead in high season (daily 6.30am–6.30pm; F$167 including golf cart; club hire F$65, shoe hire F$20). The club also has four all-weather synthetic tennis courts and six grass courts (daily 7am–9pm; F$20/1hr; racquet hire F$10).

Nadi Airport Golf Club Wailoaloa ☎675 9711. A little rough around the edges, but the hilly setting at Wailoaloa and views of both the ocean and airport runway make this an entertaining round (Sun–Fri 11am–5pm, Sat 10am–5pm; F$30 for 18-holes; club hire F$30, cart hire F$30).

SCENIC FLIGHTS

★**Heli-Tours Fiji** Port Denarau ☎675 0255, ⓦhelitoursfiji.com. Large-window scenic helicopter flights giving the best views of the islands and mountains from a quick 10-minute spin around Denarau (F$205), to 25-minute trips to the offshore coral cays (F$528) or to view the mountains and waterfalls of the Mt Evans Range ($528) – these last two can be combined in one thrilling 40-minute voyage (F$788). Minimum 2 people.

Island Hoppers Nadi Airport ☎672 0410, ⓦhelicopters.com.fj. Fly over the islands for $425 per person for 20min, or try the "tag-along" deal where you join resort transfers to an unspecified destination for F$425. Day-trips, including lunch and use of resort facilities, drop you off at either Castaway (F$612 per person), Tokoriki (F$2400 per couple) or uninhabited Yadua Island (F$2950 per couple).

VILLAGE AND EDUCATIONAL TOURS

★**Althia Tours** Nasau, Nadi Back Road ☎749 2411 or ☎944 4555. This Fijian family business offers tours with an insight into local culture and lifestyle. Popular destinations include Navala village (F$300; 6hr) or nearby Viseisei village and the Sleeping Giant orchid gardens or Tifajek Mud Pools (F$180; 3hr).

Fiji Eco Tours Lot 13, ATS Subdivision, Votualevu ☎672 4312, ⓦfijiecotours.com.fj. Half-day tours visit Nalesutale village, a 30min drive from Nadi along the Sabeto Valley, with a short forest hike to a small waterfall (Mon–Sat 9am & 1pm; F$119 includes village lunch). Full-day tours combined with the Sleeping Giant Garden or the Tifajek Mud Pools cost F$214 (daily 9am–5pm). Village stays can also be organized on request.

Flavours of Fiji Cooking School Denarau Industrial Estate ☎675 0840, ⓦflavoursoffiji.com. Learn to cook Indian thalis and traditional Fijian home-style dishes in a modern air-conditioned room, with three cooking stations. You can start the tour early with an accompanied trip to the local produce market (Mon–Sat 11am–2pm $155; with market tour F$180).

Pehicle 98 Kennedy Ave, Saunaka ☎672 4086, ⓦpehicle.com. Pehicle run Fiji's only tour to a Hindu settlement, where you can sample curries, roti and chutneys (daily 11am; F$85; 2hr 30min). On the Mystery Dinner tour, the dinner will be in an iTaukei or Indo-Fijian home (daily 6.30pm–8.30pm; F$76). All tours minimum 2 people.

WATERSPORTS

Island Surf Smugglers Cove Resort, Newton Beach ☎988 6721. To enjoy the solitude from the sea and views along the coast, Island Surf rent out SUPs (F$20/hr) or surfboards (F$40/day): it also offers organized surf trips to the world-class breaks along the Malolo Barrier Reef in the Mamanucas.

DSDS Watersports Denarau Island ☎999 3607. For a quick blast on a jet-ski, there's a 15-minute marked course alongside Denarau waterfront (F$120 solo, or F$135 tandem) or you can go on a guided 1-hour tour along Nadi's coastline (F$390 solo, or F$420 tandem). Parasailing from the beachfront costs F$255 and you can also rent kayaks (F$20/hr), SUPs (F$35/hr) or Hobie Cats (F$60/hr); lessons also available.

1

ACCOMMODATION

There are plenty of affordable hotels along the main road between **Nadi Airport** and **Downtown Nadi**. However, to get a view of the ocean, you need to stay at either Wailoaloa or Denarau Island. The backpacker centre of Newtown Beach in the heart of **Wailoaloa** has a laidback atmosphere with stunning views along the coast, and although the grey sand is not attractive, the beach is a good spot for walking at sunset. The area is in the midst of a development explosion with two large resort complexes (*Ramada Suites* and *Pullman*) planning to open in late 2017. The opulent man-made **Denarau Island**, 5km west of Downtown, with its five-star resorts, luxury homes and modern shopping centre has a hollow, plastic feel. **Vuda** (see p.67), a 20min drive north of the airport, features a couple of mid-range boutique resorts and is closer to Lautoka. For **longer stays**, *Nadi Beach Homes* (T 782 0853, W nadibeach.com) rents out excellent-value, modern one- and two-bedroom apartments with swimming pool (monthly and weekly stays available).

NADI AIRPORT AND MARTINTAR

Fiji Gateway Hotel Queens Rd, Nadi Airport T 672 2444, W fijigateway.com; map p.53. Opposite Nadi Airport, with a spacious garden, tennis courts and a large swimming pool with water slide, this is a good choice for families. The 95 a/c rooms are uninspiring but clean, and family rooms can sleep two children (free for under-12s). Day-rooms (available between 6am and 6pm) are handy for late flights. (wifi) ($) **F$215**

★ Mercure Hotel Nadi Queens Rd, Martintar T 672 2255, W mercure.com; map p.53. Great location with some of Nadi's local bars, restaurants and clubs within walking distance. The 85 modern rooms are bland but very comfortable, located in two blocks, each three storeys high, overlooking a small central swimming pool. (wifi) ($) **F$147**

Nadi Bay Hotel Wailoaloa Rd, Martintar T 672 3599, W fijinadibayhotel.com; map p.53. The original backpacker hostel in Nadi is close to the bars, restaurants and cinemas of Queens Rd. It's a pretty oasis with a large swimming pool and its cosy restaurant *Antoinette's* serves the best food of all the backpacker places in a plant-filled courtyard with wooden decking and murals. Dorms, standard rooms and apartments are all a bit pokey however, and it's directly under the flight path of the early morning 747s. Breakfast voucher included. (wifi) ($) 14-bed fan dorms **F$41**, 4-bed a/c dorms **F$46**, rooms **F$194**

NEWTOWN BEACH AND WAILOALOA

★ Aquarius 17 Wasawasa Rd, Newtown Beach T 672 6000, W aquariusfiji.com; map p.53. A converted homestead alongside the beach, this place feels homely, with hammocks, a small pool, a restaurant (see p.62) and six slightly old-fashioned rooms upstairs. The downstairs dorms have only two beds in each, ensuring the ambience here remains intimate. (wifi) Dorms **F$47**, rooms **F$160**

★ Bamboo Travellers 33 Wasawasa Rd, Newtown Beach T 672 2225, W bambootravellers.com; map p.53. With 70 rooms and more than 100 dorm beds spread across five separate properties, *Bamboo* is the "cool" place to stay and the cheapest in Wailoaloa for both dorms and doubles. The layout of the hostel is chaotic, but most rooms have been recently renovated and the mattresses are comfy enough. The building known as "Travellers" is the most popular for the hardened backpacker with large 16- and 12-bed dorms and its beach restaurant is the main hub, while "Tropic" has a more sedate feel with two quiet swimming pools. (wifi) Dorms **F$20**, rooms **F$80**

Club Fiji Resort Enamanu Rd, South Wailoaloa T 670 0150, W clubfiji-resort.com; map p.53. Quiet yet expansive beach setting at the secluded southern end of Wailoaloa, though there's no public transport here so you may feel a bit cut-off. The beachside bures have rattan furnishings, timber floors and verandas, while the restaurant and bar have a gentle, island-style atmosphere. (wifi) Bures **F$195**

Grand West Villas Wailoaloa Rd T 670 0150, W hexagonfiji.com/grand_wests.htm; map p.53. The 1- and 2-bedroom a/c units here may be a little old fashioned but they are clean and spacious with kitchens, so make an affordable base for families close to the beach. It's quiet, and there's a swimming pool and tennis courts too. (wifi) 1-bedroom **F$233**, 2-bedroom **F$317**

Smugglers Cove 13 Wasawasa Rd, Newtown Beach, T 672 6578, W smugglersbeachfiji.com; map p.53. This is the smart travellers choice: clean, organized and efficient with a swimming pool, spa and free kayaks. The 24 small rooms have modern ensuite bathrooms, while the six ocean-view rooms with verandas and the large 18-bed mixed dorm get booked up quickly. The girls-only dorm costs a few dollars extra. (wifi) Dorms **F$42**, rooms **F$245**

DENARAU ISLAND

★ Hilton Fiji Beach Resort North Beach T 675 6800, W aquariusfiji.com; map p.55. A contemporary hotel with a chain of white-washed double-storey buildings alongside the beach, which house studios and 1- and 2-bed apartments, each with barbecues on the patio and fully equipped kitchens. The three swimming pools range from toddlers to adults-only, and a live band performs most nights in the restaurant. (wifi) ($) Rooms **F$470**

★ The Palms Port Denarau T 675 0104, W thepalmsdenarau.com; map p.55. With Denarau's

1

most affordable room rates, this modern apartment block overlooks Port Denarau's shopping mall and is just a 2min walk from the marina for boat trips. The studios are spacious and well-furnished, while the larger 1- and 2-bed apartments come with kitchens and a balcony. ☞ Rooms **F$430**

Sofitel Fiji Resort North Beach ☎ 675 1111, ⓦ sofitel .com; map p.55. Popular with families, this beautifully landscaped resort has a pretty beach outlook, with most of the 296 rooms having ocean views. There are plenty of watersports available, plus a serene spa and the *V Restaurant* serves gourmet international food. ☞ ($) **F$490**

EATING

Being a tourist town, Nadi's **restaurants** offer almost every style of cuisine, though there's only one authentic Fijian restaurant, in Denarau. Prices at the independent restaurants are quite reasonable, with mains seldom topping F$40. The resort restaurants tend to be pricier but often host good-value themed buffet dinners (F$50–80 per person); they also often put on **Fijian island nights** with a meke show followed by traditional feast (see p.63). For lunch, the **Downtown** area has plenty of affordable restaurants, especially Indian and Chinese cuisine. The best value fine-dining can be found along the uninspiring commercial strip of the Queens Rd around **Martintar**, but for views and a more lively ambience head to **Port Denarau**.

DOWNTOWN NADI

★**Habibi** 10 Narewa Road ☎ 978 5893; map p.53. North of the Nadi River in a blue wooden building, this Bohemian-style restaurant is owned by a French-Tunisian couple. The ambience is laidback with rustic chairs and a flower-filled courtyard. Its Mediterranean-influenced cuisine includes mains such as *baba ganoush* (F$16) and lamb tajine (F$25). There's also a shisha bar serving a dozen fruity flavours (F$30/shisha) with cushion seats for chilling. Daily 6pm–11pm.

The Nadi Farmers Bar and Restaurant Ashram Road ☎ 777 5442; map p.54. A bar that serves great food and is known for its fresh thali-styled curries (F$17.50); the menu also features dishes such as pizzas, fish and chips and burgers. The interior is a bit bland, so head outside to the wooden tables overlooking the Nadi River. Mon–Wed 11am–11pm, Thurs–Sat 11am–3am.

Sentai Seafood Restaurant Upstairs, corner of Main St and Sagayam Rd ☎ 670 0928; map p.54. Despite being slightly pricier than its neighbours, this is the most popular restaurant among local Chinese families, who come for dishes such as seafood tofu hotpot (F$18.50) and sizzling Mongolian beef (F$20) as well as enormous portions of chow mein (around F$15). Arrive early to get one of the ten window tables looking down Main Street. Daily 10am–10pm.

Tatas Nadi Back Rd, 100 metres east of the Nadi Temple ☎ 930 8720; map p.54. Extremely popular with locals, this restaurant has atmospheric outdoor dining beneath a large mango tree, though the surroundings are a bit tatty – it dishes up cheap, authentic Indo-Fijian meat curries that are hot, quite oily and served on the bone. The food is sometimes pre-cooked in a big pot and could be served hours later, so make sure you ask first and insist your meal is freshly prepared. The chicken (F$7) and lamb (F$7) curries are bursting with delicious

spicy flavours, and they sometime have goat (F$10) and duck (F$10) curries on the menu, too. A second branch at Lodhia Street is closer to town, but little more than a hole in the wall. Mon–Sat 6.30am–9pm, Sun 8.30am–4am

★**Temple Canteen** Sri Siva Subrahmaniya Swami Temple, Queens Rd; map p.54. You can eat here at the canteen, right beside the main temple, without paying the F$5 entrance fee, and take in the calm of temple life. It serves just two good-value vegetarian dishes: a thali of three dishes with dhal, soup and roti (F$7); and masala dosa, a bread cooked with potato and spices (F$8), as well as a variety of savoury Indian snacks from F$1 each. Daily 7am–3pm.

MARTINTAR AND NAMAKA

Bird Rock Café 7 Queens Rd ☎ 672 4650; map p.53. This chic café is a good spot to take a break from the bustling nightlife, and is a hip daytime hangout for coffee and home-made cake: it also serves delicious pulled pork and beef burgers for F$16. Sun–Thurs 7am–1am, Fri & Sat 7am–5am.

★**Daikoku** Corner of Queens Rd and Northern Press Rd ☎ 670 3622; map p.53. Temple-styled restaurant serving fabulous Japanese food. There are nine *teppanyaki* tables upstairs where food is cooked in front of you – try the seafood combination (F$52), or a whole chicken cooked and served as five distinct dishes (F$44). Downstairs, in the sumptuous sushi bar, *sashimi* lovers can enjoy fine cuts of fresh, local tuna and red snapper. Mon–Sat noon–2pm & 6–9.30pm.

Indiana Nataly Building, Namaka ☎ 672 2962; map p.53. The best curry house in Nadi with kitsch Indian decor and simple tables – try goat curry, on the bone ($15), and soak up its rich juices with home-made naan bread, or sample the house speciality, which is a creamy butter chicken ($12). Daily 11am–10pm.

1

★ **Taste Fiji Kitchen** Corner of Queens Rd and Cawa Rd ☎ 672 5034, ⊕ tastefiji.com; map p.53. With random decor from an aircraft dining trolley to an imperial typewriter, this chic place is as much an art gallery as a café and is popular among expats for coffee and a muffin. The all-day breakfast menu includes dishes made from local meats and herbs, plus plenty of home-made muesli (F$14). For lunch there's an inspired mix of local and English fusion dishes including tasty seared liver on garnished mash potato (F$14). Mon–Sat 6.30am–6pm, Sun 7am–3pm.

NEWTOWN BEACH AND WAILOALOA

Aquarius 17 Wasawasa Rd, Newtown Beach ☎ 672 6000; map p.53. With outdoor tables set around the pool, this pretty spot is a good place to escape the bustle of Newtown Beach and enjoy the sea views over a romantic intimate dinner. The broad menu includes pastas and pizzas for lunch (F$17), fish and chips, curries and kokoda at dinner (F$21–$25). Daily 7am–9pm.

Bamboo Tropic Wasawasa Road, Newtown Beach; map p.53. The best of the beach resort restaurants for good Fijian food, such as *rourou* balls with grilled fish (F$15), or the vegetarian palusami-stuffed papaya pumpkin in white sauce (F$10), both of which include spinach leaves. Daily 9am–6pm.

★ **Grace Road Kitchen & Awesome Grill** Palm Rd, Newtown Beach ☎ 672 8638; map p.53. Part of a small Fijian chain owned by a Korean Christian cult, this restaurant serves healthy, organic food grown on its own farms. The Asian-inspired dishes include chilli chicken *dakgalbi* and beef teriyaki (both $13), while the "Green" and "Detox" juices are

delicious, if a little pricey at F$12. If you fancy something more meaty, you can order a burger from the next-door *Awesome Grill*, which they co-own, and eat at whichever restaurant you choose. Mon 6am–5pm, Tues–Sun 6am–11pm.

DENARAU ISLAND

Cardo's Steakhouse Port Denarau ☎ 675 0900; map p.55. Central location overlooking the placid bay surrounding Port Denarau, with lots of outdoor tables under flame trees. As well as tender steaks (expensive at around F$60), *Cardo's* makes the best thin-crust pizzas (F$19/26/39) in Nadi. It's also a good spot for coffee and a cooked breakfast. The bar usually has a lively atmosphere in the evenings, especially at weekends. Daily 8am–10pm, bar closes 11pm.

★ **Nadina Authentic Fijian Restaurant** Building C, Port Denarau ☎ 679 0290; map p.55. The appealing waterfront *Nadina* is a good local restaurant serving Fijian fish classics such as kokoda (F$16) and pan-fried *walu* steak (F$35). You may also be treated to an impromptu *kava* ceremony and some live music. Daily 7am–10pm.

★ **The Rhum-Ba** Yacht Club at Port Denarau ☎ 770 7486, ⊕ rhum-ba.com; map p.55. With Port Denarau's best views, this contemporary-styled bar/restaurant serves over 150 rums and has tables directly over the waterfront that are best booked in advance. Main courses focus mostly on fish and seafood, with seared tuna (F$42) or scallop ravioli scented with lemongrass (F$36); there are also steaks (F$52) and burgers too (F$34), as well as rum-infused desserts. Daily 11am–11pm.

DRINKING, NIGHTLIFE AND ENTERTAINMENT

For most tourists, Nadi's nightlife revolves around elaborate cocktails or a chilled "Fiji baby" (local slang for beer) at a quiet **resort bar**, with happy hours usually running from 5.30pm to 6.30pm. For more local after-hours culture, head to Martintar, popular with Nadi office workers, or Port Denarau, where the expat community relaxes. The southern end of Downtown Nadi is an edgy hangout for Fijians visiting from the rural areas, with pool bars, *kava* saloons and a couple of raucous **nightclubs**, though roaming around here late at night on your own isn't recommended. Alternatively, try the resort enclaves around Wailoaloa where meeting people, happy guitarists and *kava* evenings are more the thing. Traditional **dance shows** are held at several resorts and are usually free to watch, with a blend of animated Fijian war mekes (see box opposite), elegant Polynesian-style hula and fire-dancing; some are combined with lovo buffet dinners. Times vary, so call ahead.

BARS AND CLUBS

Bamboo Travellers Bar 33 Wasawasa Rd, Wailoaloa ☎ 672 2225; map p.53. With friendly Fijian staff, this is a welcoming place for travellers to meet for a drink on large picnic benches dotted along the beach. Daily 10am–late.

★ **Ed's Bar** Corner of Queens Rd and Kennedy St, Martintar ☎ 672 4650; map p.53. This iconic nightspot has been the place to be seen for over twenty years and remains popular with the more affluent locals. It's a great place to meet early on for a beer (F$5) and a game of pool,

or to join the crowds on the packed dancefloor as the night progresses. Bouncers keep a tight lid on things and there's occasional live music, when admission is F$5. Sun–Thurs 5pm–3am, Fri & Sat 5pm–5am.

Hard Rock Café Port Denarau ☎ 675 0032; map p.55. The standard *Hard Rock* formula with the hippest staff in town, a lively atmosphere and the usual international rock memorabilia – though disappointingly, there's no mention of any Fijian musicians. Draught beer costs F$6.50 a half-litre, with a two-for-one happy hour from 3–6pm daily. Daily 9am–10.30pm.

THE FIJIAN MEKE

One aspect of Fijian culture that retains its relevance today is the **meke**, a performing art of dance and song. Legends and tales have been passed down the generations through meke and it remains Fiji's most prominent form of artistic expression.

Traditionally, music was created only by chanting and rhythmic clapping, often with the addition of a *lali* (hollowed wood) drum hit with bamboo sticks. More recently the guitar and ukelele have been introduced. Mekes are generally performed by male-only or female-only groups, although a modern introduction, the *vakamalolo*, combines the two.

At formal mekes, men may perform club and spear dances and the women perform fan dances. In village mekes, the practice of *fakawela* involves presenting the dancers with a gift in appreciation of their performance, often fine cloth or fabric. At weddings or other celebrations bringing two parties together, this usually involves encircling the dancers with long rolls of cloth. At other times, perfumes are sprayed onto the dancers and money tucked into their clothing as they perform.

Ice Bar RB Jetpoint Complex, Martintar ☏ 672 7144; map p.53. Large dancefloor popular with Nadi's office-worker crowd at weekends when things really jam, but quiet during the week when you can talk over a drink. Local DJs mixing modern hip-hop is the norm, but it's the impromptu reggae tunes and Bollywood dance classics that inevitably get the locals into another gear. Fri & Sat F$5 cover charge. Daily 4pm–5am.

Nadi Farmers Bar Ashram Road, Downtown ☏ 777 5442; map p.54. With an outdoor dancefloor and bar stools overlooking the river, as well as special events most weeks, this place keeps busy enough. There are live bands on Thursdays and Saturdays plus an all-night happy hour Fridays, when local beers are just $4.80. Mon–Sat 5pm–2am.

DANCE SHOWS AND KAVA EVENINGS

Fijian dance performances generally feature fire-dancing and song as well as meke – traditional dance – and range from free to F$110 per person including a traditional buffet dinner. If you just want a taster, the shopping mall at Port Denarau stages daily performances from 6.30pm to 7.30pm, although the sound system could do with improvement.

★**Bamboo Tropic** Newtown Beach ☏ 672 2225; map p.53. Puts on free casual tourist-orientated *kava* sessions,

accompanied by harmonious guitar tunes and singing. Daily 7.30pm–10pm.

Smugglers Cove Wailoaloa ☏ 672 6578, ⓦ smugglersbeachfiji.com; map p.53. Check out the mixture of free entertainment in an informal beach setting, including Fijian mekes (Fri from 7.30pm), Polynesian hula performances with enthralling fire-dances (Wed & Sun from 7.30pm), plus *kava* drinking and singing with Tai and the Kavaholics (Tues, Thurs & Sat from 7pm).

Sofitel Fiji Resort Denarau Island ☏ 675 6800; map p.55. A colourful Fijian meke is performed weekly beside the pool for diners at this family-orientated resort. F$89 including traditional lovo dinner. Tues at 6pm.

★**Westin Denarau Resort** Denarau Island ☏ 675 0777; map p.55. Fijian firewalking in an impressive staged amphitheatre, combined with a meke featuring fabled songs of love and loss. F$111 including a traditional lovo dinner. Wed & Sat at 6.30pm.

CINEMA

Life Cinema Jetpoint Centre, Martintar ☏ 672 7888, ⓦ lifecinemas.com.fj. Shows the latest Hollywood blockbusters. Tickets F$8.50. Daily 10am–11.55pm.

SHOPPING

Nadi has a decent selection of **shops** and its department stores are handy for stocking **electronic goods** such as memory cards for digital cameras. General shopping hours are from 8.30am to 5.30pm weekdays, and 8.30am to 1pm on Saturday. Most shops at the open-air Port Denarau shopping centre are open daily including Sundays from 7am to 7pm, closing at 9pm on Friday and Saturday.

CRAFTS AND JEWELLERY

When looking at craft items, be aware that war clubs, printed designs on *masi* (bark cloth), *tanoa* drinking bowls and priest dishes are authentic Fijian designs, while face masks and animal carvings are simply tourist gimmicks imported from Asia.

Handicraft Market Koroivolu Ave, Downtown; map p.54. If you're good at haggling, this attractive little strip of stalls is the place to pick up reasonably priced wooden carvings, woven baskets and Fijian *sulus*. Mon–Sat 8am–5pm.

Jack's Main St, Downtown ☏ 670 0744, also at Port

1

Denarau Shopping Mall ⓦjacksfiji.com; map p.54. Dependable department store with faux-rustic decor, selling locally produced oils, essences and Fijian crafts; it's also the best place to find good quality Indian saris. They will pack and post worldwide. Downtown Mon–Sat 8am–6pm, Sun 8am–5pm; Port Denarau daily 7.30am–9pm.

Nagindas Main St, Downtown ☎670 3049, also at Port Denarau Shopping Mall ⓦsnagindas.com; map p.54. Clothing store that's a good source of Bula shirts, Fijian mumus (long dresses), traditional men's *sulus* and colourful women's sarongs. Clothes from Nagindas' own fashion label, Cloudbreak, are all made at its factory in Nadi so prices are competitive. If you can't find what you're after, check out the local competitor, Harrisons, directly opposite across the road. Downtown Mon–Fri 8.15am–6pm, Sat 8am–4.30pm; Port Denarau daily 7.30am–7pm.

FOOD
Municipal Market Between Market Rd & Hospital Rd, Downtown; map p.54. Atmospheric covered market, with enticing piles of fresh seasonal fruit and veg and a whole section dedicated to the sale of *yaqona* roots and pounded *kava* – an essential purchase if you're making a village visit (see box, p.31). If you're after a quick snack, Indo-Fijian boys sell peanuts, curried beans and roti parcels at the main entrance on Market Rd. Mon–Fri 7am–5pm, Sat 6am–4pm.

SNORKELLING AND DIVING EQUIPMENT
If you're planning on doing much snorkelling, it's worth buying your own equipment, as many budget resorts either rent them for F$20 for a few hours, don't supply them at all or have rather old leaky kit. When you're done, the gear makes a fantastic gift to a local villager, which also saves lugging them home. It will set you back about F$80 for a snorkel and mask and F$55 for a pair of fins.

The Yacht Shop Port Denarau Shopping Mall ☎979 1207; map p.55. Convenient for the ferry terminal, this tiny shop is stuffed with all sorts of useful beach equipment including snorkel sets, reef shoes and life jackets. Mon–Sat 8am–5pm, Sun 9am–2pm.

DIRECTORY

Banks All the following have ATM machines, but expect lengthy queues on Thursday afternoon and Friday after payday, and possibly no cash at all at weekends: Westpac, corner of Main St and Vunivau Rd, Downtown, also at Namaka Lane and Port Denarau (all Mon–Thurs 9.30am–3pm, Fri 9.30am–4pm), plus a 24hr branch at Nadi Airport Arrivals Concourse; ANZ Bank, Main St, Downtown, and at Namaka Lane (both Mon–Thurs 9.30am–3.30pm, Fri 9.30am–4pm). If bank machines run out of cash, try the ATM inside *Macdonald's* in Saunaka village between Martintar and Downtown, or outside the Midwest Superette at Newtown Beach in Wailoaloa.

Hospital Nadi Hospital, Nadi College Rd, Downtown (☎670 1128).

Internet access 3d's Internet Café, Main St, Downtown, opposite Hospital Rd, has 20 terminals in an a/c room (Mon–Sat 7.30am–7 pm, Sun 9.30am–6pm; F$2/hr).

Medical centres Zen's Medical Centre, 40 Lodhia St, Downtown (doctor 24hr; dentist Mon–Fri 8am–5pm, Sat 8am–1pm; ☎ 670 3533) and at Namaka (doctor 24hr; ☎672 2288); both can perform some surgical procedures. Zen's has a third clinic at Denarau opposite *Sheraton Villas* (Mon–Sat 8am–5pm; ☎675 0211) plus a 24hr ambulance service (☎839 5160).

Pharmacy Island Pharmacy, Main St opposite Clay St, Downtown (Mon–Sat 8am–7pm, Sun 9am–2pm; ☎670 6506).

Police Emergencies ☎917. The main police station is at Koroivolu Ave in Downtown (☎670 0222), with suburban stations at Nadi Airport (☎672 2172) and Totogo Lane in the CAAF Compound, Namaka (☎672 2222).

Post office At Koroivolu Ave, Downtown and at Nadi Airport (Mon–Fri 8am–4pm, Sat 8am–noon). Both offer poste restante (see p.44).

Telephone There are public phones at Nadi Airport and in front of the post office in Downtown.

Around Nadi

The area around Nadi offers access to Viti Levu's rural interior, which is dominated by sugarcane farms stretching far up its river valleys. To the east, the flats of the Nadi River eventually yield to the outstanding mountain scenery of the alpine **Nausori Highlands**. North towards Lautoka, the Queens Road passes the scenic **Sabeto River Valley** then continues on to the northern tip of Nadi Bay, **Vuda Point**, with a small beach and marina. A few kilometres beyond, the busy industrial port of **Lautoka** offers good shopping and access to the north coast. In the distance, the shapely **Koroyanitu National Park** beckons through the haze.

Momi Bay

Twenty minutes' drive **south** of Nadi along the Queens Road is the turn-off to **Momi Bay**, site of one of Fiji's most attractive large resorts: the road junction is a good place to pick up fresh, cheap fruit from local stalls. As you drive, you'll pass through the hilly coastal region of Momi, which consists of a mixture of sugarcane farms, coastal forest and scrubland. Five minutes down the Lomawai Road towards Momi Bay, you'll see a small track signposted to the **Momi Guns** (daily 9am–5pm; F$5; ☎628 4356), two six-inch World War II coastal artillery guns aimed at Navula Passage in anticipation of a Japanese invasion. The site is run by the National Trust and has a lovely view of the southern Mamanucas Islands.

Zip Fiji Momi

Tau Village, Momi Hills ☎ 672 6045, ⓦ zip-fiji.com • Tours (3hr) start at 9am and 2pm and include lunch • Zip wire F$235; zip wire and abseiling F$245; Cave tour F$155 • Free pick-ups are provided from all hotels around Nadi

The fastest and most varied of the Nadi's two zip wire operations, **Zip Fiji Momi** is set among Momi's mountainous tropical forests, with sixteen zip wires stretching over 5km and offering great views of the canopy and surroundings. You can also visit several of the **limestone caves** of Tau village, which can be explored either on foot or by abseiling down one of four 35-metre lines.

ARRIVAL AND DEPARTURE   MOMI BAY

By taxi Only a couple of buses daily travel to Momi so your best bet to visit is to take a taxi from Downtown Nadi (40min; F$40).

ACCOMMODATION

Fiji Marriott Resort Momi Bay ☎670 7000, ⓦmarriott.com; map p.52. Influenced by traditional Fijian architecture, this massive new resort has 250 rooms of different sizes and styles, including its signature bungalows built over the water. There's also a fine-dining restaurant enclosed by a man-made lagoon. Although the entire resort environment is highly sculptured, there's a decent white-sand beach and the surrounding countryside is the complete opposite, wild, raw and remote. ☎($) **F$725**

The Nausori Highlands

Towering over the coastal flats **inland** from Nadi are the high peaks of Koromba to the south and Koronayitu in the north, both over 1000m and forming part of the spectacular **Nausori Highlands**. With your own transport, a stunning **drive** starts from halfway along the Nadi Back Road along the Nausori Highlands Road. Head along this road for 14km, and after a steep and unmistakable hairpin bend, keep an eye out for a walking track on the left-hand side (you can park 50m beyond at a roadside clearing on the right); the track leads up past a triangular survey marker to a steep cliff with superb views over the Sabeto River Valley and out over Nadi to the offshore islands. If you have a 4WD vehicle, you can continue from here on to the pretty highland village of **Bukuya**, beyond which the dirt road heads either north to Ba via Navala village (see p.130), or south to Sigatoka via the stunning and winding River Valley Road – you'll need at least eight hours to complete either loop back to Nadi.

Sabeto Valley

The nicest scenery of the lush **Sabeto Valley** is along the Sabeto Road, 4km north of the airport. South of the Sabeto River, the distinct outline of the **Sleeping Giant** rock formation is clearly visible from the road, which is tar-sealed for its first 5km. Beyond the Masimasi Hindu Temple, the road turns to dirt before entering the southern section of the Koroyanitu National Heritage Park (see p.70), then continuing east for another 30km through the steep Nausori Highlands to the remote **Vaturu Dam**.

1

Sleeping Giant Zipline and Orchid Falls Walk

Holika Road 📞 666 7935 or 📞 999 6360, 🌐 ziplinefiji.com • Daily 9am–5pm • F$189, children (4–12yrs) $94.50, including unlimited goes on the zip wire, a guided walk to Orchid Falls, lunch and a fruit juice; Orchid Falls only $50 • Take the Sabeto Rd for 8km, then turn left down the signposted dirt track across the river and continue for another 2km • Free return transfers from Nadi Downtown hotels and Port Denarau, with pick-ups at 8.30am & 1pm

A 35-acre rainforest adventure park, the **Sleeping Giant Zipline** features an array of zip wires, where you can fly through the jungle at speeds of 60km/h. Also in the park, at the pretty **Orchid Falls** waterfall, you can swing on ropes, swim in pools and spot parrots: you can either walk to the falls independently, or go on the one-hour guided walk which is included in the price – either way, it's worth the trip alone even if you don't fancy the high-adrenaline zip wires.

Garden of the Sleeping Giant

Wailoko Road • 📞 672 2701, 🌐 gsgfiji.com • Mon–Sat 9am–5pm, Sun 9am–noon • F$16 • Turn inland off the Queens Rd, 1km north of the Sabeto Rd, onto the Wailoko dirt road; the entrance is 2km down the road

Founded by actor Raymond Burr (aka Perry Mason), the **Garden of the Sleeping Giant** boasts a wonderful collection of orchids and other flowering plants as well as gentle trails meandering through the landscaped grounds and into the lowland rainforest abutting the Sleeping Giant escarpment.

Tifajek Mud Pools and Hot Springs

Wailoko Road 📞 839 1478 • Daily 9am–5pm • F$20 • Turn inland off the Queens Rd, 1km north of the Sabeto Rd, onto the Wailoko dirt road; the pools are about 4km along here, some 2km beyond the Garden of the Sleeping Giant

The **Tifajek Mud Pools and Hot Springs** were first discovered in the 1940s when US soldiers used them to bathe in. Today, you can indulge in a full rejuvenating and body cleansing routine: the first procedure is to wallow in the pools and smother your body in black mud. After sun-drying the mud to a plaster, you wash off in a stream and then submerge yourself in the sulphur-infused volcanic hot pool to cleanse your skin. If that's not relaxing enough, you can pay extra for a body massage afterwards.

ACCOMMODATION   **SABETO RIVER VALLEY**

Stoney Creek Lodge 6km up the Sabeto Rd, just beyond Masimasi Hindu Temple 📞746 4669, 🌐 stoneycreekfiji.net; map p.52. This offbeat rural retreat, with dreamy views looking up the Sabeto Valley, is only 20min drive from Nadi Airport. It boasts a swimming pool, restaurant, quiet bar and plenty of dogs – though it can be somewhat disorganized. Activities on offer include mountain treks and cycling. 📶 Dorm F$55, rooms F$145

Lomolomo

The most scenic region around Nadi's extensive flatlands lies along a rural stretch of the Queens Road running north towards Lautoka, dotted with tranquil villages and backed by forested hills. Some eight kilometres north of the airport, the rocky tongue of the Sabeto Hills descends dramatically towards the base of **LOMOLOMO** village. From here, you can explore a delightful **walking track** over the hills and back to the Wailoko dirt road. The trail starts from Esivo Road, 1km beyond the village just beyond the timber mill. Three hundred metres down this dirt road, a small track leads uphill following the ridge inland towards the seldom-visited **Lomolomo Guns**. It takes thirty minutes to walk to these World War II artillery guns from the main road: once here, you'll be rewarded with a fine view overlooking Nadi Bay and the surrounding mountains.

Vuda Historic Site

Vuda Back Road • Mon–Sat 9am–4pm • F$30 for 1–2 hr guided tour • Turn right off the Queens Rd along the Vuda Back Rd (just before the Vuda River): after 2km on the right side, you'll see a small wooden house where the caretaker lives

Entwined around a massive hillside boulder complex, the ancient village of **Vuda** is

1

said to have been founded by Lutunasobasoba. As you explore the overgrown paths around the old village site, keep an eye out for the ancient **rock platforms** where homes were built, and for clearings with accumulated pottery shards and *kai* shells where the common people cooked. The high chiefs, and supposedly Lutunasobaso himself, lived on top of the highest rocky bluff, guarded by a hundred Fijian warriors.

Viseisei village

Head north on the Queens Rd towards Lautoka: just after the Vuda River, turn left into Viseisei Rd • Village tour F$5

According to Fijian legend, the chiefly village of **Viseisei** is where Lutunasobasoba, the first inhabitant of Fiji, landed his canoe, the *Kaunitoni*, having sailed all the way from Tanzania (see p.218).

Park on the roadside at the school end of the village, and local women at the seafront **craft stalls** will arrange a walking tour, taking in the **Methodist church**, the exterior of the chief's thatched house and the totemic breadfruit tree. Arrive at 10am on Sunday, and you'll hear wonderful a cappella singing in the church.

Vuda Marina and around

☎ 666 8214, ⓦ vudamarina.com.fj

On the brow of the hill past Viseisei village, a scenic road turns left and runs for 3km to **Vuda Point**, home to a quaint marina and several boutique resorts. Considered the safest anchorage for yachts in Fiji, **Vuda Marina** has a general store (daily 7am–6pm) and a relaxed oceanfront restaurant (see below).

ARRIVAL AND DEPARTURE   VUDA MARINA AND AROUND

By ferry Ferries from Vuda Marina run to *Beachcomber Island* (daily; 25min), *Octopus Resort* (daily; 1hr 30min) and *Treasure Island* (daily; 20min).

By bus The bus from Lautoka arrives at the police post beside the marina. Buses from Nadi stop at the Vuda Point junction; from here, you can either walk for 25 minutes along the scenic road down to the marina or hope a carrier van is waiting.

ACCOMMODATION AND EATING

Boatshed Restaurant Vuda Marina ☎ 666 8214; map p.52. Elegant, open-plan restaurant well placed for sunset views, serving dishes such as seafood *kovu* cooked in coconut broth (F$23) and good old-fashioned pork crackling and lamb roasts to share (F$58 for 2 people). Don't miss the excellent-value F$10 lunch specials (Mon–Fri) or the popular live bands on Sunday afternoons (2–7pm). Daily 10am–10pm.

The Fiji Orchid Saweni Beach Rd, North of Vuda ☎ 628 3099, ⓦ fijiorchid.com; map p.52. Once the home of film star Raymond Burr with a fine 5-hectare garden of orchids and other tropical plants that became the love of his life. The six stylish bures have polished wooden floors, large bathrooms and a safari-style canopy roof that makes you

feel closer to the surrounding lush gardens. The original homestead is now a fine-dining restaurant, and Saweni beach is just five minutes' walk away. ⓦ Bures F$660

★**First Landing Resort** Vuda Marina ☎ 666 6171, ⓦ firstlandingfiji.com; map p.52. Adjacent to the marina and fronting a coral-sand beach, this is one of the only small beach resorts in the Nadi area and has magnificent mature gardens dominated by huge rain trees. Bure rooms are in duplex plantation-style cottages, while the modern three-bed apartments have kitchens and are ideal for families. There's an excellent restaurant overlooking the beach serving wood-cooked pizzas, and snorkelling in the lagoon. ⓦ Bures F$315, villas F$595, apartments F$695

Lautoka

Half an hour's drive north of Nadi, and just twenty minutes from the airport, **LAUTOKA** is Fiji's second largest city and an important port. It's a surprisingly low-key affair – the city centre is more compact than Downtown Nadi, with most of its 55,000 inhabitants living in the light industrial suburbs. Although there is little to admire

1

architecturally, Lautoka is a good place to wander, with plenty of leafy avenues and diverting **Indo-Fijian stores** and market stalls – the latter a far cry from Nadi's touristy souvenir shops.

Lautoka established itself around the **sugar industry**. In 1903, the Australian-owned Colonial Sugar Refinery Company set up headquarters here, attracted by a deep-water harbour. The **sugar mill** they built is still the largest in Fiji and employs more than a thousand people. The rambling corrugated sheds and chimney stacks of the mill are fed by an endless parade of cane trucks and trains between July and December, eventually pumping raw molasses along pipes to container ships moored at **Lautoka Port** – it's not a place to linger in the crushing season, with the stench of sugar sludge filling the air: a series of ten posters on the walls at the Waterfront Road roundabout provide a colourful history detailing the influence of sugar on the city.

In recent years, Lautoka has become a second home for the people of the **Yasawa Islands** who, without secondary schools or work opportunities, send their children here for education and jobs.

The city centre

The organized city centre is laid out in a grid pattern with one-way streets, flanked by beautiful tree-lined Vitogo Parade and parallel Naviti Street. A walk around this one-square-kilometre centre takes in the majority of **shops**, the Municipal Market and an impressive **mosque**. East of the mosque, **Vitogo Parade** is home to an endless line of fashion stores selling good-quality suits, shirts, saris and costume jewellery. Opposite the central bus station, the shops along **Naviti Street** sell a bizarre array of odds and ends, mostly cheap imports from China, but you'll find plenty of colourful saris and *sulwar kameez* (Punjabi dress), as well as tailors who can make clothes at bargain rates. Across Naviti Street under a Brutalist concrete dome is the **Municipal Market** (Mon–Fri 7am–5.30pm, Sat 5am–4pm), one of the most largest and least claustrophobic markets in Fiji.

For a pleasant detour away from the downtown shopping area, head south along Tavewa Avenue, opposite Shirley Park. Midway down you can stop for a swim or a beer at the colonial-style **Northern Club** (see below) before continuing on past the Sri

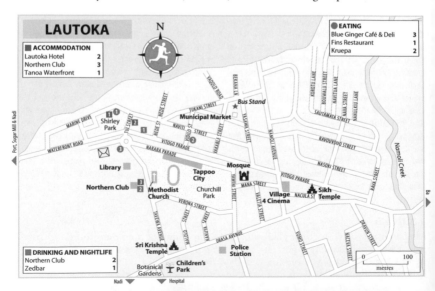

LAUTOKA ORIENTATION

Approaching from Nadi, the Veitari roundabout, full of mango sellers from August to December, splits the **Queens Road** in two. The right fork, along **Drasa Avenue**, passes through Lautoka's residential area, bypassing downtown and joining the Kings Road to Ba town at the north end of the city. The left fork heads down **Navutu Road** along the industrial section of Lautoka into downtown; the road passes South Pacific Distilleries (where Fiji's famous rum is concocted), the fishing port and the sugar mill.

Krishna Temple to Lautoka's superbly kept **botanical gardens** (Mon–Fri 8am–6pm, Sat & Sun 10am–6pm; free.

ARRIVAL AND DEPARTURE   LAUTOKA

By bus and minivan Arriving by bus or minivan, you'll be dropped at the bus stand between Tukani and Naviti streets behind the Municipal Market in the heart of the city.
Destinations Ba (124 daily; 30min–1hr); Nadi (40 daily;

25–50min); Suva via Rakiraki (13 daily; 6hr); Suva via Nadi and Sigatoka (24 daily; 5hr 30min).
By boat The Lautoka Jetty along Waterfront Rd is where the cheap local fibreglass fishing boats to the Yasawa Islands leave from.

ACCOMMODATION

Lautoka Hotel Corner of Naviti and Tui streets ☎ 666 0388, ✉ lautokahotel@cjsgroup.com.fj. Handy location and the best spot for backpackers. The budget rooms and ten-bed dorms are simple windowless boxes with plywood walls, but the deluxe rooms surrounding the pool are pretty and good value, and come with a/c and Sky TV. Can get noisy at weekends when a nightclub operates in the premises. Dorms F$20, standard rooms F$70.
★**Northern Club** 11 Tavewa Ave ☎ 666 2469, ⊕ thenorthernclubfiji.com. This pleasant colonial-style establishment is both a gentleman's watering hole

and a weekend playground for local families, but it's close to downtown and set in nice landscaped gardens with a pool and tennis courts. The six studio units are a bit old-fashioned and the bathrooms are tiny, but with a/c, TV, cooking stove and fridge they offer good value. F$125
Tanoa Waterfront Marine Drive ☎ 666 4777, ⊕ tanoawaterfront.com. Located across the road from the ocean, this is Lautoka's only upmarket hotel. It has a large landscaped swimming pool, but remains predominantly frequented by business people. ☎ Rooms F$150, poolside suites F$210

EATING, DRINKING AND ENTERTAINMENT

CAFÉS AND RESTAURANTS
Blue Ginger Café & Deli Elizabeth Square ☎ 907 6553. This endearing and friendly Indian-run café is brightly coloured inside and out, and serves the town's best coffee and cakes (F$5), as well as healthy salads (F$8.80) and *quesadillas* ($14.20). Mon–Sat 8am–6pm.
Fins Restaurant Tanoa Waterfront, Marine Drive ☎ 666 4777. Lautoka's only fine-dining restaurant has a handful of outdoor tables with ocean views, although the modern interior is café-style. The broad but overpriced menu includes beer-battered fish and chips (F$24), grilled local market fish (F$29), curry of the day (F$30) and local beef fillet (F$49). Daily 6am–10pm.
Kruepa Vidilo St ☎ 666 0591. Popular among the Indo-Fijian community, this authentic vegetarian restaurant serves a selection of thalis ($10) and Punjabi *parathas* (F$7–9.50). The interior decor is colourful but the waiters

can be a little aloof. Sun–Wed 9am–9pm, Thurs–Sat 8am–10pm.

BARS AND CLUBS
Northern Club 11 Tavewa Ave ☎ 666 0184. The bar of this social club is a good place to meet locals over a cheap draught beer, or play snooker on a full-sized table for 50¢ a game. Also serves bar snacks and meat pies. Daily 2pm–midnight.
Zedbar Vitogo Parade ☎ 935 3694. Popular with the affluent young residents of Lautoka, this nightclub has pool tables and satellite TV showing sports or music. DJs play on Fri & Sat nights, when there's a F$5 entrance charge. Mon–Sat 8pm–1am.

CINEMA
Village 4 Cinemas 25 Namoli Ave ☎ 666 3555. Shows the latest Hollywood blockbusters. Tickets F$7. Daily 10am–11pm.

1

LISTINGS

Banks All the listed banks have 24hr ATM machines and foreign currency exchange: ANZ Bank, 165 Vitogo Parade (Mon 9.30am–4pm, Tues–Fri 9am–4pm, Sat 9am–1pm); Westpac, Provident Plaza, Naviti Street (Mon–Fri 9.30am–4pm).

Internet access *Mega Café,* near the mosque on Vitogo Parade (daily 8am–10pm; F$1 per hr), is air-conditioned.

Library Western Regional Library, Tavewa Ave off Elizabeth Square (Mon–Fri 10am–5pm; ☎ 666 0091).

Medical care Lautoka Hospital off Thompson Crescent (☎ 666 0399) caters for emergencies. Alternatively, several general practitioners are based at the Bayly

Clinic, 4 Nede St (Mon–Fri 8am–1pm & 2–4.30pm, Sat 8am–1pm for private doctor or dentist; ☎ 666 4598).

Pharmacy Hyper Pharmacy, 101 Vitogo Parade (Mon–Sat 8am–8pm, Sun 9am–2pm & 6–8pm; ☎ 665 1940).

Police At Drasa Ave opposite Yawini St (☎ 666 0222). There's also a police post in the city centre on Tui St beside Shirley Park.

Post office Elizabeth Square (Mon–Fri 8am–4pm, Sat 8am–noon).

Sports Northern Club, 11 Tavewa Ave (☎ 666 0184), is a social club with swimming pool (F$3), tennis (F$1.50/30min) and squash (F$1/30min).

Telephone At the post office on Elizabeth Square.

Koroyanitu National Heritage Park

Some 15km southwest of Lautoka, **Koroyanitu National Heritage Park**, with its accessible walking trails and waterfalls, was created in 1992 to preserve the area's natural forests and endemic birdlife from clearing for pine forest and encroaching grasslands.

At the **Abaca visitor centre** you can pick up pamphlets, and organize a compulsory guide for the two **walking trails** that start from here. The most challenging is the Batilamu Track, which snakes uphill through forest for two hours until it reaches the summit of the 1163m **Mount Batilamu**. The mountain forms the belly of the Sleeping Giant (see p.66), and from the summit you can see all the way back to Lautoka and across to the Yasawa Islands. Alternatively, an easy two-hour loop trail follows a grassy ridge to **Savuione Falls**, which tumble 80m in two tiers to a deep swimming pool. The trail then descends into dense *dakua* forest back to Vereni Falls, close to Abaca village.

ARRIVAL AND DEPARTURE   KOROYANITU NATIONAL HERITAGE PARK

By car Access to the park is by 4WD from Lautoka via Tavakubu Rd off Drasa Ave; it takes 30min to reach Abaca village, travelling up a steep dirt road past the dramatic volcanic escarpment of Castle Rock.

By public transport There's no public transport to Abaca

and taxis are unwilling to make the trip due to the road conditions: the best option is to contact local guide George Prince (see tours below) who provides transfers to the park from Lautoka for F$30 one way.

INFORMATION AND TOURS

Entry fee F$40, plus compulsory guide to Savuione Falls (F$30; 3hr) or Mt Batilamu (F$40; 5hr).

Visitor centre ☎ 664 5431 or ☎ 992 1517. Mon–Sat 8am–4.30pm, Sun by request only.

Tours Guided treks led by George Prince (☎ 664 5431, ✉ abacaecopark@yahoo.com) are the best way to

appreciate the park. A full-day guided tour including a local Fijian village lunch costs F$150, while overnight options include a hut stay on top of Mt Batilamu for F$260, or a night in a Fijian village for F$230. All tours are for a minimum of 2 people and include return transfers from Lautoka, meals and park fees.

THE STORY OF ABACA

Abaca got its name by accident. The original village was called Nagara but in 1931 a **landslide** hit the village, leaving only three survivors. Thankful to be alive, the three went in search of a new home. On their journey they came across a large stone emblazoned with the letters ABC. The letters had been painted by a missionary in the 1830s while teaching the alphabet to the people of Nagara. Inspired by this prophetic sign, the survivors decided to name their new village "Abaca", an acronym in the local dialect for "the beginning of eternal life after a miracle".

ACCOMMODATION

Nase Lodge Arrange via the visitor centre (see opposite); map p.52. In a wilderness setting near the visitor centre, this wooden cabin has two large bunk rooms and a communal lounge and kitchen – you're likely to be the only guest, though school groups sometimes book the whole hut, so call ahead to check. Meals can be arranged at the village: breakfast F$15, lunch F$15, dinner F$30. Camping **F$35**, dorms **F$50**

The Mamanucas and Yasawa Islands

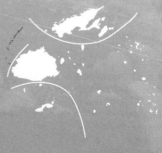

REEF IN THE MAMANUCAS

The Mamanucas and Yasawa Islands

Extending in an arc off the coast of Viti Levu, the Mamanucas and Yasawa Islands are a chain of beautiful palm-fringed islands with perfect white sandy beaches, placid lagoons and picturesque resorts. This is Fiji's tourism gem, attracting thousands of visitors, especially from Australia and New Zealand. Thankfully, though, the islands remain remarkably undeveloped – no building rises higher than a coconut palm and even on the most popular islands it's possible to wander a short distance to find a secluded stretch of beach. The focus here is on relaxation. Most visitors spend their days sunbathing, snorkelling or scuba diving, with sightseeing limited to hiking between small villages or trekking to a hilltop to see the sunset. Evenings are spent around the resort bar and restaurant which, apart from at a couple of backpacker resorts, tend to wind down around 10pm – this is no Bali or Ibiza, though there are plenty of opportunities to try *yaqona* (*kava*).

The thirty or so small islands of the **Mamanucas** lie just off the coast from Nadi making them the most popular day-trip destination in Fiji. Budget accommodation and small **boutique resorts** are scattered evenly around the group, some on tiny uninhabited **coral islands** and the majority in secluded bays. Honeymooners, families and singles flock here between June and October when Australia and New Zealand are gripped by winter; finding accommodation can be difficult during this time.

Extending to the north of the Mamanucas is a long, thin string of fifteen volcanic masses that make up the **Yasawa Islands**. These islands are slightly larger and more dramatic in appearance than their southern neighbours and, being further out from the tourist hub of Nadi, are less commercialized. The **beaches** here are exquisite and the best way to see them is by hopping on and off the fast *Yasawa Flyer* passenger ferry – the most popular **backpacker trail** in Fiji – and staying at some of the many budget resorts along the way. For a little more luxury, consider taking an overnight or week-long **cruise**, putting ashore at secluded beaches and anchoring at fabulous coral reefs for snorkelling.

Brief history

Before the arrival of tourists, the Mamanucas mostly served as fishing and egg-gathering grounds for its landowners from Viseisei and Nadi on Viti Levu. The majority were never inhabited due to the lack of fresh water. Only three of the larger volcanic islands – Malolo, Yanuya and Tavua – supported small **fishing villages**. With poor farming conditions, life was tough and the majority of islanders sought out new opportunities on the mainland. Today, their fortunes have reversed and these iTaukei households all earn money through hotel land rent, with at least one family member

WAYA ISLAND

Highlights

①Musket Cove Marina Light a barbecue overlooking the beach, grab a cocktail and watch the yachts sail by. **See p.82**

②Mana Island Luxury rooms, dorm beds, beaches, hilltop views, easy-to-arrange diving trips, even sand-spit outings – whatever your bag, this island makes a great base. **See p.86**

③Monuriki Island Take a trip to Monuriki Island with its high volcanic rocks, deep lagoons and coral reefs. The little island was the setting for Tom Hanks' desert island solitude in the movie *Castaway*. **See p.88**

④Overnight cruises Splash out on a multiday cruise to the Yasawas with fabulous

sightseeing, snorkelling and village visits along the way. **See p.92**

⑤Snorkelling Most islands have healthy coral reefs which are accessible directly from the beach: to spot tip reef sharks head to Mouya Reef, while manta rays congregate in Drawaqa Passage. **See p.93 & 96**

⑥Waya and Wayasewa Explore these stunning volcanic islands along scenic coastal and ridge trails. **See p.94**

⑦Sawa-i-Lau Caves Dappled with unusual light and shrouded in legend, these exciting swim-through caves are an iconic attraction. **See p.99**

HIGHLIGHTS ARE MARKED ON THE MAP ON P.76

MAMANUCAS AND YASAWA ISLANDS

HIGHLIGHTS

1. Musket Cove Marina
2. Mana Island
3. Monuriki Island
4. Overnight cruises
5. Snorkelling
6. Waya and Wayasewa
7. Sawa-i-Lau caves

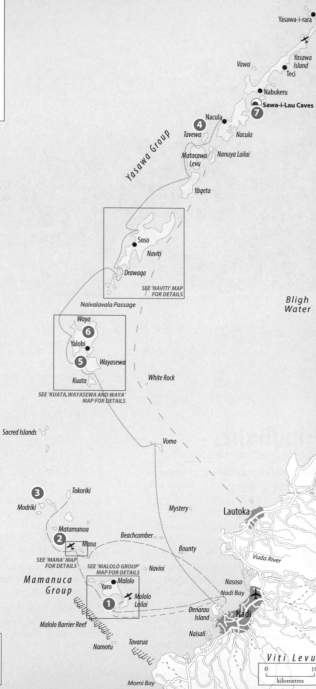

Yasawa-i-rara

Vawa

Yasawa Island

Teci

Nabukeru

Sawa-i-Lau Caves 7

Nacula 4

Tavewa

Nacula

Matacawa Levu

Nanuya Lailai

Yaqeta

Yasawa Group

Viwa

Soso

Naviti

Drawaqa

SEE 'NAVITI MAP FOR DETAILS

Bligh Water

Naivalavala Passage

SOUTH PACIFIC OCEAN

Waya 6

Yalobi

5

Wayasewa

Kuata

SEE 'KUATA, WAYASEWA AND WAYA' MAP FOR DETAILS

White Rock

Sacred Islands

Vomo

Tokoriki 3

Modriki

Mystery

Lautoka

Matamanoa

Mana 2

Beachcomber

Bounty

Vuda River

SEE 'MANA' MAP FOR DETAILS

SEE 'MALOLO GROUP' MAP FOR DETAILS

Navini

Mamanuca Group

Yaro 1 Malolo

Mololo Lailai

Nasoso

Nadi Bay

Denarau Island

Nadi

Malolo Barrier Reef

Namotu

Tavarua

Naisali

Viti Levu

Momi Bay

Malolo Cat
South Sea Cruises
Tavewa Seabus
Yasawa Flyer

0   10
kilometres

working in the tourist industry. Food supplies are now shipped in on fast boats from the mainland.

Conditions were better on the larger Yasawa Islands. Thanks to the presence of natural spring water and more fertile soils, a greater number of coastal villages were established here. The southernmost islands of the chain, Kuata and Wayasewa, are aligned to the mainland village of Viseisei, being part of its *yavusa* or district and sharing its dialect. All other islands give allegiance to the high chief or **Tui Yasawa** who resides in Yasawa-i-Rara village at the northernmost tip of the group. Little is known about the early history of the Yasawa people except that they were deeply feared as warriors by the inhabitants of eastern Fiji. In 1789 **Captain William Bligh** (see p.218), having been cast adrift in a small rowing boat by the *Bounty* mutineers, rowed through the Yasawas and was chased by several war canoes. Fortunately for him, a squall blew in and the pursuing Yasawans retreated. The choppy passage through which he escaped is known as Bligh Water.

The Mamanucas

Referred to by Fijians as the "Magic Islands", the **MAMANUCAS** are a stunning collection of two dozen beach-fringed islets, surrounded by a translucent expanse of ocean strewn with coral reefs. Situated in the lee of the main island of Viti Levu, and sometimes visible from Nadi, the islands boast the finest weather in Fiji – year-round sunshine, calm seas and gentle breezes. Given the ease of travel and the wide choice of resorts, this is the South Pacific's prime beach holiday destination.

The **coral islands**, lying immediately offshore from Nadi and Lautoka, comprise a dozen picturesque tiny **coral cays**, which feature heavily in the tourist brochures, and each house one resort. More prominent from the mainland, are the larger volcanic islands of the **Malolo Group**, with rolling, grassy hills framing beautiful **beaches**, and the surrounding seas bobbing with yachts and ferries. There are plenty of **activities** available here, including game fishing, jet-skiing and kayaking, as well as excellent **scuba diving** and world-class **surfing**.

Forming the western border of Fiji, the remote **Mamanuca-i-Cake Group** is also volcanic in appearance but has more rugged coastlines and steeper hills covered in light forest. Being further from the mainland, these islands are less busy – with just three small boutique beach resorts, they appeal mostly to honeymooners, and as a stop on overnight cruises.

ARRIVAL AND GETTING AROUND   THE MAMANUCAS

The bulk of visitors arrive on the **fast catamarans** running from Port Denarau at the southern end of Nadi, although there are also **water taxis** and a dedicated **boat service** to Mana from Wailoaloa, in Nadi Bay. For fantastic sightseeing along the way, you could consider transferring to the islands by **seaplane** or helicopter – it's not always prohibitively pricey, if you're in a group. Once in the Mamanucas, all the resorts have speedboats for **inter-island transfers**, but these are expensive – the short 10min hop between Malolo and Malolo Lailai, for example, might cost F$90 one way. It's a lot cheaper catching one of the fast catamarans between the islands; *South Sea Cruises* have the most frequent connections. Note that the Coral Islands and Matamanoa-i-Cake group can also be visited as part of a longer Yasawas cruise (see p.92).

MAMANUCAS ON A BUDGET

Although many backpackers find it cheaper to base themselves in Nadi and visit the Mamanucas on day-trips, it is possible to stay on the islands, with affordable dorm accommodation on both Mana (see p.87) and Malolo (see p.85). It's a good idea to stock up on water and snacks in Nadi before boarding the boat, since these are sold at resort prices on the islands as well as in Port Denarau, so do your shopping in advance. If you're not on a pre-paid, all-inclusive tour, load up on cash in Nadi, as the only ATM hereabouts is on Malolo Lailai.

2

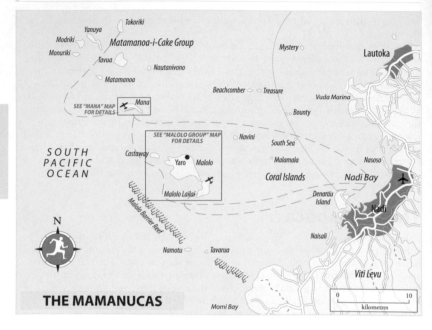

THE MAMANUCAS

BY BOAT

The following companies all offer free hotel pick-ups and drop-offs in the Nadi area; some resorts run their own speedboat transfers and this will be arranged when you book. Note that the Mamanuca-i-Cake Group lies beyond the fast catamaran route from Port Denarau, although there are regular connections by smaller outboard boats.

Malolo Cat Port Denarau ☎675 0207, ⓦmalolocatfiji .com. Four daily fast, non-stop catamaran services between Port Denarau and Malolo Lailai.

Mana Flyer Newton Beach, Wailoaloa ☎997 1885, ⓦmanaflyerfiji.com. Small daily boat serving the backpacker resorts in the Mamanucas.

Sea Fiji Port Denarau ☎672 5961, ⓦseafiji.net. A 24hr water taxi service from Port Denarau to all island resorts, in distinctive bright-orange catamarans and mono-hulls. Transfers to the inner islands start from F$500 for up to eight people.

South Sea Cruises Port Denarau ☎675 0500, ⓦssc .com.fj. Services (4–5 daily) to most Mamanucas resorts – one boat runs to the Coral Islands, Malolo, Castaway and Mana, and another to Matamanoa and Tokoriki.

BY PLANE

Island Hoppers Nadi Airport ☎672 0410, ⓦhelicopters.com.fj. Helicopter flights to most islands in the Mamanucas from Nadi Airport, Denarau Island and various resorts along the Coral Coast; prices start from F$300 per person one-way. They also have a plane, which can get you to Mana or Malolo Lailai.

Pacific Island Air Nadi Airport ☎672 5644, ⓦpacificislandair.com. Four- and eight-seater seaplanes, taking off from Nadi Airport and splashing down in the resort lagoons. Prices start from F$390 per person one-way (min 2 passengers), and you're allowed 20kg of luggage.

Turtle Airways Newton Beach, Wailoaloa ☎672 1888, ⓦturtleairways.com. Turtle Airways offers low-flying seaplane transfers to resorts in the Mamanucas (journey time around 15min). Prices start from F$330 per person one-way (min 2 passengers), with departure times tailored around international flights: discuss your baggage requirements in advance as the planes from Nadi have a 460kg weight limit (including passengers).

The coral islands

The **CORAL ISLANDS** comprise twelve tiny cays, surrounded by a shallow lagoon. These islands seldom rise more than 5m above sea-level, are covered with light scrub vegetation and until recently were all uninhabited. Apart from the resorts that are now built on them, there's not an awful lot to distinguish one from another, except for

SCUBA DIVING IN THE MAMANUCAS

With fast boat transfers and a wide choice of operators, **divers** can easily sample all dive sites in the Mamanucas while staying at a single resort. The islands are a great spot to **learn to dive** with sheltered lagoons, water temperatures seldom dropping below 24˚C and excellent visibility, usually at least 30m.

The dozen or so shallow patch coral dive sites in the northern **coral islands** are ideal for beginners. More advanced divers come here for the two popular **wrecks** – a partially intact World War II B26 bomber at 26m; and the 40m-long cruise ship, *Salamander*, lying at 12–28m and covered in soft corals and anemones. In the southwest of the Mamanucas, the 30km-long **Malolo Barrier Reef** has several deep drop-offs suitable for experienced divers – turtles, lion fish, rays and large sharks are common. The reef is a fifteen-minute boat ride from Malolo Lailai.

The reefs surrounding **Mana** have some exceptional sites for beginner to intermediate divers. The most raved about site is "Supermarket", offering regular **shark encounters** from white tips to greys, as well as a drift dive along a wall with an abundance of lionfish and moray eels. Other sites include "Gotham City", named for its abundance of batfish, and "Barrel Head", a wide bommie where you can drift along a wall with massive sea fans and plenty of turtles. Heading west to the Mamanuca-i-Cake Group, **Tokoriki** has several interesting sites with gorgonian **sea fans** featuring prominently at "Sherwood Forest", along with a fine selection of soft corals, nudibranchs and anemones.

DIVE OPERATORS

The operators below charge similar prices – usually around F$580 for a two-day scuba course, F$710 for a two- or three-day advanced PADI certificate, up to F$825 for a full four-day open-water course. Single-tank dives start at F$140, with two-tank ones around F$270. It's very easy to arrange dive trips in Nadi too, especially around Wailoaloa Beach – ask at your accommodation.

Ratu Kini ☎ 666 9309, ⊚ ratukinidiveresort.com.fj. Budget operator for Mana Island backpackers; they run five- and seven-day trips, including accommodation in dorms or private rooms.

Reef Safari ☎ 675 0950, ⊚ reefsafari.com.fj. International operator with a base at South Sea Island.

Subsurface Fiji ☎ 666 6738, ⊚ subsurfacefiji.com. Dominant dive operator with bases at most resorts in Malolo, Malolo Lailai and Matamanoa-i-Cake.

Viti Watersports Port Denarau Marina ☎ 670 2413, ⊚ vitiwatersports.com. Based in Matamanoa, but also operates fast, covered boats for day-trippers from Denarau Island to the Malolo Barrier Reef.

Namotu and Tavarua in the southeastern tip of the Malolo Barrier Reef, which have world-class **reef surfing**, though this is best accessed from the Malolo islands (see box, p.85). The northern coral islands are the most accessible, with transfers from both Port Denarau and Vuda Marina taking less than twenty minutes.

South Sea Island

The tiny speck of **South Sea Island** is the smallest of the coral islands and takes just 25 minutes to reach from Port Denarau. It's the first stop on the main catamaran routes, making it a busy little place with both day-trippers from Nadi and backpackers heading to and from the Yasawas. It's rather a cramped island, not even a hundred paces in width, and takes less than five minutes to walk around. The snorkelling is disappointing: it's so close to Nadi Bay that the reefs have been damaged by runoff from the sugarcane farms and rivers on Viti Levu. There's not much to do except bask on the beach and cool off in the resort's swimming pool – **day-trippers** are sometimes enticed by the offer of unlimited beer or house wine.

Bounty Island

Five minutes northwest of South Sea Island, **Bounty Island** is the largest of the Mamanucas coral cays at 48 acres, and the best for exploring; it was the idyllic location for reality TV show *Celebrity Love Island*. Bounty is a popular spot for **backpackers**

2

ISLAND NAMES

Resorts on the smaller coral islands have a higher profile than the islands themselves and in most cases the **traditional Fijian name** has been ditched in favour of an alluringly exotic title – the actual names of Beachcomber, Bounty, Castaway, South Sea and Treasure islands are Tai, Kadavu, Qalito, Vunivadra and Elevuka, respectively. However, we've used the **resort names** throughout, as this is what you will see on transport information and timetables.

---

heading to and from the Yasawas. Kayaks and catamarans are available for rent, and **kayakers** can circumnavigate the island in an hour paddling in a crystal clear lagoon. The north lagoon facing the resort has reasonable **snorkelling**, with shallow waters good for beginners, and there are several massive coral heads with plenty of small reef fish barely 30m from shore. You'll also find **walking** trails meandering through light scrub (good for bird-spotting), and interesting **beachcombing** with lots of shells, driftwood, hermit crabs and wonderful views looking back to Vuda Point and the mountains of Viti Levu.

Treasure Island

Three kilometres to the west of South Sea Island is fourteen-acre **Treasure Island**, home to a family-orientated resort (see opposite). There's a **turtle sanctuary** (see box opposite) in the centre of the island, and a few hundred metres off the south beach sits a tiny sand islet with some good snorkelling.

Beachcomber Island

Facing Treasure Island, less than a kilometre to the west, **Beachcomber Island** is home to a somewhat hedonistic resort (see opposite). Organized party nights with pumping music, limbo dancing, crab races and lots of young gap-year travellers may not be everyone's idea of fun, but in season the island raves past midnight, which is something of a rarity in Fiji. There are also plenty of activities to fill the days, including parasailing, sailing, waterskiing, jet-skiing and banana-boat rides, all of which can be sampled on an action-packed day-cruise.

Navini Island

A tiny coral cay encircled by a white sandy beach, **Navini Island** is off the regular ferry route in a secluded spot between Beachcomber and Malolo. With just ten beachfront bures, no day-trippers and extremely attentive staff, it makes for a perfect **honeymoon destination**. Just offshore is a great snorkelling lagoon.

Namotu and Tavarua

At the southern end of the Mamanucas, on the eastern edge of the Malolo Barrier Reef and facing Momi Bay on Viti Levu, are two coral cays, **Namotu** and heart-shaped **Tavarua**. Both islands are home to upmarket **resorts** run by US-based companies, though it's also possible to access the world-class surf breaks here from Malolo or Malolo Lailai (see box, p.85). This section of the Malolo Barrier Reef is also a popular playground for pods of bottle-nose **dolphins**, which can be seen on organized dolphin-watching cruises from Malolo Lailai (see p.83) and Nadi.

ARRIVAL AND GETTING AROUND

CORAL ISLANDS

Day-trips Most visitors, especially budget travellers, visit the islands on day-trips run from Nadi (see p.50); sample prices are around F$160 to Bounty and South Sea, including transfers and lunch.

By boat *South Sea Cruises* (see p.78) and Awesome Fiji's *Yasawa Flyer* (p.90) run large, comfy catamarans from Port Denarau to South Sea (F$95), Bounty (F$95), Treasure (F$110) and Beachcomber (F$110). Services leave Denarau daily at 8.30am, 9am, 12.15pm and 3.15pm; the journey can be quite spectacular, and the boats wait while passengers load and unload from the smaller boats needed for transfer to these tiny isles.

SEA TURTLES IN THE MAMANUCAS

Five of the world's seven species of **sea turtle** can be found in Fiji – the green, loggerhead, leatherback, hawksbill and Olive Ridley: of these, the green, loggerhead and hawksbill lay their eggs on the small coral islands of the Mamanucas. At around the age of 25, female turtles return to the same beach where they hatched to lay their eggs, burying them deep in the sand in batches of up to two hundred. This happens at night between September and January. After sixty to seventy days, the eggs **hatch** en masse, again at night, and the hatchlings make their way to the sea. As few as one in a thousand reach full maturity, and their odds of survival are further reduced by light and noise pollution from resorts.

Despite a national ban on **hunting turtles** for meat – an essential ingredient in ceremonial feasting – locals in the outlying islands continue to do so. In an effort to revive populations and promote ecological awareness, *Treasure Island Resort* (see below) has set up a small **turtle sanctuary** to nurture baby sea turtles before releasing them back into the ocean. If your timing's right you may be able to participate in their feeding and release, which generally occurs between November and March.

2

Destinations from Port Denarau Beachcomber (4 daily; 45min); Bounty (4 daily; 35min); Castaway (3 daily; 1hr 50min); South Sea (4 daily; 30min); Treasure Island (4 daily; 45min).

By boat Cheaper than the catamarans is the small *Mana Flyer*, which leaves Newton Beach, Wailoaloa, daily at 10.30am (F$75).

ACCOMMODATION

Beachcomber Island Resort ✆ 666 1500, ⓦ beachcomberfiji.com. Accommodation is spread over three dorms (one huge, one small and one female-only), private double rooms and comfy, highly colourful bures with en-suite, hot-water bathrooms. Not for nothing is it known as the party island – it's loud, raucous and you don't come here for a good night's sleep. You can often get all-inclusive specials when booking, but otherwise beware: meals and drinks are pricey. 🛜 Dorms F$41, rooms F$262, bures F$400

Bounty Island Resort ✆ 666 7461, ⓦ fiji-bounty.com. A laidback resort on Bounty Island's north beach. The 22 simple a/c wooden and bamboo huts have en-suite bathrooms and are strung out along the beachfront, while dorm rooms (also a/c) are set back from the sea in a large cement building and share hot-water showers. A restaurant and swimming pool abut the beach, and they've kayaks and catamarans for rent. 🛜($) Dorms F$47, island bures F$172, beachfront bures F$208

Navini Island Resort ✆ 666 2188, ⓦ navinifiji.com.fj. Deluxe bures come with spa baths and a private courtyard overlooking the beach. Fishing trips, village visits and use of watersports equipment are included in the price, as are two hearty meals. 🛜 F$962

South Sea Island Resort ✆ 675 0500, ⓦ awesomefiji.com. Youth-orientated accommodation on a miniscule island: there's just one large wooden dorm room (32 beds) above a restaurant, with two toilets and an open sink smack in the middle, making it rather devoid of privacy. Rates include meals, and there's usually a three-night minimum stay. F$175

Treasure Island Resort ✆ 666 6999, ⓦ www.treasureisland-fiji.com. Accommodation here is in 68 a/c family rooms, set 30m back from the beach. There's a fantastic all-day kids' club, plus mini-putt golfing, a spa, and nightly entertainment. Same-day transfers from the airport. 🛜($) F$800

The Malolo Group

Twenty kilometres from Nadi, the coral cays give way to four large volcanic islands making up the **MALOLO GROUP**. This is the heart of the Mamanucas tourism experience, with the busiest and most popular resorts. **Malolo**, the largest island in the group at just over 2400 acres, and its little sister **Malolo Lailai** have a smattering of resorts, a **marina** and the chiefly village of **Yaro**. Along with beautiful **Castaway Island**, these islands form a cluster protected to the south by the stunning Malolo Barrier Reef. Just a fifteen-minute boat ride away, there's excellent surfing in the passages, and advanced scuba divers can enjoy the challenging wall-dives on the outer edges of the reef. Six kilometres to the northwest of Malolo is **Mana**, the liveliest island for backpackers, which also has lovely **beaches** to explore.

2

SPOTTING THE SOUTHERN CROSS

Free from excessive ambient light, Southern Hemisphere **stargazing** is outstanding in Fiji, especially on small islands such as the Mamanucas. As dusk fades, look toward the south and slightly east to see the **Southern Cross** as it rises above the horizon. It's a small series of five stars, most easily located by Alpha and Beta Centauri, the two brightest stars low on the horizon. Draw an imaginary line from the lower star to the upper one and extend it a little in an arc to the lowest star of the horizontal cross. Be careful not to confuse it with the false cross, slightly higher in the sky, of about the same size but not as bright.

ARRIVAL AND INFORMATION   THE MALOLO GROUP

By boat Although it's possible to walk between Malolo and Malolo Lailai at low tide, the two islands are actually on separate catamaran routes. To Malolo Lailai, the non-stop *Malolo Cat* (see p.78) leaves Port Denarau at 7.30am, 10.30am, 2pm & 5.30pm (F$80 one way or same-day return; 1hr), returning from Musket Cove Marina at 5.45am, 8.45am, 12.15pm & 4pm. To Malolo and Castaway, *South Sea Cruises* (F$125; see p.78) leave Denarau daily at 9am, 12.15pm (both taking 2hr, via various coral islands) and 3.15pm (50min, direct); return departures from Malolo are at 11am, 2pm (both 50min), and 4.10pm (2hr). You can also use these *South Sea* services between Malolo and Mana (F$60; 35min).

By plane The tiny airstrip on Malolo Lailai is used by Pacific Island and Island Hoppers services (see p.78); Turtle Airways' seaplanes (see p.78) plop down in the waters nearby.

Money There's an ATM by the entrance to the *Musket Cove Resort* lobby on Malolo Lailai.

Malolo Lailai

The third-largest of the Mamanucas Islands, **Malolo Lailai** is surrounded by picturesque sandy beaches. On its west side is a sheltered bay separating the island from its larger sister, Malolo. Tucked into the bay are several resorts, restaurants and the **Musket Cove Marina**. In mid-September the Fiji sailing season culminates here in the week-long **Musket Cove Regatta**, featuring race days as well as plenty of partying. The low grassy hills on the north side of Malolo Lailai are crisscrossed with walking tracks, with stunning views looking back to Viti Levu and out over the Mamanucas.

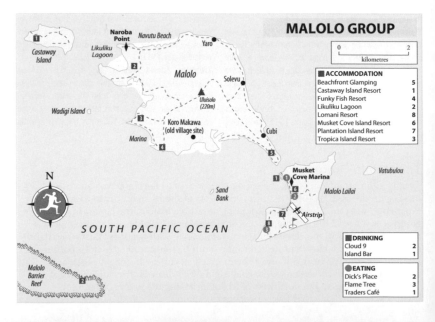

MALOLO GROUP

0 ———— 2
kilometres

■ ACCOMMODATION
Beachfront Glamping	5
Castaway Island Resort	1
Funky Fish Resort	4
Likuliku Lagoon	2
Lomani Resort	8
Musket Cove Island Resort	6
Plantation Island Resort	7
Tropica Island Resort	3

■ DRINKING
Cloud 9	2
Island Bar	1

● EATING
Dick's Place	2
Flame Tree	3
Traders Café	1

Naroba Point · Navutu Beach · Yaro · Likuliku Lagoon · Castaway Island · *Malolo* · Solevu · *Uluisolo (220m)* · Wadigi Island · Koro Makawa (old village site) · Marina · Cubi · SOUTH PACIFIC OCEAN · Musket Cove Marina · Vatubulou · Malolo Lailai · Sand Bank · Airstrip · N · Malolo Barrier Reef

When Australian prospector **John Thompson** sailed to Fiji in 1872 he purchased Malolo Lailai for fifty muskets and five hundred pieces of gold from the landowners on the neighbouring island of Malolo. In 1903 the island was leased to the Won Ket family who worked the land as a successful copra plantation for 63 years using Chinese labourers – a **Chinese cemetery** can be seen in the hills. In 1966, with the collapse of copra prices, the island was sold to its present owners, the Smith and Raffe families, both of whom pioneered the region's tourism industry, building successful holiday resorts.

2

ACCOMMODATION   MALOLO LAILAI

Lomani Resort ☎666 8212, ⊛lomaniisland.com. With just two dozen Mediterranean-style whitewashed suites, and a lovely swimming pool with decked outdoor restaurant, this is a good choice for honeymooners. The serene plantation-style setting is at the quieter end of Malolo Lailai's main beach, with a lagoon deep enough for swimming and snorkelling. ☎ F$1030

Musket Cove Island Resort ☎666 2215, ⊛musketcovefiji.com. Varied accommodation, including standard hotel rooms, traditional thatched bures with hammocks, and villas on an artificial island with over-water decks. There's a large pool, and free snorkelling excursions are offered. ☎ Rooms F$370, bures F$600, villas F$1000

Plantation Island Resort ☎666 9333, ⊛plantation island.com. Large, slightly dated-looking resort bustling with young families. The palm-fringed beach is stunning, and they have three swimming pools plus windsurfing boards and kayaks to borrow, as well as restaurants, bars and an espresso and juice bar. ☎($) F$620

EATING

One of the delights of staying on Malolo Lailai is its choice of **restaurants**. For **food shopping**, The Trader (daily 8am–7pm), beside the *Musket Cove Resort* lobby, stocks a good selection of groceries (but no alcohol); prices are just about fair for a Mamanucas island.

Dick's Place Musket Cove Resort ☎664 0805. This resort restaurant has an excellent menu, including delicious New Zealand lamb shanks, *ika vakalolo* (fish cooked in coconut cream) and risotto; most mains are F$55–70, or around half that for veggie options. Daily 7.30am–5pm & 6.30–10pm.

Flame Tree Lomani Resort ☎666 8212. This is a good choice if you want to get away from the hordes, and kids – it's adults only here. The seafood is excellent (though the service can be a little frosty), with kokoda (see p.29) a great snack for F$21; steaks start at F$52. Payment by card only, or they can charge it to your room at any local resort. Daily noon–2pm & 6–9pm.

Traders Café Musket Cove Marina ☎666 2215. This stylish, relaxed place has a pretty setting overlooking the marina, as well as good coffee (from F$8) and pizza (from F$26); in addition, their pies (F$7.5) are just about the cheapest belly-fillers on the island. Daily 8am–8pm.

ACTIVITIES ON MALOLO LAILAI

Activities at both *Musket Cove Resort* and *Plantation Island Resort* are available to non-guests; they include waterskiing, parasailing, banana-boat rides, sport fishing, island-hopping and surfing. Subsurface Fiji (see p.79) offers a full range of **scuba diving** courses, including Nitrox, and the PADI Bubblemaker for kids. Thousands of tiny reef fish congregate around the sandbar, a kilometre offshore in Malolo Bay, but you'll need to join a **snorkelling trip** by boat to get there, organized by all resorts on Malolo Lailai (F$90 per person).

For **sailing** or speedboat charters, the best option is Take a Break Cruises (☎925 9469, ⊛takeabreakcruises.com; F$120 per person, minimum six people), who have bases at *Musket Cove* and *Plantation*. They also run **dolphin-watching cruises** on board the luxury sailing catamaran *Take A Break* (Mon–Thurs 9.15am–noon; F$69, minimum nine people), as well as game fishing (F$250 per person) and sport fishing (F$570 for the boat; 3hr minimum).

The activity bure (daily 8am–5pm) beside Musket Cove Marina rents out **bicycles** for F$30 per day. There's also a flat nine-hole **golf course** behind *Plantation Island Resort* with nice sea views (F$40 including clubs and trolley plus F$2/6 per used/new ball).

2

DRINKING

★**Cloud 9** Malolo Barrier Reef ☎ 869 7947, ⓦ cloud9 .com.fj. Yes, you read the address right, and no, the map location is not a misprint – this bar is located out in the sea, perched above the reef. As you might expect, it's a trendy spot with pulsing lounge music and pricey drinks. You can get there on their own boat (leaves Port Denarau at 9am, returning at 3pm; F$229, including F$60 worth of food and drink vouchers), or on transfers run by most of the area's resorts. Card only. Daily 10am–5pm.

Island Bar Musket Cove Marina ☎ 666 2215. Atmospheric bar on an artificial island connected to the marina by pontoon. It's a great spot to sip a sunset beer (from F$7) or local rum (F$8, or F$24 for a sampler set) overlooking Malolo Bay. Daily 11am–9pm, sometimes later.

Malolo

Malolo is the largest island in the Mamanucas, and boasts a full array of accommodation – from glamping to opulent resorts. The 220m-high hillfort of **Uluisolo** looks down on the island's rich vegetation and white beaches, and though these won't change much in the foreseeable future, a mammoth new construction project on the west of the island will begin to attract wealthy sailors and their yachts into a brand-new marina over the next few years.

The east coast

Sitting pretty on the east coast, **Solevu** is known as the "shell village", though many of the shells on sale here are imported from Asia. Fifteen minutes further south, the tiny settlement of **Cubi** is inhabited by a community from Fulaga (see p.182) in the Lau Group – the men are renowned woodcarvers and you can buy fine samples of *tanoa* bowls and war clubs. From Cubi, it's a ten-minute walk to the southern lagoon (see below), or you can follow the inland trail to Uluisolo (see below).

The southern lagoon

The southern point of Malolo juts out into a shallow **lagoon** almost touching Malolo Lailai – you can walk between the two islands at low to mid-tide. Although not practical for swimming or snorkelling (the reefs have been extensively damaged by fishing), the southern lagoon is great for **kitesurfing**, with southeasterly trade winds creating almost perfect conditions between May and October.

Inland Malolo

The real beauty of Malolo lies inland, and there are plenty of **walking tracks** around the island, including several ascending to the 220m-high **Uluisolo**. At the summit is a US-built World War II **lookout post** offering fabulous views of the entire Mamanucas and as far north as Matacawalevu in the northern Yasawas. It

---

THE DESTRUCTION OF SOLEVU VILLAGE

In July 1840 a flotilla of six **US Navy warships** was sent to the South Pacific to survey the islands and assure the safety of American whalers in the region. Having toured Tonga, Samoa, New Zealand and most parts of Fiji, the ships arrived at Malolo Island. A small boat was sent to Solevu village to bargain for much-needed food provisions but the crew was ambushed and two officers killed. Outraged by this unprovoked attack, the captain of the flotilla, Charles Wilkes, set about revenge. First, the bodies were recovered and buried in an unmarked grave on tiny Kadavu Island (currently home to *Bounty Island Resort*); then the village of **Solevu** was burned to the ground, garden plantations ripped apart, canoes sunk and 57 men slaughtered. The attack proceeded to neighbouring Yaro where the village elders hastily surrendered by prostrating themselves as a sign of humility. Wilkes ordered the villagers to supply his ships with water, yams, a dozen pigs and three thousand coconuts – a huge task considering the damage caused by the attack and the poor farming conditions of the region. Wilkes was subsequently court-martialled for his severe actions – the first military strike in Fiji carried out by Western forces.

SURFING MALOLO

Surfing at **Malolo Barrier Reef** is exceptional, with waves up to 5m high, crystal-clear water and smooth right- and left-hand breaks. The most famous breaks are the left-handers "Cloudbreak" and "Restaurants", and the right barrel of "Wilkes" and "Desperations".

Funky Fish on Mololo (see below) often offer week-long deals including free transfers out to the breaks. Alternatively, the activities hut at *Plantation Island Resort* on Malolo Lailai (see p.83) runs a boat daily during high tide (sometimes twice daily). Choose one of seven breaks, according to the conditions and your level of ability; the trip takes around four hours (F$70–90).

Other resorts offering boat trips to the reefs include *Castaway Island* (see below) and *Mana Island* (see p.87). There's also direct access from *Rendezvous Fiji* on the mainland, a twenty-minute drive south of Nadi.

Note that most of the breaks are at their best in the **morning** before the winds freshen up and the prime season for monster waves is between April and November. Surfing here is not for beginners – waves can be huge and, with **sharp coral heads** just a few metres below the surface, any untimely wipeout could lead to severe cuts or grazes.

2

takes just under an hour to reach the top: the best approach is from the east, since the trails from north and south can be tricky, but note that there is little shade along the way.

ACCOMMODATION   MALOLO

Beachfront Glamping ☎ 679 722 7094. Bookable on Airbnb, these two snazzily-furnished tents sit right by the beach on the deserted southern tip of the island, an easy wade from Musket Cove at low tide. At other times, you'll have to phone for a kayak pick-up, or perhaps hitch a ride on a yachtie's dinghy – loads of fun. Meals available on request. **F$150**

★**Funky Fish Resort** ☎ 679 900 1323, ⓦ funkyfishresort.com. A great-value resort tucked away on its own on the south coast. The cute little huts are arranged along the shoreline, while the dorm provides a rare budget option, and a hammock of some kind is never too far away; there's a sea-view pool, and the daily special meals (included with rooms, but not dorms) are of decent quality. A good place to chill out, or go surfing (see box above). ⓦ Dorms **F$52**, rooms **F$393**

Likuliku Lagoon ☎ 672 0978, ⓦ likulikulagoon.com. In a delightful crescent-shaped bay with tidal beach, this resort oozes elegance. The eighteen hand-crafted beachfront bungalows are exquisite, with massive bathrooms plus plunge pools and daybeds. The pricey overwater bungalows have good snorkelling direct from the steps leading down into the lagoon. Rates include meals. ⓦ **F$1990**

★**Tropica Island Resort** ☎ 665 1777, ⓦ tropicaisland .com. Gorgeous boutique resort, with a variety of rooms and beachfront bures – the latter are a delight, with thatched roofs, plus swing benches and hammocks, and even the cheapest rooms have private plunge pools and outdoor showers. Food is outstanding (all meals extra), there's an indulgent spa, and activities include watersports, basket weaving and crab races. ⓦ **F$895**

Castaway Island

Lying less than a kilometre off the northwest tip of Malolo, steep, rocky **Castaway Island** has a stunning powdery sand point, and a gorgeous turquoise lagoon. The island also boasts one of the best **walking trails** in the Mamanucas. Starting from the back of *Castaway Island Resort* (see below), a narrow path climbs for five minutes before levelling out and meandering through light natural forest. After twenty minutes, the trail emerges on the rocky slopes of the east side of the island where you're graced with wonderful **views** overlooking the small uninhabited Mociu Island and beyond to Mana and Matamanoa.

ACCOMMODATION   CASTAWAY ISLAND

Castaway Island Resort ☎ 666 1233, ⓦ castawayfiji .com. A popular choice for families and older couples, with dozens of traditional thatch bures located on the beautiful sand point. There's a tennis court, two swimming pools and a spa in the landscaped gardens, as well as exceptional snorkelling from the beach. ⓦ **F$1185**

2

Mana

Unlike most islands in this area, little **Mana** has some decent budget accommodation, making it the de facto choice for backpackers and those travelling on a shoestring. Prices aside, it's one of the best islands in the Malolo Group to explore, flanked by gorgeous sweeping beaches, and with a couple of hilly peaks providing an outstanding view of the surrounding islands. Occupying much of the western side of the island is the largest resort in the Mamanucas – now host to stacks of Chinese visitors, thanks to Mana's use as a location on a popular Chinese reality show.

Around the coast

While the private resorts topping and tailing the island make circumnavigating Mana on foot impossible, there are a few beaches open to all. One is the **South Beach**, home of the backpacker resorts – it's not great for swimming, but 50m out there's a nice drop-off with great visibility for **snorkelling**, coral heads teeming with fish and the chance to spot the occasional turtle. The other public beaches are **North Beach** and **Sunset Beach**, up on the north coast: the path to them runs through the grounds of the *Mana Island Resort* then along the airport runway – if you are approached by any resort staff, just tell them you are going to the beach. Sunset Beach, unsurprisingly, is best for sunsets, while North Beach has better snorkelling, with a steep drop-off 50m from shore.

Inland Mana

There are several nice walks along the hilly ridges inland. Easy-to-find trails head up from the *Mana Island Resort* to **Sunset Lookout** and **Tuilawa Lookout**, both fifteen-minute ambles through light forest to viewpoints with great sunset views. Another trailhead starts behind *Ratu Kini's* and follows the eastern ridgeline to the summit of **Ului Koro Navou**, with superb views overlooking the rocky islands of the Mamanuca-i-Cake Group.

ARRIVAL AND GETTING AROUND   MANA

By boat *South Sea Cruises* catamarans (see p.78) depart Denarau daily at 9am, 12.15pm and 3.15pm (F$130; 1hr 30min, whichever way around the loop goes); from Mana, departures are at 10.25am, 1.30pm and 4.45pm. You can use these services to connect to Malolo too (F$60; 35min). Cheaper than the catamarans, the small (but covered) *Mana Flyer*

departs Newton Beach, Wailoaloa, at 10.30am, then returns from Mana at around 12.30pm (F$75 one way; 50min).
By plane Mana's minuscule airstrip is used by Pacific Island and Island Hoppers services (see p.78), while Turtle Airways' seaplanes (see p.78) splash down in the waters off South Beach.

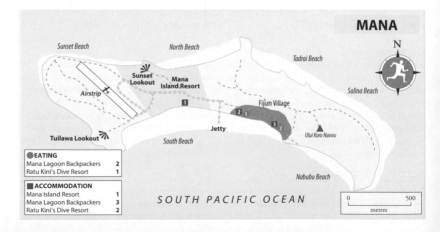

MANA

N

Sunset Beach

North Beach

Tadrai Beach

Sunset Lookout

Mana Island Resort

Salina Beach

Airstrip

1

Fijian Village

2 1

3 2

Jetty

Ului Koro Navou

Tuilawa Lookout

South Beach

Nabubu Beach

● **EATING**
| Mana Lagoon Backpackers | 2 |
| Ratu Kini's Dive Resort | 1 |

■ **ACCOMMODATION**
Mana Island Resort	1
Mana Lagoon Backpackers	3
Ratu Kini's Dive Resort	2

SOUTH PACIFIC OCEAN

0   500
metres

Tours The backpacker resorts run various tours, including snorkelling trips to nearby islands (F$70), and a very interesting jaunt to a nearby sandbar: Mana Lagoon Backpackers charge F$40 per person to get you out there, while for F$90 per head *Ratu Kini* throw in four beers per person, plus a barbecue. You can stay the night there, if you wish – your own private island, for a relative pittance.

ACCOMMODATION

Mana Island Resort ☎ 665 0423, ⓦ manafiji.com. With 150 rooms and bungalows, this is the largest of the Mamanuca resorts, though you wouldn't know it, as it's spread out over three hundred acres of landscaped gardens, fronting both South and North beaches. There are loads of amenities and water activities on offer, and a wide range of accommodation options from rooms, apartments and bungalows. ⓦ($) F$565

Mana Lagoon Backpackers ☎ 929 2337. Cheerful backpackers' hostel with a large and lively sand-floor beachfront restaurant (see below) and two rather stuffy dorm lodges at the back; some guests love it, some move out after the first night. Rates include simple meals, which aren't a patch on the restaurant's paid-for ones; if you bring your own food, dorm beds go for F$30. ⓦ($) Dorms F$55, rooms F$140

★ **Ratu Kini** ☎ 672 1959, ⓦ ratukinidiveresort.com .fj. Long-established backpacker hostel. The restaurant and bar are right over the beach, with the units set in a cement building 30m behind and the lodge rooms and larger dorms right at the back of the village abutting the hill. Interiors are clean and there's a lively atmosphere at night, with themed entertainment when there are enough guests. They also have a fully equipped dive shop (see p.79). Rates include breakfast. ⓦ($) Dorms F$35, rooms F$190

EATING AND DRINKING

Mana Lagoon Backpackers ☎ 929 2337. This budget place has decent cheapish food – try the superb fish curry (F$24), or *ika vakalolo* (F$27). It's open all hours, at least in theory – some guests drink so many beers that they end up sleeping on the beach, surrounded by empty bottles. ⓦ($) Daily 24hr.

Ratu Kini ☎ 672 1959, ⓦ ratukinidiveresort.com.fj. The food here is better than at *Mana Lagoon*, and the set-up a little smarter – though it's often just as lively. The fish and chips (F$24) provides a substantial feed, while their handful of Fijian dishes cost around F$35. ⓦ($) Daily noon–1.30pm & 6–7.30pm.

The Mamanuca-i-Cake Group

Only two of the thirteen islands belonging to the enchanting **MAMANUCA-I-CAKE GROUP** have resorts – **Matamanoa** and **Tokoriki** – and there are traditional fishing villages on **Tavua** and **Yanuya**. Otherwise, the islands are completely uninhabited. **Monuriki** was made famous in the 2001 film *Castaway* starring Tom Hanks, but its equally stunning neighbour **Modriki** is relatively unvisited; the more remote **Sacred Islands** remain way off the tourist trail, only visited briefly by an overnight cruise company or by private yachts.

ARRIVAL AND DEPARTURE   MAMANUCA-I-CAKE

By boat *South Sea Cruises* catamarans depart Denarau daily at 9.15am and 3pm for Tokoriki and Matamanoa (F$115; 1hr 30min), returning soon after arrival at 10.45am and 4.30pm.

On a tour To get to Yanuya, Monuriki and Modriki, most people join a tour – unless you're staying on Matamanoa or Tokoriki, these are best and most easily done from Mana (from F$70), but they're also possible from Nadi and the coral islands. The "Seaspray" tour run by *South Sea Cruises* (F$240; see p.78) includes snorkelling off Monuriki, a *kava* ceremony and village visit on Yanuya, plus lunch and all-you-can-drink beer and wine on board.

Matamanoa

Small, rocky **Matamanoa** is covered in thick forest, with a gorgeous beach on its eastern flank. Bird Rock, a few hundred metres off the southern coast, teems with seabirds, mostly noddies, terns and frigates, and is a fantastic spot for snorkelling and scuba diving; trips are operated by Viti Watersports, who are based on the island (see p.79).

A steep **trail** from the *Matamanoa Island Resort*, starting behind the tennis court, winds its way up to the island's summit where several huge boulders seem to balance precariously; it's easy to scale these for one of the most impressive **views** in Fiji – a 360-degree panorama with small islands in all directions. Directly north is **Tavua**, the third-largest island in the Mamanucas with a single village on its west coast, lined with lush coconut trees which stick out among its sunburnt barren hills. If you come in the evening or early morning, there's a good chance of spotting fruit bats and doves, which feed in the forests, and possibly the elusive crested iguana, which is usually well camouflaged in the canopy.

ACCOMMODATION   MATAMANOA

★**Matamanoa Island Resort** ☎672 3620, ⓦmatamanoa.com. If you're looking for a (relatively) good-value romantic getaway, this is the place to stay. The resort's spacious thatch bures are raised slightly from the beach, giving fabulous ocean views; there are also a/c rooms at the back in a single-storey block. ☜ Rooms F$595, bures F$945

Tokoriki

Surrounded by a fringing reef, hilly **Tokoriki** has two resorts either side of a rocky outcrop that divides a long stretch of beach on the west side of the island. In recent years the island has suffered from beach erosion and large amounts of seaweed washing up on certain tides, although the resorts remove it before it gets too whiffy. The offshore reefs are unaffected by the seaweed and **snorkelling** is excellent about 200m from the beach at both resorts. From May to July the lagoon teems with tiny bait fish, attracting both **seabirds** which circle and dive-bomb from above, and locals from the neighbouring villages casting fishing nets from small boats.

ACCOMMODATION   TOKORIKI

Sheraton Resort ☎664 7707, ⓦsheratontokorikiisland .com. Overlooking a turquoise lagoon, this resort has undergone substantial renovation since Cyclone Winston hit (see box, p.26). With over one hundred opulent rooms, it's a relative whopper as far as the Mamanucas are concerned; some units come with private plunge pools, though the infinity pool outside is open to all, as is the excellent on-site spa. ☜ F$375

★**Tokoriki Island Resort** ☎672 5926, ⓦtokoriki .com. An upmarket, adults-only retreat with a gorgeous infinity pool overlooking the ocean, and several beach bures. Perched against the hillside at the far end of the property are a series of private villas ranking among the most delightful in Fiji, each with handcrafted wooden interiors and their own plunge pools. ☜ F$1295

Yanuya, Monuriki and Modriki

Tokoriki is owned by the people of neighbouring **Yanuya**, a long, thin island with several knolls. The cute little village here is renowned for its **pottery making**; you can visit on a day-trip from nearby resorts, or on the daily *Seaspray* sailing cruise from Mana Island (see p.86) which comes ashore for a traditional *kava* ceremony and village craft market.

Off the west side of the village are the islands of **Monuriki** and **Modriki**; the former was used as the setting for the 2001 film *Castaway*, so don't be surprised if someone has arranged a bunch of coconut shells to spell out "HELP ME" on the beach. With steep, craggy rock faces and thick forests, it's difficult to explore these islands, but with a guide you can reach the summit of the long flat rock-face of Monuriki on which Tom Hanks looked out in despair, seeing nothing but ocean (though in reality there are several islands visible from here, including Modriki within swimming range). The beaches on the eastern side of both islands are beautiful, with fine white sand backed by tall palm trees; day-trips here allow time for some fine snorkelling.

The Sacred Islands

Ten kilometres north of Tokoriki, the seven uninhabited **Sacred Islands** (or Mamanuca-i-Ra) rise out of the ocean in breathtaking splendour. Between May and September a handful of yachts are usually anchored in the protected bays here enjoying the solitude. Apart from the weekly visit by Captain Cook Cruises (see p.92) on its way up to the Yasawas, few other people venture this way, except the occasional TV crew – several series of *Survivor* have been filmed on the islands.

2

> ## THE LEGEND OF THE SACRED ISLANDS
>
> The **Sacred Islands** are owned by the people of Tavua. Their oral history, still recalled locally in dance, recounts the **legend** of the canoe *Rogovaka* arriving with Fiji's first inhabitants, led by Tui Na Revurevu. These new arrivals were said to have settled on the largest of these islands and called it Vanua Levu, translating to "big island" (not to be confused with its much larger namesake in northern Fiji). The legend goes on to tell of a second wave of immigrants who, finding Vanua Levu already settled, continued on to Vuda on Viti Levu (see p.66). A village thrived on Vanua Levu for a while, but as the island has no source of spring water, it was later abandoned. An archeological excavation revealed ancient **Lapita pottery**, which seems to back up the legend's authenticity. The people of Tavua hold the island sacred; to this day, it's expected that anyone setting foot on Vanua Levu should lay a traditional gift of *yaqona* roots in a small cave found behind the row of coconut palms on the eastern side of the sand spit.

The reef alongside the picturesque 200m-long sand spit on **Vanua Levu** has fantastic **snorkelling**, with extensive coral gardens, but the beach is difficult to land on. Neighbouring **Navadra** is more accessible, with a good swimming beach. The islands are important nesting grounds for migrating seabirds, particularly terns and noddies.

The Yasawa Islands

The volcanic hilly **YASAWA ISLANDS** attract a constant stream of visitors, drawn to their tranquil bays, stunning white sandy beaches and colourful snorkelling lagoons. Connected by a fast daily catamaran from Nadi, the islands are easy to visit and popular among **island-hopping backpackers** who are well catered for by twenty or so beach hostels between Kuata and Nacula islands: some have a party-style atmosphere and others a more traditional Fijian focus. A handful of more luxurious boutique resorts pull in married couples and families, while small ship cruises anchor overnight in the quieter parts of the islands visiting traditional villages, remote beaches and snorkelling reefs along the way.

The group of thirty islands has three distinct zones. The southern islands of **Kuata**, **Wayasewa and Waya** have jagged peaks etched with dramatic rock faces and fantastic walking tracks. These three islands are the closest to the mainland, only two hours by fast catamaran, and are by far the most interesting to visit, with villages tucked into deep bays, a stunning sand spit connecting the two Wayas and the region's best **scuba diving**. In the central zone is the largest island in the group, **Naviti**, with rolling grassy hills and a small cluster of islands off its southern end where **manta rays** congregate between late May and September. Fifteen minutes' sailing north of Naviti is the start of the expansive **northern Yasawas** with tranquil Blue Lagoon Bay being the Yasawas' most developed tourist region and home to a variety of beach accommodation.

ARRIVAL AND GETTING AROUND · THE YASAWA ISLANDS

Passenger ferry **catamarans** depart daily from Port Denarau in Nadi and from Lautoka to the majority of the Yasawa Islands. A few resorts offer direct transfers from Lautoka, which can be cheaper and quicker than the catamarans, though these smaller boats can feel unstable in choppy waters. The cheapest travel to the islands is aboard local fibreglass **fishing boats** which leave from Lautoka Jetty along Waterfront Rd, although these are much slower, less comfortable and not as safe or stable as the catamarans. Taking a multiday **cruise** can be the most convenient way to experience the Yasawas; both cruises listed below anchor at sublime snorkelling reefs and visit secluded beaches or traditional villages.

BY BOAT

YASAWA FLYER

Services and tickets The *Yasawa Flyer* catamaran, operated by Awesome Adventures (☎675 0499, ⓦ awesomefiji.com), departs from Port Denarau daily at 8.30am and returns at 5.45pm, stopping in both directions at all Yasawa resorts as far north as Nacula, as well as several islands in the Mamanucas. Tickets start

THE YASAWAS BACKPACKER TRAIL

Once the Yasawa people decided to open up their region to independent travellers in 1987, a few **backpacker resorts** sprang up on Tavewa, followed by similar developments on Waya and Wayasewa and Fiji's first community-owned resort at Wayalailai. In the early days, passage to the islands was by small fishing boat, usually with ageing engines and no life jackets. In 2001, the fast passenger ferry *Yasawa Flyer* was launched, changing travel to the region dramatically. Today, the bustling backpacker trail supports the livelihoods of many iTaukei families who also benefit from the health and social volunteer projects that have been established here (see p.38) – though the downside of the tourist influx is the degradation of local coral reefs and fishing lagoons.

ACCOMMODATION

More than half of the Yasawas' budget resorts are run by the islanders' themselves, either as individual businesses or community projects. Others have been bought by foreign investors and become "flashpackers", highly organized outfits that have lost much of their Fijian authenticity. Most travellers visit several resorts during their trip, often spending just 1 or 2 nights at each place – to really get to know the culture of the islands, try staying longer at one of the Fijian-owned places, where you may end up spear-fishing in a lagoon or visiting the family gardens to pull some cassava. Many resorts can be booked via the Awesome Adventures Combo Pass (see box, p.92), though it tends to be slightly cheaper to book the Fijian-owned properties direct, especially during the quieter summer months or if booking last-minute by phone.

COSTS AND ACTIVITIES

Compared to the mainland, **costs** on the islands are high. Most resorts charge F$120 for a dorm bed including three meals, while a 1.5-litre bottle of water or small bottle of beer costs around F$6. Wi-fi is only available at some resorts, and usually costs around F$5/hr. Some resorts also charge F$10 a day for snorkelling gear, so it's worth bringing your own. There are no shops to spend money in so your only other outlay will be on **activities**, such as kayak hire (generally F$20 per day), guided hikes to mountain lookouts (roughly F$40pp), and snorkelling trips to the outer lagoons and village (around F$50pp); in the northern islands, the must-do activity is a trip to swim in the limestone caves (F$50–90pp).

SERVICES, HYGIENE AND FOOD

Hygiene at the budget resorts has improved over the years, although you're still likely to run into the odd creepy-crawly, especially in the thatch bures. Humidity can also be a problem and bedding can feel damp at times. While sheets are always provided, not all places have towels so you should bring your own. **Drinking water** is mostly collected in rain-tanks and generally tastes OK: it's not UV-filtered, however, so it's a good idea to bring a supply of bottled water or, if you're staying for a long time, your own water filter jug. At the smaller resorts, shower water may not be hot, electricity limited to evenings only and **internet** access either not available or expensive, so you may want to pre-purchase your own SIM and data plan – Digicel and Vodafone both offer reasonable connectivity throughout the islands.

At backpacker resorts **meals** are included in the price and usually consist of breakfast, lunch, dinner and sometimes afternoon tea; the more basic resorts serve a simple buffet, often repeated daily, which can become mundane so it's worth bringing some snacks. Flashpacker resorts tend to charge extra for a compulsory meal plan (F$100–200 per person per day) that includes breakfast, lunch and dinner, and generally has a small choice of dishes on the menu. Drinks are always paid extra and added to your bill on check-out. Most special diets are catered for if pre-warned, but you should check beforehand and bring your own basic foodstuffs just in case.

from F$150 for a one-way trip to Kuata (2hr) up to F$180 all the way north to Nacula (4hr). All resorts meet their guests directly off the *Yasawa Flyer*; mostly these small fibre-glass boat transfers are free, but some charge F$10–20 for the service.

The Bula Pass You can buy single tickets between the islands on the *Flyer*, although if you're going to island-hop, the best option is to purchase the Bula Pass (F$420 for 5 days, F$530 for 7 days, F$650 for 10 days, F$710 for 12 days, or F$775 for 15 days), which allows unlimited trips on the *Flyer* until you return to Port Denarau.

Destinations from Port Denarau Yasawa Islands, Kuata to Nacula (daily; 2–5hr).

2

TAVEWA SEABUS

The chunky 46-seater *Tavewa Seabus* catamaran (T 666 2648, W seabusfiji.com) is not as comfortable as the *Yasawa Flyer* but just about stable enough when seas are rough. It departs daily at 8am from Lautoka Jetty off Waterfront Road and heads straight to Yaqeta in the northern Yasawas without stopping, then on to Tavewa where it arrives around 11.30am before heading back to Lautoka at 1pm. Tickets cost F$100 one way; transfers to/from Nadi hotels cost $7 one way.

Destinations from Lautoka Yasawa Islands, Yaqeta to Tavewa (daily; 3–3hr 30min).

BY PLANE

To Yasawa Island The only airstrip in the Yasawas is on the northernmost island, Yasawa Island, but the grass runway is used exclusively by the upmarket *Yasawa Island Resort*.

To Naviti and Nanuya Levu Turtle Airways (T 672 1888, W turtleairways.com) provides daily seaplane transfers (minimum 2 people) between Wailoaloa in Nadi direct to various Naviti resorts (25min; F$380 one way) and also to Nanuya Levu in the northern Yasawas (35min; F$380 one way): for the latter you must pre-arrange for your resort to pick you up by boat from the Turtle Island dock on Nanuya Levu.

ON A CRUISE TRIP

Blue Lagoon Cruises T 675 0500, W bluelagoon cruises.com. Offers two trips to the Yasawas, which leave Port Denarau every Mon & Fri at 3pm on board the *Fiji Princess*: the three-night "Explorer Cruise" (from F$2995 per person) and four-night "Wanderer Cruise" (from F$3995 per person) can be combined into a seven-night cruise.

★ **Captain Cook Cruises** T 670 1823, W captaincook cruisesfiji.com. Spanning four levels and with a maximum of 90 guests, this cruise ship is surprisingly spacious on board. The ship has a swimming pool, sauna and sundeck, plus lively entertainment. The three-night

RESORT ROUND-UP

When island-hopping, many backpackers want to experience a few different types of resort. Here is an at-a-glance round-up of the Yasawas resorts reviewed in this guide, arranged geographically from south to north, so that you can choose in advance whether you want to be at party central, chill-out on a beach or gain an insight into some authentic Yasawa culture. Many of the resorts can be booked on the *Yasawa Flyer* as you travel to the islands using the Awesome Adventures Combo Pass (T 675 0499, W awesomefiji.com), which includes unlimited boat travel (see p.91) and is valid at a variety of backpacker resorts. The pass can be pre-purchased in two versions: the one-coconut version is valid for simple cheaper accommodation, while the two-coconut version costs more and allows you to stay at the smarter, more expensive resorts.

Name	Island Group	Combo Pass	Ownership	Accom Style	Ambience
Barefoot Kuata (p.95)	Kuata	2-Coconut	Foreign	Flashpacker	Mixed
Naqalia Lodge (p.95)	Wayasewa	1-Coconut	Fijian Community	Backpacker	Quiet
Wayalailai Resort (p.95)	Wayasewa	1-Coconut	Fijian Community	Backpacker	Mixed
Yalobi Village Stay (p.95)	Waya	N/A	Fijian Individual	Village	Quiet
Octopus Resort (p.95)	Waya	2-Coconut	Foreign	Holiday Resort	Quiet
Paradise Cove (p.97)	Naviti cluster	N/A	Foreign	Holiday Resort	Quiet
Mantaray Island (p.96)	Naviti cluster	2-Coconut	Foreign	Flashpacker	Party
Barefoot Manta (p.96)	Naviti cluster	2-Coconut	Foreign	Backpacker	Quiet
Botaira Beach (p.96)	Naviti	N/A	Fijian Individual	Holiday Resort	Quiet
White Sandy Beach (p.97)	Naviti	1-Coconut	Fijian Individual	Backpacker	Quiet
Navutu Stars (p.100)	Yaqeta	N/A	Foreign	Holiday Resort	Quiet
Long Beach Resort (p.100)	Matacawalevu	1-Coconut	Fijian Individual	Backpacker	Quiet
Nanuya Island (p.100)	Nanuya Lailai	N/A	Foreign	Holiday Resort	Quiet
Gold Coast Inn (p.100)	Nanuya Lailai	1-Coconut	Fijian Individual	Backpacker	Quiet
Coconut Beach (p.100)	Tavewa	N/A	Foreign	Holiday Resort	Quiet
Nabua Lodge (p.100)	Nacula	1-Coconut	Fijian Individual	Backpacker	Party
Oarsmans Bay (p.100)	Nacula	2-Coconut	Fijian Individual	Backpacker	Quiet
Nacula Village Stay (p.100)	Nacula	N/A	Fijian Community	Village	Quiet
Yasawa Island (p.101)	Yasawa Island	N/A	Foreign	Holiday Resort	Quiet

"Southern Yasawa Cruise" visits the Sacred Islands and Waya (from F$2295 per person), while the four-night "Northern Yasawa Cruise" goes up to the Sawa-i-Lau Caves and stunning beaches of Yasawa Island (F$3,100 per person). Cruises leave Port Denarau every Tues & Sat at noon. 🛜

Kuata, Wayasewa and Waya

The three volcanic islands of **Kuata**, **Wayasewa** and **Waya** are the most striking of the Yasawa Islands and on a clear day can be seen from Nadi jutting out on the distant horizon. The 50km journey by boat from Port Denarau takes just under two hours.

2

Kuata

Kuata, the most southerly island of the Yasawas, has been designated a **nature sanctuary** by its owners on adjacent Wayasewa. Pleasant **walking trails** meander around the oddly shaped hills and rocky outcrops, and you might come across the elusive boa constrictor here. A deep ocean wall immediately off the island's west coast has fantastic **scuba diving** including a shark dive site where you may encounter bulls and tigers. There's an unusual figure-of-eight swim through pinnacles and caves off the east coast. Dive operators are based at both *Barefoot Kuata* (the only operator doing the shark dive) and neighbouring *Wayalailai Resort* on Wayasewa (see p.95), or you can dive with Captain Cook Cruises (see above). Snorkelling is also very good here, while **Mouya Reef**, some fifteen minutes by boat from either Kuata or Wayasewa, is a magnet for small reef sharks.

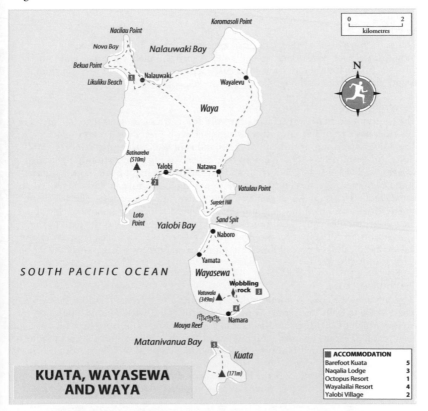

■ ACCOMMODATION	
Barefoot Kuata	5
Naqalia Lodge	3
Octopus Resort	1
Wayalailai Resort	4
Yalobi Village	2

Wayasewa

Across the passage from Kuata, **Wayasewa** is dominated by the towering 350m-high twin peaks of Vatuvula and Vatusawalo, with the old village of **Namara** sitting directly beneath their sheer rock faces. In 1985, after heavy rain, a landslide brought several huge boulders tumbling down the hillside to within inches of people's homes. The village was declared unsafe and relocated to the north side of the island at **Naboro**. It didn't take long, though, for some families to return home and when the adjacent community-owned backpacker resort opened in the 1990s, more villagers moved back to Namara. Today, the majority of Namara's houses are again occupied, although most families with young children prefer living close to the new primary school at Naboro.

Inland Wayasewa

The forty-minute **hike** from the back of *Wayalailai Resort* to the summit of **Vatuvula** is a must, especially at sunset. The well-trodden track ascends steeply through forest and up a narrow crag before opening out onto a rocky escarpment that leads to the summit. It's hard going after rain and crossing the 10m-long boulder to reach the sheer-cliff summit is a little nervy, but for conquerors there are fabulous views looking directly down on the resort and over the bay to Kuata and the Mamanucas. The return leg passes another island icon, the **wobbling rock**, balancing precariously on a much larger boulder. Alternatively, you can hike across the middle of the island and down to Naboro with its delightful 200m-long **sand bridge** exposed at low tide connecting it to Waya Island.

Waya

Dramatic **Waya** has a strange, contorted appearance, with knife-edge ridges, monumental rock protrusions, several unbelievably photogenic **beaches** and some fantastic **hiking trails**. From its western coast, a giant's face seems to peer out from the island, slanting back as though floating in the sea.

The south side of the island

The southern point of Waya, facing the sand bridge that connects it to Wayasewa at low tide, has a beautiful inwardly curved beach with pretty **coral reefs** to both sides. The only place to stay at this end of the island is in **YALOBI**, twenty minutes' walk along the western coast. Set in a deep bay, it's one of Fiji's most stunningly located villages, with a sandy beach in front and backed by a massive buckled cliff almost 500m high, with green veins of rainforest growing in the fissures and valleys. Yalobi is the chiefly village of Waya, home to around five hundred people, a health centre and a primary school. You can climb the pointed Mount Batinareba towering above the village, though you'll need to hire a local **guide** (F$60/3hr) as the path to the summit can be difficult to follow. Also with a guide, you can walk the pretty inland tracks that meander between the island's four coastal fishing villages; make sure you carry plenty of water.

The northwest coast

Waya's northwest coast is home to the *Octopus Resort* in pretty Likuliku Bay, from where **walking trails** head into the undulating hills and, with a guide, you can explore much of the interior. There's also a great coastal walk from here that you can do unguided. From the north end of **Likuliku Beach**, walk around the rocky ledge of Bekua Point to secluded Nova Beach. At low tide, you can rock-hop around Nacilau Point for a sweeping view of the north coast of Waya Island. Just before you reach Nalauwaki village, climb over the hills and back down to *Octopus Resort* – the complete circuit takes two to three hours.

ACCOMMODATION   KUATA, WAYASEWA AND WAYA

KUATA

Barefoot Kuata ☎ 776 2092, ⓦ thebarefootcollection
.com/kauta-island. This budget resort has pretty dorm
rooms right on the beachfront, plus four elegant safari
tents sleeping two people with stylish outdoor
bathrooms. There are three tiny swimming pools
beside the restaurant in case you tire of the excellent
snorkelling in the lagoon. A marine biologist runs the
dive operation here. Rates include meals. ☞ Dorms
F$159, safari tents F$554

WAYASEWA

Naqalia Lodge ☎ 746 7888, ⓦ naqalialodge-fijiresort
.com. Run by local villagers, with traditional-style bures
and a twelve-bed dorm. Great swimming above the coral,
and a pleasant relaxed atmosphere. Limited cold water and
electricity, and the evenings are tranquil: it's not one for the
party crowd. Rates include meals. Camping (with own tent)
F$90, dorms F$130, bures F$325
★**Wayalailai Resort** Namara ☎ 603 0215 or ☎ 932
3446, ⓦ wayalailairesort.com. Community-owned with
a lively atmosphere, this place is set over three terraced
levels with lawns and provides lots of activities, yet retains
a charming laidback Fijian ambience. The 24-bed dorm

lodge overlooks ten small en-suite bures which gaze down
onto the beach. There's a large deck restaurant abutting
the hill, with stunning views over to Kuata and unobscured
stargazing. Rates include meals. ☞ ($) Camping (with
own tent) F$90, dorms F$130, rooms F$295, bures F$340

WAYA

★**Octopus Resort** Likuliku Bay ☎ 666 6337,
ⓦ octopusresort.com. Appealing to families, couples and
the more refined backpacker, this efficient resort sits
alongside one of the most stunning beaches in Fiji with
snorkelling reefs right off the shore. Good food, a
swimming pool and guided hikes add to its appeal. Rates
include meals. ☞ ($) Dorms F$154, bungalows F$467,
bures F$617
Yalobi Village Stay Yalobi ☎ 834 2601. Simeli Bale's
family have two basic guest bures at the western end of the
village with a shared outdoor bathroom. With access to a
kitchen, but no fridge, you can bring along supplies to cook
yourself; otherwise, the family will prepare meals:
breakfast (F$5), lunch (F$10), dinner (F$10). Guides
available for hiking. A *sevusevu* should be presented to the
chief or headman on arrival and village protocol observed
(see box, p.40). Cash only. Bures F$120

Naviti and the southern cluster

Less intriguing than Waya but blessed with almost a hundred delightful white-sand
beaches, most backed by dense vegetation and steep hills, **Naviti** is the largest of the
Yasawa Islands, home to nine villages and the region's only boarding school. The
island is shaped somewhat like a lobster with two elongated arms reaching out to
the north and a cluster of small islets forming a tail to the south, known as the
southern cluster.

Naviti

A little over halfway along Naviti's west coast is **Natuvalu Bay**, a beautiful long
stretch of sandy beach peppered with tall coconut trees and a couple of resorts.
The bay is tidal and almost empties of water at low tide, but if you walk ten minutes
over the northern point you'll find **Honeymoon Beach**, a great swimming and
snorkelling spot (a F$2 fee is payable here). For even more seclusion, continue
walking north around the rocky bluff to find a series of charming, sandy cove
beaches. On your way back, just past the summit of the small hill leading down to
the resorts, look out for a track on the right: it follows a wooded ridge and after ten
minutes opens out to a lookout with fabulous **views** of both Natuvalu Bay and
Honeymoon Beach.

The southern cluster

The best of Naviti's resort beaches is alongside *Botaira Beach Resort* on the island's
southwest side: from here, a gradual climb into the hills and along a grassy ridge to
the southern point of the island presents an inspiring view looking down on the
lagoon encircling **the southern cluster** with its translucent hues of blue. The coral
reefs here offer excellent **snorkelling**, and between May and October it's possible to
swim with **manta rays**, which feed around the rich current-fed passages, particularly

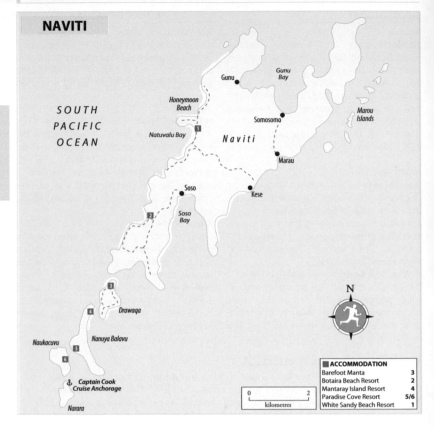

off Drawaqa Island. All the Naviti resorts offer boat trips to swim among the manta rays on the incoming tide, though you can find up to sixty people, plus boats, in the water at the same time. The *Barefoot Manta* resort (see below) has its north beach facing the **Drawaqa Passage** and its onsite marine biologist tries to pick a time to visit when no one else is around.

ACCOMMODATION — NAVITI AND THE SOUTHERN CLUSTER

★**Barefoot Manta** Drawaqa, southern cluster ☎670 3040, ⓦthebarefootcollection.com/manta-island. Set on a stunning point with beaches on two sides lined with thatch bures. As well as the usual Fijian activities – lovo dinners and night fishing – you can also assist in the village for a day; longer volunteer projects are also possible, such as working in local schools or environmental projects around the island. An open-water dive course costs F$780. Rates include meals. ⓦ Dorms F$159, rooms F$378, safari tents F$554

Botaira Beach Resort Soso, Naviti ☎603 0200, ⓦbotaira.com. Welcoming *Botaira* couldn't have a nicer beach, with hammocks strung between palm trees, deep white sand and good snorkelling. The eleven bures have thatched roofs and varnished timber floors. Rates include meals. Dorms F$180, bures F$629

Mantaray Island Resort Nanuya Balavu, southern cluster ☎664 0520, ⓦmantarayisland.com. This long-established backpacking favourite has lots of activities including scuba diving and waterskiing and is consistently the Yasawas' liveliest nightspot. The restaurant and bar are perched on a hill overlooking the lagoon with satellite TV and themed party nights. Bures have beautiful en-suite bathrooms, while quaint treehouses are tucked among light scrub and share bathrooms with a 32-bed dorm, which is subdivided into boxed cubicles, each with two bunk beds. Rates include meals ⓦ($) Dorms F$155, treehouse F$405, bures F$719

Paradise Cove Resort Naukacuvu, southern cluster ☎708 8414, ⌨paradisecoveresort.com.fj. The Yasawa Islands' largest resort fronts a pretty beach with an excellent snorkelling lagoon. The bures are beautifully decorated, most with open-air bathrooms and the suites have private plunge pools overlooking the beach. The 2-bedroom villas are popular with families, but there's also a large adults-only section of the resort with its own swimming pool. For complete isolation, take one of the four beach houses across the lagoon where you can feel like a marooned observer looking back to the resort at night. Rates include meals

📶($) Bures F$896, 2-bed villas F$1547, suites F$1797, beach house F$2179

White Sandy Beach Resort Natuvalu Bay, Naviti ☎666 4066, ⌨whitesandybeach_diveresort@yahoo.com. Just three simple cottages – one sleeping up to five people – and a basic thatch dorm lodge sleeping twelve. Meals are well presented and served on a wooden veranda overlooking the beach at sunset. Scuba diving is the speciality here with the owner's son operating the PADI dive shop. Rates include meals. Camping (with own tent) F$70, dorms F$110, bures F$260

The northern Yasawas

The 5km choppy Naivalavala Passage separates Naviti from Yaqeta, the most southerly of a cluster of a dozen islands that make up the **NORTHERN YASAWAS**. The islands' remote position gives them an exotic aura but, in fact, it's the most tourist-orientated region of the Yasawas, particularly around **Blue Lagoon Bay** between Matacawalevu and Nacula islands: here, there are ten small resorts, with **yachts** congregating around the sheltered bay between May and October. Typically low-lying in nature – the highest point is just under 300m – the main attractions are the beaches, with snorkelling or scuba diving along an intricate network of coral reefs never far away. Intriguing limestone caves shelter the largest island of the group, the long thin **Yasawa Island**, with undulating hills, sea-cliffs and sweeping, fine, white sandy beaches used as picnic stopovers by luxury overnight cruises.

Yaqeta

Shaped like a hammerhead shark, the island of **Yaqeta** is surrounded by a string of uninhabited white sandy beaches. The island's solitary village, also called Yaqeta, is surrounded by one of the Yasawas' few areas of fertile flat land. The **north side** of the island boasts a beautiful turquoise lagoon, overlooked by the elegant *Navutu Stars Resort* (see p.100).

Matacawalevu

In a shallow turquoise passage between Yaqeta and the hilly island of **Matacawalevu** lies the region's most beautiful lagoon. Popular with locals for net fishing, the lagoon is fronted by a long curved sandy beach, home to the Fijian-owned *Long Beach Resort* (see p.100). Just offshore from the resort sits the triangular rocky island of **Deviulau**, which can be climbed for fantastic views of the beach and bay; it also offers good snorkelling along its southern point. You can walk to the island at low tide, though look out for stingrays lurking in the water.

A twenty-minute track from the resort leads across to the east coast village of **Vuake**. The village's picturesque **Catholic church**, perched on a hill overlooking the shallow tidal waters of Nasomo Bay, is a wonderful place to experience the full volume of a Fijian Sunday church service. From Vuake, walking tracks lead up into the hills, where village gardens are planted with *dalo* and *yaqona*, or you can walk north along the coast to the island's second village, the Methodist enclave of **Matacawalevu**, also on the east coast.

Blue Lagoon Bay

Flanking the north and east coast of Matacawalevu are the small islands of Nanuya and Tavewa, with the larger island of Nacula forming the northern enclosure of **Blue Lagoon Bay**. The bay is named partly for its dream-like turquoise waters but also to capitalize on the semi-erotic 1980 film *The Blue Lagoon*, starring Brooke Shields, filmed

2

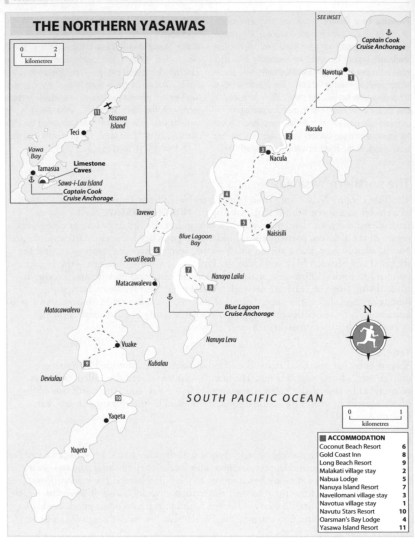

partly on Nanuya Levu. Around this sheltered bay is the highest concentration of **backpacker resorts** in the Yasawas, making it a handy place for island hopping and exploring by kayak.

Nanuya Levu and Nanuya Lailai

The twin Nanuya islands are separated by the long, deep Blue Lagoon Bay. The privately owned **Nanuya Levu** (big Nanuya) is off-limits unless you're staying at the ultra-exclusive *Turtle Island Resort*, though there's more down-to-earth accommodation on **Nanuya Lailai** (Little Nanuya), the northern of the two islands. The **best beach** on Nanuya Lailai is the Blue Lagoon Beach on the sheltered west coast, with excellent **snorkelling** just off the beach along a 30m coral wall drop-off.

Tavewa

The island of **Tavewa** was originally owned by the people of neighbouring Nacula, but was given as a dowry to William Dougherty, a Scottish copra planter who married a local girl of status from the village. Today the island has been subdivided into many small parcels of land distributed among Dougherty's descendants.

There's no village on Tavewa, but a couple of resorts and a handful of resident shacks line the eastern beachfront. The west coast, as with Matacawalevu, is rugged and inaccessible. There's a fantastic **coral wall** fringing Tavewa's northeastern side, and there's a good chance you'll see reef sharks and sometimes tonnes of harmless jellyfish. The nicest **swimming lagoon** is around the sheltered **Savuti Beach** at the southern tip of the island, just beyond *Coconut Beach Resort* (see p.100) – it was recently declared a protected marine area and the sea life has blossomed since: look out for baby black-tip reef sharks scouring the shallow waters beside the beach.

Nacula

Covered mostly by wild grasses, hilly **Nacula** is the third largest of the Yasawa Islands. Its chiefly village, also named Nacula, is on the west coast where the white sand is brilliantly fine. Some 2km north of Nacula village, is Malakati village, where you can stay overnight in one of the island's three **village stays** (see p.100), all of which are connected by walking trails. Nacula's southern side also has lovely beaches, including the kilometre-long crescent sands alongside *Oarsman's Bay Lodge* (see p.100), where good snorkelling reefs start within twenty metres from the shore. At low tide you can walk south around **Sandy Point** to an even longer stretch of beach, home to *Nabua Lodge* (see p.100). Between the two, a walking track leads up to the 238m-high summit of **Naisau** from where, on a clear day, you can see the entire Yasawa chain.

Sawa-i-Lau

Off the north coast of Nacula, the island of **Sawa-i-Lau** sits in a pretty bay hugging the southern point of Yasawa Island and is home to some partially flooded **limestone caves**. Locals believe the ten-headed **snake god**, Uluitini, resides deep inside the caves and folklore warns that any pregnant woman, however slight, will be unable to fit through the entrance. The main chamber is 15m high, with limestone pillars and natural sunlight streaming in from above. Boys from nearby Nabukeru village usually climb to the top and jump into the crystal-clear **pool** here; the other challenge is to swim underwater for ten seconds to a series of smaller darker chambers where **petroglyphs** can be seen incised on the walls.

The best way to visit the caves is with local boatman Joe (Mon–Sat; ☎839 4841; F$90 for a 1hr trip), who picks up from the resorts around Blue Lagoon Bay; he also offers transfers between resorts in the region and private tours to Yasawa Island (see below).

Yasawa Island

The long, thin **Yasawa Island** has impressive **cliffs** and pristine, powdery white-sand beaches along the west coast, one of which can be visited on the Captain Cook Cruise (see

---

KAYAKING IN THE NORTHERN YASAWAS

A fantastic way of seeing the remote side of the northern Yasawas is to join one of the **kayaking trips** run by South Sea Ventures (☎02 8901 3287 in Australia, ⦿southernseaventures.com; 7 nights for A$2370). Group trips run May to October, and involve three to four hours of paddling a day in single or twin sea-kayaks. The kayak tours paddle between Matacawalevu and Sawa-i-Lau, camping in two-man tents alongside beaches, on an uninhabited island and at Navotua village (see p.100). Trips are suitable for novice or experienced kayakers, although a reasonable level of fitness is needed.

p.92). The island is synonymous with the luxurious *Yasawa Island Resort* (see opposite), beautifully positioned on a long secluded stretch of beach on the northwest coast.

Six traditional villages are found on the east coast. The fishing village of **Teci** is one of the most authentic in Fiji, with over half its homes being traditional thatch-roof bures. At the northern tip of the island is the chiefly village of **Yasawa-i-Rara**, close to stunning Vulawalu Beach: the journey here from Blue Lagoon Bay takes over an hour by boat.

2

ACCOMMODATION   THE NORTHERN YASAWAS

YAQETA

Navutu Stars Resort ☎ 664 0553, ⓦ navutustarsfiji .com. Run by a young Italian couple, this resort serves up superb meals, using herbs and fruits grown in the organic gardens. There are little corners of solitude everywhere, including a treehouse-style yoga platform and a simple spa hut. The contemporary whitewashed villas have a Balinese feel and the grand bures on the hill have beautiful sunken spa baths and wonderful views of the bay. Closed Feb. ⓦ($) **F$810**

MATACAWALEVU

★**Long Beach Resort** ☎ 603 1020, ⓦ longbeachfiji .com. One of the most authentic laidback resorts in the Yasawas, *Long Beach* fronts a beautiful 1km stretch of powdery white sand and is run by welcoming hosts from the local village. You can get a traditional Fijian massage here or visit nearby Vuake village for the day. Two en-suite bures with ceiling fans and tiled floors overlook the beach with another three set back in the gardens: one houses an eight-bed dorm. Cash only. Rates include meals. Dorms **F$120**, bures **F$280**

NANUYA LAILAI

Gold Coast Inn ☎ 776 0212, ⓦ goldcoastfiji.com. This small beachside retreat has just four bures with beautifully thatched roofs, plus a wooden dorm cottage sleeping five people. The warm-hearted Fijian family cook three organic meals a day, usually including fish caught from the lagoon and supplemented with fruit and vegetables from their gardens; solar lamps are provided at night. Rates include meals. Dorms **F$120**, bures **F$280**

Nanuya Island Resort ☎ 666 7633, ⓦ nanuyafiji.com. Tucked behind a seawall after losing its beach to erosion, this resort has an airy restaurant serving organic food and a stunning hilltop bar with panoramic views of the bay. The somewhat pricey accommodation is in wooden bures perched among trees on a hillside and accessible via steep steps, or in one of the more spacious villas sleeping up to four people squeezed along the foreshore. ⓦ($) Bures **F$522**, villas **F$854**

TAVEWA

★**Coconut Beach Resort** ☎ 945 7505, ⓦ coconut beachfiji.com. Having taken over the long-standing *Otto &* *Fanny's* next door, this small boutique resort retains all the grace of its former coconut plantation. The palm-fringed Savuti Beach, fronting the resort, is delightful and few places in the Yasawas have such an open and breezy feel about them. The four spruced-up cottages, each split into two rooms and with delightful open-air en-suite bathrooms, are great value. Rates include meals. ⓦ($) Bures **F$570**

NACULA

Nabua Lodge ☎ 666 9173 or ☎ 990 7294, ⓦ nabualodge-yasawa.com. A lively budget retreat where Fijian hospitality gels well with the more rowdy backpacker crowd. Of the nine bures, three have en-suite bathrooms and sleep up to four people; two are dorms sleeping 22 people in single beds. Rates include meals. Dorms **F$120**, bures **F$280**

★**Nacula Village Stay** Malakati ☎ 906 0241, Naveilomani ☎ 945 9109, Navotua ☎ 946 7325, ⓦ yasawahomestays.com. Connected by paths, Nacula Island's three village stays offer a unique way to experience Fijian life. The tiny community-run *Malakati* has the prettiest beach and snorkelling reef: its accommodation is in two private bures sharing an outdoor bathroom, and guests are invited to eat their meals in one of the village homes. Ten minutes' walk along the coast, *Naveilomani* is in Nacula's large chiefly village, making it a good spot to interact with village life – visitors stay with a host family in a cement cottage with two en-suite guest rooms, and meals are served by the host family. Along the more remote north coast, *Navotua* has three private bures sharing an outdoor bathroom, with meals served on the veranda. All three village stays accept cash only, have limited electricity and require a *sevusevu* and village protocol (see box, p.40). Rates include meals. *Malakati* **F$150**, *Naveilomani* **F$170**, *Navotua* **F$150**

Oarsman's Bay Lodge ☎ 628 0485, ⓦ oarsmanbayfiji .com. This picturesque resort with accessible snorkelling is popular with the more discerning backpacker as well as couples and families. The eight simple wooden cottages with outdoor showers are excellent value, and the wooden-decked restaurant serves decent food. There's also an eight-bed a/c dorm above the restaurant. Rates include meals. Camping (with own tent) **F$139**, camping (with hired tent) **F$166**, dorms **F$154**, bures **F$451**

YASAWA ISLAND

★**Yasawa Island Resort** ☎672 2266, ⓦyasawa .com. Superb high-end resort on a gorgeous beach with a deep lagoon for swimming. The eighteen a/c bures have elegant minimal interiors and wooden decks with day-beds, and the beachfront spa offers treatments and facials. Tailor-made private excursions are its forte from an uninhabited island picnic to a visit to the local school. Air transfers extra. Rates include meals. 🛜 Bures F$2162

Rural Viti Levu

HUTS, NAVALA VILLAGE

Rural Viti Levu

Given that Fiji is renowned for its tiny coral islets, many visitors are struck by the sheer size of Viti Levu, the country's main island. Covering just over ten thousand square kilometres, and roughly half the size of Wales, "Big Fiji" offers a wide range of scenery, from sunburnt yellow sugarcane fields along the dry north coast to the verdant blanket of rainforest spread over the eastern half of the island. With the exception of the Nadi-to-Lautoka corridor and the urban sprawl between Suva and Nausori, Viti Levu is distinctly rural in character, with only a handful of small market towns along the coastal road circling the island. Most such towns are found at the mouths of rivers, which in turn connect the isolated – and seldom visited – mountainous interior.

3

Viti Levu can be hastily explored in two days, either by public bus or rental car, but a week is recommended to have a chance to meet some of the exceedingly hospitable characters who will welcome you along the way. More time will allow you to branch off the main roads to explore and **hike** among some of the most beautiful countryside in the South Pacific.

The Queens Road, the main artery connecting Nadi and Suva, travels along **South Viti Levu**, a relatively well developed tourist region. The first stop is the small town of Sigatoka, close to the absorbing Sigatoka Sand Dunes National Park. Further east are the beach resorts of the Coral Coast and the adventure sports capital of Pacific Harbour. Beyond Suva (see Chapter 4; p.134), **East Viti Levu** is the least developed area on the mainland, and still mostly covered by rainforest; its main attraction is the picturesque Tailevu Coast, accessed on a remote dirt road. In stark contrast to the southern coast, **North Viti Levu** appears rather barren, its often-spectacular scenery dominated by sugarcane farmland, interspersed with the market towns of Rakiraki, Tavua and Ba. Inland, however, is Fiji's most attractive village, Navala, as well as the country's highest point, Mount Tomanivi; offshore are the budget resorts of Nananu-i-Ra island.

Climate

Viti Levu's **climate** splits into two zones. The area around Suva catches the brunt of the southeasterly trade winds, which roll in off the ocean and cause cloud build-up over the mountains. Consequently, everything east of a fairly distinct line extending from Rakiraki to Sigatoka lies in the **wet zone**, with high rainfall, dense forests and often-unbearable humidity. Once the clouds have blown over the mountain range – the highest point of which reaches 1323m at Mount Tomanivi – they fall, cool and dissipate, leaving the other half of the island with almost perpetual sunshine. This is the **dry zone** – or the "Burning West", as it is ridiculed by umbrella-clad Suva-ites.

REEF SHARK, OFF PACIFIC HARBOUR

Highlights

❶ Sigatoka Sand Dunes National Park
Explore the wild beachfront where ancient
Fijians once lived; shards of bone and
ancient pottery are regularly revealed by
the wind. **See p.110**

❷ Shark diving Extreme-adventure fans can
come face to face with tiger and bull sharks on
these world-famous dives, best accessed from
Pacific Harbour. **See p.118**

❸ River rafting Journey along the lush
waterfall-lined rapids of the Navua River either
by kayak, longboat or river raft. **See p.120**

❹ Tailevu Coast Travel along the remote and
seldom-visited east coast with winding bays and
delightful, friendly Fijian villages. **See p.121**

❺ Tavua and Ba Charming Indo-Fijian market
towns, both well off the tourist trail. **See p.126
and p.128**

❻ Mount Tomanivi Climb Fiji's highest peak for
a spectacular view of the surrounding forests.
See p.127

❼ Navala village Fiji's sole surviving traditional
thatch village on the Ba River is truly
breathtaking and on a grand scale. **See p.130**

HIGHLIGHTS ARE MARKED ON THE MAP ON PP.106–107

SEE "TAVUA" MAP FOR DETAILS

SEE "BA" MAP FOR DETAILS

SEE "SIGATOKA & AROUND" MAP FOR DETAILS

HIGHLIGHTS

1 Sigatoka Sand Dunes National Park
2 Shark diving, Pacific Harbour
3 River rafting
4 Tailevu Coast
5 Tavua and Ba
6 Mount Tomanivi
7 Navala village

Bligh Water

Vatia Peninsula

Tavaua E

Tavua

YAQA

Vatukoula

Vomo

Mamanuca Group

Mana

Treasure Island

Tivua Island

Lautoka

KINGS ROAD

KOROYANITU NATIONAL HERITAGE PARK

Mount Koronayitu (1192m)

BA

Ba River

Navala

Nagatagata

Na

Bounty Island

Saweni Beach

Vuda Point

Vuda River

Mount Batilamu

Sabeto River

Nadele

Vaturu Dam

Bukuya

Nanoko

Nubutautau

Nadi Bay

Nasoso

Nadi International Airport

Nadi River

Nausori

Draiba

Korolevu

Denarau Island

Nadi

NAUSORI HIGHLANDS

Naisali

QUEENS ROAD

Yavuna

Uciwai Hills

Momi Bay

Mount Koroba (1076m)

Sigatoka River

Vunamoli

Tonga

Bourewa Beach

Mavua

Mount Tuvutau (933m)

Navua River

Robinson Crusoe Island

Likuri Lagoon

NADROGA

Nabukelevu

Natadola

Cuvu

Sigatoka

Korotogo

Vatukarasa

Biausevu

SERUA

Korotogo Beach

Korolevu

Namatakula

Namagumagua

Coral Coast

N

SOUTH PACIFIC OCEAN

Vatulele

0   10
kilometres

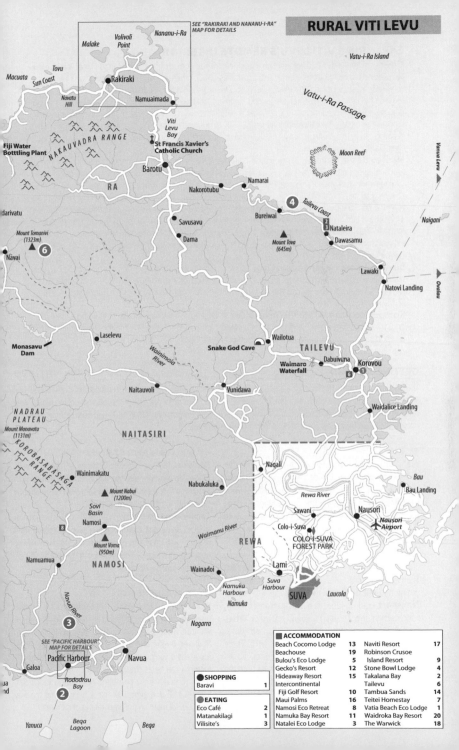

Malake
Volivoli
Point
Nananu-i-Ra
Vatu-i-Ra Island

Macuata
Tovu
Sun Coast

Rakiraki
Navatu
Hill
Namuaimada

Vatu-i-Ra Passage

Moon Reef

Vanua Levu

Fiji Water
Botttling Plant

NAKAUVADRA RANGE

Viti
Levu
Bay
St Francis Xavier's
Catholic Church

Barotu

RA

Namarai

Nakorotubu

Bureiwai

4

Tailevu Coast

Nataleira

Dawasamu

Naigani

darivatu

Mount Tomanivi
(1323m)

6

Savusavu

Dama

Mount Tova
(645m)

Navai

Lawaki

Natovi Landing

Ovalau

Monasavu
Dam

Laselevu

Wailotua

Snake God Cave

Wainimaia
River

TAILEVU

Dabuivuna

Korovou

Waimaro
Waterfall

6

1

Naitauvoli

Vunidawa

Waidalice Landing

NADRAU
PLATEAU

Mount Monavatu
(1131m)

NAITASIRI

KOROBASABASAGA
RANGE

Wainimakatu

Naqali

Bau

Nabukaluka

Bau Landing

Rewa River

Sawani

Nausori

Mount Nabui
(1200m)

Sovi
Basin

Namosi

8

Colo-i-Suva
Fiji Golf Resort

Nausori
Airport

Mount Voma
(950m)

NAMOSI

Waimanu River

REWA

COLO-I-SUVA
FOREST PARK

Namuamua

Wainadoi

Lami

Navua River

Suva
Harbour

SUVA

Laucala

3

Namuka
Harbour

Namuka

Nagarra

Pacific Harbour

Navua

Galoa

2

Rododrau
Bay

Yanuca

Beqa
Lagoon

Beqa

■ **ACCOMMODATION**

Beach Cocomo Lodge	13	Naviti Resort	17
Beachouse	19	Robinson Crusoe	
Bulou's Eco Lodge	5	Island Resort	9
Gecko's Resort	12	Stone Bowl Lodge	4
Hideaway Resort	15	Takalana Bay	
Intercontinental		Tailevu	6
Fiji Golf Resort	10	Tambua Sands	14
Maui Palms	16	Teitei Homestay	7
Namosi Eco Retreat	8	Vatia Beach Eco Lodge	1
Namuka Bay Resort	11	Waidroka Bay Resort	20
Natalei Eco Lodge	3	The Warwick	18

● **SHOPPING**
Baravi   1

● **EATING**
Eco Café   2
Matanakilagi   1
Vilisite's   3

EXPLORING VITI LEVU'S REMOTE INTERIOR

The less-travelled dirt roads of the interior provide a genuine insight into **rural Viti Levu**. None of the routes below is served by buses, and although all can be navigated by a regular car with good suspension in good weather, 4WD is recommended. Before you leave, check your tyres (including your spare) and take plenty of drinking water; *yaqona* roots are also good to carry as a village *sevusevu* (see box, p.40). If you don't want to drive yourself, Talanoa Treks (**☎**947 2732, **Ⓦ**talanoa-treks-fiji.com) run regular hiking trips around the interior, from day-trips to a four-night "Full Monty" trek across the island.

Nadi to Ba via Navala Start from the Nadi Back Road, climbing into the grassy hills of the Nausori Highlands. The scenery is barren and very remote, with panoramic views along most of the road until you hit Navala, home to over a hundred traditional thatch bures (see p.130). Overnight stopover: *Bulou's Lodge* (see p.131).

Navua to Suva via Namosi Highlands Start from Namosi Rd along the Queens Rd, 11km east of Navua town. The road meanders through dense tropical forest into the Namosi Highlands (see p.120), past traditional villages with stunning mountain views along the way. Overnight stopovers: *Namosi Eco Retreat* (see p.120) or *Colo-i-Suva Lodge* (see p.148).

Suva to Tavua via Monasavu Dam This route journeys through the heart of Viti Levu, past the lush Sovi Basin and Monasavu Dam towards Mount Tomanivi, Fiji's highest mountain, before heading downhill into the farming valleys surrounding Tavua. Overnight stopover: *Stone Bowl Lodge* (see p.128).

Korovou to Rakiraki via the Tailevu Coast Travel along the secluded, winding Tailevu coastline, passing rivers, seldom-visited villages and scenic bays. Overnight stopovers: *Natalei Eco Lodge* (see p.122) or *Takalana Bay* (see p.122).

GETTING AROUND   RURAL VITI LEVU

The Queens Rd connects Nadi and Suva along the south coast (4hr), while the less-travelled Kings Rd connects Nadi and Suva via Lautoka along the north coast (6hr); between them the roads cover the 460km circumference of the island. Stray cattle (especially at night), kids playing on the roadside, speeding minivans, over-laden trucks and deep potholes make the roads occasionally hazardous, though things are certainly improving.

BY BUS

Public **buses** are the safest way to travel, and offer lovely views of the countryside from the high windows. Most buses originate from either Lautoka or Suva, travelling between the two cities on the Kings Rd along the north coast, or on the Queens Rd along the south coast, stopping at towns and most large hotels along the way. Services are cheap (around F$19 from Lautoka to Suva), and buses stop frequently en route. The larger, more comfortable services include **Sunbeam Transport** (**☎**666 2822, **Ⓦ**sunbeamfiji.com), who run along both the Queens Rd and Kings Rd; **Pacific Transport** (**☎**330 4366, **Ⓦ**pacifictransport.com.fj), which serves the Queens Rd only; and **Inter Cities** (**☎**338 2296, **Ⓦ**intercitiesfiji.com), whose buses serve the Kings Rd only and have free wi-fi. These services are supplemented by scruffier local buses, often running shorter routes, and as such on both the Queens Rd and Kings Rd you're unlikely to be waiting more than 40min or so for the next ride.

BY MINIVAN AND CARRIER VAN

Minivans Minivans operate between all towns, usually picking up passengers at bus stands. They are quicker than buses and cost approximately the same, but can be slightly unnerving to ride, especially at night.

Carrier vans Open-backed carrier vans travel to interior villages along dirt roads, bringing produce to and from market – ask among the market vendors and you should be able to hitch a bumpy ride squashed in the back for F$1–7, depending on the distance.

BY TAXI AND RENTAL CAR

It can often be a good idea to rent **taxis** for short-distance rides, and they're easy to find in all towns along the way – you can make bookings through your accommodation. However, they're also worth considering for longer rides, especially if you're travelling in a group – negotiated off-meter, it can be as cheap as R$100 all the way between Nadi and Suva. It's also possible to **rent cars** in Nadi (p.57), Suva (p.142) and almost all major towns along the way (see p.25 for more on the practicalities of car rental).

South Viti Levu

The scenic Queens Road passes through countless fishing villages alongside the winding bays of **South Viti Levu**. A fabulous beach, **Natadola**, lies within an hour's drive south of Nadi. East of that is the region's main town, **Sigatoka**, a lively market centre which acts as a springboard to several worthy attractions, including the **Sigatoka Sand Dunes National Park** and **Tavuni Hill Fort**. Beyond Sigatoka the sunny climate and sugarcane fields give way to cloud-clad mountains, which descend towards the picturesque lagoons of the **Coral Coast**. Graced by white sandy **beaches**, this was where tourism first began in Fiji; it's still home to a wide range of resorts, from large family-friendly complexes to budget places tucked away in secluded bays. Further east is **Pacific Harbour**, with the fabulous **Beqa Lagoon** offshore for scuba diving and game fishing, and the oppressive virgin rainforest of the **Namosi Highlands** offering remote riverside villages, pristine waterfalls and whitewater rafting. From here, the bustling, rain-drenched capital city of Suva (see Chapter 4) is just forty minutes' drive along the coast.

3

Natadola Beach and around

One of Viti Levu's most picturesque beaches, white-sand **Natadola** is hidden away off the Queens Road, less than an hour's drive south of Nadi. A long, sweeping crescent fringing an emerald sea, it is one of the few **bodysurfing** beaches in Fiji – one small surfing break, on the south side close to the river-mouth, is popular with local kids, while there's a more challenging one at the channel entrance. All in all, Natadola makes an excellent day-trip from Nadi, despite the persistent touts from the local village who will try to sell you handicrafts or a ride on a mangy horse. It's also the departure point for transfers to the lively backpacker resort, **Robinson Crusoe Island** (see below).

ARRIVAL AND DEPARTURE   NATADOLA BEACH AND AROUND

By car The initial journey from Nadi passes through flat featureless sugarcane fields for 17km before cutting inland through dense pine forests just after the Momi Bay turn-off. The longer, winding old coastal road from Momi Bay to Likuri Harbour is far more scenic. When the old coastal road rejoins the Queens Rd, it's only another 4km to the Natadola turn-off.
By bus Paradise Transport buses connect Natadola with Sigatoka (4 daily; 1hr; F$3.25).

ACCOMMODATION

Intercontinental Fiji Golf Resort ☎673 3300, ⓦ fiji.intercontinental.com; map pp.106–107. Large, snazzy, pricey resort; even the smallest of their 200-plus rooms is pretty massive, and luxuriously appointed. It's popular with those who come to play at the nearby Natadola Bay golf course – one very highly rated by golf pros themselves. Online discounts make the resort just about affordable, though breakfast is not included in the cheapest rates. 🛜 F$510

Robinson Crusoe Island Resort ☎776 0999, ⓦ robinsoncrusoeislandfiji.com; map pp.106–107. Set on a small island, this lively resort boasts attractive traditional-style bures and lodges, plus a 13-person dorm. Features lots of organized activities and pseudo tribal entertainment (which may not be everyone's cup of tea), but there's good snorkelling on the outer reef. Rates include meals; transfers from Nadi are F$99 per person. Dorms F$128, bures F$320, lodges F$410

Cuvu Beach

East of Natadola and backed by the Queens Road, **Cuvu Beach** has become popular with budget travellers of late, thanks to the presence of a couple of lower-end resorts; the resort may be less manicured than the Yasawas' backpacker spots, but it offers a more realistic insight into the Fijian way of life. The presence of small **Voua village** nearby also means that you can dine and drink in the local manner, should you so desire, and it's also the departure point for one of Fiji's most unique attractions – a ride along the coast in an old **sugar-train**.

Coral Coast Railway

Departs from the station by *Gecko's Resort* • F$70 to Sigatoka • ⓣ 652 0434

Fiji's south-coast railway was primarily constructed to transport sugarcane to processing facilities and ports. A passenger service was introduced in 1915, and though this has long since been discontinued, occasional **Coral Coast Railway** services now make short runs in old sugarcane trains to destinations along the coast to Sigatoka. The experience is a pleasant one: the carriages chunter through the countryside, passing various villages on the way. However, staff have been known to pester passengers into buying lollies for schoolkids – if you want to give gifts, bring more wholesome materials such as schoolbooks or crayons instead.

ARRIVAL AND DEPARTURE

CUVU BEACH

By bus Sunbeam and Pacific services between Nadi (1hr away) and Suva (3hr) stop by Cuvu Beach on request. There are also juddery local services to and from Sigatoka (30min; F$1.60).

By train The Coral Coast Railway (see above) runs from Cuvu to Sigatoka (around 30min) at least once a week, and there are other shorter services from Cuvu too; call the company for details.

ACCOMMODATION

Gecko's Resort ⓣ 652 0200, ⓦ geckosresort.com; map pp.106–107. This good-value resort has surprisingly attractive rooms and is aimed at the middle market, with fire dances, massage facilities and a small pool. The on-site restaurant is affordable, too. ($) F$200

★**Namuka Bay Resort** ⓣ 707 0243; map pp.106–107. You'll need your own wheels and a firm posterior – or a brave taxi driver – to get to this secluded, family-run coastal spot, sat all on its own west of Cuvu Beach. Even the dorm beds are just a quick sprint from the waters, and the meals (often featuring produce from the resort garden) are uniformly excellent given the remote location. Power not available 24hr. Meals included in the rates. Dorms F$95, villas F$180

Sigatoka and around

Dominated by Indian traders, the busy market centre of **SIGATOKA** (pronounced "singa-TO-ka") is located 4km inland on the banks of the Sigatoka River, and acts as a hub for the region. Although it's quite attractive, the accommodation options here are rather grim – they're far better on the nearby Sunset Strip (see p.114). However, quite a few foreigners drop by either en route to somewhere else, or while visiting nearby attractions. In general, it's a pleasant little window into urban life in provincial Fiji, with a bustling **market** at the centre, small-scale shops filling a tight network of streets, and plenty of curry restaurants.

To the west is the **Sigatoka Sand Dunes National Park**, where ancient Lapita pottery shards lie buried in the sand; walking trails crisscross the dunes, and there's good surfing offshore. Inland, the Sigatoka River, the longest in Fiji, winds north for 120km to Nadarivatu at the foothills of Mount Tomanivi (see p.127). The lower portion of the river valley makes for good exploring by car, but there are no designated walking trails other than the steep track weaving around **Tavuni Hill Fort**.

Sigatoka market

Market Rd • Mon–Sat 7am–5pm

Pleasantly unhurried and hassle-free, Sigatoka's little municipal **market** remains the focal point of the town. You'll smell the Indian spices which are on sale, as well as the usual fruit and veggies, plus the ubiquitous *yaqona* (sachets from F$10). Outside, on the eastern flank, small shacks sell tasty Indian sweets.

Sigatoka Sand Dunes National Park

Visitor centre Mon–Fri 8am–4.30pm, Sat & Sun 8am–4pm • F$10 • ⓣ 652 0243 • Accessible on Queens Road buses, or around F$8 by taxi from Sigatoka

Five kilometres west of central Sigatoka, the **Sigatoka Sand Dunes National Park**

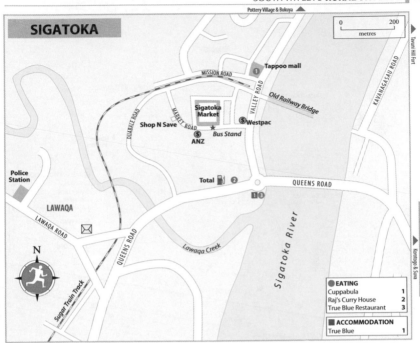

SIGATOKA

makes for an inspiring outing. The mighty dunes cover an area of 650 hectares, stretching for 3km and petering out to a sand spit at the mouth of the Sigatoka River. In places they rise to 80m, with fantastic views of the crashing surf along the beach.

The **visitor centre** has an informative display highlighting the fragile ecology and archeological importance of the region, and can also provide guides. There are two designated **walking trails** from here: an hour's stroll through forest to the beach; and a two- to three-hour walk which takes you along the ridge of the dunes. Along the beachfront you'll find plenty of driftwood and, if you look carefully, you'll come across small shards of **Lapita pottery**, evidence of human settlement from over two

FIJIAN POTTERY

The discovery of fired earthenware has been the single most important way of tracking the migration of people across the South Pacific; for Fijians, the trail commences with the introduction of **Lapita pottery**, a distinct form of geometric patterning impressed on clay pots by finely saw-toothed blades prior to firing. The oldest examples of Lapita, dating back to 1220 BC, were found at Bourewa Beach on the southeast coast of Viti Levu, while the highest concentration has been found at Sigatoka Sand Dunes National Park (see above).

In pre-European times, pottery formed the basis of Fijian homewares, with clay vessels used as water containers, *yaqona* bowls, and pots for baking, steaming and frying food. Today, potters around the islands retain traditional motifs, some using woven mats to create patterns, others using carved paddles or leaves. The potters, almost exclusively **women**, knead the clay with fine sand using the heels of the feet, beat it into shape using a wooden mallet, crudely fire the pots and then glaze them for waterproofing by rubbing over with the hot wax-like gum of the *dakua* tree, which was also used as a candle in pre-European times.

SIGATOKA AND AROUND

thousand years ago (see box, p.111). Unusually large human bones are regularly found here, suggesting that the fish diet and lifestyle of the early settlers was very healthy.

Sigatoka River Valley

Early morning mists rising from the **Sigatoka River** fill the surrounding valley, giving it a surreal atmosphere. Along the river's banks is some of the most fertile farming land in Fiji, with plantations of fruit, vegetables and sugarcane. Dirt roads travel either side of the river from Sigatoka town. The west side of the valley, known as the Valley Road, extends from Sigatoka town all the way to Bukuya village (see p.65); here the road branches off to Nadi, or continues across the centre of Viti Levu to Ba on the north coast. The east side of the valley is less travelled, and goes only as far as Mavua village. Alternatively, you can fire straight up the centre of the valley on jet-boat tours (see opposite).

The Valley Road

Nakabuta village tour daily 8am–5pm • ☎ 650 0929 • Tour by donation, approx F$5 • Daily bus from Sigatoka to Draiba at 12.30pm; 2hr; F$3

The **Valley Road**, on the west side of the river, makes an excellent **walking track** and passes many villages and viewpoints along the way. The initial 6km from Sigatoka town is sealed, passing immediately through Sigatoka village and hugging close to the river. A further kilometre leads to **Nakabuta village**, where tours of the village including a *yaqona* ceremony, **pottery-making** demonstrations and Fijian dance are performed for impromptu arrivals. There's also farm-stay accommodation in the valley (see below).

Tavuni Hill Fort

Beside the village of Naroro, 5km from Sigatoka town, accessed via the Kavanagasau Rd on the Suva side of the Sigatoka bridge • Mon–Fri 8am–5pm, Sat 8am–4pm • F$12, guide additional F$3 • Bus (2 daily) or carrier (every hour or so) from Sigatoka (F$1); taxi from Sigatoka around F$10

Five kilometres up the rough dirt road on the east side of the valley is **Tavuni Hill Fort**, a fascinating example of Fiji's tribal past. In the eighteenth century, Tongan invaders began to push further into Fijian territory and established a base on this fantastically steep hill overlooking the Sigatoka River. They waged wars on the surrounding settlements until 1876 when they were subdued by native troops under British control. What remains is a well-excavated and easily accessible hillfort with stone foundations, rock barricades, ceremonial grounds and the chilling *vatu-ni-bokola*, or killing stone, where victims' heads were smashed with a war club. The **views** from the hilltop are worth the visit alone, and make for great panorama shots.

3

ARRIVAL AND INFORMATION

By bus Sunbeam Transport and Pacific Transport buses pass through Sigatoka town several times daily on the south coast route, and there are plenty of local services heading along the Queens Road too – all use the town-centre terminal, though you may have to ask

around for the precise boarding point if you're heading to a local village.

Destinations Nadi (1hr 20min); Navua (1hr 45min); Pacific Harbour (1hr 30min); Sunset Strip (20min); Suva (2hr 30min).

TOURS AND SERVICES

Tours Sigatoka River Safari (☎650 1721, ⓦsigatokariver.com) offers entertaining jet-boat "safari" tours (F$249) of the Sigatoka River Valley, including village visits with *kava*, Fijian food and dance. Coastal Inland Tours (☎650 1161, ⓦcoastalinlandtours .com) have several options including a waterfall tour

(F$170), a cannibal-cave journey (F$219) and a river cruise (F$189); all are four hours long and include a *kava* ceremony at local villages.
Banks There are Westpac and ANZ banks (Mon–Fri 9.30am–4pm), both with ATMs, on Market Rd in Sigatoka, and another ANZ ATM at the Total petrol station.

ACCOMMODATION

TOWN CENTRE

True Blue Queens Rd ☎650 1530; map p.111. If you really need to stay in Sigatoka town, this is the pick of a dire bunch. The top-floor en-suite rooms are adequately furnished with ceiling fans and some with a/c (F$10 extra will get you a TV) – they are the least noisy of the rooms too, since the *Sigatoka Club* is on the ground floor. F$55

SIGATOKA RIVER VALLEY

★**Teitei Homestay** Valley Rd, km19 ☎863 8944; map pp.106–107. The cock-a-doodle-doos will wake you early at this Airbnb-bookable farm-stay, located just across the river from Mavua village (villagers sometimes swim across, since there's no road for miles). It's basic, and you can forget about hot showers for a while, but the friendly family ensure that there are few better places in which to take the slow pulse of life in the Fijian boondocks. Meals available on request; three-night minimum stay. Per person F$100

EATING

For budget eats, try one of the simple places west of the market; here, the Shop N Save supermarket (see map, p.111; Mon–Sat 7am–7pm, Sun 7am–2pm) has a good selection for self-caterers, plus an attached bakery.

★**Cuppabula** Tappoo Mall, Sigatoka Valley Rd ☎650 0199; map p.111. By far the most urbane place for coffee and Western food in Sigatoka is this cheery little café; meals are pricey and not that great, but the coffee (from F$5) really hits the spot, as do their cakes. Mon–Fri 7.30am–5pm, Sat 7.30am–4pm, Sun 8.30am–3pm.

Raj's Curry House Queens Rd ☎650 1470; map p.111. Tiny and a little grubby, but a winner with locals for its cheap curries – veggie set meals go for just F$9, *kai* curries (made with river mussels, a local favourite) for F$15, and meat curries for a little more. You get a good sample of Indo-Fijian food here, but avoid the

pre-cooked counter meals. Mon–Sat 8.30am–8.30pm.
True Blue Queens Rd ☎ 650 1530; map p.111. Part of the eponymous hotel, this restaurant looks pretty horrid, but they serve good meals, and some tables have great river views – your safest bet is the yummy fish and

chips (F$10), though you could also try a curry, or the masala crab (F$54). In the afternoons, the downstairs drinking hall opens up, though you can grab a beer in the main restaurant at any time (from F$6). Daily 7.30am–10pm.

Korotogo Beach and Sunset Strip

Eight kilometres beyond Sigatoka town, past the final stretch of sugarcane fields, is **Korotogo Beach**. The beach itself is ordinary and not great for swimming, but the pleasant 2km-long road towards it, known as the **Sunset Strip**, has a few restaurants, budget motels and holiday homes and makes a convenient base for exploring the sights around Sigatoka (see p.110).

Kula Eco Park

Just across the Queens Rd from the Sunset Strip · Daily 10am–4pm · F$30 · ☎ 650 0505, 🖥 fijiwild.com

The absorbing **Kula Eco Park** holds Fiji's largest collection of native wildlife, and is nicely situated in a temperate forest with self-guided boardwalks meandering through aviary cages, reptile enclosures and a reef fish aquarium. Large crested iguanas (see box, p.194) are its highlight: endemic to Fiji, they are rarely seen and limited to only a couple of islands off Vanua Levu and Yasawa.

ACCOMMODATION　　　　KOROTOGO BEACH AND SUNSET STRIP

Casablanca Sunset Strip ☎ 652 0600; map p.112. The cheapest private rooms on the strip – they won't win any prizes for design or features, but they're not that bad, and all face out onto a small swimming pool and the beach. Negatives are a general air of neglect, occasionally misfiring showers, and a club next door which can make sleep tricky on Friday and Saturday nights. F$85

Crow's Nest Sunset Strip ☎ 650 0230, 🖥 crowsnes tresortfiji.com; map p.112. Attractive individual wooden villas set into the steep grassy terrace facing the sea. The nautical theme permeates throughout, and there's even a little museum of whaling and sailing memorabilia. Their restaurant (see below) specializes in Italian food and seafood dishes. 🖥 ($) F$279

Outrigger Off Queens Rd ☎ 650 0044, 🖥 outrigger .com; map p.112. Five-star resort set in forty acres of beautifully landscaped grounds. The reception and most

of the 207 rooms are perched on a hill overlooking the deluxe bures below – the latter all come with a butler to pamper you. Rooms have all the mod cons you expect and there are three fabulous restaurants on site. The beach is not great, close to a swiftly flowing passage with riptides – instead guests relax around a large swimming pool, or head uphill to the spa. 🖥 $ Rooms F$460, bures F$780

★ **Tubakula Beach Resort** Queens Rd ☎ 650 0097, 🖥 fiji4less.com; map p.112. This quiet place provides excellent value as well as some of the only dorm beds on the south coast. Their A-frame bungalows, all neatly set in gardens between the beach and swimming pool, are pretty huge for the price. The only TV here is in the lobby and there's no wi-fi, making this a wonderful spot in which to simply wind down. Dorms F$32, bungalow F$146

EATING

Baravi Bar Outrigger ☎ 650 0044; map p.112. Offers a "culinary journey" through India, Thailand, Singapore and China; mains are F$30 or so. For more intimate evening dining, the hotel's *Ivi Restaurant* serves Pacific/ Continental cuisine starting from F$35, though children under 13 are not permitted. Daily noon–9.30pm.

★ **Beach Bar & Grill** Sunset Strip ☎ 902 5979; map p.112. Café-bar with a cute courtyard garden, and a varied menu featuring thin-crust pizzas, fish curry, grilled beef and catch-of-the-day (most mains F$18–40). Splash out on the very large "open shell" appetiser, which is something like a seafood chowder with coconut milk

served in a coconut (F$16.50); the pancakes and ice cream are a winner, too. Licensed (happy hour 5–8pm) and BYO. Daily 3–10pm.

Quarter Deck Crow's Nest ☎ 650 0230; map p.112. Styling itself as the "Amalfi Korotogo", this ocean-view restaurant whips up great Italian food, with pasta and pizzas from F$18; the extensive menu also features curries, East Asian dishes and all-day breakfasts, at affordable prices, though these are more hit-and-miss. Licensed, but it's better to hit the bar at the bottom of the resort, and take your drinks to the grassy area abutting the beach. Daily 6.30am–10.30pm.

The Coral Coast

Driving along the **Coral Coast**, loosely defined as the 60km section of the Queens Road between Korotogo Beach and Pacific Harbour, is perhaps the most pleasant drive in Fiji. The name, inspired by the exposed offshore reefs, was used to market Fiji's first collection of tourist resorts, which were set up here in the 1960s. The Coral Coast begins in the province of Baravi, passing through the small settlement of **Korolevu**, where Fiji's first tourist hotel once stood; along the coastline here are a dozen **beach resorts**. Beyond Korolevu, the scenery becomes more intense as the highway climbs inland over the mountains of **Serua**, which shield several deep bays with secluded budget retreats. There are few specific attractions on the Coral Coast apart from its scenery, but its situation, midway between the sites of Sigatoka and the activities of Pacific Harbour, makes it a good base.

Vatukarasa and around

Beyond Korotogo Beach, the Queens Road hugs the coastline for 30km all the way to Namatakula village. One of the finest coastal views is found 15km beyond Sigatoka, past Malevu village, overlooking the peaceful **Sovi Bay** with its pounding surf. There's plenty of roadside parking and you can scramble down the rocks to the grey sandy beach for a walk (though with unpredictable currents, swimming is not advisable).

On the far side of the bay is the pretty **Vatukarasa**, once settled by Tongans and with several beautifully thatched bures surrounding the village green, plus an excellent handicraft shop (see p.116).

Korolevu and around

Biausevu village and waterfall F$25 including horse-ride and *kava* ceremony • Taxis F$10 one-way from Queens Road junction

At **Korolevu**, 15km east of Vatukarasa, there's a Pacific petrol station with a small shop. Visible in the undergrowth behind is a small airport control tower, evidence of the old airstrip that served guests heading to the Korotogo Beach Hotel, Fiji's first tourist resort. The hotel was the pinnacle of tourism in the early 1970s, before the Queens Road was tar-sealed, but closed in 1983. A dirt road running parallel to the disused grass runway leads inland for 5km through lush tropical forest to **Biausevu village**. From the village, a flattish, thirty-minute trail crisscrosses a small stream before ending at the pretty **Savunamatelaya Waterfall**, where you can swim in the natural pool.

Namatakula and around

Nine kilometres beyond Korolevu is the village of **Namatakula** in the province of **Serua**; it's a so-so, shopless kind of village, where life dawdles by at a snail's pace. A little beyond here, the Queens Road cuts inland for 20km to climb over steep hills draped in thick **rainforest**. On the first ascent, a small dirt road leads to *Mango Bay Resort*, with a beach backed by incredibly tall coconut palms. There's another pretty beach with good snorkelling at **Namagumagua**, accessed down a 4km dirt road signposted to *The Wellesley Resort*, 10km further along the Queens Road.

ACCOMMODATION	**THE CORAL COAST**

VATUKARASA AND AROUND

★**Beach Cocomo Lodge** ☎650 7333, ⓦbeach cocomofiji.com; map pp.106–107. Set on a small hill overlooking the ocean and with steps leading down to a secluded sandy beach, this little-known spot is a real gem for those seeking seclusion. The two wooden cottages with polished wooden floors are tastefully decorated and have hot-water en-suite bathrooms; the only downside is that they back onto the main road. Delicious meals are served in a breezy thatched bure overlooking the sea. 📶($) F$188

Hideaway Resort ☎650 0177, ⓦwww.hideawayfiji .com; map pp.106–107. Once you're behind the prison-like walls barricading this large resort from the highway, the atmosphere is rather quaint, albeit a bit cramped. The bures are prettily painted and set in landscaped grounds; interiors are bright and airy, most with a/c and some with outdoor courtyard showers. The beach is adequate, and there's good reef-surfing in the passage either side of high tide. Rates include breakfast. 📶($) F$385

Tambua Sands ☎650 0399, ⓦwarwicktambuasands .com; map pp.106–107. With just 25 bures, this sleepy spot is relatively small for a Coral Coast resort. The ocean and garden bures are comfortable, with high roofs, ceiling fans and plenty of open space between them. If you're looking for something simple, with a small swimming pool and good restaurant, this pretty beachfront resort is great value. Rates include continental breakfast. 🛜($) **F$230**

KOROLEVU AND AROUND

★**Maui Palms** ☎650 7082, 🌐mauipalms-accommodation.com; map pp.106–107. This relatively new option has become a real hit, with a range of impeccably designed villas surrounding an infinity pool, kayaks and snorkelling equipment for free use, and a general air of supreme calm. The beds are just about the comfiest in Fiji, too. 🛜 **F$345**

Naviti Resort ☎653 0444, 🌐warwicknaviti.com; map pp.106–107. Liveliest of the large hotels in the area, probably thanks to its excellent-value inclusive packages, many of which include alcohol. Within the resort are 220 a/c rooms, five tennis courts, a nine-hole pitch-and-putt golf course and two swimming pools. Staff are very attentive, especially with children, and there's also a kids' club and babysitting service. 🛜($) **F$280**

Waidroka Bay Resort ☎330 4605, 🌐waidroka.com; map pp.106–107. This place is distinctly laidback, as you'd expect of a surfing and scuba diving retreat. It's

tucked 4km down a dirt road, screened by thick jungle but without a beach. The five simple terrace rooms are set on a hill with fine views, with six cosy bures and a swimming pool in the gardens overlooking the sea. The Beqa Lagoon dive sites are 20–30min away in one of their five fully equipped fast boats; Frigates Passage surfing is a 45min trip, while three local surf spots are within 10min of the resort. 🛜 Rooms **F$295**, bures **F$395**

NAMATAKULA AND AROUND

★**Beachouse** ☎0800 653 0530, 🌐fijibeachouse.com; map pp.106–107. The most popular stop on the Coral Coast – nay, the entire south coast of Viti Levu – with independent travellers. Located on what's effectively a private beach, backed by tall coconut palms, it's great if you're after a social atmosphere. There's a good swimming pool and bar, the food is tasty and there's loads to do, from waterfall hikes to sea-kayaking and shark dives. Rates include breakfast and dinner. 🛜 Dorms **F$88**, rooms **F$235**

The Warwick ☎653 0555, 🌐warwickhotels.com/fiji-resort; map pp.106–107. With 247 rooms, this is a whopper – despite its size, they still manage to get the small details right, from the opulent-looking waterside dining areas to the manicured gardens, as well as the cane furnishings and stylish prints in the rooms. One bar here boasts a real Fiji rarity – shisha pipes to smoke. 🛜 **F$590**

EATING AND DRINKING

★**Eco Café** Korolevu ☎653 0064; map pp.106–107. For those heading along the Coral Coast, this is a treat worth pausing for. This ramshackle-looking beachside place may look like a bit of Thailand exiled to Viti Levu, but they serve up excellent pasta and wood-fired pizza (from F$20), plus Fijian specials too, if you call ahead; you can also drop by for a cocktail. Fri–Tues 1–9pm.

Vilisite's Korolevu ☎653 0054; map pp.106–107. Once the most popular seafood spot in Sigatoka town, this restaurant has moved to a secluded part of the Coral Coast instead. Pride of place goes to their fish and chips (F$10 for a "small" portion), though you may well be tempted by eggplant in *lolo* (F$10), kokoda (F$17) or a full lobster (F$72). Daily 9am–9pm.

SHOPPING

Baravi Vatukarasa ☎652 0588; map pp.106–107. On the Suva side of the village, this is the larger and more commercial of Vatukarasa's two handicraft shops, with a wide range of wood carvings and jewellery made all

around Fiji. Also serves surprisingly good coffee (F$5), cakes and cold drinks. Mon–Sat 7.30am–6pm, Sun 8am–5pm.

Pacific Harbour and around

Purpose-built in the early 1970s, **PACIFIC HARBOUR** was drained from swampland and laid out meticulously with suburban driveways and intermittent luxury villas. Today, it is known as Fiji's **adventure sports** hub (see p.118) – the **Navua River**, some 10km to the east, boasts stunning waterfall hikes and longboat excursions, while further inland, the high mountains of the mysterious **Namosi Highlands** offer fantastic 4WD driving, whitewater rafting and remote village treks. Offshore is the phenomenal **Beqa Lagoon**, with world-class scuba diving, including raved-about shark dives, and serious game fishing.

TRADITIONAL FIJIAN COSTUME >

3

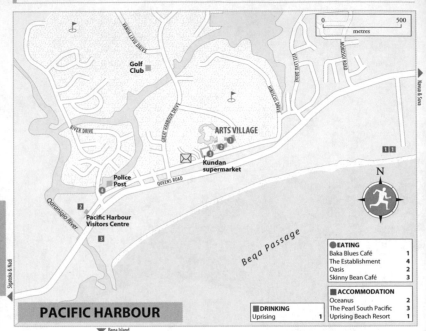

The Arts Village

Hibiscus Drive • Meke and fire-dance Wed–Sat at 7pm • F$80 (minimum eight people) • ☎ 345 0065, ⓦ artsvillage.com.fj

Apart from its offshore activities, Pacific Harbour's main attraction is the **Arts Village**, which once boasted around thirty boutique shops selling quality crafts. Things have taken a dive under the present owners (day-trippers from Nadi walk around looking underwhelmed), but there are still a few good restaurants here (see p.120), plus a couple of little cafés serving cheap roti wraps and sandwiches – and the colonial-style atmosphere of the wood-panelled buildings is hard to beat. Also here is the kitsch but fun **Cultural Centre**, a mock-traditional Fijian village with an artificial lake that you can be punted around in a canoe. You can also explore the replica *bure kalou*, or sacred temple, to hear about ancient customs and legends.

ARRIVAL AND INFORMATION

PACIFIC HARBOUR

By bus Sunbeam Transport and Pacific Transport buses pass through Pacific Harbour several times daily on the south coast route.

Destinations Nadi (2hr 30min); Navua (30min); Sigatoka (1hr 30min); Suva (1hr 20min).

Information For general information and to make bookings for any activities or tours (see below), try the Pacific Harbour Visitors Centre (☎ 808 5920; daily 9am–5pm), just east of the bridge at the western edge of town.

Money ANZ and BSP have banks, with ATMs, in the Arts Village.

TOURS AND ACTIVITIES

BUGGY RIDES

Terratrek Off main road by Uprising ☎ 928 2397, ⓦ terratrektoursfiji.com. Fun buggy rides along two main mountain courses; those on the waterfall route leave at 9.30am (4hr; F$349), while the shorter "scenic rides" depart at 2pm (2hr; F$249).

DIVING

Some 12km south of Pacific Harbour, Beqa Lagoon is renowned for its **shark-feeding dives**, which attract divers from across the world. On a good day you may see up to a hundred sharks, including reef sharks, silvertips, tawny nurse sharks, sicklefin lemon sharks, menacing-looking bull sharks and the occasional tiger shark, as well as schools of other large fish taking advantage of the free food (mostly tuna heads from a nearby factory). Both of the companies below claim an excellent safety record, but for a more sedate experience there are also soft coral and wreck dives available in the lagoon on the days that the sharks are not fed.

★**Aqua Trek Beqa** Club Oceanus ☎345 0324, ⓦaquatrek.com. Professional dive operator with top-of-the-range gear and boats. Shark dives cost F$370 and depart Pacific Harbour at 8.30am on Mon, Wed, Fri & Sat, with coral diving around Beqa Lagoon available on other days for F$290.

Beqa Adventure Divers ☎345 0911, ⓦfijisharkdive .com. Local operator conducting shark dives departing at 8.30am Mon, Tues & Thurs–Sat (two-tank dive F$325), and coral dives Sun–Fri (two-tank F$325; snorkelling F$90).

GAME FISHING

Xtasea ☎345 0280, ⓦxtaseacharters.com. Game fishing charters aboard a well-equipped 20m game fishing boat (F$1800 for half-day; max 4 anglers but up to 8 people). Heads south of Beqa to the deep channels trawling for billfish and tuna. Includes breakfast and lunch.

GOLF

Golf course Great Harbour Rd ☎990 8125, ⓦgolf .thepearlsouthpacific.com. One of Pacific Harbour's star attractions is its underutilized championship golf course (daily 9am–6pm; F$75 green fee; carts, caddies and rental equipment available). The 18-hole course is mostly flat but provides stunning views.

JET-SKI TOURS

Jetski Safari Pacific Harbour ☎345 0933, ⓦjetski-safari.com. Guided jet-ski tours circumnavigating Beqa Island (daily 8am–noon; solo ride F$580, dual

ride F$640). The tour includes a picnic lunch on one of Beqa's deserted beaches, and a snorkel on one of the stunning reefs.

RIVER TRIPS

Discover Fiji Tours Navua, by market stalls ☎345 0180, ⓦdiscoverfijitours.com. Guided river trips departing from Navua, just east of Pacific Harbour (see p.120). One option (F$249) includes a jet-boat ride up to and past a waterfall, then an inflatable-raft ride back down to the falls, plus a barbecue. Another tour features rides on a *bilibili* (a raft of bamboo poles strapped together using vines), plus *kava* and lovo (F$155).

WHITEWATER RAFTING

★**Rivers Fiji** East of Arts Village ☎345 0147, ⓦriversfiji.com. American-run operator offering thrilling year-round whitewater rafting on the Upper Navua River (Mon, Wed & Fri 6.45am–5pm; F$399); the journey downstream passes over exciting Grade II-III rapids, and through a stunning canyon whose sheer rock walls overflow with waterfalls. They also offer more sedate inflatable-kayak tours heading down the Middle Navua River (Tues, Thurs & Sat; half-day tour F$299).

ZIP WIRES

★**Kila Eco Adventure Park** Near Navua ☎331 7454, ⓦkilaworld.com. Large adventure park with all manner of attractions, including zip wires, rope walks and swings (one of the latter is truly Tarzan-esque), "eco-walks", and waterfall-fed bathing pools. F$170/122 for a full-/half-day; eco-walks F$12.50.

Zip Fiji Between Navua and Suva ☎930 0545, ⓦzip-fiji.com. Zoom 30m above the ground through the forest canopy on one of this operation's near-2km of squeal-worthy zip wires, one of which is over 200m in length. F$235 per person, including transfers from Pacific Harbour.

ACCOMMODATION

★**Oceanus** Atoll Place ☎345 0498, ⓦcluboceanus .com. This mid-budget spot is a great deal. The starting point for most shark dives in the Beqa Lagoon (see opposite), it boasts a string of large, affordable rooms with powerful a/c, as well as a small pool, and a restaurant which whips up surprisingly good food. Rates include breakfast. ☞($) Dorms F$50, rooms F$190

The Pearl South Pacific Queens Rd ☎345 0022, ⓦthepearlsouthpacific.com. An iconic Pacific Harbour resort with a fresh, contemporary look – the six lavish suites are something else, draped in exotic linens and with themed decor from provincial French to Indian. There's an intricately designed pool, and it's right on

the beach with views of Beqa and breezes off the ocean. ☞ Rooms F$420, suites F$935

★**Uprising Beach Resort** Off Queens Rd ☎345 2200, ⓦuprisingbeachresort.com. This affordable beachside resort fits in seamlessly with Pacific Harbour's adventure label, offering plenty of activities. The large, rather grand-looking dorm is set back from the beach, the pine-panelled, wooden-floored bures boast cute bathrooms and outdoor showers, while the villas are on a grander scale and come with all mod cons. The curved bar is also a popular hangout (see p.120). Dorms F$60, bures F$285, villas F$385

3

EATING

For self-caterers, the Kundan supermarket in the Arts Village (Sun–Thurs 7am–7pm, Fri & Sat 7am–8pm) has plenty of choice, and a booze corner.

Baka Blues Café Arts Village ☏ 345 0041, ⓦ bakabluescafe.com. The most notable of the Arts Village's lakeside restaurants, with a menu featuring Tex-Mex temptations such as ribs (F$30), pulled pork burgers (F$28), and some great beef chilli (F$22). Pleasingly, you can also wash your food down with Southern Comfort and Jack Daniels; the N'orleans-style piped music gives way to cheesy American live music most evenings. Mon–Sat 11am–10pm.

The Establishment Off Queens Rd ☏ 831 0109. Relatively new spot priding itself on its burgers, served with a curious variety of international fillings (all F$17.50), as well as good pizza and pasta. Swing by at weekends for their brunch specials, which include pancakes any way

(F$16) or Central American *tostadas* (F$18). Mon–Fri 11am–10pm, Sat & Sun 8am–10pm.

Oasis Arts Village ☏ 345 0617. Decent restaurant serving hearty international meals, including Asian mains such as fried rice and teriyaki steak (from F$18). For a more local flavour, try the kokoda (F$14) or catch-of-the-day (F$25). Daily 9am–9pm.

★**Skinny Bean Café** Arts Village ☏ 358 9869, ⓦ skinnybeanfiji.com. For the best coffee in town (from F$5), head to this urbane spot facing the main road; their cakes (also from F$5) are hard to resist, as is the free wi-fi, though the place (even its outdoor yard) can become a bit of a heat-trap when there's no breeze. ☏ Mon–Sat 7am–7pm, Sun 7am–4pm.

DRINKING

Uprising Uprising Beach Resort, off Queens Rd ☏ 345 2200. This funky resort bar-restaurant can get rowdy at weekends with locals and international students from the university in Suva. No real surprise,

since it's the best place for a drink in Pacific Harbour, with seating between the beach and swimming pool, draught beer from F$7 and cocktails from just F$10. Daily 11am–9pm.

Navua and the Namosi Highlands

NAVUA, 10km east of Pacific Harbour on the Suva side of the Navua River, is a dusty market centre, its population a mix of Indo-Fijian rice farmers from the delta and Fijian highland villagers. The only reason to come here is to catch a boat to Beqa Island (see p.152), or to explore the **Namosi Highlands**, looming large to the north above the river floodplain.

Longboats line the riverbanks between the market and bridge, before journeying up the murky **Navua River** to the highland villages. Guided longboat and whitewater rafting trips (see p.119) head off from here through stunning scenery towards Wainimakatu; this remote region fronts the massive **Sovi Basin**, an amphitheatre of lowland rainforest surrounded by mountain ridges with an abundance of endemic birdlife – this is Fiji's largest and most important protected nature reserve.

With a 4WD vehicle, it's possible to drive from Navua along the Namosi Road, following the Waidina River through remote forests. The most picturesque village along the road is **Namosi**, sitting beneath the 950m-high sheer cliff peak of **Mount Voma**. Climbers can quite easily scale Mount Voma without ropes in around three hours, and will be graced on a clear day with sweeping views of the surrounding mountains.

ARRIVAL AND GETTING AROUND NAVUA AND THE NAMOSI HIGHLANDS

By bus Most buses between Nadi and Suva stop at the bus stand in Navua for a 15min rest stop.
Destinations Nadi (3hr 20min); Pacific Harbour (30min); Sigatoka (2hr); Suva (45min).

By boat Boats head upriver from Navua to Namuamua and Nukusere (from 10am; 2hr; $15). Bear in mind that you may not be able to return till the following morning.

ACCOMMODATION

Namosi Eco Retreat Navunikabi ☏ 928 9378, ⓦ facebook.com/namosieco. This cluster of simple bures provides a real off-the-grid experience – no electronic equipment is used on site, bar the

solar-powered lights which come on in the evening. Rafting and swimming are two suitably natural activities in which you can partake while you're here. Breakfast included. Bures F$250

East Viti Levu

The hilly, tropical countryside of **East Viti Levu** is the least-visited part of the big island. Here you'll find some of the prettiest roadside landscapes in Fiji, particularly around **Viti Levu Bay** along the northeast coast. North of Suva, the **Kings Road** races across the fertile, flat farming land of the mighty Rewa River, cutting 20km inland through deep tropical rainforest alongside the Wainibuka River – along this route you may see locals heading downstream on precarious-looking *bilibilis*, rafts made from bamboo poles, sometimes laden with market goods – before rejoining the coast near the village of **Barotu**, by Viti Levu Bay. An alternative track from Korovou heads along the undulating hills and bays of the remote **Tailevu Coast**, then over the high Nakorotubu Range before hitting Barotu.

Korovou and around

The dictionary definition of a one-street town, little **KOROVOU** forms the intersection of the Tailevu Coast Road and Kings Road. While the town is essentially a convenient bus-stop, with bathroom facilities for passengers in need, the presence of a charming little hotel, plus a ramshackle market and a couple of stores, makes this appealingly grubby town a fun – and totally tourist-free – base for a couple of nearby sights, including **Waimaro Waterfall** and the **Snake God Cave**.

Waimaro Waterfall

Kings Rd, 15km west of Korovou • F$2

Just west of Dakuivuna village, at the scenic **Waimaro Waterfall**, steps lead down to a stream and picnic bench surrounded by forest: there are toilets and changing facilities here, but no lockers, so keep an eye on your belongings. Local kids are often on hand to demonstrate the best spots for jumping into the pool below the falls.

Snake God Cave

Wailotua, Kings Rd, 18km northwest of Korovou • F$15

At Wailotua, a large cave, known as the **Snake God Cave**, is cut into the steep mountain abutting the village. Inside is its star attraction, a bulky stalagmite said to resemble a six-headed **snake god**. In pre-European times chiefs would meet and consult here. Sadly, the ancient stone is now coarsely scribbled with the names of local tourists.

ARRIVAL AND DEPARTURE   KOROVOU AND AROUND

By bus As well as the Sunbeam express buses that follow the Kings Rd (see above), several local minibuses head inland from Korovou to Vunidawa.
Destinations Ba (4hr); Lautoka (4hr 45min); Rakiraki (2hr 30min); Suva (1hr 10min); Tavua (3hr 25min).

By minivan Public minivans run north to Natovi Landing (every 30min; F$2), and you may be able to persuade the driver to continue 40min on to Natale-i-Ra (see p.122) for another F$25 or so; a couple of daily minibuses head all the way.

ACCOMMODATION AND EATING

★ Tailevu ☎ 343 0028, �� facebook.com /tailevuhotel; map pp.106–107. Tucked away up a hillside west of the roundabout marking the northern edge of town, this is a lovely little place, boasting half-a-dozen comfy, en-suite rooms with a/c. Breakfast is included, and they'll sometimes let you join in the family dinner too; wi-fi and drinks are available in the bar/ lobby area. 🛜 F$85

Matanakilagi South of the roundabout; no phone; map pp.106–107. The best restaurant in town (and one of the only ones, too), serving cheap staples like fish *lolo* or burger and chips for F$8 and under. Mon–Sat 7am–6pm.

The Tailevu Coast

The most scenic route between Korovou and Viti Levu Bay heads along an 80km dirt track hugging the remote **Tailevu Coast**. With its lovely coastal scenery, secluded villages, hiking tracks and offshore dolphin-spotting, this seldom-visited region is an exceptional place to explore. In the southern portion, 10km from Korovou town, **Natovi Landing** is the departure point for ferries to Ovalau and Vanua Levu (see p.186).

Natale-i-Ra

The pretty village of **Natale-i-Ra** makes a lovely base for visiting one of the area's great attractions, **Moon Reef**, which is around forty minutes away by boat. As well as offering fantastic snorkelling, the reef is one of only a couple of reliable places in Fiji to spot and swim with bottlenose **dolphins**. Other activities, which you can organize through the local accommodation (see below), include a two-hour hike through light forest to the summit of **Mount Tova** (645m), a volcanic plug with panoramic views.

Bureiwai to Namarai

The daily bus from Suva terminates north of Natale-i-Ra at **Bureiwai**, though drivers can continue further north along the highly **scenic** road to Namarai, meandering around a series of beautiful bays covered in coconut palms. Keep an eye out for a small signpost for the Church of the Latter-day Saints; a small track on the opposite side of the road heads out to a lovely **viewpoint** from a cliff overlooking the bay. Once in **Namarai**, a neatly laid out village in a small bay, you'll be warmly received by the locals, although note that this is a traditional, strongly Methodist area so dress appropriately.

ARRIVAL AND DEPARTURE   THE TAILEVU COAST

By bus You can reach Natale-i-Ra by public transport from Suva, but not from Rakiraki. Lodoni Transport (☎ 339 2888) has two buses departing Suva on weekdays at 1.30pm and 2.30pm, and one bus on Saturday at 1pm, heading to Korovou, Natovi Landing and beyond Natale-i-Ra as far as Bureiwai (3hr), where both buses spend the night before returning early in the morning to Suva.

By taxi Buses run regularly from Suva to Korovou, where you can hire a taxi to Natale-i-Ra or *Takalana Bay Beach Resort* for F$40.

By car Access to the Tailevu Coast road is easy to miss from the Kings Rd: at a turning 1km south of Barotu, head east onto the poorly signposted Nakorotubu Rd. Shortly afterwards turn left again at Luci's Shopping Centre. The steep road to the coast is best tackled by 4WD, although cars with good tyres and high clearance will usually do the job.

By boat From Natovi Landing, passenger and car ferries operated by Patterson Brothers (☎ 331 5644, ⓦ fijisearoad.com) depart for Ovalau (3.30pm, daily though not always on Sun) and Naubouwalu on Vanua Levu (daily; 3hr 30min–4hr). *Interlink Shipping* (☎ 999 2026, ⓦ interlinkshipping.com.fj) departs for Naubouwalu (5 weekly; 7hr), and Savusavu on Vanua Levu (2 weekly; 12hr).

ACCOMMODATION

Natalei Eco Lodge Natale-i-Ra ☎ 972 1832; map pp.106–107. Thatch bures alongside the beach, as well as cottages with en-suite cold-water showers and flush toilets. Located right on the edge of the village, the lodge has little privacy, but cultural interaction is without doubt the focus here. Activities include weaving lessons, *yaqona*-drinking, hiking and waterfall treks and, with larger groups, meke performances. A restaurant overlooks the beach and local-style meals are included in the rates, though it's best to bring snacks too: cold drinks are available, but no alcohol, so bring your own. Dorms F$85, bures F$185

★**Takalana Bay Beach Resort** 1km north of Natale-i-Ra ☎ 991 6338, ⓦ takalana.blogspot.com; map pp.106–107. There are just a couple of bures at this simple spot, though facilities are homely and well decorated, with en-suite hot-water bathrooms and cooking stoves. The retreat is surrounded by private land descending to the coast, with unobscured views towards Naigani and Ovalau islands: for F$60 they'll take you out for a dolphin-spotting excursion. Rates include meals. Dorms F$115, bures F$250

Viti Levu Bay

From Barotu, the Kings Road loops north towards Rakiraki around the northeastern corner of Viti Levu; from here there are impressive views of the Nakauvadra Range tapering off into deep **Viti Levu Bay**. Thanks to volcanic activity, the coasts to the north and south of the bay are steep and irregular, with numerous promontories.

St Francis Xavier's Catholic Church

Naiserelagi village, 8km south of Namuaimada • Small donation appreciated • Accessible on Kings Rd buses

At the base of the bay, buffered by mangrove forests, **St Francis Xavier's Catholic Church** perches on a hilltop overlooking the school in Naiserelagi village. Inside are three beautiful **murals** painted by Jean Charlot in 1962. Challenging European colonization and superiority of the time, the centrepiece, a 10m-high fresco, depicts a crucified Black Christ wearing *masi* cloth, while two side altar panels, one with indigenous Fijians and the other with Indo–Fijians, show unique cultural scenes of *tabua* and *yaqona* offerings to Christ. There is also a mural of St Peter Chanel, Fiji's first martyred saint, holding a symbolic war club.

Namuaimada

Dwarfed by the high mountains, and hugging the exposed northerly point of the bay, is the pretty beachside village of **Namuaimada**. Lodged between two bluffs, the beach here bears the brunt of the trade winds and is a renowned **kitesurfing spot**. The village is a little rough around the edges but it's a friendly place, with a pleasant mix of traditional thatch bures, wooden lodges and modern cement buildings surrounding the church. Guides from the village offer **trekking** in the mountains as well as hand-line **fishing** on the reef (both around F$10).

3

North Viti Levu

At first glance **North Viti Levu**, with its rolling sunburnt hills and succession of dusty inland towns, might appear rather dreary; delve a little deeper, however, and you'll discover some unexpectedly charming sites around what is now being promoted as the **Suncoast**. Off the undulating coast northeast of **Rakiraki**, the tranquil island of **Nananu-i-Ra** has fabulous diving and is a retreat popular with budget travellers. Further west and inland is Fiji's highest mountain, **Tomanivi**, which can be conquered on a pleasant but arduous half-day hike. Pressing on west again, and also inland, the raw **Ba hinterland** is home to **Navala**, Fiji's most spectacular traditional village.

Rakiraki and around

Fiji's northernmost settlement is the small market town of **RAKIRAKI**, also known as Vaileka. It evolved from a tiny village to a town of around 1500 following the expansion of the **Penang Sugar Mill**, originally built in 1880, and the place remains dominated by sugarcane farming to this day. Bar its small market, Rakiraki has little to entice tourists, but nearby is the pretty **Volivoli Point** and the beautiful offshore island of **Nananu-i-Ra**, both of which boast some lovely places to stay.

Volivoli

The placid hills of **Volivoli** mark the northern point of Viti Levu and look out on the offshore islands of Malake and Nananu-i-Ra. Taking advantage of this serene landscape are two small resorts, both with good scuba-diving operators. The beach at Volivoli Point is non-existent at high tide, but as the waters retreat, a **sand spit** emerges with space for sunbathing and bonfires.

ARRIVAL AND SERVICES   **RAKIRAKI AND AROUND**

By bus Sunbeam and Inter Cities (see p.108) provide the most luxurious services between Rakiraki and other towns on the Kings Rd, though there are plenty of more basic buses doing the rounds too.

Destinations Ba (1hr 45min); Lautoka (2hr 10min); Suva (3hr 40min); Tavua (55min).

Banks There are four banks with ATMs on Rakiraki Rd, south of the bus station.

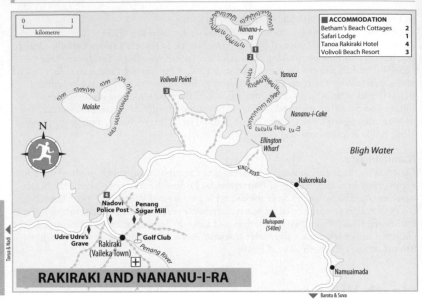

RAKIRAKI AND NANANU-I-RA

ACCOMMODATION AND EATING

RAKIRAKI

Tanoa Rakiraki Hotel Kings Rd, 3km from the town centre ☎ 669 4101, ⓦ tanoahotels.com. Heavily damaged by Cyclone Winston (see box, p.26), this surprisingly large hotel is currently undergoing repair in its main blocks and dorms; however the rooms that remain are highly appealing, and there's a pleasant swimming pool and good restaurant. Breakfast included. ☎ **F$185**

VOLIVOLI

★**Volivoli Beach Resort** Volivoli Rd ☎ 669 4511, ⓦ volivoli.com. It's hard to believe that this plush, family-friendly spot started life as a backpacker guesthouse. It's now a fully-fledged four-star resort, complete with swimming pool, and a selection of luxuriously appointed villas, all with jaw-dropping views out over the bay – some of the best vistas in Fiji, no less. Rates include half-board. ☎ **F565**

Nananu-i-Ra

Fifteen choppy minutes by boat from Ellington Wharf (see opposite) lies delightful **Nananu-i-Ra**, a hilly island surrounded by beautiful white sandy beaches. Cyclone Winston (see box, p.26) gave the island a real wallop, wiping out one of its few small budget resorts, and scuppering plans for larger developments. Things have recovered with admirable speed, though tourism had already been in decline since Nananu's heyday as a buzzing backpacker base in the 1990s; what remains is a hidden gem – a far-flung, under-visited spot for **diving**, **windsurfing** or simply hanging out.

Lomanisue Beach

Long, curving, palm-fringed and pretty much unspoiled **Lomanisue Beach** (also known locally as Back Beach or Three-Quarter Mile Beach) is a real beaut; it's home to the *Safari Lodge* (opposite) – guests arrive straight here on the transfer boat – and

---

WATERSPORTS IN RAKIRAKI AND NANUI-RA

Ra Divers at the *Volivoli Beach Resort* (see above) is a long-established operator offering open-water courses for F$850 and 2-tank dives for F$330, plus full-day game-fishing charters for F$1980.

The Safari Lodge on Nananu-i-Ra (see opposite) runs open-water courses (F$890), discover dives (F$180) and the like, as well as renting out kayaks and windsurfing equipment.

a short walk over a tiny crest from *Betham's* (see below). Swimming on this side of the island is good though it's constantly buffeted by winds, making it one of Fiji's best **windsurfing** spots.

Northern Nananu-i-Ra

From the north end of Lomanisue Beach, you can walk around the rocky headland at low tide to the secluded bay on the **north side** of the island – the centuries-old stone wall formations lining the shore here were built to catch fish on the outgoing tide. The bay can also be accessed via tracks, which lead up the lightly wooded hills; easiest to find and follow is the ridge-path heading back to *Betham's* on Front Beach.

ARRIVAL AND DEPARTURE   **NANANU-I-RA**

To Ellington Wharf Nananu-i-Ra is accessed from Ellington Wharf, 10km east of Rakiraki along the Kings Rd (15min); express buses will drop you at the wharf junction, as will local services from Rakiraki (F$2.80). It's a near-2km walk from said junction to the wharf, so if you have heavy luggage, your best bet is to hire a taxi from Rakiraki (F$15);

phone numbers are also left at the junction bus-stop by enterprising local taxi drivers.

To Nananu-i-Ra Both the resorts listed here offer pick-up boat transfers for F$50 return; you'll have to be at the wharf before 5pm, though, since they won't travel after dark.

ACCOMMODATION AND EATING

Both the places listed here can knock up meals, though they also have cooking facilities for guests, so most visitors self-cater. The nearest supermarket is in Rakiraki town, though a cute little shop by Ellington Wharf sells a modest array of provisions at fair prices.

Betham's Beach Cottages ☎ 669 4132, ⊕ bethams .com.fj. The pick of Nananu-i-Ra's mini-resorts has a handful of simply furnished beachfront cottages, a few private rooms and one room with dorm beds. They can whip up simple meals on request, and there's alcohol for sale. Dorms F$40, rooms F$116, cottages F$170
Safari Lodge ☎ 669 3333, ⊕ safarilodge.com.fj. In the

process of changing its name to *Kalo Kalo*, this beachfront option is a little rough around the edges (and the meals are largely to be avoided), but it's the best base for budget travellers wanting to dive, windsurf and chill. They are currently in the process of becoming self-sufficient, by growing their own veggies and installing solar panels. Dorms F$30, room F$100, bures F$315

The Nakauvadra Range

The journey west along the Kings Road from Rakiraki to Tavua passes through the vast cattle farmland of **Yaqara**. The scenery here resembles a mini Wild West, with cowboys rounding up the herds and the rugged mountain scenery of the legendary **Nakauvadra Range** in the background. Around 28km southwest of Rakiraki is the turn-off for the impeccably sterile bottling plant for **Fiji Water**, which since its inception in 1996 has become Fiji's most recognized global brand; water is sourced from a well fed from the Nakauvadra Range, said to be the home of Degei, the most powerful of Fijian gods (see box below).

DEGEI, GOD OF GODS

Near the summit of Uluda, the northern peak of the Nakauvadra Mountains, is a cave. It is no ordinary cave, for it is said that **Degei**, the most important god in Fijian folklore, resides here. To the early Fijians, Degei was the creator of the world, creator of men and god of anger and war. He took the form of a **snake** and, when he moved, the earth shook. Noise irritated him so the bats were chased away from the cave, birds were ordered to sleep away from the summit and the waves crashing onto the nearby reef were silenced. Throughout Fiji, and particularly on Viti Levu, the snake god ruled supreme and was offered the first bowl of *yaqona* as a matter of respect. In the hills of Viti Levu you may still see the first bowl of grog poured outside in his honour.

3

Navatu Hill

Seven kilometres west of Rakiraki, **Navatu Hill** is topped by the remains of an ancient **fort** boasting fabulous panoramic views. Accessible via a rough trail on the east side of the hill, the fort was used as a defence from the fearsome **Udre Udre**, a chief from Rakiraki who, as folklore recalls, ate nothing but human flesh. You can see Udre Udre's **grave** beside the Kings Road, 100m from the Nadovi Police Post – the 872 stones placed here supposedly represent the number of people he ate.

Tavua and around

The Kings Road passes straight through **TAVUA**, making it feel busier than it is – step off the main drag and you'll find that this Indian-dominated market centre makes a wonderful place in which to soak up the region's friendly rural atmosphere. The cramped **market** is at the eastern end of town; you can easily spend an idle hour here chatting to locals, without being pressured to buy a single thing.

Eight kilometres inland from Tavua, the Vatukoula **gold mine** is Fiji's largest, and a major source of employment. Further inland is the high plateau around **Nadarivatu**, base camp for exploring Fiji's highest peak, **Mount Tomanivi**. South of here you can traverse the **Nadrau Plateau** to visit the historically infamous village of **Nubutautau** (see box opposite).

Nadarivatu

The old colonial settlement of **NADARIVATU**, once the penal colony for Fiji, lies around 25km inland from Tavua and is one of the access points for climbing Mount Tomanivi (see opposite). It's a wonderfully cool and peaceful setting, located in a large depression surrounded by mountains and pine forests above the heat of the coast. The journey up here is quite spectacular, accessed 3km east of Tavua town via a dirt road. The trip can be done in fifty minutes but with wonderful views along the way, particularly on the steep ascent from pretty Waikubukubu village, it will probably take longer. Nadarivatu

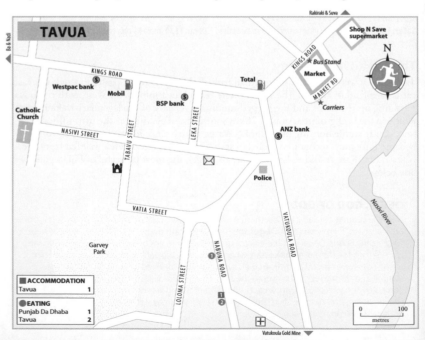

■ ACCOMMODATION	
Tavua	1

● EATING	
Punjab Da Dhaba	1
Tavua	2

translates as "the stone bowl", which refers to a small black stone found beside the road close to the health centre – legend tells of water sprouting from the stone in times of drought and its being the source of the mighty Sigatoka River.

Mount Tomanivi

Guides to summit F$30, plus F$25 admission fee which goes towards village projects • Buses and carriers from Tavua to Navai village (see p.128); drivers will need 4WD • Organized treks run by Talanoa Treks (see box, p.108)

At 1323m, **Mount Tomanivi** – also known as Mount Victoria – is the highest point in Fiji. At this high elevation, however, the mountain appears to be nothing more than a hill, although the two-hour hike to the top can certainly be strenuous. The **trail** starts from **Navai village**, 8km south of Nadarivatu (see opposite); enquire in the village about homestays. The walk is best attempted on a dry day, setting off from Navai around 8am – any later and the trail becomes swelteringly hot, any earlier and the summit is likely to be obscured by morning mist. The lower part of the trail is extremely muddy, passing plantations and crossing a couple of streams. About halfway up, it enters the government-leased **Tomanivi Nature Reserve**, where you'll probably see masked shining parrots, long-legged warblers and hear whistling doves. From here on up the route follows an exceptionally steep ridge over boulders and contorted tree roots – it's quite a scramble but thankfully the trail is hemmed in by thick forest. There are a couple of clearings along the way with glimpses of the surrounding countryside, and the panorama from the top is exceptional. On a clear day you'll see the stark contrast between the dry valleys in the distant north and the rugged tropical mountains draped in rainforests to the south.

The Nadrau Plateau and Nubutautau

Guide to Nubutautau around F$40 • Buses and carriers to Nagatagata from Tavua (see p.128)

It's possible to head deep into the Viti Levu interior on a **two-day trail** traversing the **Nadrau Plateau** and visiting the notorious village of **Nubutautau**. The trail starts from **Nagatagata** village, accessible on a 15km-long dirt track which branches off to the right just south of Nadarivatu. Walkers should aim to arrive at Nagatagata in the morning and ask for a **guide** for the three-hour trek to remote Nubutautau; it was here in 1867 that the Reverend Thomas Baker was killed and devoured by the villagers (see box below), and the steel axe used in the attack is still kept in the village.

REVEREND BAKER AND THE CURSE OF NUBUTAUTAU

In 1867, having spent eight years in Fiji and speaking the language fluently, the English clergyman the **Reverend Thomas Baker** was appointed Missionary of the Interior. His job was to persuade the fierce hill people of Viti Levu to convert (or *lotu*) to the Christian faith. The odds were stacked against Baker as the hill people, or *Colo*, were great enemies of Cakobau, King of Fiji (see box, p.149) who had already converted to Christianity, making them suspicious of the new religion.

By 20 July, Baker had reached the village of **Nubutautau**. Wishing to cross over to western Viti Levu, he presented a *tabua* to the chief, Nawawabalavu, requesting safe passage. However, Nawawabalavu had already received a *tabua* from the people of Naitasiri village, lower down the valley, requesting him to kill the missionary. The following morning, while leaving the village, Baker and his party of nine men were ambushed by Nawawabalavu's warriors, clubbed to death and then eaten – Baker's gnawed footwear can still be seen in Suva's Fiji Museum (see p.139). Another version of the story maintains that the attack was in revenge for Baker insulting the chief by removing a comb from his hair, although there is no evidence that this happened. News of the event reached the European stronghold of Levuka, and pressure was put on **Cakobau** to punish the murderers. Reluctantly, eight months after Baker's death, Cakobau led his forces towards Nubutautau but was ambushed, losing almost a hundred men including several influential chiefs.

The people of Nubutautau eventually succumbed to Christianity but for many years it was believed their land was **cursed** as drought consumed the hills. It wasn't until November 2003 that reconciliation was complete, with the invitation of Reverend Baker's relatives to a formal *soro*, or forgiveness ceremony, conducted by the then Prime Minister, Laisania Qarase.

If you wish to continue along the trail, you should present a *sevusevu* in order to stay the night in Nubutautau. With a guide from the village, you can head along the difficult but scenic six-hour walk to the highland village of **Korolevu** (not to be confused with Korolevu on the Coral Coast), crossing the **Sigatoka River** several times along the way – this is really only practical in settled weather during the dry winter months (May–Oct). Once at Korolevu, you can catch the daily early-morning carrier van for the 75km journey down to Sigatoka on the south coast (see p.110).

ARRIVAL AND SERVICES
TAVUA AND AROUND

By bus Bus services connect Tavua with Ba and Lautoka to the west, and points east all the way to Suva; they stop around the market.
Destinations Ba (45min); Lautoka (1hr 20min); Rakiraki (1hr); Suva (4hr 40min).
Banks ANZ and Westpac have banks, with 24hr ATMs, in the centre of town.

GETTING AROUND

By bus and carrier Buses and carriers serve the inland villages. Nadan (☏668 0150) runs buses to Nagatagata (Mon–Sat at 3.30pm; F$7.50) and Navai (Mon–Sat at 3pm; F$6), both via Nadarivatu (F$3.50). Carriers run these routes from behind Tavua market more regularly (ask around for approximate departure times), though all services are at the mercy of the weather and tend not to depart on Sundays; you can rent an entire carrier to Nadarivatu for around F$50, though you'll pay a fair bit more to go any further.

ACCOMMODATION

TAVUA

★**Tavua** Nabua Rd ☏668 0522. What really gives Tavua an edge over its neighbours is this charmingly whitewashed colonial-style hotel, a 5min stroll uphill from town, and also known as the *Gold Town Hotel*. Its airy en-suite rooms come with a/c, ceiling fans and TVs, and there's also an on-site swimming pool, a bar and a good restaurant (see below). F$140
Vatia Beach Eco Lodge Vatia Beach ☏625 4737, ⓦvatiabeach.com; map pp.106–107. Set on a deserted beach some way west of Tavua, this excellent budget base is pleasingly rough around the edges. Accommodation is in simple, fan-free huts or dorm beds in the main block; decent meals are available for just F$13, and breakfast is included for non-dorm guests. They also rent out kayaks and snorkelling equipment. It's F$20 from Tavua (or Ba) by taxi, or a 3km hike from the Kings Rd junction. ⓦ($) Dorms F$40, bungalow F$60

NADARIVATU

★**Stone Bowl Lodge** ☏877 8497; map pp.106–107. Similar to the *Tavua* hotel (see above), this is a real period piece, having been a mountain retreat for expat workers in the 1920s. At an altitude of almost 1000m, its wood-panelled rooms are a real bargain, and the wood fires help to keep out the chills. Tours around the plateau are on offer, and full board (highly recommended) is available for F$30 per day. Cottages F$50

EATING

★**Punjab Da Dhaba** Nabua Rd, Tavua; no phone. If Fiji's curries have left you disappointed with their narrow range of options, this shack will come as a godsend. While it's barely big enough to accommodate the couple who run it, they do an astonishing job whipping up delicious butter chicken, *rogan josh*, *paneer tikka masala* and more, all for F$7 or less. These and the roti are all freshly made to order – you'll have to wait 30min or so, but you can wait in the adjacent park, whose benches also make a fine place to dine (there being no tables at the restaurant). A real find. Daily 8am–8pm.
Tavua Nabua Rd, Tavua ☏668 0522. The hotel restaurant is far and away the most elegant place to eat in town. The menu is surprisingly broad (mains F$15–24); try a fish *lolo*, chilli chicken rice, or the hearty but decidedly unhealthy "Tavua chicken", rather like a chicken Kiev. Daily 7am–9pm.

Ba

Separated from the ocean by a huge mangrove estuary, **BA** is an easy place to like – and not just because of its terse, rather comical name. The fifth largest town in Fiji, with a population of around 15,000 (mostly Indo–Fijians), its scruffy atmosphere and lack of

PATHWAYS OF THE SPIRITS

Viti Levu, particularly the grasslands between Rakiraki and Ba, is crisscrossed with **ancient pathways** known as *tualeita*. Dating back centuries before European contact, most of the paths run along the highest ridges allowing walkers to spot enemy war parties and to avoid being followed. The paths played an important role in the Fijian colonization of Viti Levu, linking pioneer settlements to the main chiefly villages. Before the widespread conversion to Christianity, *tualeita* also held a religious importance. It was believed that the spirits of the dead followed the trails on their journey back to their origins, and thence on to the afterlife. Most walking tracks today follow *tualeita*.

formal attractions mean that it's rarely visited by package tours – adventurous, independent travellers, however, will enjoy this relaxed, unhurried place, with a hugely appealing **market**. Many of Ba's residents are Muslim, and the town **mosque** is a major landmark; the only other significant building is the large sugar mill south of the centre. There is one quirky sight on the way out of town – a giant football sitting by the river, a reference to the fact that the local team are national champions more often than not.

Ba market

Off Rarawai Road, near the bus stand • Mon–Sat 6am–5pm; grog section stays open til 9pm

Ba's only real attraction is the town **market**, one of Fiji's largest and best – it's not much smaller than the more vaunted one in Suva, and with less of the dodgy undercurrent. Browsing its stalls is almost entirely hassle-free; should any stall-owner engage you in conversation, they'll most likely be simply wanting a chat. Another plus-point over Suva's market is the **grog section**, busy most of the day with friendly locals knocking back *kava* in a refreshingly natural, non-ceremonial manner – no hand-claps to imitate, no preceding fire-dance, just Fijians being Fijian. It's a lovely place.

ARRIVAL AND SERVICES   BA

By bus A local bus service runs between Nadi and Ba several times daily (F$3), while the plusher Sunbeam Transport and Inter Cities services pass through Ba on their north-coast route between Lautoka and Suva.

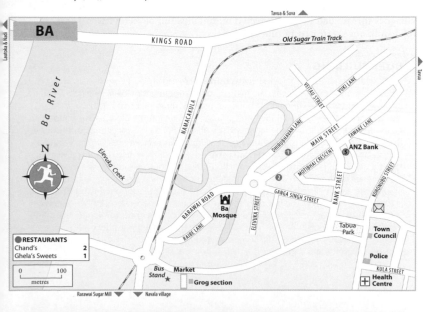

Destinations Lautoka (45min); Nadi (1hr 20min); Navala (1hr 30min); Rakiraki (1hr 45min); Suva (6hr 10min); Tavua (45min).

Banks ANZ bank (Mon–Fri 9.30am–4pm), on Bank St, has an ATM.

ACCOMMODATION AND EATING

Ba's only official accommodation, a single grimy hotel, has been mothballed ever since its owner landed up in jail on embezzlement charges. If you really want to stay in town, get chatting to people at the market, and you'll most likely be able to wangle an ad-hoc homestay in no time.

Chand's Main St. The locals' favourite restaurant, located one floor up with views down onto the street; tasty South Indian curries go from F$15 (or F$12 for the excellent vegetarian thali), and they also serve Chinese-style food. Daily 10am–9pm.

Ghela's Sweets Main St. The best place in town for Indian sweets and snacks. You'll pay next to nothing for a belly full of Delhi; $3 buys a few samosas and bhajis, a couple of luminous milk sweets, and a mug of *masala* tea. Daily 7.30am–7pm.

3

Navala

Village fee F$25

The hinterland south of Ba town provides a scenic, mountainous route between Nadi and North Viti Levu. The most interesting feature on this road is the remote village of **NAVALA**, home to almost two hundred traditionally thatched bures, and an iconic symbol of Fiji. Back in 1950, the community decided to reject modern building materials and to encourage all school leavers to learn the art of traditional bure making (see box below). The result, sixty years on, is the last remaining **thatch village** in Fiji. The only cement structures are the church, school, and a few generator huts.

To visit the village, introduce yourself to the first person you come across on the roadside – they will take you to the village headman where you pay the village entry fee, which represents a *sevusevu* and goes towards upkeep of the housing. Strolling around is a delightful experience; the chiefly bures have elaborately designed rooftops and are set in a neat line facing the village green, while commoners reside in the more disorganized clusters of bures on the lower slopes of the Ba River. The village is surrounded by grass-covered mountains, full of secret caves where townsfolk once retreated in times of war.

BURE BUILDING

Traditional Fijian homes – known here as **bures** – are usually built communally by members of the same *mataqali*. The main wooden structure is made from a hardwood tree, often *vesi*. Bure shapes vary slightly between regions: most are broadly rectangular, although in Lau they have rounded ends similar to those found in Tonga. The wooden posts are joined together with *magimagi* (see box, p.183), a fibrous coconut string, rather than nails or bolts. There is no central post, ensuring a large open-plan living area and a high ceiling for ventilation. The walls are usually made from bamboo, sliced and woven together. A raised platform makes up the floor, and this is laid with straw as a cushion and woven mats for decoration. The roof is thatched using a reed called *sina* and lasts for around five years before being replaced. Across the top of the roof, or piercing either side, is a black post known as the *balabala*; this fern tree trunk is decorated with white cowrie shells to indicate various forms of chiefly status. Roofs of lesser huts or kitchens are made from the leaf of the coconut tree, and will last from three to ten years depending on the quality of weaving. Bures are usually laid out around a central *rara*, or village green, used for ceremonial events and – these days – daily rugby practice.

ARRIVAL AND DEPARTURE

NAVALA

By bus The only way to reach Navala by public transport is from Ba town, though it's not very practical for a day-trip. Buses (Mon–Sat; F$4.25; 1hr 30min) leave from the bus stand at 12.30pm, 4.30pm & 5.15pm, although the last of these reaches Navala after dark, and you won't be able to return the same day. Buses from Navala back to Ba leave at 6am, 7.30am & 1.45pm.

By taxi or day-tour Taxis from Ba quote around F$70 including waiting time, or you can visit on a day-tour from Nadi (see p.50).

ACCOMMODATION

Bulou's Eco Lodge ☎ 628 1224, ✉ sipirianotui@gmail.com; map pp.106–107. Perched on the banks of the Ba River a 5min walk south of the village, the ten-bed dorm lodge forms part of Bulou's house and is a bit cramped, but you're likely have it to yourself (bring a small *sevusevu*). The two en-suite bures are set down a small trail on a hillside clearing overlooking the river. The lodge can arrange treks, horse-rides, raft-building and guided walks in the hills, which are likely to be a highlight of your visit. Rates include bountiful Fijian meals. Dorms **F$80**, bures **F$180**

3

Suva and around

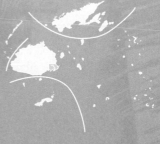

SAILING BOATS, SUVA HARBOUR

Suva and around

Sitting on a 5km-long peninsula in the southeast corner of Viti Levu, Suva is a somewhat neglected capital city. Fiji's seat of government, this lively city remains rather off the tourist radar, bar the occasional squad of camera-toting cruise ship passengers. However, despite the often humid and rainy climate, Suva has a lot going for it. Visually it's one of the most attractive of all the South Pacific ports, with pretty colonial buildings in the centre and moody weather rolling in off the ocean, covering the surrounding rugged peaks in thundery clouds. The culinary scene is good and the nightlife lively – plus, with a population of around 90,000 and double that again in the wider urban sprawl, it's large enough to sustain cinemas, shopping malls and other things you may have forgotten about on your way around Fiji.

Apart from the quaint **museum** and stately buildings, there are few standout attractions in central Suva. However, spend some time here and you'll discover a vibrant **cosmopolitan** city with strong community bases from all corners of the Fijian archipelago and across the entire South Pacific. Organizations from throughout the region have their headquarters here and the University of the South Pacific attracts students from all over the world.

Inland, the lush tropical rainforest of Naitasiri quickly takes hold – the peaceful **Colo-i-Suva Forest Park** is only twenty minutes' drive from downtown. Suva's poorer neighbourhoods sprawl north along the Kings Road in an almost constant parade of busy satellite towns to Nausori, an industrial and farming centre home to Suva's domestic airport along the banks of the imposing **Rewa River**. The river and its surrounding mangrove estuaries have long been Fiji's tribal power-base, with both the Burebasaga Confederacy of Rewa and the Kubuna Confederacy of **Bau** based in the region.

Brief history

The name **Suva** means "little hill", and refers to a mound in Thurston Gardens (p.139) where the temple of Ro Vonu once stood, in what was then a small village. In the 1840s, said village became embroiled in a dispute that was to have far-reaching consequences for the whole of Fiji.

The 1841 massacre

Qaraniqio, a fearsome chief from Rewa, visited Suva in 1841 and stole a pig. Qaraniqio and his warriors were caught in the act, and one of his men was killed. In retaliation the Rewans attacked the village, killing over three hundred men, women and children; the bodies were carried by canoe to Rewa for a celebratory feast. On hearing of the massacre, **Cakobau**, chief of **Bau**, demanded retribution – Suva came under his protection, since the chief of Suva village had married a woman from Bau twenty years earlier. His revenge attack on Rewa eventually sparked the eleven-year **war** that decided the fate of the islands (see p.149).

Indian firewalking p.141
Safety in Suva p.143
Dining on the cheap at Suva's food
  courts p.144

The rise of Bau Island and King
Cakobau p.149

TOBERUA ISLAND

Highlights

❶ Grand Pacific Hotel Now restored to something approaching its original splendour, this grand old dame is a great place to stay if you can afford it – if it's beyond your budget, just pop in for a coffee or cocktail. **See p.139**

❷ Fiji Museum Come face to face with Fiji's cannibal past, including the half-chewed shoe of the Rev Thomas Baker. **See p.139**

❸ Firewalking at Mariamma Temple Experience this engrossing and hugely passionate Hindu firewalking ceremony, held in August. **See p.141**

❹ Global cuisine If you've been circling Viti Levu, Suva's array of international restaurants may come as a pleasant change – take your pick from Japanese, Korean, Western brunches and a great array of Chinese and Indian dishes. **See p.144**

❺ Suva nightlife Take a bar-crawl along Victoria Parade to sample the best nightlife in the South Pacific. **See p.146**

❻ Toberua Island This warm and welcoming island resort is an ideal spot for diving, snorkelling, birdwatching and pure relaxation. **See p.149**

HIGHLIGHTS ARE MARKED ON THE MAPS ON P.136, P.138 & P.140

Australia moves in

Having achieved victory and crowned himself King of Fiji, Cakobau faced even greater problems. On July 4, 1849, at Nukulau Island off Suva, the house of US commercial agent **John Williams** (see p.222) accidentally caught fire during Independence Day celebrations. Following Fijian custom, the locals looted everything inside. The US government held Cakobau accountable and demanded US$42,000 in compensation. In 1868, when the first instalment was due, the Australian-owned **Polynesian Company** offered to pay off the debt in exchange for 200,000 acres of land around Suva Point. Under threat of US naval attack, Cakobau had little choice but to accept; by 1870, 170 Australians had arrived to farm cotton in the area, but they soon discovered that the soil was too thin and the climate too humid, and sugar was planted instead. Fiji's first **sugar mill** was built to process the crop, although this too failed to profit.

Suva becomes the capital

After Fiji was ceded to Britain in 1874, officials began to survey the islands in order to build a **new capital**. The Polynesian Company promised ample freehold land should they choose Suva; this, together with Suva's deep-water harbour, led the British to favour it over its nearest rival, Nadi. By 1882, the move from the old capital of Levuka was completed. The dense jungle tumbling from the hills was cleared, the swamps were filled in, and **Victoria Parade** – named after the monarch of the time – became the heart of the new town.

SUVA AND AROUND

0   5
kilometres

N

Viwa

Naqali

Kasavu

Bau
Bau Landing

Rewa River

Verata

Toberua
Kaba Point

Sawani

Nausori

Buretu

Wailoku Waterfall

Colo-i-Suva

COLO-I-SUVA FOREST PARK

Nausori Airport

Nakelo Landing

Nine Miles

Wainibokasi Landing

Caubati

Kalabo

Burebasaga

Lami Town

Suva Harbour

SUVA

Laucola Bay

Laucola

SEE "SUVA SUBURBS" MAP FOR DETAILS

Nukulau

Makuluva

SOUTH PACIFIC OCEAN

■ **ACCOMMODATION**	
Colo-i-Suva Eco Lodge	2
Toberua Island Resort	1

HIGHLIGHTS

4 Global cuisine

6 Toberua Island

Twentieth-century and present-day Suva

In its early days as capital, Suva was little more than a backwater trading port but gradually it grew, securing wealth and new impressive **colonial-style buildings**. In 1914, gracious living finally arrived with the completion of the *Grand Pacific Hotel*, which boasted vintage champagne, haute cuisine and a manager from London's *Savoy*. Not quite as swish were the merchant quarters around **Cumming Street**, fronted by *kava* saloons and brothels. Many devout citizens called for the street to be cleansed of its evil, and just that happened in February 1923 when a rampant **fire** spread through the area.

By 1952, Suva covered an area of fifteen square kilometres and was proclaimed Fiji's first official city. A year later, a tsunami caused by an offshore earthquake smashed into the shoreline, killing eight people and causing damage to the city centre. In 1987 and again in 2000, Suva hit the world headlines after political **coups** threw the city into chaos with widespread looting. The 2006 coup was less fiery, with the army quickly assuming control of the streets.

City centre

Lively **central Suva** is where the best of the city's eating, shopping and strolling opportunities are focused. The northernmost sight of note is the large **Municipal Market** (see below), southeast of which a cluster of Chinese and Indian **merchant shops** can be found around **Mark Street** and **Cumming Street**; crammed with an array of astoundingly colourful clothing, these are great places to poke around in. Beyond the Nubukalou Creek is **The Triangle**, one of two tiny, three-sided parks popular with locals for relaxing; south of here, **Victoria Parade** is the administrative centre of Fiji, with modern malls and high-rise office towers interspersed with some wonderful old buildings. The first you'll come to is the **Old Town Hall**, with its cast-iron-columned veranda, and a couple of restaurants (see p.144), while a few hundred metres to the south, the solemn-looking **Old Parliament** – built in 1939 – faces pretty **Albert Park**. Press on a little further, and you'll find Thurston Gardens, home to the charming **Fiji Museum**.

The Municipal Market

South end of Rodwell Rd • Mon–Sat 6am–6pm • Free

The colourful **Municipal Market** (see p.147) is the largest in Fiji, with a huge variety of fruit and vegetables for sale. Upstairs are the *yaqona* and spice stalls; although *kava* drinking has been banned by the City Council, ask around and someone will soon slip you some grog under the table. On Friday and Saturday mornings, Fijians come from miles around to visit the market, which spills out into the streets among the barbecue sellers and shoe-shine boys. Keep an eye out for pickpockets at these times.

The Triangle

Junction of Scott St and Renwick Rd

A good starting-point for a trip around Suva is **The Triangle**, a tiny park where locals meet to gossip under an impressive *ivi* tree. Fijian history buffs will notice three of the four inscriptions on the concrete historical marker here are incorrect: Cross and Cargill, the first missionaries to land in Fiji, arrived on October 12 (not October 14) 1835; the government approved the move from Levuka to Suva in 1877 (not 1882); and the Public Land Sales of 1880 were not proclaimed under the current *ivi* tree, but one further down the street towards the Morris Hedstrom store.

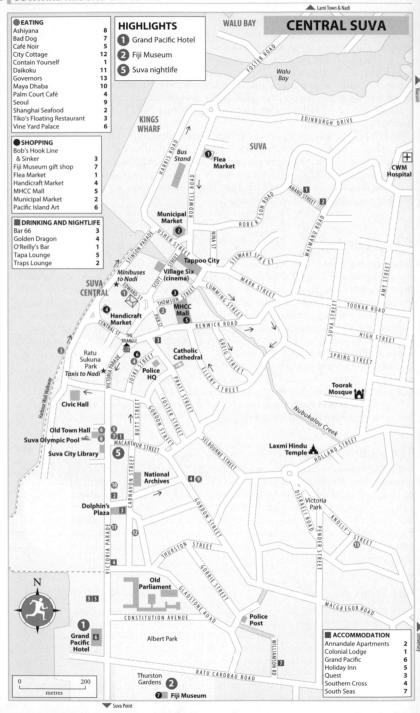

Lami Town & Nadi

CENTRAL SUVA

WALU BAY

EATING

Ashiyana	8
Bad Dog	7
Café Noir	5
City Cottage	12
Contain Yourself	1
Daikoku	11
Governors	13
Maya Dhaba	10
Palm Court Café	4
Seoul	9
Shanghai Seafood	2
Tiko's Floating Restaurant	3
Vine Yard Palace	6

HIGHLIGHTS

1 Grand Pacific Hotel

2 Fiji Museum

5 Suva nightlife

SHOPPING

Bob's Hook Line & Sinker	3
Fiji Museum gift shop	7
Flea Market	1
Handicraft Market	4
MHCC Mall	5
Municipal Market	2
Pacific Island Art	6

DRINKING AND NIGHTLIFE

Bar 66	3
Golden Dragon	4
O'Reilly's Bar	1
Tapa Lounge	5
Traps Lounge	2

ACCOMMODATION

Annandale Apartments	2
Colonial Lodge	1
Grand Pacific	6
Holiday Inn	5
Quest	3
Southern Cross	4
South Seas	7

FOSTER ROAD

Walu Bay

EDINBURGH DRIVE

Nasori

KINGS WHARF

SUVA

Bus Stand

HARRIS ROAD

RODWELL ROAD

Flea Market

CWM Hospital

ANAND STREET

WAIMANU ROAD

ROBERTSON ROAD

Municipal Market

USHER STREET

NINA ST

STEWART STREET

MARK STREET

SCOTT STREET

STINSON PARADE

Tappoo City

Minibuses to Nadi

Village Six (cinema)

THOMSON STREET

CUMMING STREET

SUVA STREET

TOORAK ROAD

AMY STREET

SUVA CENTRAL

EDWARD ST

PIER ST

MHCC Mall

RENWICK ROAD

HIGH STREET

Handicraft Market

CENTRAL ST

Catholic Cathedral

GREIG STREET

SPRING STREET

Ratu Sukuna Park

THE TRIANGLE

JOSKE STREET

ELLERY STREET

Toorak Mosque

Taxis to Nadi

VICTORIA PARADE

Police HQ

PRATT STREET

Harbour Wall Walkway

Civic Hall

BUTT STREET

GORDON STREET

FOSTER STREET

SELBOURNE STREET

Nubukalou Creek

Old Town Hall

Suva Olympic Pool

MACARTHUR STREET

Suva City Library

Laxmi Hindu Temple

HOLLAND STREET

CARNAVON STREET

National Archives

Dolphin's Plaza

GORDON STREET

Victoria Park

DISRAELI ROAD

KNOLLY'S STREET

PENDER STREET

THURSTON STREET

GORRIE STREET

N

Old Parliament

GLADSTONE ROAD

MACGREGOR ROAD

CONSTITUTION AVENUE

Police Post

WILLIAMSON RD

Grand Pacific Hotel

Albert Park

RATU CAKOBAU ROAD

0	200

metres

Thurston Gardens

Fiji Museum

Suva Point

Sacred Heart Cathedral

Pratt St • Open access; services Mon–Fri 6.30pm, Sat 1pm, Sun 7am, 8.30am, 10am, 5pm & 7pm • Free

The imposing **Sacred Heart Cathedral** is Fiji's only cathedral, and one of just eighteen in the entire South Pacific. Construction of the twin-towered building began in 1895, with stone shipped in from the Hunter Valley in Australia, and the timber flooring sourced from Quebec in Canada. The first Mass was held in 1902, but the cathedral wasn't fully completed until 1935 – 22 years after the death of its instigator, Bishop Julian Vidal of Australia.

Albert Park

Off Victoria Parade • Daily 24hr • Free

A fine, colonial-looking stretch of lawn, **Albert Park** was host to a little bit of history in 1928, when Charles Kingsford Smith and his crew touched down here after the second leg of the first-ever successful flight across the Pacific. Today, the park is used as a sports ground – albeit a rather muddy one after the heavy rains – and there's usually a rugby game or cricket match going on here. The park also hosts provincial *soli*, or fundraising events, with handicraft stalls and meke performances, and in the August school holidays it becomes the main venue for the Hibiscus Festival (see p.34).

Grand Pacific Hotel

Victoria Parade • ☎ 322 2000, ⓦ grandpacifichotel.com.fj

Overlooking the park on Victoria Parade is the **Grand Pacific Hotel** (see p.143), recently revamped to its former glory after a period of dereliction. It was built in 1914 to service the luxury cruise ships which provided the main means of long-haul travel in those days. Famous guests included Queen Elizabeth II, Somerset Maugham and James A. Michener, the latter thus describing the hotel in *The World Is My Home*: "The barefoot Indians who served the meals had a grace that few hotels in the world could offer and none surpass." The hotel closed in 1992, and spent two decades rotting forlornly; thankfully, it was spared the bulldozer, and after major refurbishment it reopened with great pomp in 2014.

The Fiji Museum

Thurston Gardens, accessible from Ratu Cakobau Rd • Mon–Thurs & Sat 9.30am–4.30pm, Fri 9.30am–4pm • F$10 • ☎ 331 5944, ⓦ www
.fijimuseum.org.fj

Suva's most rewarding attraction, the neatly laid-out **Fiji Museum**, is set within **Thurston Gardens**, Suva's spacious and elegant botanical gardens. If you have even a slight interest in Fiji's history or want to see some wicked war clubs and **cannibal forks**, or the largest surviving piece of the **HMS Bounty**, then it's worth the trip to Suva.

Lower level

The first hall you'll come to displays a double-hulled **war canoe**, some impressive 12m-long oars, a piece of eight from the *Eliza* shipwreck (see p.220), and lots of intriguing everyday items such as tattooing tools and wigs. Beyond the excellent gift shop (see p.146), the adjoining gallery maps out the arrival of the first Europeans and includes part of the **HMS Bounty**'s rudder. It also features a small exhibition on the Reverend Thomas Baker, eaten by cannibals in 1864 (see box, p.127): don't miss the gnawed remnants of his shoes.

Upper level

Upstairs, the **Indo-Fijian Gallery** recounts the history of Indian indentured labourers brought to Fiji between 1879 and 1916: on display is the figurehead of the *Syria*, a ship which sank off Viti Levu in 1884, killing 59 from the subcontinent. Elsewhere on this upper level are some beautiful *masi* (weavings made from tree bark), and a curious hall extolling the virtues of "Heavenly Culture, World Peace, Restoration of Light", a shadowy Korean religious sect

– quite blatantly paid for by said Christian group, it purports to chart the global spread of peace from a peninsula which, in reality, is still technically at war with itself.

The suburbs

Suva's **suburbs** are mostly residential areas, but there are several sights worth exploring in this wide area. **Government House** and **Parliament House** lie just to the south of the Fiji Museum, and you can stroll between the two on the paved **Nasele Walkway**, which hugs the stone seawall all the way to Suva Point and provides suitably romantic spots for courting couples. Heading around the point brings you to the eastern side of the peninsula, and after a short while you'll see the **National Stadium**, with a capacity of close to twenty thousand; just inland from the arena is the Fiji campus of the **University of the South Pacific** (USP), established in 1968. Cutting further inland will bring you to Rewa Street, home to two intriguing places of worship – a church for the city's **Rotuman** community, and the **Mariamma Hindu Temple**, occasional host to spellbinding firewalking ceremonies (see box opposite).

Government House

Off Victoria Parade

Built in 1928, **Government House** is the private residence of the President of Fiji, its entrance guarded by the much-photographed, long-suffering presidential guards, each

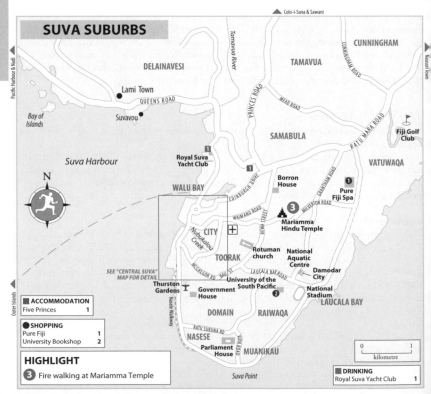

SUVA SUBURBS

ACCOMMODATION
Five Princes — 1

SHOPPING
Pure Fiji — 1
University Bookshop — 2

HIGHLIGHT
③ Fire walking at Mariamma Temple

DRINKING
Royal Suva Yacht Club — 1

sporting a red tunic and white serrated *sulu*. Nearby is the upmarket residential area of **The Domain**, sitting prettily on a hill with large houses hidden behind security fences and thick tropical landscaping.

Parliament House

Battery Rd · ☎ 330 5811, ⓦ parliament.gov.fj · Free tours bookable online

Suva's **Parliament House** was designed to resemble a Fijian bure, though one made of steel and topped with a bright orange roof; more traditional elements include the *masi* bark-cloths (see box, p.157) found draping much of the place. The building was commissioned by Sitiveni Rabuka (who instigated the 1987 coup), and it was duly completed in 1992, before becoming the venue for another coup – it was here that George Speight seized control of the government in 2000. The building lay idle after parliament was dissolved after a further coup in 2006, but is now fully functioning once more; to look around, phone or email in advance, or ask the guard on the gate. It's particularly interesting to visit when parliament is in session; you'll find a calendar of relevant dates on the website above.

University of the South Pacific

Laucala Bay Rd · ☎ 323 1000, ⓦ usp.ac.fj

While not terribly interesting as a tourist sight, the **University of the South Pacific**, or **USP**, as it's universally referred to, is of great importance to the wider South Pacific region. Jointly owned by the governments of twelve Pacific nations, it's become a melting pot of bright minds from Samoa, Kiribati, Tuvalu, Tonga and the like – as well as East Asia and the West. It's a good place for a stroll, and if you've some spare time, look into one of the **cultural exhibitions** or the university **bookshop** (see p.147).

Mariamma Hindu Temple

Howell Rd, off Rewa St · Daily 6am–7pm · Prayers daily at 7am

Though considerably less showy than its counterpart in Nadi (see p.53), the **Mariamma Hindu Temple** is by far the most attractive in Suva. A little out of the way, it attracts precious few visitors outside morning prayer time, so you may well be able to admire the colourful decorations in perfect solitude.

ARRIVAL AND DEPARTURE   **SUVA**

The most pleasant way to arrive in Suva is **by boat**, cruising into the deep-water harbour surrounded by majestic mountains. The majority of visitors, though, arrive at and depart from the grimy **bus stand** in central Suva; from here, public buses travel from and to Lautoka, either along the north coast (Kings Rd) or south coast (Queens Rd), stopping at all towns en route. Nausori Airport is the departure point for all **flights**.

INDIAN FIREWALKING

Between April and September every year, Dravidian Hindus around Fiji seek favourable omens from the gods during the replanting of crops. To test their faith and devotion, many take part in one of the eighty or so Indian **firewalking ceremonies** that occur throughout rural Fiji. The build-up to any ceremony is a two-week-long process of denial and self-discipline to attain purification, culminating in a night of passionate dedication when the fire pit is lit. Before crossing the pit, the yellow-clad participants undergo body piercings, notably through the tongue and cheeks, bathe in either a river or the ocean and are finally physically whipped into a frenzy before strutting across the hot embers – not surprisingly a few participants end up in hospital. The most accessible of the ceremonies is held in July or August at the **Mariamma Hindu Temple** (see above).

BY PLANE

Nausori Airport 20km north of Suva, Nausori International Airport has few facilities (bar an exchange booth), no information counter and no lockers, although the *Air Café* (daily 5am–6.30pm) sells decent coffee. As well as domestic flights with Fiji Link and Northern Air, it handles a few international services.

Getting into town The taxi journey from Nausori Airport to Suva takes 30min–1hr (F$30). To travel by local bus, you need to head to the main road and catch a service into Nausori town (every 30min 6am–6pm; F$1), and then catch a Suva-bound bus from there (every 15min 6am–6pm; F$1.80). Note that traffic can be bad along the Suva–Nausori road and the journey may take an hour at peak times.

Destinations Cicia (1 weekly; 1hr); Gau (1 weekly; 30min); Kadavu (1 weekly; 40min); Labasa (3–4 daily; 40min); Lakeba (2 weekly; 1hr 15min); Levuka (6 weekly; 15min); Matei, Taveuni (1–2 daily; 1hr 5min); Moala (1 weekly; 40min); Nadi (3–6 daily; 30min); Savusavu (5 weekly; 1hr); Vanua Balavu (1 weekly; 1hr 10min).

BY BUS

Buses into Suva arrive at and depart from the hectic bus stand beside the Municipal Market.

Express buses Express bus services run roughly every hour or so to and from Nadi (along the Queens Rd) and Lautoka (along the Kings Rd): they are operated by Sunbeam, Inter Cities and Pacific (see p.108), as well as a host of smaller operators. Alternatively, a comfortable tourist coach operated by Coral Sun leaves Suva's *Holiday Inn* (see opposite) daily at 7am, returning from Nadi Airport at 1pm (F$20; 4hr).

Destinations Ba (6hr 10min); Korovou (1hr 10min); Lautoka (6hr); Nadi (4hr, via the Queens Rd); Navua (50min); Pacific Harbour (1hr 20min); Rakiraki (3hr 40min); Sigatoka (4hr); Tavua (4hr 40min).

BY MINIVAN AND SHARE-TAXI

Minivans heading to Nadi (F$17) congregate near the Post

Office on Edward St; those heading north collect behind the New World supermarket opposite the bus stand. Share-taxis to Nadi depart from the eastern flank of Ratu Sukuna Park (F$25 per passenger, or F$100 for whole vehicle).

BY CAR

There are two main roads into Suva. From Nadi, the southern Queens Rd enters the city via Lami Town, passing industrial Walu Bay, turning right at the roundabout and past the bus stand into the city centre. From Nausori, the Kings Rd heads through the congested suburbs of Nine Miles, Nabua and Samabula before descending down Edinburgh Drive to the same roundabout at Walu Bay (keep left for the city centre).

BY BOAT

All cargo boats (see box, p.179) dock at Walu Bay, west of the city centre, and serve the outer islands of Lau, Lomaiviti and Rotuma on an irregular monthly timetable – contact Fiji Shipping Corporation (☎331 9383) for the latest schedule. The more central Kings Wharf, overlooking the Municipal Market, welcomes cruise liners and container ships. Connecting buses from Suva bus stand to Natovi Landing (see p.122), some 90min north of Suva, link with Interlink and Patterson Brothers ferries to Ovalau, Savusavu, Taveuni and south to Kadavu; the journey times below for these destinations include bus connections.

Ferry operators Goundar Shipping (☎330 1035, ⓦ goundarshipping.com), Interlink Shipping (☎999 2026, ⓦ interlinkshipping.com.fj), Lehona Shipping (☎354 3833 or ☎893 9203, ⓔ ben_cavu@yahoo.com.au), Patterson Brothers (☎331 5644, ⓦ fijisearoad.com) and Victoria Marine (☎330 0711, ⓔ victoriamarinelimited@gmail.com).

Destinations Kadavu (1 weekly; 8–12hr); Koro (2 weekly; 8hr); Northern Lau Group and Lakeba (1 weekly; 1–5 days); Ovalau (2 weekly; 6hr); Rotuma (1 monthly; 2 days); Savusavu (2 weekly; 12hr); Southern Lau Group (1 monthly; 2–6 days); Taveuni (2 weekly; 16hr).

GETTING AROUND

On foot With a compact city centre and few attractions beyond, walking is the best way to get around Suva by day (see box opposite, for information on safety after dark). Thankfully, most streets have canopies to keep out the rain, although the condition of the pavements is not wheelchair- or pram-friendly.

By bus Local buses are exceptionally cheap – most inner city fares cost just F$1 – and meander around Suva to all satellite towns on a frequent schedule between 6am and 6pm, with a more limited service running until 10pm.

By taxi Taxis are the only safe way to get around at night (see box opposite). Luckily, they are cheap and ubiquitous, with half a dozen taxi stands in the city centre alone: Carnarvon Taxis (☎331 5315) in Carnarvon St behind Dolphin Plaza, Black

Arrow Taxis (☎330 0139) in Central St opposite Westpac Bank, and Usher Taxis (☎331 2977) in Usher St beside the market are the most convenient. Fares are calculated by a fixed-rate meter with a flagfall of F$1.50 (F$2 from 10pm–6am; F$5 from the airport) plus ten cents for every 100m travelled. A journey across the city shouldn't cost more than F$5.

By car Central Rental, 293 Victoria Parade (☎331 1866, ⓦ www.central.com.fj), and Budget, 123 Foster Rd, Walu Bay (☎338 1555, ⓦ www.budget.com.fj), have rental depots in the city and at Nausori Airport. Metered parking spaces are available along most streets (20¢ for 15min), or there's longer-stay parking (F$1 per hour) along the vacant foreshore behind Civic Hall, accessible from either Stinson Parade or Victoria Parade beside Civic Tower.

SAFETY IN SUVA

Although Suva centre is safe during the day, you should exercise caution **after dark**, when taxis are recommended to get around, even if you're only going a few hundred metres down the street. Female travellers should avoid going out unaccompanied after dark.

ACCOMMODATION

As you'd expect, the capital has a decent variety of **accommodation**, although it's the one place in Fiji you won't find palm-fringed resorts, due to the lack of nearby beaches. The only time it's difficult to find a room is at Christmas or during the Hibiscus Festival (usually the school holidays in Aug). **Suva South** and **Central** are the best options for most visitors, being close to the top restaurants and bars as well as the Fiji Museum. **Suva North** is distinctly seedier, with several hotels offering rooms by the hour to a largely local clientele. For **long-term rentals**, the classified pages of the *Fiji Times* or *Fiji Sun* are your best bet; try and get a local to call, as they are more likely to get a discount.

CITY CENTRE

Annandale Apartments 265 Waimanu Rd ☎331 1054; map p.138. One of the few passable budget deals in town, with acceptably clean rooms (usually) and harbour views. Accommodation for tourists is set aside from the locals' area, and facilities include a/c, TV and hot-water bathrooms. Deluxe rooms have kitchens, and are ideal for long-term stays. F$65

★**Colonial Lodge** 19 Anand St ☎330 0655, ⓦfacebook/colonialloge; map p.138. This charming, historic wooden house is run as a B&B for backpackers, students, volunteers and scholars. It feels homely, with an airy lounge and wooden floors throughout: you can choose from dorms, single rooms with a shared bathroom, en-suite doubles or a fabulous self-contained studio in the garden. Guests can use the family kitchen, and there are discounts for longer stays. Rates include breakfast; home-cooked dinners are F$15. Dorms F$38, singles F$50, doubles F$96

★**Grand Pacific** Victoria Parade ☎322 2000, ⓦgrandpacifichotel.com.fj; map p.138. By far the best choice in Suva, this heritage property counts as a tourist sight in its own right (see p.139). The rooms are immaculately appointed, all with small balconies and thick carpeting; guests also get a ten-minute free neck massage while they check in, and most end up repairing of an evening to the hotel bar. F$445

Holiday Inn Victoria Parade ☎330 1600, ⓦihg.com; map p.138. The location is perfect for both tourists and business people, opposite the Old Parliament building and facing the ocean with beautiful harbour and mountain views: there's also a nice swimming pool. The rooms are practical, if rather uninspiring, though the sea-view ones have small balconies. Breakfast included. ☎($) F$360

★**Quest** Corner of Renwick Rd and Pratt St ☎331 9117, ⓦquestapartments.co.nz; map p.138. Superb apartments popular with the diplomatic and business crowds, and perfectly adequate for travellers too (two-night minimum stay). Each apartment comes with a kitchenette, washing machine and DVD player, and there's an on-site gym. ☎($) F$260

Southern Cross 63 Gordon St ☎331 4233; map p.138. Close to the city centre and nightlife, and boasting a mock-marbled foyer, this hotel represents decent value for money, though their rooms (all a/c) can be scruffy at times. Up on the top floor is *Seoul*, a great Korean restaurant (see p.144). F$185

South Seas 6 Williamson Rd ☎331 2296, ⓔsouthseas@fiji4less.com; map p.138. The cheapest accommodation in Suva, in a pleasant colonial-style wooden house, although its location is a bit isolated. The rooms all share bathrooms down pokey corridors, and are furnished with plastic bunk beds. There's a communal kitchen and lounge area with TV. Dorms F$26, singles F$50, doubles F$63

SUBURBS

Five Princes 5 Princes Rd ☎335 1575, ⓦfiveprinceshotel.com; map p.140. Suva's boutique choice is on a colonial estate, with rooms, self-catering bures and a self-catering villa set in tropical gardens. It's a hike from downtown Suva, but there's a lovely saltwater pool and a gourmet restaurant. Rooms F$240, bures F$280, villa F$400

EATING

The most popular **restaurants** in Suva are **Chinese** and **Indian**, and many of these serve up over-the-counter meals from around F$6. However, with variable hygiene standards, this kind of fast food is best avoided unless purchased from one of the city's **food courts** (see box, p.144). Otherwise, there's a good variety of cuisine on offer, from European to Indian via Korean and Japanese; prices seldom exceed F$30.

CAFÉS

Café Noir Victoria Parade ☎310 0071; map p.138. This café is by far the most stylish in Suva, an air-conditioned haven dishing up good breakfasts (including eggs Florentine; F$11.50), panini (from F$7.50), excellent coffee, and fruit juices. Mon–Sat 8am–7pm.

Contain Yourself Off Edward St ☎948 1681; map p.138. For something completely different, head to this pun-tastic café, housed in shipping containers, with a corrugated roof that makes a splendid racket if – oh, this is Suva – when it rains. The coffee's good (F$3.20–6), as are the brownies, cakes and make-your-own sarnies. Daily 7.30am–9pm.

Palm Court Café QBE Courtyard, off Victoria Parade ☎330 4662; ⊛palmcourtfiji.com; map p.138. Attractive bistro in a leafy courtyard setting – there's no sign, so keep your eyes peeled. The cooked breakfast costs F$15.50, steak or home-made fish burgers are F$8.20, or you can simply sit and relax over a coffee (flat whites F$5.50), herbal tea or a thick shake. Mon–Fri 7am–4.30pm, Sat 7am–2pm.

RESTAURANTS

Ashiyana Old Town Hall, Victoria Parade ☎331 3000; map p.138. A favourite with the Indian community, this tiny, unpretentious restaurant serves eye-wateringly hot curries. Mains such as *murgh tikka* cost from F$12. Tues–Sat 11.30am–2.30pm & 6–10pm, Sun 6–10pm.

Bad Dog Victoria Parade ☎330 2884; map p.138. If you've been in the Fijian sticks for a while, you'll appreciate this snazzy spot with icy air-conditioning and eclectic cuisine, including pizzas, steak, sushi and seafood (mains F$12–25). The desserts are yummy (try the lemon-lime cheesecake), and you can move on to the bar for after-dinner drinks. Mon–Wed 11am–11pm, Thurs–Sat 11am–1am, Sun 5–11pm.

City Cottage 47 Carnarvon St, no phone; map p.138. This unassuming-looking restaurant is one of the only reliable places in Suva for Fijian-style food – there it is, sitting on the counter, going slowly cold (if it's meant to be hot) or warm (if it's supposed to be cold). Try fish in coconut cream (F$10), kokoda (F$8), *kai* shellfish in coconut cream (F$2.50 each), or some Indian-style *bhajis* (F$0.20 each), and eat them all out on the wooden veranda. Mon–Sat 7am–10pm.

Daikoku FNPF Place, Victoria Parade ☎330 8968; map p.138. Cosiest of the three Japanese restaurants in town, with five *teppanyaki* tables (griddled portions from F$15), as well as fresh sushi (from F$6 for two). They also have a good range of sake (from F$16.50 for a small jar), with a tasting guide on the drinks menu – take your first steps towards being a rice-wine connoisseur. Mon–Sat noon–2pm & 6–10pm.

★**Governors** 46 Knolly St ☎337 5050, ⊛governorsfiji.com; map p.138. Suva's current expat place of choice, and no wonder – within a colonial building snazzed up with South Sea flourishes, staff serve rounds of delectable Western food, including burgers and cake. It's best as a brunch spot, with the eggy dishes particularly recommended – have them Solomon-style (with chilli spinach), Indian (spiced), or Chinese (with oyster sauce and spring onions). Sun–Tues 9am–2.30pm, Wed–Sat 9am–2.30pm & 6–9.30pm.

★**Maya Dhaba** 281 Victoria Parade ☎331 0045; map p.138. Fine Indian dining in a contemporary setting. The number of dishes on offer makes selection difficult – try the subtle North Indian goat *masala*, on the bone with whole spices, or the South Indian chicken *dora*, rolled in rice pancakes. Mains cost F$15–25, though the lunch thalis (your choices are Punjabi or South Indian) are even better value at under F$15. There's also a cheaper outlet in the MHCC food court (see box below). Daily 11am–3pm & 6–10pm.

★**Seoul** 63 Gordon St ☎330 3605; map p.138. Providing great views from the top floor of the *Southern Cross* hotel, this Korean restaurant is a real find. Dishes include hot-stone *bibimbap* (mixed rice, spice and veggies; F$20), *bibim guksu* (cold spicy noodles; F$20), wholesome *jjigae* broths (from F$18), and barbecued meat (from F$18 a portion); they're all extremely authentic, and to seal the

DINING ON THE CHEAP AT SUVA'S FOOD COURTS

After time in the wilds of Viti Levu, Suva can seem like a sort of culinary paradise. Fiscal necessity, however, may force budget travellers to avoid the tantalizing international options dotted around town, yet hygiene concerns will prompt most Suvans to tell you to steer clear of the cheaper eateries – if this sounds like a hard square to circle, then **food courts** come as a saving grace. All the city's malls have them; the best is the one atop the **MHCC Mall** (see p.147), which has a winning mix of local and international staples, including a budget branch of *Maya Dhaba*, the best curry restaurant in town (see above). The food court on the top floor of **Tappoo City** on Thomson Street (Mon–Wed 9am–6pm, Fri & Sat 9am–8pm, Sun 11am–5pm) isn't far behind. The advent of these air-conditioned mall courts are leading the slow demise of the city's older-style food courts, though an excellent one survives just south of the centre – **Dolphin Plaza** (Mon–Sat 8am–5pm), on the corner of Victoria Parade and Loftus St, almost has the air of a Singaporean hawker market, with cheap curries and Chinese dishes, a stall selling Indian sweets, and a stand dishing up cheap sushi and California rolls from *Daikoku* Japanese restaurant (see above).

deal you'll get a few free *banchan* side-dishes to munch on while you wait. Daily noon–3pm & 6–10pm.

Shanghai Seafood Corner of Thomson and Pier streets ☎ 331 4865; map p.138. Popular Chinese restaurant with an extensive numbered menu and food that's neither too spicy nor too salty; mains are F$15 or so. Try to bag a table on the colonial-era veranda. Daily 11.30am–2.30pm & 5.30–10.30pm.

★**Tiko's Floating Restaurant** Stinson Parade ☎ 331 3626; map p.138. The speciality of this boat-restaurant is (as you might expect) freshly caught seafood, including mud crabs, king prawns, octopus and lobster, as well as excellent kokoda (F$16). Local walu fish comes in as many

forms as Bubba Gump's shrimp – have it grilled in lemon butter, in red Thai curry, or poached in coconut milk (all around F$38). Service is impeccable, there's a wide selection of wines, and the creaking noises of the ship add to the South Seas atmosphere. Mon–Fri 11.30am–2pm & 5.30–10pm, Sat 5.30–10pm.

Vine Yard Palace Old Town Hall, Victoria Parade ☎ 331 5111; map p.138. For a good feed on a budget, this all-you-can-eat Chinese buffet (weekday lunchtimes; F$15.80) is hard to beat, and is hugely popular with a ravenous Fijian crowd. The à la carte menu is okay too (most mains around F$10), and the setting rather grand. Mon–Sat 11.30am–2.30pm & 6–10pm.

DRINKING AND NIGHTLIFE

One of Suva's most enduring charms is its lively **nightlife**. Most of the bars and clubs are in one block around Victoria Parade and Carnarvon St, making it easy to hop from one to another and sample the different atmospheres. Fijians like to drink **communally**, as if drinking *yaqona* – if you buy a Fiji Bitter "long neck", which is more economical, it will be shared by passing round a small glass to down in one. It's a quick way of getting drunk, and brawls occasionally break out in the wilder places. However, the locals are very protective of foreign visitors, and on most occasions you'll be well looked after. **Taxis** are advisable for the ride back to your hotel (see box, p.143). For **music**, you can catch live bands at *Traps Lounge* (see below), or go for some more elegant jazz or R&B at the *Holiday Inn's Tapa Lounge* (see below).

BARS

O'Reilly's 5 MacArthur St, corner of Victoria Parade ☎ 331 2322; map p.138. Popular with tourists and university students, this bar has loud music, a large-screen TV and a pool table at the back; it's also the only place in Fiji you'll find Guinness on tap. The bouncers here keep a tight grip on proceedings. Mon–Sat 11am–midnight, Sun 5–11pm.

Royal Suva Yacht Club Queens Rd, Walu Bay ☎ 330 4201; map p.140. A bit out of the way – 2km from the city centre in Walu Bay – but with a lovely beer garden overlooking the sea, it's a pleasant spot to enjoy the views across the harbour towards the Viti Levu highlands. Especially great for sunsets, and the bar snacks are good too. Mon–Thurs 8am–10pm, Fri–Sun 8am–midnight.

Tapa Lounge Holiday Inn, Victoria Parade ☎ 330 1600, ⊛ ihg.com; map p.138. Despite recent competition from the *Grand Pacific* down the road, the *Holiday Inn's* bar remains the most upmarket drinking spot in town, although it's inevitably somewhat pricey (beer from F$9, cocktails from F$17). You can take your drinks out by the pool, while there's live music in the evenings (Tues–Fri). Daily 9am–11pm.

★**Traps Lounge** 305 Victoria Parade ☎ 331 2922; map p.138. The main bar at the front is the place to be seen for an after-work tipple. There's a pool bar at the back, a non-smoking chill-out lounge at the top and a buzzing dancefloor with live music (Wed and Thurs from 10pm). F$5 admission some weekends. Mon–Sat 5pm–1am.

CLUBS

Bar 66 Dolphin Plaza, Victoria Parade, entrance on Loftus St ☎ 870 6071; map p.138. Hangout for the hip under-25s, with DJs playing pop and reggae, and a dancefloor which was upgraded to "bouncy" in 2015. It doesn't get going until after 11pm and it's usually the last place to close, picking up the crowds from *Traps* (see above) after midnight. Tues–Sat 9pm–late.

Golden Dragon 379 Victoria Parade ☎ 331 1018; map p.138. Long-standing favourite among the islanders with live music on Wed and Thurs, mostly reggae-influenced, and lots of university students out for a laugh – you'll often see Polynesians dancing the hula here. Fri & Sat after 9pm admission F$5. Mon–Sat 7pm–midnight.

SHOPPING

Suva has witnessed a profusion of **malls** in recent years, and it's easy to get the feeling that before too long the whole city centre will be an enclosed, air-conditioned space full of bland stores. Still keeping it old-school, scruffy but characterful Cumming St has Suva's best selection of **clothes shops**, where you can buy fine Indian attire, and fabric by the metre. One of the street's many tailors can then whip you up a suit or shirt, or try the same at the Flea Market (see opposite).

BOOKSHOPS

Fiji Museum gift shop Thurston Gardens ☎ 331 5944; map p.140. Useful for historical titles and *Domodomo*

(F$6), the museum's monthly journal. They also sell postcards of old photographs (those of tribal chiefs are understandably popular), wooden carvings, jewellery and souvenirs. Mon–Thurs & Sat 9.30am–4.30pm, Fri 9.30am–4pm.

University Bookshop Laucala Bay ☏ 323 2500; map p.140. A selection of titles about the Pacific, on topics ranging from history and culture to law, legend, language and song. Mon–Fri 8am–5.30pm, Sat 8.30am–1pm.

CLOTHING AND COSMETICS

Pacific Island Art QBE Courtyard, off Victoria Parade ☏ 664 0085, ⌨ pacificislandsart.com; map p.140. Tahitian-owned shop selling colourful, tropical-looking clothes which have proved popular with female students from nearby USP, and also elements of Fiji's highly visible gay community. Mon–Fri 9am–5pm, Sat 9am–4pm.

Pure Fiji Karsanji St; map p.140. A weekly factory outlet sale of Fiji's favourite products: lotions, potions, shampoos and sugar rubs made with coconut oil and other natural flower extracts. They make great gifts. Sat 10am–1pm.

MARKETS AND MALLS

Flea Market Usher St at Rodwell Rd; map p.140. Behind the post office, this small market is filled with tiny stalls, all selling pretty much the same stuff and vying for your attention. Prices here start high, so you'll have to bargain to get a good deal. Mon–Sat 8am–6pm.

Handicraft Market Facing Stinson Parade; map p.140. This street market is where locals come to buy mats, *masi* and garlands for traditional ceremonies, and to get shirts and dresses tailor-made. Mon–Sat 8am–6pm.

MHCC Mall Renwick Rd; map p.140. Bland but useful, this air-conditioned mall remains the best in town, despite plenty of recent competition. It's full of sports shops, fast-food outlets (see box, p.144) and fronted by a *Gloria Jean* café: it also boasts a well-stocked supermarket. Daily 9am–10pm.

Municipal Market South end of Rodwell Rd; map p.140. Selling a cornucopia of seasonal fruit and vegetables, this market is great for a browse even if you're not buying. Behind Usher St are the fish stalls, with fresh seafood supplied direct by Suva's fishing fleet – grab some lobsters for next to nothing. At the far end of the market, the Women's Centre sells crafts, clothes and great shopping bags made from bright, recycled fabrics. Mon–Sat 6am–6pm.

SNORKELLING AND FISHING EQUIPMENT

Bob's Hook Line & Sinker Harbour Centre, 14 Thomson St ☏ 330 1013; map p.140. The best place in town to buy water-related gear, including snorkelling and fishing equipment. Mon–Sat 9am–5.30pm.

SPORTS AND ACTIVITIES

Golf Fiji Golf Club, 15 Rifle Range Rd, North Samabula (☏ 338 1184, ⌨ fijigolfclub.com.fj) has a flat eighteen-hole course; non-members can play any day except Sat (daily 7am–5pm; F$30 per round; trolley, clubs and shoes extra).

Rugby Catch a game of Sevens, Fiji's national sport (some would say obsession), at the National Stadium on Laucala Bay Rd; check ⌨ fijirugby.com for fixtures. Somehow, Fiji is not currently a stop on the world Sevens calendar, though this oversight will hopefully be rectified soon. Outside game time, you can watch burly chaps practising in Albert Park (see p.139).

Spa therapy If you're after a pampering, try the Pure Fiji Spa, part of the world-famous cosmetics company's HQ on Karsanji St (daily 10am–10pm; ☏ 338 3611). Cane sugar, green papaya and lemongrass are among the ingredients used to invoke a feeling of wellness, right from the free foot-soak on arrival.

Swimming The ocean around Suva is too polluted for swimming: the city's most conveniently located swimming pool is the attractive open-air 1925-built Suva Olympic Pool, off Victoria Parade (April–Sept Mon–Fri 10am–6pm, Sat & Sun 8am–6pm; Oct–March Mon–Fri 9am–8pm, Sat & Sun 7am–8pm; ☏ 330 5599), where you can swim all day for F$3. You can also swim at Laucala Sports City, Laucala Bay (☏ 331 2177), where there's an Olympic-sized indoor swimming pool at the National Aquatic Centre (daily 6am–7pm; F$5).

Watersports Suva's closest snorkelling reef is at Nukulau Island (see p.148), and a mediocre surfing break lies off Suva Point. For water activities it's best to head west to Pacific Harbour (see p.116), 45 minutes along the Queens Road, or to the offshore islands of Toberua (see p.149) or Caqalai (see p.175), both popular weekend destinations for city dwellers.

DIRECTORY

Banks Westpac, corner of Scott and Central streets (Mon–Thurs 9.30am–3pm, Fri 9.30am–4pm); ANZ Bank, 25 Victoria Parade (Mon 9.30am–4pm, Tues–Fri 9am–4pm), also at Centrepoint and USP.

Cinemas Village Six on Scott St (☏ 330 6006) is a long-established central cinema showing mainstream and Bollywood films; tickets F$7. Newer and more popular is Damodar City, on Grantham Rd (☏ 327 5100, ⌨ damodareventcinemas.com.fj); tickets from F$7, or F$20 for premium seats.

Dentist Daily Care Dental, Rodwell Rd (Mon–Fri 9am–5pm, Sat 9am–"tooth-hurty", just like the kids' joke; ☏ 943 7495).

Doctors Mitchell Clinic, 4F Tappoo City, Thomson St (☏ 337 1133).

Embassies and high commissions Australia, Princess Rd ☏ 338 2211; France and EU Schengen States, 7F BSP Life Centre Building, Thomson St ☏ 331 0526; Federated States of Micronesia, Loftus St ☏ 330 4566; Indonesia, Gordon St ☏ 331 6697; Kiribati, McGregor Rd ☏ 330 2512; Nauru, Ratu Sukuna House, MacArthur St ☏ 331 3566; New

Zealand, Pratt St ☎ 331 1422; Papua New Guinea, Gordon St ☎ 330 4244; Tuvalu, Gorrie St ☎ 330 1355; UK, Gladstone Rd ☎ 322 9100; US, Princess Rd ☎ 331 4466.

Hospitals CWM Hospital, Waimanu Rd ☎ 870 4905; MIOT Pacific Hospital, 120 Amy St ☎ 330 3404.

Immigration 969 Rodwell St (Mon–Fri 8.30am–12.30pm; ☎ 331 2622).

Libraries Suva Library, 196 Victoria Parade (Mon–8am–4.30pm, Fri 8am–4pm; F$20 non-Suva resident membership fee; ☎ 331 3433). University Library, USP Campus, Laucala Bay (Mon–Thurs 8am–10pm, Fri 8am–6pm, Sat 9am–6pm, Sun 1.30–6pm during term time; Mon–Fri 8am–4pm during holidays; F$20 temporary membership fee to access the extensive Pacific Collection; ☎ 323 2402). The National Archives on

Carnarvon St (Mon–Thurs 8am–4.30pm, Fri 8am–4pm; free; ☎ 330 4144) was once the print works for the *Fiji Times* and hosts a comprehensive collection of historical documents for public browsing, including *Fiji Times* newspapers dating back to the first issue in 1869 and many old photographic albums.

Pharmacies Superdrug Pharmacy, Central Building, Renwick Rd (Mon–Fri 8am–6pm, Sat 8am–3pm; ☎ 331 8755); Nasese Pharmacy, Ratu Sukuna Rd (Mon–Sat 8am–5pm & 7–9pm, Sun 10am–1pm & 7–9pm; ☎ 331 4450).

Police Corner of Pratt and Joske streets ☎ 991 or ☎ 331 1222. There are 24hr manned police posts at Market St (☎ 331 1122) and Gorrie St (☎ 330 9822).

Post office Edward St (Mon–Fri 7.30am–5pm, Sat 8am–1pm).

Around Suva

There are plenty of attractions around Suva worth exploring on day-trips, or even by staying overnight. Off Suva Point is **Nukulau Island**, which has the only sandy beach and snorkelling reef in the vicinity. Inland, the tranquil forest park of **Colo-i-Suva** forms a boundary between Suva and the wet, mountainous interior of Viti Levu. The mountains feed the impressive Rewa River, which drains to the north of Suva through Nausori town and into the vast, mangrove-lined **Rewa Delta**. This region, and the coast to the north, is home to the chiefly villages of Rewa and **Bau** – the latter once home to Cakobau, the only King of Fiji – and remains the most influential power-base in Fiji.

Colo-i-Suva Forest Park

Daily 8am–4pm • F$5; guides F$30 for a 2hr walk • ☎ 332 0211 • Take a Saweni- or Serea-bound bus from the Suva bus stand (hourly; 30min; F$1.10) or a taxi (20min; F$15)

Around 25 kilometres north of Suva is **Colo-i-Suva Forest Park**, a pristine area of low-altitude rainforest. Pronounced "tholo-ee-Suva", it's a pretty place dominated by mahogany trees, their trunks thick with parasitical tree ferns. There's a good chance of spotting **wild orchids** in the park as well as endemic **birds**, including the pink-billed parrotfinch. An easy one-hour **nature trail** leads to a couple of small **waterfalls**, with good swimming pools and nearby picnic benches.

Unfortunately, the park has a reputation for car theft and occasional muggings, though at the time of writing this hadn't happened for a fair few years – if you're worried, the attendant at the park entrance can arrange a **guide** and look after valuables.

ACCOMMODATION   COLO-I-SUVA FOREST PARK

★ **Colo-i-Suva Eco Lodge** Just before the entrance to park ☎ 332 0562, ⓦ coloisuva.com.fj; map p.136. A pleasant, ecofriendly retreat with a good range of accommodation – bures with verandas overlooking the lake, studio apartments by the pool, and private rooms

with shared facilities – enveloped by lush surrounding forest. The lodge has an excellent restaurant, well worth dining at even if you're not staying here, though prices are a little high – no surprise, since it's the only place to eat for miles around. � Rooms F$88, bures F$200

The Rewa River delta

East of Suva, the landscape is dominated by the snaking tributaries and mangroves of the **Rewa River delta**, dotted with small fishing villages. At the eastern end of the river is **Kaba**

THE RISE OF BAU ISLAND AND KING CAKOBAU

Despite its modest size, **Bau Island** played a key role in the history of Fiji. Up until the eighteenth century, Verata (10km north of Nausori) and its rival **Rewa** had ruled the archipelago, the latter being the head of the aristocracy of Burebasaga, one of the three founding clans. In 1760, a tiny island named Ulu-ni-Vuaka ("the head of the pig"), barely 300m from the shore of Viti Levu, was settled by warriors of Verata lineage; in time, it became known as Bau. The island's first chief erected **sea walls** to protect it from invasion, and built stone canoe docks, making the island a powerful seafaring base. In 1808 a Swedish "beachcomber" (see p.220) named **Charlie Savage** – who five years later would end up in the cannibals' pot – visited Bau and brought with him **firearms**, until then never possessed by Fijians. Using these new, terrifying weapons, the ruling chief, Naulivou, fought a series of wars with Verata, 15km to the north. When Verata was weak, Rewa grew in strength; between the two, they battled the upstarts from Bau for supremacy. Bau grew more powerful under the rule of the brutal cannibal chiefs of **Tanoa**, and later **Cakobau**. The chiefs seized upon the right of *vasu* (see p.245), claiming wide support from villages throughout Fiji. At its peak, the island boasted three thousand inhabitants and twenty temples.

By 1871, with the backing of the European merchants of Levuka, Cakobau had proclaimed himself **King of Fiji**. Three years later he ceded the islands to Britain. Today, the chief of Bau remains one of the most powerful in Fijian political life. As for Rewa, the aristocrats managed to retain their hold over their far-flung subjects, and Burebasaga remains the largest and most powerful of Fiji's three ancient confederacies.

Point, where the great war between Rewa and Bau came to its bloody conclusion in 1855 with a battle involving five thousand warriors and a hundred war canoes (see above).

4

Bau Island

Punts F$2 for locals, but usually more like F$6 for foreigners • Permission to visit is not usually necessary, but you can try calling the village spokesman (☎ 362 4028) just in case • Buses from Suva to Bau Landing (hourly; F$1.50)

Seven kilometres north of Kaba Point is Bau Landing, access point for the chiefly island of **Bau**. To visit the tiny island, reached by punt from here, you once needed to ask the *Turaga-ni-Koro* or village spokesman for permission; though this is no longer necessary, bring *yaqona* roots or powder, and dress respectably. Though small, the island has over two hundred houses and a fascinating history (see box above). The mound in the centre is where the chiefly families live, while around the perimeter are subclans: craftsmen from Lau, warriors from Botoni and fishermen from Kadavu. The island's Methodist **church**, dating from 1859, was the first to be built in Fiji. It was erected under the orders of King Cakobau, the fierce chief of the island who converted to Christianity in 1854. All the ancient temples on Bau were destroyed, and their stone used in the construction of the church. The baptismal font beside the altar is reputed to be Cakobau's killing stone, where the skulls of his captives were smashed before being eaten.

Toberua Island

Three kilometres off Kaba Point is the four-acre **Toberua Island**, home to one of Fiji's first boutique island resorts (see below). There are colourful coral formations and **reef sharks** at nearby Toberua Passage, which is excellent for both snorkelling and scuba diving. The resort will organize your transport to the island, as well as twice-weekly boat trips to **Mabualau**, a tiny limestone islet 5km to the east, dedicated as a nature reserve and packed with large white fluffy **boobies**.

ACCOMMODATION	TOBERUA ISLAND
★**Toberua Island Resort** ☎ 347 2777, ⊚ toberua .com. This delightful resort has built its reputation around its friendly staff, many of whom have worked here their entire lives, and guests often return year after year. The	fifteen bures have wonderfully spacious, traditionally decorated interiors, with airy outdoor showers. The resort's PADI dive outfit runs trips to over twenty dive sites, from coral heads to walls and crevasses. **F$480**

Beqa, Vatulele and Kadavu

BEQA ISLAND FIREWALKERS

5

Beqa, Vatulele and Kadavu

Beqa, Vatulele and Kadavu, the three main islands south of the Fijian mainland, present world-class scuba diving, hair-raising reef-surfing, and record-breaking game fishing. If that's not enough to entice you, several of Fiji's most beautiful beaches are located here, with shallow lagoons offering fabulous sea-kayaking and deep bays sheltering fishing villages.

The rugged island of **Beqa** has long been known for its firewalkers, though today more visitors come for the adrenaline-pumping shark dives just offshore in its huge lagoon, accessed from Pacific Harbour (see p.118). West of Beqa is the famous **surfing break** of Frigates Passage, opposite the small island of **Yanuca**; further west again lies the delightful limestone island of **Vatulele**, a centre for **tapa cloth** making, and home to several unusual attractions including ancient rock carvings and a cave full of bizarre red-coloured prawns. The furthest from Viti Levu of the southern islands – and the largest of the three – is **Kadavu**, barely a forty-minute flight from Nadi and closer still from Suva, but a world away from the tourist trail. With its twisting **Astrolabe Reef** and dramatic mountain scenery, this is the place to visit for adventure on the water, and to immerse yourself in Fijian culture.

Beqa

If not shrouded by clouds, the roughly contoured profile of **BEQA** (pronounced "Mbenga") can be seen clearly from Suva. It's closer still to Pacific Harbour, from where small boats bump across 12km of open sea to reach it. The island is roughly circular in shape, with steep forest-clad mountains rising sharply from a meandering coastline. Its large lagoon, protected by a 30km-long barrier reef, is renowned for **shark dives** and deep-sea game fishing; most trips leave from Pacific Harbour, and are covered in Chapter Three (see p.118).

Beqa's most distinctive feature is its **firewalkers** (see box, p.155). You can often see them perform on Viti Levu, especially at the Arts Village in Pacific Harbour (see p.118), but nothing beats witnessing the real thing on home soil – Rukua, Naceva and Dakuibeqa on the southeastern side are the main firewalking villages.

The island's 1400 inhabitants live in nine coastal villages. There are no roads on the island, but several **walking tracks** between villages make for pleasant exploring. The easiest route runs from Waisomo on the northern tip of the island to Rukua along the west coast. You can also hike to one of the island's **three mountains** – Korolevu (439m), towering over Lalati village on the north coast, is the highest and most challenging. The best way to explore the coastline is from a kayak; *Lalati Resort* (see p.154) runs a delightful kayaking trip to tranquil Malumu Bay, which bites deep into the west coast, almost severing it from the main bulk of Beqa.

ARRIVAL AND DEPARTURE   BEQA

By boat Most visitors arrive on Beqa via pre-arranged resort transfers from Pacific Harbour, but boats also leave from Navua (Mon–Sat) between 11am–2.30pm (30min; F$40 per person one way), returning from Beqa between 6–7am – this, of course, means you have to stay the night. Note that the schedules are far from gospel, and you may have to wait a day or more if the weather is bad, or if there are too few passengers. At the time of writing, it looks like a scheduled

The legend of Beqa's firewalkers p.155   **Watersports on Kadavu** p.162
The making of tapa cloth p.157

Highlights

❶ Surfing, Frigates Passage Surfers shouldn't miss the strong left-hand break at Frigates Passage on the little island of Yanuca. **See p.155**

❷ Beqa firewalkers Watch the locals amble over white-hot stones during traditional ceremonies in the village of Dakuibeqa. **See p.155**

❸ Vatulele Head to the hard-to-reach island of Vatulele, long famed for its tapa cloth making. **See p.156**

❹ Manta rays, Vuro With a span of over six metres, these vast but harmless creatures are

some of the biggest fish in the ocean – snorkelling trips to Vuro allow you to see them at close range. **See p.157**

❺ Astrolabe Reef, Kadavu The third biggest reef in the world and one of the best dive sites anywhere, this reef is home to colourful soft corals, fast channels and large fish. **See p.160**

❻ Kayak around Kadavu Explore the indented bays, mangrove forests and traditional villages along Kadavu's rugged coastline. **See p.162**

HIGHLIGHTS ARE MARKED ON THE MAP ON P.154

5

ferry service may start up from Pacific Harbour, perhaps even daily – ask around in Pacific Harbour for details.

Day-trips Beqa and its lagoon are also accessible from Pacific Harbour on a day-trip: cruises can be booked through Paradise Beach (F$249; ☎ 998 1000, ⓦ paradisebeachfiji.com), with flexible itineraries, so you can choose from jungle walks, village visits, snorkelling or simply hammock-time. They also sometimes run sunset tours featuring firewalking; contact them for details. Alternatively, you can visit Beqa from Pacific Harbour by jet-ski with Jetski Safari (see p.119).

ACCOMMODATION

It's not too hard to organize homestay accommodation on Beqa – ask at Paradise Beach travel agency (see above), the tourist information kiosk in Pacific Harbour (see p.118), or even the boat drivers, one of whom runs a particularly good option in Rukua village.

Lalati Resort Malumu Bay ☎ 347 2033, ⓦ lalatifiji .com. Sitting pretty on the northeast coast, with thirteen spacious villas, suites and cottages strung along the shore, and a few more up on the hillside. On site are a swimming pool, a spa and a nice bar, and gourmet meals are included in the rates. Usually a three-night minimum, with cheaper

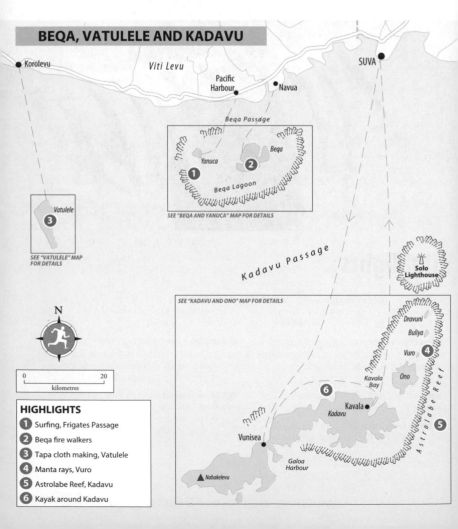

BEQA, VATULELE AND KADAVU

Korolevu

Viti Levu

Pacific Harbour

SUVA

Navua

Beqa Passage

Yanuca

1

Beqa

2

Beqa Lagoon

SEE "BEQA AND YANUCA" MAP FOR DETAILS

Vatulele

3

SEE "VATULELE" MAP
FOR DETAILS

Kadavu Passage

Solo
Lighthouse

SEE "KADAVU AND ONO" MAP FOR DETAILS

Dravuni

Buliya

Vuro

4

Kavala
Bay

Ono

Astrolabe Reef

N

6

Kavala

Kadavu

5

0   20
kilometres

Vunisea

Galoa
Harbour

▲ Nabakelevu

HIGHLIGHTS

1 Surfing, Frigates Passage

2 Beqa fire walkers

3 Tapa cloth making, Vatulele

4 Manta rays, Vuro

5 Astrolabe Reef, Kadavu

6 Kayak around Kadavu

ACCOMMODATION

Lalati Resort	1
Lawaki Beach House	3
Yanuca Island Resort	2

BEQA AND YANUCA

0 — 5
kilometres

rates for longer stays. ☎ F$920
★**Lawaki Beach House** ☎331 8817, ⊕www
.lawakibeachhouse.com. Run by a Fiji–Swiss couple, this
relatively cheap option is on the west coast, at the end of a

long stretch of beach. The bures have en-suite hot-water
bathrooms, while guests in the five-bed dorm lodge share
a cold-water one. Rates include meals. Camping with own
tent F$100, dorms F$1300, bures F$290

Yanuca

Some 12km west of Beqa, **Yanuca** (pronounced "ya-noo-tha") is a relatively low island,
with light forest, gentle hills and a solitary village on its east coast. The main reason to
visit is the excellent **surfing** available at **Frigates Passage**, an extremely consistent and
powerful left-hand break that's one of the best surfing spots in the South Pacific; rides
of 100m are not uncommon. Surfers can chill out on coarse coral beaches, with
hammocks strung between coconut palms, and a deep lagoon with good snorkelling.

ARRIVAL AND DEPARTURE   **YANUCA**

By boat Small boats leave Pacific Harbour at 3pm
returning from Yanuca early in the morning the

following day. As with all services to the southern
islands, delays are possible: the boatmen in Pacific

THE LEGEND OF BEQA'S FIREWALKERS

Unlike Hindu firewalking (see box, p.141), **Beqa's firewalkers** perform purely for
entertainment rather than religious purification. The legend of how the islanders obtained
mastery over fire has been passed down through the generations.

Once there was a famous storyteller named **Dredre** who lived in the ancient mountain
village of Navakeisese on Beqa. His tales would captivate the villagers throughout the night
and it was customary to bring small gifts as a token of appreciation. One evening, Dredre
requested all present to bring him the first thing they encountered when out hunting the next
day. The following morning, a young warrior named **Tui** went fishing in a mountain stream
and pulled out what he thought was an eel from the mud. To his surprise, the eel assumed the
shape of a *vu*, or spirit god, and Tui knew that Dredre would be most pleased with his gift. The
spirit god pleaded for its life offering all sorts of tempting powers, but only when Tui was
promised the **power over fire** did he succumb. The spirit god dug a pit, lined it with stones
and lit a huge fire upon it. When the stones were white hot, the spirit god leaped in, showing
no effect from the heat. Tui followed and to this day his descendants from the Sawau tribe
re-enact the same performance of walking on white-hot stones.

5

Harbour hang out at a blue-and-green hut between the main road and *Oceanus* resort, so check the likely departure time with them.

Day-trips Some resorts along the Coral Coast run day-trips to Yanuca; *Beachouse* near Namatakula (see p.116) runs a good one that also includes time on Vatulele (F$150).

ACCOMMODATION

Yanuca Island Resort ☎ 997 8958, ⓦ facebook.com /YanucaIslandResort. Run by surfers, for surfers, this resort and its four spartan bures make a grand place to chill out while waiting for the optimum left-hand barrel

conditions to develop. It's set in a small cove backed by jungle and fronted with a stretch of glorious sand, and the meals (included in the price) are usually excellent; for beer, you'll have to pop down to the shop by the harbour. **F$190**

Vatulele

The flat yet intriguing island of **Vatulele**, or "the ringing rock", lies 32km south of Viti Levu. Covering 31 square kilometres, the island boasts ancient rock art, sublime beaches, a sparkling lagoon and four villages completely absorbed with making **tapa cloth**. Although petroglyphs on the western tip of the island show evidence of human habitation for over three thousand years, Vatulele was first recorded in written history in 1799, when the American schooner *Anne and Hope* spotted villagers along its coastline. It had a brief period of tourist popularity while the luxury *Vatulele Island Resort* was open; since its closure in 2012, however, there has been nowhere to stay on the island, so the only way for visitors to explore its smattering of interesting sights is on a day-trip (see below).

The four villages on Vatulele lie within a thirty-minute walk of each other along the flat **east coast**. The famous **petroglyphs**, carved into the limestone cliffs at a height of 10m, are over on the **west coast**; designs include hands, faces and animals such as roosters. Just south of here is another island icon, the **sacred deep-red prawns** in the tidal cave of Korolamalama – eating the prawns is strictly forbidden, and islanders believe that anyone who harms them will be shipwrecked. A steep ten-minute walk up from the petroglyphs, you can climb to the solar-powered **lighthouse**, perched on the cliff edge, for a fabulous view of lush green forest, and of the eagles and swiftlets that thrive among the craggy cliffs.

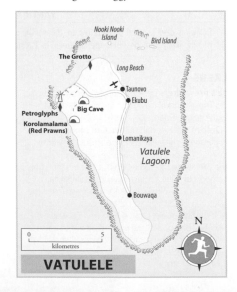

ARRIVAL AND DEPARTURE
VATULELE

By air There are currently no scheduled flights landing at the grass airstrip on the east side of Vatulele.

By boat Small outboard village boats leave from Korolevu (see p.115) on the Coral Coast every Tues, Thurs and Sat, generally around noon (45min; F$30 one-way): however, since they return in the early morning you'd have to stay the night, and there's currently no accommodation on the island – the only real option is to try asking the boatmen about homestays, or seeing if you can charter a whole vessel for a day-trip.

Day-trips *Beachouse* near Namatakula (see p.116) on the Coral Coast runs occasional tours to Vatulele and Beqa Island (F$150; 6-person minimum) which include lunch, a village visit, *kava*-drinking, snorkelling, and a visit to the famous red prawns.

5

THE MAKING OF TAPA CLOTH

From sunrise to sunset, the deep resonating thump of wood beating against wood echoes around the villages of Vatulele. This is the sound of **tapa cloth** production, a fine paper made from the bark of the **mulberry tree**, or *masi* in Fijian. The cloth was traditionally used as clothing, wrapped around the waist and draped over the shoulder of people with chiefly status. It also represented a conductor between the spirit and living world, and was hung from the high ceiling of the *bure kalou*, or temple, and used by the priest to mediate with the gods. Today, it is used in decorative **artwork** and gift-wrapping sold in boutique shops around Fiji; for many, the best chance to see the real thing is in the Fiji Museum (see p.139).

Tapa cloth is almost exclusively created by women. The first step is to slice and strip the long, thin bark of the mulberry tree into single pieces, which are then soaked in the sea for four nights. Once supple, the bark is beaten into a **pulp** using hardwood slabs and heavy wooden sticks, then woven with other strips to make a single piece of cloth. Dried in the sun, the cloth is eventually **decorated** using patterned stencil designs depicting the origin of the artist, and figurative icons relevant to a clan's totemic god – often a turtle or shark. Once stencilled, the cloth is known in Fijian as *masi*. Only two or three colours are used – brown dye is obtained from the bark of the mangrove tree; the black dye comes from charcoal; while the red dye that is sometimes used is obtained from seeds. For the villagers on Vatulele, tapa is the main **cash crop**, generating an average annual income of F$2000 per household, although for some tapa artists this can reach F$6000, equalling the basic salary of a Fijian civil servant.

Kadavu and Ono

Jutting from the sea like a serrated chunk of emerald, **KADAVU** (pronounced "Kan-davu") is the fourth-largest island in Fiji – snaking 57km from east to west, its rugged coastline littered with deep bays. **West Kadavu** is dominated by the volcanic cone of Nabukelevu at its western end, while to the east is Kadavu's only expanse of flat land, taken up by the small airstrip and the government centre of **Vunisea**. **Central Kadavu**, east of Vunisea, has the island's best **beaches**, as well as the fantastic Namalata Reef off the north coast. **East Kadavu** overlooks part of the immense Astrolabe Reef – one of the world's longest barrier reefs – and its handful of **dive resorts** are backed by steep tropical rainforest, and a sprinkling of waterfalls. Most resorts can arrange a guide to help you spot Kadavu's four **endemic bird species** (the Kadavu fantail, Kadavu honeyeater, velvet fruit dove and Kadavu musk parrot), though you may well see specimens flitting from tree to tree in any case.

There are just over ten thousand inhabitants on Kadavu, primarily engaged in subsistence farming and fishing, making it one of the best places to immerse yourself in **Fijian culture**. Most of the island's coastal villages are hidden in bays or among mangrove estuaries, and obscured from view when travelling along the coast by boat. Some of the villages are connected by walking trails, though many of the trails are only accessible at low tide.

Off the northeastern tip of Kadavu and surrounded by the Astrolabe Reef is **ONO ISLAND**, home to two small villages and several beautiful beaches. Surrounding Ono are a dozen smaller islands, including **Vuro**, where **manta rays** congregate.

Brief history

In 1792, William Bligh became the first European to chart Kadavu and its dangerous coral reefs, but for the next few decades the islanders had little contact with the outside world. This peaceful isolation was shattered in 1829, when the island was **conquered** by warriors from Rewa in southeastern Viti Levu. As such, Kadavu was brought under the influence of the powerful Burebasaga Confederacy, and forced to assist Rewa in the 1840s war against Cakobau (see box, p.220).

Thirty-five years after Bligh's encounter, French commander Dumont d'Urville almost ran aground on the reefs north of Ono and so named them after his ship, *L'Astrolabe*.

5

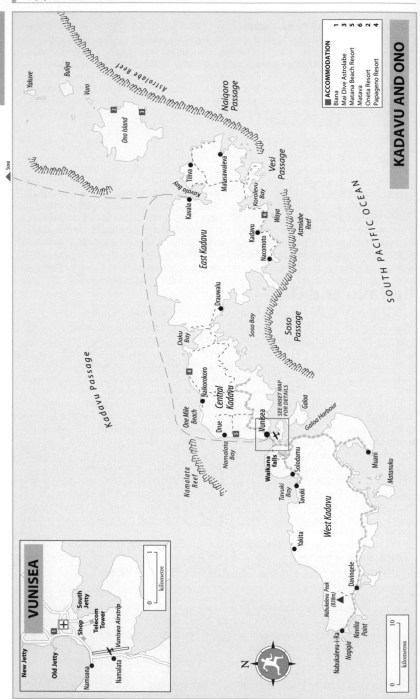

ACCOMMODATION

Biana	1
Mai Dive Astrolabe	3
Matana Beach Resort	5
Matava	6
Oneta Resort	2
Papageno Resort	4

SOUTH PACIFIC OCEAN

Astrolabe Reef

Naiqoro Passage

Vesi Passage

Soso Passage

Kadavu Passage

Namalata Reef

East Kadavu

Central Kadavu

West Kadavu

Ono Island

Yakuve

Buliya

Vuro

Yaukuve

Tiliva

Matasawaleva

Kavala

Kavala Bay

Korolevu Bay

Wiya

Kadavu

Nacomoto

Drauwalu

Soso Bay

Daku Bay

Naikorokoro

One Mile Beach

Drue

Namalata Bay

Waikana falls

Vunisea

Solodamu

Tavuki Bay

Tavuki

Yakita

Galoa

Galoa Harbour

Muani

Matanuku

Davinqele

Nabukelevu Peak (838m)

Nabukalevu-i-Ra

Nagigia

Navilila Point

SEE INSET MAP FOR DETAILS

Sova

VUNISEA

New Jetty

Old Jetty

South Jetty

Shop

Telecom Tower

Vunisea Airstrip

Namuana

Namalata

0   1   kilometre

N

0   10   kilometres

After publishing his journals, which described the discovery of endless supplies of the Chinese delicacy **bêche-de-mer** (sea cucumber), Kadavu began to attract overseas traders. Galoa Harbour, on the southern side of present-day Vunisea town, became a busy port, and it wasn't long before American **whalers** moved into Tavuki Bay on the north coast. Land was briskly traded with the locals for firearms and alcohol, while merchants from China and Europe set up stores and began planting cotton. Galoa reached its peak in 1871, but within a few years it had become a virtual ghost town when Levuka, backed by Cakobau, established itself as the main port for trade.

Many of the **Chinese** traders remained, marrying into local Fijian families, and the Chinese link remains strong today. Kadavu's largest export is *kava*, reputed as the finest and strongest in Fiji. The fourteen provincial chiefs on Kadavu remain relatively autonomous from the Burebasaga Confederacy, and are among the most powerful local chiefs in Fiji.

Vunisea

You're most likely to be swept in and out of tiny **VUNISEA** (pronounced "vuni-see-ah") on your way to one of Kadavu's resorts. Making a convenient base for exploring the attractions of west Kadavu, the township has a pretty setting between Namalata Bay on the north coast and Galoa Harbour on the south coast. In pre-European days, warriors would slide their war canoes on rollers over the isthmus separating the north and south bays, saving themselves the long journey around the coast.

Namuana village

Beside the airstrip and fronting the beach at Namalata Bay is pretty **Namuana village**, famous for its **turtle calling ceremony**, though this now only happens occasionally. The turtles, said to represent two maidens of the village lost to sea, are summoned to the surface by a chant sung by the women. If a turtle doesn't appear, it's said to be because a person from the bitter rival village of Nabukelevu is present. A twenty-minute trail from the village leads up to the saddle of the hill, with great views of both bays, and continues to secluded **Waikana Falls**, where you can swim in a shallow pool.

West Kadavu

A rough but scenic dirt road heads across the isthmus from Vunisea along the **south coast** of west Kadavu, all the way to **Nabukelevu-i-Ra** village on the **western tip** of the island. Along the way it passes several beautiful bays, and the towering peak of **Nabukelevu**, also known as Mount Washington. It's possible to climb to the 838m-high summit in a full day, starting out from Davinqele village on the south coast. From the top you'll see the dramatic north face of the peak tumbling down to the sea.

Central Kadavu

East of Vunisea, a dirt road – perhaps better for walking than driving – meanders inland to the dense tropical rainforest of **central Kadavu**. Roughly 8km in, a side-road heads north, following an undulating valley to a series of five beautiful sandy **cove beaches**, beside the picturesque village of **Naikorokoro**. West of the village, and within walking range (at low tide) of the enviably located *Matana Beach Resort* (see p.162), is **One Mile Beach**, a secluded beauty with deep sand and massive coconut palms. The beach marks the start of a 10km-long **trail** along the northern coastline, passing Naikorokoro, a couple of small rocky headlands and Naivakarauniniu village on the way, and ending up at *Papageno Resort* (see p.162) and its forests. High up in the forest there's a sweeping lookout over **Daku Bay** and, forty minutes' walk inland, a small **waterfall** with swimming pool.

5

East Kadavu

Beyond Daku Bay lies the heavily indented coastline of **east Kadavu**, difficult to access other than by sea. Kavala Bay on the north coast, and Korolevu Bay on the south coast, form great basins surrounded by steep mountains. Their river estuaries are lined with **mangrove forests**, and you can explore parts of this incredibly peaceful environment by **kayak**. However, it's the underwater spectacle of the **Astrolabe Reef** that attracts most visitors here; the reef hugs the southeast side of Kadavu all the way to Galoa Harbour, and extends 40km north in open sea. Divers are well catered for at east Kadavu's **dive resorts**.

Kadavu village

Village entry F$10

The village of **Kadavu** lies hidden behind mangrove estuaries, hemmed in by steep mountains. At the back of the village, a high **waterfall** has carved and hollowed a russet-coloured rocky chamber into unusual shapes, with a deep swimming pool below – when visitors arrive, energetic village kids swarm in to show off their courage by jumping from the 20m-high rock faces surrounding it.

Nacomoto

From Kadavu you can hike for an hour through rainforest to **Nacomoto**, where village stays can be arranged (see below). If you want to see grey **reef sharks** and large schools of barracuda, jacks and emperors, Nacomoto Passage is as good a bet as anywhere in Fiji, with dive boats from *Matava* (see p.162) diving the site frequently.

ARRIVAL AND DEPARTURE   KADAVU

By plane Vunisea is home to the island's only airport, served by Fiji Airways flights from both Nadi (6 weekly; 45min) and Nausori (1 weekly; 30min); the latter are usually far cheaper, and all services are in dinky 19-seater prop-planes.

By boat The large, and surprisingly comfy *Goundar Shipping* ferry (☎330 1035, ⊛goundarshipping.com; F$44 economy one way, F$70 for first class, F$170 for a

cabin) leaves Suva at 10pm each Wed, arriving in Vunisea at either 6am or 11am on Thurs, depending on whether or not it stops first at Kavala Bay. It then returns to Suva at around 3pm, arriving at 9pm.

Getting to Ono Island There are no direct boats to Ono; transfers from Vunisea can be arranged directly with the island's resorts.

GETTING AROUND AND SERVICES

By resort boat Each resort has its own fleet of boats, which connect with carrier trucks meeting pre-booked guests at Vunisea Airport or the ferry jetty. Boats heading to the south coast resorts depart from Galoa Bay, over the rise from the airport, on the other side of Vunisea town. Note that the seas can be rough, especially along the exposed south coast, and not all boats carry life jackets. It takes 35 minutes to reach the far western point of Kadavu from Vunisea, and an hour to reach Ono or the Astrolabe Reef in good weather – maybe double that if seas are rough.

By road The winding roads on Kadavu are unsealed, making them impassable after heavy rains. There are no buses, and no rental cars available, but several minivans and trucks shuttle around Vunisea between the airstrip and jetties, and can be hired for exploring further.

Services Apart from at the resorts, facilities are limited: there are no banks, ATMs or restaurants, and only a few shops. Other than Vunisea's two supermarkets and fruit-and-veg market, plus a smattering of basic village shops selling mostly tinned food and kerosene dotted around the island, you'll be reliant on your accommodation for food.

ACCOMMODATION

Village homestays in Nacomoto in east Kadavu can be organized through either *Matava* (see p.162) or Tamarillo Expeditions (see p.162). Homestays can also be arranged at Solodamu village in west Kadavu (☎362 3009); a contribution of at least F$40 per person should be given to help pay your way.

VUNISEA AND WEST KADAVU

Biana Vunisea ☎368 6010. Mostly used by government workers and those suffering flight cancellations, this basic cottage overlooking the old jetty has three rooms, sharing a lounge, kitchen and cold-water bathroom. The beach here is sandy, and there are good snorkelling reefs in the

5

WATERSPORTS ON KADAVU

Life on the water is such an integral part of Kadavu that it's little wonder watersports are the main attraction for visitors – in particular scuba diving on the phenomenal 100km-long **Astrolabe Reef** and the **Namalata Reef** off the north coast of Vunisea, which may be smaller but is equally impressive and diverse.

DIVING AND SNORKELLING

The Astrolabe Reef can be divided into two distinct sections: the 50km northern loop, forming a figure of eight shape, is all in open water, entwined with canyons, arches and other spectacular seascapes; while the section of reef hugging the east and south coast of Kadavu to Galoa Harbour has five rich current-fed passages, all featuring a profusion of **soft corals**. There are strong drift dives at Naiqoro, shallow corals at Vesi, **sharks** at Nacomoto, **fans** at Soso and **manta rays** at Galoa.

Pretty much every resort on Kadavu and Ono can organize diving or snorkelling (see p.35 for an idea of dive and PADI certificate prices): the **Mad Fish Diver Centre** at *Matava* resort (see below) and **Dive Kadavu** at the *Matana Beach Resort* (see below) are both recommended and the latter can also be used by non-residents.

SURFING

The passages at Soso and Vesi have unpredictable but sometimes massive **surfing breaks**, most easily accessible from *Matana Beach Resort* on the southeast coast. The best spot for surfing, though, is off the western tip of Kadavu; here you can surf the gnarly left at King Kong, or head around the point to Daku Beach, where there are both reef breaks and a beach break for beginners.

KAYAKING

It's possible to **kayak** around Kadavu in seven days, staying in villages or bedding down at a budget resort along the way. New Zealand outfit Tamarillo Tropical Expeditions (☎360 3043, 🌐tamarillo.co.nz; 7-day all-inclusive round-island packages NZ$2595 per person) have well-organized itineraries and great contacts with the local villages, with guided two-person sea kayaks and support boats. It can be hard work, with a minimum of five hours of paddling in sometimes choppy seas (working muscles you'd previously never knew existed), but it's a great way to experience the island's remote coastlines and villages. Less strenuous overnight packages, and day-trips exploring the mangrove estuaries, run on demand from the base camp at Korolevu Bay on the southeastern corner of Kadavu.

FISHING

Game fishing charters using top-of-the-range gear are available from *Matava* on the southeast coast of Kadavu (F$1000/2000 for half-/full-day). You can cast in the surrounding reefs for Giant Trevallys, or trawl between 1000m and 3000m of water for marlin, tuna and sailfish. More casual hand-line fishing can also be organized from all resorts.

bay, but you'll need to bring your own gear. Rates include breakfast; the owners cook and serve other meals by prior arrangement. Per person F$100

CENTRAL KADAVU

Matana Beach Resort ☎368 3502, 🌐matana beachresort.com. With the Namalata Reef offshore, *Matana* is primarily a dive resort, and it's often known by the name of the owners' dive business, Dive Kadavu. It has ten bures with polished timber floors and large windows, in a beautiful setting. Rates include meals and transfers. 📶($) F$520

★**Papageno Resort** ☎603 0466, 🌐papagenoresort .com. Set in 346 acres of serene tropical forest, this is a

nature lover's paradise. Accommodation is in rooms, villas and colonial-style bures, and food is outstanding, sourced from locally grown organic ingredients. Divers have the option of either the Astrolabe or Namalata reefs and there are regular snorkelling trips to visit the manta rays at Vuro Island, plus game fishing off Nabukelevu. Rates include meals; transfers are free if you stay three or more nights. 📶($) Villas F$400, bures F$600

EAST KADAVU

★**Matava** ☎333 6222, 🌐matava.com. Tucked into a small, beachless bay enclosed by rocky Waya Island, this resort is fantastically well organized but retains a village-style atmosphere, with welcoming hosts and a fine blend of European and Fijian cuisine. It's excellent value for money, especially the "backpacker" beds, which are essentially dorm beds in a classy bure. As well as its own dive operation, they've some of the finest snorkelling in Fiji just ten minutes away by boat at Vesi Passage, with soft coral gardens and thousands of exotic reef fish. Rates include breakfast and use of snorkel gear; optional lunch-and-dinner plans cost extra F$85 per head. (wifi) ($) "Backpacker" beds **F$100**, bures **F$540**

ONO ISLAND

Mai Dive Astrolabe ⓣ 603 0842, ⓦ maidive.com. Aussie–Fijian option that's a great choice for dive enthusiasts, who may want to opt for one of the week-long packages. Accommodation is in inviting bungalows with lots of timber, verandas and hammocks. The food is excellent, especially given the remote location. Five-night minimum stay; rates include meals, but return transfers from Vunisea cost F$70 per person extra. **F$675**

★ **Oneta Resort** ⓣ 603 0778, ⓦ onetaresort.com. This resort enjoys a wonderful beachside location, where you can lounge in a hammock or wander the tropical garden around your bure. The food – and the nearby fishing – is sensational. Rates include meals, though transfers from Vunisea are pricey at F$75 each way, and double that if you stay less than five nights. **F$680**

Lomaiviti and Lau

BAY OF ISLANDS

Lomaiviti and Lau

A world away from the beach resorts of the Mamanucas and Yasawa islands, the historically fascinating Lomaiviti and the remote Lau islands radiate from the east coast of Viti Levu, eventually dissipating before a massively deep ocean trench separating Fiji from Tonga. Those who visit these enchanting islands step into the Fiji of old, where islanders fish the lagoons as a matter of necessity and travel the open seas in small boats.

As a tourist destination, the inner islands of the **Lomaiviti Group** are relatively developed, particularly Ovalau, home to Fiji's charming former capital, **Levuka**. In comparison, the Outer Lomaiviti and the entire expanse of the **Lau Group** offer few facilities, but will captivate the minds of the most curious of travellers. Once the battlegrounds between warring tribes from Fiji and Tonga, this overlooked area has a rich Tongan heritage and is now popular with visiting yachts drawn to its spectacular limestone islands and bays. With over sixty islands to visit across a wide expanse of ocean, virtually no accommodation and limited transport, time and patience are the main requisites for successfully exploring this region.

Brief history

The Lomaiviti and Lau islands played a key role in the struggle for supremacy over the Fijian archipelago. By the mid-nineteenth century the ruthless **Ratu Seru Cakobau**, high chief of Bau, had brought much of Fiji under his control. However, the Tongans held a long association with the Lau Group, which in most parts are closer to their islands than Viti Levu. In 1848, **Enele Ma'afu**, a Tongan prince, was sent to Lakeba in Lau under the guise of protecting the missionaries established there. By supporting Cakobau's enemies and plying his own brand of fierce warfare, Ma'afu soon began to dominate the region, even gaining control of Vanua Levu and Taveuni. By the 1870s, Cakobau concluded that Ma'afu had the upper hand. Fearful of a direct confrontation he decided to cede Fiji to Britain, which he believed would halt the Tongan's conquest. The British were reluctant to accept Cakobau's terms as he didn't represent the united people of Fiji. So, in 1871, Cakobau rallied a few white settlers in Levuka, and, with the backing of his allied chiefs, announced himself **King of Fiji**. After much debate and tension, **cession to Britain** was completed on October 10, 1874, and **Levuka** became the administrative capital of the new colony. Ma'afu, his aspirations of control of Fiji halted, reluctantly accepted administration over the Lau Group.

Lomaiviti Group

The sixteen islands of the **Lomaiviti Group** form a neat triangular cluster in the heart of the Fijian archipelago, 20km east of Viti Levu and 50km south of Vanua Levu. In the nineteenth century the island of **OVALAU** became the centre of European trade, with whalers and merchants setting up camp beside the village of **Levuka**, which eventually became Fiji's first capital. Levuka remains the region's main tourist draw yet visitor numbers are blissfully insignificant. North and east of Ovalau, a handful of **small**

Highlights

❶ Historic Levuka Soak up the colonial atmosphere of Fiji's hugely welcoming old capital, with its colourful facades and laidback demeanour. **See p.169**

❷ Ovalau's north coast The scenic hilly coast wrapped around north Ovalau is home to walking trails, waterfalls, endemic birds and fishing villages, plus three delightful budget retreats. **See p.174**

❸ Lovoni Hike your way up to the historic village of Lovoni, dramatically sited in a volcanic crater and once home to a famously fierce hill tribe. **See p.175**

❹ Caqalai Island Look out for banded sea-snakes, or just take it easy at this tiny, classic backpackers' resort. **See p.175**

❺ Bay of Islands Marvel at the unusual limestone formations, caves and snorkelling reefs at these fascinating islands off Vanua Balavu. **See p.181**

❻ Southern Lau Explore the seldom-visited, remote Southern Lau Group of islands on an adventurous small-ship cruise, or the truly intrepid traveller can hop on a local cargo boat. **See p.181**

HIGHLIGHTS ARE MARKED ON THE MAPS ON P.168 & P.169

6

islands lie entwined within coral reefs, boasting secluded white sandy beaches and **ancient hillforts** hidden in the forests. Unfortunately these small islands, including Makogai, Naigani and Wakaya, along with the two larger islands of Gau and Koro, were badly hit by **Cyclone Winston** in 2016 (see box, p.26), and travel around them remains difficult with resorts closed and infrastructure decimated. The southern waters off Ovalau, however, were less affected and several tiny **coral islands** here with beach huts, along with a handful of budget retreats on Ovalau itself, make a refreshing alternative **backpacker route** to the well-travelled Yasawa Islands.

Ovalau

From a distance, **OVALAU** resembles a giant meringue with its top bitten off. The missing top of the island is, in fact, a blown-out volcanic crater, 400m deep with three lakes and the proud village of **Lovoni** lying at the bottom. Just under eight thousand people live on the island, over half of them based in and around the characterful seaside town of **Levuka**, protected by UNESCO World Heritage status and hemmed in by sheer rainforest-covered mountains midway along the east coast. The drier coastline of **north Ovalau** has rolling grassy hills, stunning viewpoints and a pleasant beach at Arovudi, while forested **south Ovalau** boasts excellent kayaking and snorkelling in the protected lagoon sheltered by the long thin Moturiki lying just offshore. The east coast of Ovalau has few specific attractions, although you're likely to pass through to access the island's airstrip, wharf, or to travel the road to Lovoni.

ARRIVAL AND DEPARTURE   OVALAU

BY PLANE
The airstrip at Bureta on the southwest side of Ovalau is

served only by Northern Air (☎ 347 5005, ⊛ northernair .com.fj), whose daily flight from Nausori Airport, Suva,

HIGHLIGHTS
5 Bay of Islands
6 Southern Lau

LOMAIVITI AND LAU

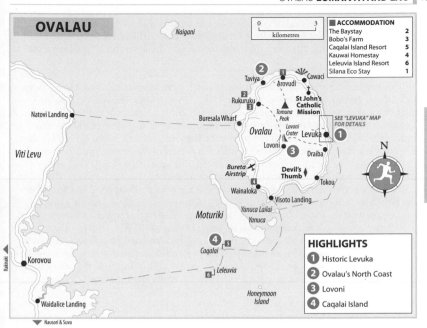

takes twelve minutes. A minibus shuttles passengers to Levuka for F$10.

BY FERRY

From Natovi Landing Patterson Brothers ferries (☎ 331 5644, ⓦ fijisearoad.com; F$24.65 one way) depart daily at 3.30pm from Natovi Landing, an isolated spot midway up the east coast of Viti Levu, to Buresala on the west coast of Ovalau, from where a free connecting bus runs into Levuka; the ferry returns to Natovi at 6am the following morning.

A Patterson Brothers connecting bus runs between Suva and Natovi, departing at 1pm from Bay 6 at the Suva bus stand (F$10).

From Caqalai or Leleuvia If you're heading from Viti Levu direct to the small backpacker resorts on Caqalai or Leleuvia (see p.176), onward small boats run from both islands to Levuka (around F$40; 40min). The boat journey can be done in either direction, making a round trip incorporating Ovalau a popular option with budget travellers.

GETTING AROUND

By bus Ovalau's only public bus is the school service, which leaves Bureta at 6am (Mon–Sat; F$2) for St John's Catholic Mission via Levuka, returning along the same route around 3pm.

By taxi Taxis are easy to find around Levuka and are fine for travelling around the island's circular coastal dirt road but not to Lovoni. A taxi from Levuka to Bureta Airport or to Arovudi costs F$30.

By village truck Village trucks are the most common way to travel around the island and have a base in Levuka beside the seawall opposite the Church of the Sacred Heart. Carrier trucks originate from most villages (the village name is usually

written on its canopy) and run twice, if not three times a day into Levuka: the morning and afternoon school-runs plus a lunch-time shopping trip. Travel is in the back of the truck on wooden benches running along its side and costs $3 per trip. For trips from Levuka to Arovudi or Rukuruku, contact Manasa (☎ 923 5812) or Junior (☎ 991 5855).

By 4WD tour To explore the island further, contact local English expat David Kirton, who runs Tutus Tours (☎ 923 5812, ✉ levukaheritage@connect.com.fj) and offers transfers, sightseeing tours around the island (F$130 for a half-day; $150 full-day), trips to Lovoni village ($100), plus kayak and snorkel gear rental.

Levuka

Once a wild whaling outpost, diminutive **LEVUKA** is now a charming seaside town with some two thousand residents. Its laidback atmosphere is epitomized by its untidy, weathered yet colourful clapboard buildings, most of which now function as Indian-run

6

stores, so packed full of goods it's difficult to poke around without bumping into someone. Local residents meet for a gossip along Levuka's main thoroughfare, misleadingly named **Beach Street**, which runs between the rocky seawall and the town's most historic buildings.

Brief history

With a protected harbour and a welcoming chief, Levuka village hosted a small band of British and American **whalers** during the 1830s. In return for shelter, the whalers gave gifts of muskets which the villagers used to fend off their rivals, the fierce hill people of Lovoni. Soon to follow the whalers were a motley crew of fugitives, blackbirders and beachcombers, with zealous Victorian **missionaries** hot on their heels. By 1871, when the great warrior Cakobau declared Levuka the **capital of Fiji**, it was home to more than two thousand European residents and 52 hotels and bars. It was joked that ships would navigate into port by following the bobbing rum bottles.

Levuka's short life as a South Pacific metropolis came to an abrupt end in 1881 when the British moved the capital to Suva. The rejected town once again became a sleepy trading port for the outer islands, and it was not until 1976 that it gained a new lease of life when the PAFCO **tuna cannery** set up here. During the 1980s, with the emergence of **tourism**, Levuka found itself as a curio, a relic of Fiji's colonial past. It also realized its unique status as a town of Fijian firsts: the first Methodist church, the first hotel, the first bank, school and newspaper are but a few of its proud claims. In 2013, the town's unique colonial architecture became protected as a **UNESCO World Heritage Site**.

Morris Hedstrom building

Beach St • Mon–Fri 8am–1pm & 2–4.30pm, Sat 8am–1pm • F$2 • ☎ 344 0356

Standing proudly at the southern end of town, Beach Street's most iconic site is the **Morris Hedstrom building**, which opened in 1868 as a grocery store. Morris Hedstrom built up a trading empire that thrived during the colonial era, finding its way to every corner of the archipelago. You'll still find Morris Hedstrom supermarkets in most Fijian towns but this original store was donated to the National Trust in 1980 and today houses the **Levuka Community Centre** (see box below), as well as a tiny **museum** exhibiting a random collection of relics from the colonial era. A useful notice board here displays tourist brochures, and you can pick up the handy Firsts of Fiji trail map at the counter.

Church of the Sacred Heart

Midway along Beach Street • Always open • free

The picturesque Catholic **Church of the Sacred Heart** with a domed roof was built in two stages: the main section for worship was crafted from local timber in 1858 with the arrival of the first Catholic missionaries, while the imposing **clock tower** was erected forty years later, using thick limestone blocks baked from coral. The church is worth a peek inside for its gruesome yet humbling series of fourteen **paintings** depicting Christ's crucifixion.

WALKS AND WATERSPORTS AROUND LEVUKA

Worthwhile **hikes** around Levuka include **The Peak trail**, a tough two-hour trek through forest culminating in a panorama over the eastern coastline from the large peak which rears up behind Levuka. Guided treks along the trail are run by the affable Nox (book through *Levuka Homestay*; ☎ 344 0777; F$25); he also runs a plantation walk including information on local medicine and a swim in a natural pool (F$20), plus impromptu two-hour **walking tours** through Levuka's less-explored parts (F$10). Alternatively, curators at the Levuka Community Centre lead informative two-hour walking tours of the town (☎ 344 0356; Mon–Fri at 10am and 2pm; F$10).

Ovalau's only **diving** operator is based at *Kauwai Homestay* (☎ 732 4330; F$80 for 1-tank) along the south coast. There's also good **snorkelling** off Kauwai and around Rukuruku Bay on the north coast of Ovalau, but nothing near Levuka town.

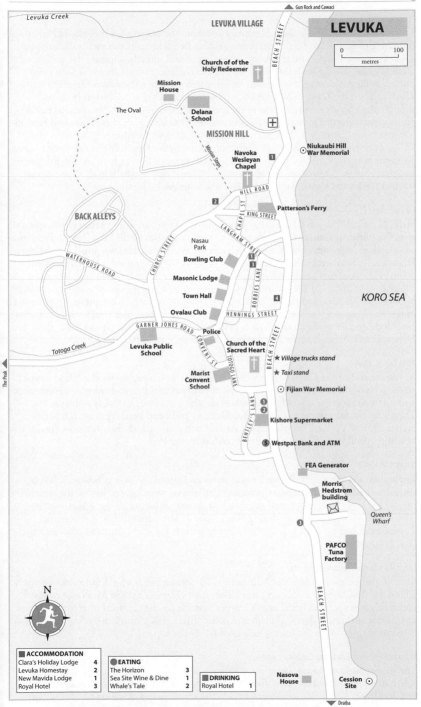

6

Gun Rock and Cawaci

Levuka Creek

LEVUKA VILLAGE

LEVUKA

0   100
metres

**Church of the
Holy Redeemer**

**Mission
House**

The Oval

**Delana
School**

MISSION HILL

**Niukaubi Hill
War Memorial**

**Navoka
Wesleyan
Chapel**

BACK ALLEYS

HILL ROAD

Patterson's Ferry

KING STREET

CHAPEL ST

WATERHOUSE ROAD

CHURCH STREET

LANGHAM STREET

Nasau
Park

Bowling Club

Masonic Lodge

ROBBIES LANE

Town Hall

Ovalau Club

HENNINGS STREET

KORO SEA

GARNER JONES ROAD

Police

Totoga Creek

The Peak

**Levuka Public
School**

CONVENT ST

**Church of the
Sacred Heart**

BEACH STREET

TOTOGA LANE

★ **Village trucks stand**

★ **Taxi stand**

**Marist
Convent
School**

⊙ **Fijian War Memorial**

BENTLEY'S LANE

Kishore Supermarket

Ⓢ **Westpac Bank and ATM**

FEA Generator

**Morris
Hedstrom
building**

Queen's
Wharf

**PAFCO
Tuna
Factory**

N

BEACH STREET

**Nasova
House**

Cession ⊙
Site

■ ACCOMMODATION	
Clara's Holiday Lodge	**4**
Levuka Homestay	**2**
New Mavida Lodge	**1**
Royal Hotel	**3**

● EATING	
The Horizon	**3**
Sea Site Wine & Dine	**1**
Whale's Tale	**2**

■ DRINKING	
Royal Hotel	**1**

Draiba

6

Nasau Park and around

Inland from Beach Street along Hennings Street are the playing fields of **Nasau Park**, once the venue of King Cakobau's headquarters on his frequent visits to Levuka. Before you reach the park, a small bridge crosses Totoga Creek and directly opposite the bridge is the quaint double-storey **Town Hall**, built in 1898 to commemorate Queen Victoria's silver jubilee. Adjacent to it are two derelict buildings: to the left is the town's former famous drinking hole, the **Ovalau Club**, which was flattened by Cyclone Winston in 2016, though plans for its restoration are in progress; while the burnt-out Neoclassical building on its right is the old **Masonic Hall**, desecrated in 2000 by a mob of two hundred fired-up villagers from Lovoni who believed it to be a place of devil worship.

Continuing on past the Bowling Club leads to the back of the colonial-era *Royal Hotel*, a pleasant spot for afternoon tea; to reach the hotel entrance turn right at the intersection of Langham Street. Alternatively, head north into Chapel Street, which leads to the quaint **Navoka Wesleyan Chapel**, founded in 1862 and with thick limestone walls.

Mission Hill

From Navoka Wesleyan Chapel, 190 steps lead up to the summit of **Mission Hill**, named after Fiji's first mission school, built here in 1852 by the Reverend John Binner. From the top step a grass path continues to **Mission House**, where Cakobau was proclaimed King of Fiji in 1871. Further up the hill to the left is the flat hilltop known as the **Oval**, where colonial-era residents once gathered on Saturdays for a spot of horse racing. It's now a rugby field with fabulous **views** overlooking Levuka and out towards the offshore islands of Makogai, Wakaya and Batiki. Look out for **pilot whales**, which are present year-round in the Koro Sea – if you're exceptionally lucky you may spot a humpback whale between June and September. From the Oval, a gravel road continues back down to the coast, past Delana Public School, to the hospital at the northern end of Beach Street.

The back alleys

At the far end of the Oval, a narrow bush track winds its way down the hill to Levuka's alluring **back alleys**. A confusing network of pathways and small bridges meander back and forth connecting the old wooden houses where many of Levuka's residents live. There's no obvious route to follow but as long as you keep heading downhill you'll eventually end up back in town. Alternatively you can explore this area from town by heading uphill from Waterhouse Road behind Nasau Park.

Niukaubi Hill

Jutting out into the sea splitting Levuka town and Levuka village is **Niukaubi Hill**, a small bluff where the Supreme Court and Parliament were located before the capital moved to Suva. In its place now stands a **war memorial** listing all the Fijian soldiers who died fighting for Britain during World War I. The adjacent bay is where the *Leonadis* docked on March 3, 1879, bringing with it Fiji's first shipload of indentured Indian labourers.

Levuka village and Gun Rock

Three hundred metres north of Niukaubi Hill, beyond the hospital, is **Levuka village** where the first Europeans set up camp. The small village is backed by a large exposed rockface known as **Gun Rock**, used as target practice by the cannons of HMS *Havanah* to impress and intimidate Cakobau and other chiefs. Ask around the village for a guide to accompany you on the twenty-minute hike to the top.

Nasova House and the Cession Site

The grand **Nasova House**, once the residence of the British Governor, lies at the southern end of Levuka, some five minutes' walk south of the tuna cannery. Nearby, in what looks like a tidy graveyard beside the coast, is the ceremonial spot where

King Cakobau signed the **Deed of Cession** on October 10, 1874, handing over not only sovereignty to Great Britain but also his iconic war club. A public re-enactment of this occasion is performed every year on the same date, coinciding with the town's weeklong heritage festival, "Back to Levuka". A stone embedded with a plaque was laid to mark the **Cession Site** in 1935, and two further stones accompanied this – the one in 1970 to commemorate Independence was presided over by Prince Charles, who stayed in the beautiful **thatch bure** across the road.

ACCOMMODATION   LEVUKA   6

Although there are less than fifty rooms in Levuka, the only time you'll struggle to find a place to stay is during "Back to Levuka" week (mid-Oct), when booking is essential.

Clara's Holiday Lodge Beach St ☎ 344 0013, ✉ claras holidaylodge@rocketmail.com. By far the cheapest accommodation in town, this quaint colonial-style home with a cream-coloured picket fence looks pretty and charming from the outside. Its interior, however, is very bland, with a featureless hallway leading to twelve tiny rooms sharing cold-water bathrooms. Rates include breakfast. Dorms **F$25**, rooms **F$50**

★ **Levuka Homestay** Church St ☎ 344 0777, 🌐 levuka homestay.com. This delightful modern homestay ranks among Fiji's best. Run by an Australian couple, it has just four guest rooms staggered up the hillside, with cosy furnishings and large bathrooms. The breakfast is an event in itself, with freshly made fruit smoothies, fruit, home-made muesli, a cooked breakfast, fresh tea or brewed coffee. Rates include breakfast. 🛜 ($) **F$188**

★ **New Mavida Lodge** North Beach St ☎ 344 0477, ✉ newmavidalodge@connect.com.fj. This mock-palatial modern building – with glittering chandeliers and shiny ceramic floors– seems completely out of place in Levuka. All fourteen rooms have a/c, and the clinical ten-bed dorm is exceptionally good value, with his-and-hers hot-water en-suite bathrooms. There's even a laundry service. Rates include breakfast. 🛜 ($) Dorms **F$27**, rooms **F$65**

Royal Hotel Robbie's Lane ☎ 344 0024, ✉ royal @connect.com.fj. Fiji's oldest hotel, the *Royal* first opened in the 1860s but was rebuilt in 1916 after a fire. The main building has plenty of colonial character, and the fifteen rooms upstairs come with slanted wooden floorboards, creaking four-poster beds and tiny bathrooms. The eight modern two-bedroom cottages in front of the swimming pool are a lot more comfortable and the best option in Levuka for families. Rooms **F$58**, cottages **F$157**

EATING AND DRINKING

Levuka has just enough **restaurants** for a short visit, but with only a trickle of tourists and few residents dining out, they lack panache. **Groceries** can be bought at Kishore Supermarket (Mon–Sat 6.30am–6.30pm, Sun 7–11am), next to the *Whale's Tale* restaurant on Beach St. The only licensed **bar** is at the *Royal Hotel* where you can enjoy a quiet afternoon tipple from 4pm on and play snooker on its full-size table for $1.

The Horizon Beach St ☎ 344 0429. Located almost opposite the tuna cannery in what looks like a community hall, this restaurant specializes in pizza, in particular tuna pizza (F$15.50); highlights of the otherwise uninspiring menu include fish and cassava chips (F$12) and curry chicken (F$11). Daily 11am–9pm.

Sea Site Wine & Dine Beach St ☎ 344 0553. Despite its dungeon-like setting at the back of a canteen, this place serves a variety of great food from delicious tuna-inspired *ceviche* and *sashimi* ($10) to spicy lamb curry (F$12).

Licensed and with a/c. Mon–Sat 10am–3pm & 6–11pm, Sun 6–11pm .

★ **Whale's Tale** Beach St ☎ 929 5820. A charming nautical ambience and delightful home-cooking in one of Levuka's most photographed buildings make this the town's perennial top choice. Choose dishes from a blackboard menu that changes daily depending on what's available at market – the lunchtime fish and chips is spot-on, and there's a good-value two-course dinner for F$26.50. Mon–Sat 9.30am–2pm & 6–9pm.

DIRECTORY

Banks Westpac Bank (Mon–Fri 9.30am–12.30pm & 1.30–4pm) on Beach St is the town's only bank. There's also an ATM machine (ANZ) beside the Levuka Community Centre.

Hospital Beach St, at the northern end of town (Mon–Fri 8am–4.30pm ☎ 344 0221 or a/h ☎ 344 0152).

Police On the corner of Totogo Lane and Garner Jones Rd (open 24hr; ☎ 344 0222).

Post office On Queens Wharf Lane leading down to the port (Mon–Fri 8am–1pm & 2–4pm).

Telephones Outside the post office, in front of Kishore Supermarket on Beach St.

6

North Ovalau

North of Levuka, it's a pleasant 7km walk along the dirt road clinging to the coast to the large Catholic mission and boarding schools of **St John's College** at **Cawaci**. On the southern boundary of the mission, sitting on a bluff overlooking the sea, is the **Bishop's Tomb**, final resting place of Bishop Julien Vidal from France, Fiji's first bishop. From the tomb there's an impressive view north along the coast towards Cawaci's centrepiece, the twin-towered **Church of St John the Baptist**, built in 1897, with its thick whitewashed coral stone walls standing out against the green mountains.

Arovudi village

At Ovalau's northernmost point, 14km from Levuka, one of the island's few white sandy beaches fronts the village of **Arovudi**. Between the beach and the village is an impressive rock foundation where once stood a *bure kalou* or priest's temple. At the western end of the beach is a large collection of jet-black **volcanic stones** used by the women of the village to make an unusual flavouring known as *kora*: grated coconut is wrapped in banana leaves and placed under the stones, where it ferments slowly for four days, a salty flavour being added with each incoming tide.

Rukuruku Bay

Less than 5km west of Arovudi along the coast road, **Rukuruku Bay** has an unusual black-sand beach beside the village and excellent snorkelling along the outer reef. The local women are renowned for catching sardines in the lagoon here, which are chased by giant trevally fish into awaiting nets. A mostly flat 25-minute walking trail heads inland from the village to **Navuwai Waterfall**, a popular spot for a swim surrounded by rainforest and a good place for viewing birds, including the golden fruit dove and occasionally the wattled honeyeater.

ACCOMMODATION   **NORTH OVALAU**

★The Baystay Rukuruku Bay ☎803 8789, ✉lizaditrich@hotmail.com. This quiet, well-organized retreat alongside a narrow beach has just three bamboo and thatch bures (one is a dorm) with en-suite hot-water showers, plus a communal kitchen. From here you can explore the nearby village, walk to Navuwai Waterfall, snorkel off the reef, or just watch movies under the stars. The former owner of the Levuka's *Whale's Tale* restaurant (see p.173) prepares delicious meals on request: breakfast and lunch F$17.40 each, 2-course dinner F$25. Dorms F$35, bures F$116

Bobo's Farm Between Taviya and Rukuruku ☎947 2277, ⓦbobosfarm.com. This five-hundred-acre private farm, run by Bobo and his German wife Karin, is located slightly inland and surrounded by tranquil rainforest. Bobo is passionate about the medicinal values of local vines, roots and leaves, while Karin cooks organic meals using ingredients sourced from their gardens and serves them in the farmhouse. The single wooden solar-powered cottage has two guest rooms, a lounge and a cold-water bathroom. F$93

NAIGANI ISLAND

Some 10km off the northwest coast of Ovalau, **Naigani Island** has an interesting history, which is typical of the region's volatility. The islanders trace their roots back to **Verata** on Viti Levu, to which they remain politically aligned. Verata was one of the two traditional enemies of Bau, so when the island was invaded by Cakobau in 1860 a thousand of the islanders were killed and carried off to Bau to be eaten – only two people were left alive. A few years later, an Australian named **Riley** was given a portion of the island as a dowry, having married the daughter of a Verata chief. Today, Naigani has a population of around fifty, descendants of the two surviving islanders and Riley's offspring. They live in a village on the north coast, lodged between two volcanic peaks. The **original village** is found in the hills, protected by a rim with a killing stone at its entrance and a large **hillfort** higher up. Large amounts of Lapita pottery have been discovered around the island dating back more than two thousand years. There's no accommodation on Naigani, but all the north Ovalau resorts listed above can organize trips here with local boatmen – it's a thirty-minute boat ride.

Silana Eco Stay Arovudi village ☎835 9260, ⓦsala
_nagalu@yahoo.com. Bubbly Fijian couple, Seru and Sala
rent out a single clean cottage with cold-water shower plus
camping beside the beach a short walk east of the village.
There's a range of activities on offer, including traditional
mat weaving, fishing trips (F$20) and a hike to a large
hillfort on top of Tomuna Peak (F$30 including lunch;
minimum two people). Rates includes hearty Fijian meals.
Camping F$50, cottage F$150

South Ovalau

The coast of **south Ovalau** is rugged and covered in tropical forest. Jutting out above
Tokou village is the dramatic volcanic plug nicknamed the **Devil's Thumb**. Heading
around the southwest coast, flanked offshore by Moturiki Island, you'll find the village
of **Wainaloka**, founded by freed Solomon Island slaves in the middle of the nineteenth
century. A few kilometres beyond Wainaloka is the Bureta airstrip.

Lovoni

From the Bureta airstrip, a dirt track winds inland, following the Bureta River to **Lovoni**
village, one of the island's star attractions. The village was made infamous by the fierce
tribe (see box below) who lived behind an impregnable hillfort in the centre of the
volcanic crater here (they've since moved to a more practical location just to the side).

The easiest way to visit is on a seven-hour guided trip with Epi's Tours (☎977 9977,
ⓔepibole@yahoo.com; F$80 including lunch; tours pick up from Levuka hotels
Mon–Sat at 10.30am; booking essential), which involves a bone-crunching ride in the
back of a carrier van. A more rewarding alternative is to take a **guided hike** with Nox
(see box, p.170) starting from Draiba village, a few kilometres south of Levuka. This is
the shortest trail from the coast but it still takes a tough couple of hours through thick
rainforest before you reach the dramatic setting of the crater – arrange for a carrier van
to bring you back by road. You can also approach Lovoni from *Bobo's Farm* or *Silana
Eco Stay* (see above), although these are both full-day hikes.

ACCOMMODATION   **SOUTH OVALAU**

★**Kauwai Homestay** South coast, north of
Wainaloka ☎732 4330, ⓦkauwai.com. This holistic
retreat specializes in healthy food, occasional yoga
weekends and generally being at one with nature. The
guesthouse has four rooms with a shared cold-water
bathroom, plus a private cabin sleeping up to ten for
families or groups. There's no beach here but the views
from its raised position are therapeutic and a passage cuts
through the mangroves to a protected bay where you can
kayak, snorkel and fish; boat tours (F$40pp) and scuba
diving (F$80 1-tank) can be arranged too. Eta, from the
local village, cooks wonderful meals ($25pp per day).
Rates include breakfast. Camping (own tent) F$25, rooms
F$40, cabin F$350

Caqalai and Leleuvia

Two small islands along Ovalau's south coast, **Caqalai** and **Leleuvia**, possess beach
resorts and are becoming popular with **backpackers** keen to avoid the increasingly

---

CAKOBAU AND THE LOVONI TRIBE

During 1870 and 1871, **Cakobau** tried time after time to subdue the fierce **Lovoni tribe** who
had been constantly menacing the European settlers around Levuka. Unable to break through
the ring of defences protecting the village in Lovoni Crater, Cakobau sent a Methodist
missionary to Lovoni, inviting the tribe to a **reconciliation** in Levuka. Tired of being pursued
by Cakobau, the Lovoni chief consulted his priest and accepted the invitation. On June 29,
1871, the entire village came down to Levuka. A meal was prepared, but as soon as the tribe
set down their weapons to eat, Cakobau's warriors surrounded and subdued them. In time the
majority were sold off as **slaves** and dispersed throughout every corner of the archipelago.
Those that remain are a stoutly proud group, believing their village to be the only one in Fiji
not to have been conquered by Cakobau.

6

commercial Yasawa Islands trail. The nicest is **Caqalai Island**, where at low tide you can wade out to nearby **Snake Island**, which offers good **snorkelling** and the chance to spot black-and-white **sea snakes**. Although they are extremely venomous, the snakes are so timid and agile that you will have little chance of getting near them. Even better snorkelling is available at **Honeymoon Island**, a sand spit 5km to the east where you'll likely spot small reef sharks hiding among the coral.

ARRIVAL AND DEPARTURE

CAQALAI AND LELEUVIA

By resort transfer Both resorts arrange transfers from Viti Levu: Caqalai boats leave from Waidalice Landing just before Varaqa village about a 30min drive north of Nausori, while Leleuvia boats leave from nearby Bau Landing. Transfers cost F$45 per person one-way, for a minimum of two people. You can reach Waidalice or Bau Landing by taxi from Suva (F$60) or Nausori ($30); Waidalice can also be reached by bus/minivan from Nausori (F$7). From Levuka, the 40min boat journey to either Caqalai or Leleuvia costs F$55pp, minimum 2 people, and can be arranged through the resorts.

ACCOMMODATION

★**Caqalai Island Resort** ☎719 3404, ⌨fijiisland resortcaqalai.com. This laidback backpackers hangout is owned by the Methodist Church of nearby Moturiki Island, but don't let that put you off – the only drawback is that no alcohol is sold on the island, though it's fine to bring your own. In a tiny coral island setting, the fourteen bures are beautifully thatched and hidden among palm trees on the edge of the beachfront; and the bathrooms, painted in colourful murals, have cold-water showers and flush toilets. Cash only. Rates include meals. Camping (own tent) F̲$̲5̲5̲, dorms F̲$̲6̲5̲, bures F̲$̲2̲0̲0̲

Leleuvia Island Resort ☎838 4365, ⌨leleuvia.com. Caqalai's close rival, 2km to the south, has a similar setting but is a lot more flash. Choose from traditional thatched bures or the male and female 20-bed dorms. The sand-floor restaurant is well positioned overlooking the beach and activities include scuba diving, paddleboarding and outrigger canoe sailing. Leleuvia is a popular weekend retreat for Suva residents so rates are more expensive at the weekend. Rates include meals. ⌨ ($) Dorms F̲$̲1̲6̲9̲, bures F̲$̲4̲1̲3̲

Outer Lomaiviti

Few travellers reach the six islands of **Outer Lomaiviti**, especially since Cyclone Winston devastated the elaborate coral reefs that twist around the islands of **Makogai** and Wakaya. Rising out of the Koro Sea some 50km east of Ovalau are the large volcanic islands of **Koro** and Gau, the fifth and sixth largest landmasses in Fiji respectively. Both islands are blessed with rich agricultural land and large iTaukei populations, though virtually no tourist infrastructure.

Makogai

In 1911, the small hilly island of **Makogai** became a **leper colony** for sufferers of the disease from throughout the South Pacific. Under the care of Mother Mary Agnes, a community was built consisting of a large hospital, cinema, shops and a church, as well as a cemetery where 1241 leprosy sufferers now rest in peace. The colony closed in 1969, twenty years after an effective treatment for the disease was found. In 1986, Makogai was declared a **marine reserve** and is now run by the Ministry of Fisheries as a research centre with a hatchery breeding giant clams, trochus and sea turtles.

ARRIVAL AND DEPARTURE

MAKOGAI

By cruise boat There's nowhere to stay on Makogai, and the only practical way to visit this fascinating island is with Captain Cook Cruises from Port Denarau (see p.92) on its "Colonial", "4-Cultures" or "Lau" trips.

Koro

The triangular-shaped island of **Koro** lies 70km northeast of Ovalau and less than 50km south of Vanua Levu. Rising to a peak of 560m, this volcanic island has splendid views from its inland road, with bush tracks, **waterfalls** set among tropical forests and herds of wild horses in the grassy inland plains. The largest village is Nasau, midway along the east coast about 5km north of the airstrip, home to a hospital, post office and government headquarters. The women of Koro are renowned for their finely woven **handicrafts**, particularly mats and fans.

Koro was the island most affected by **Cyclone Winston** (see box, p.26) with the eye passing just to the north of the island on February 20, 2016. Three-quarters of Koro's houses were destroyed and several villages along the east coast were completely wiped out by storm surges. Eight islanders died. Today, the island is still reliant on aid and more than a quarter of the population (some 3500 people) have left Koro and moved to cities and towns around Fiji: for more information on the impact of Cyclone Winston on Koro, see ⓦkorois.org.

6

ARRIVAL AND DEPARTURE   KORO

By plane Fiji Link (☎672 0888, ⓦfijiairways.com) flies to Koro from Nausori every Monday (F$183 one way).
By boat *Goundar Shipping* (☎331 3266, ⓦgoundar shipping.com; F$40 one way) departs Walu Bay in Suva at 6pm on Mon, calling in at Muanivau Landing on the south point of Koro around 6am before heading back to Suva at 6am on Wed.

ACCOMMODATION

Koro Beach Resort ☎368 3301. The only place to stay on Koro, this small resort makes a good base to explore the island. Six simply furnished bures with en-suite hot-water bathrooms extend along the beachfront; there's also a casual restaurant. Rates include meals. Bures F$180

Lau Group

Like the flick of a paint brush, sixty tiny dots in a canvas of deep blue make up the **LAU GROUP**, a widely dispersed collection of islands forming the distant eastern border of Fiji. Only half the islands are inhabited and the people who live here are almost completely reliant on the reef-strewn sea that surrounds them. Cargo boats from Suva bring in essential supplies and connect the islands with the outside world. Otherwise, they remain untouched, **undeveloped** and seldom visited by outsiders apart from sailors anchoring in its secluded bays between May and September and the odd **small-ship cruise** visiting a few beaches and villages.

The Lau Group can be split into three regions: Northern Lau, Southern Lau and Moala. Starting some 60km off the southern coast of Taveuni, **Northern Lau** is the region most appealing to tourists, thanks to its historic island of Vanua Balavu with the spectacular Bay of Islands at its northern tip. **Southern Lau** is the most isolated part of the group – in places it's nearer to Tonga than Suva – and the most influenced by Tongan culture. These islands hold the region's seat of power at the traditional village of Tubou on Lakeba. The **Moala Group** is the nearest to Viti Levu, its three high volcanic islands sitting in an isolated sea between Southern Lau and Kadavu.

If you're coming to the Lau Group, bring plenty of cash, supplies and *kava* roots (pounded *kava* is also acceptable) as a *sevusevu* when visiting villages – there are no banks, only a handful of small village stores, and food and fuel costs are inflated due to the islands' isolation.

Brief history

Before **Captain James Cook** chartered the island of Vatoa in Southern Lau in 1774, Lau was a little-known group of remote islands where Tongans and Fijians traded, occasionally fought and often intermarried. The Tongans came for the giant *vesi* trees that flourished around the islands of Fulaga, Kabara and Lakeba. These were hollowed out to make large double-hulled canoes used for exploration, trade and war around the Tongan empire. In 1800, the *Argo*, one of the first Western merchant ships to enter Fijian waters, was **shipwrecked** on the Bukatatanoa Reef, off Oneata. Its survivors were rescued in canoes and transported to Oneata where they became the first white people

6

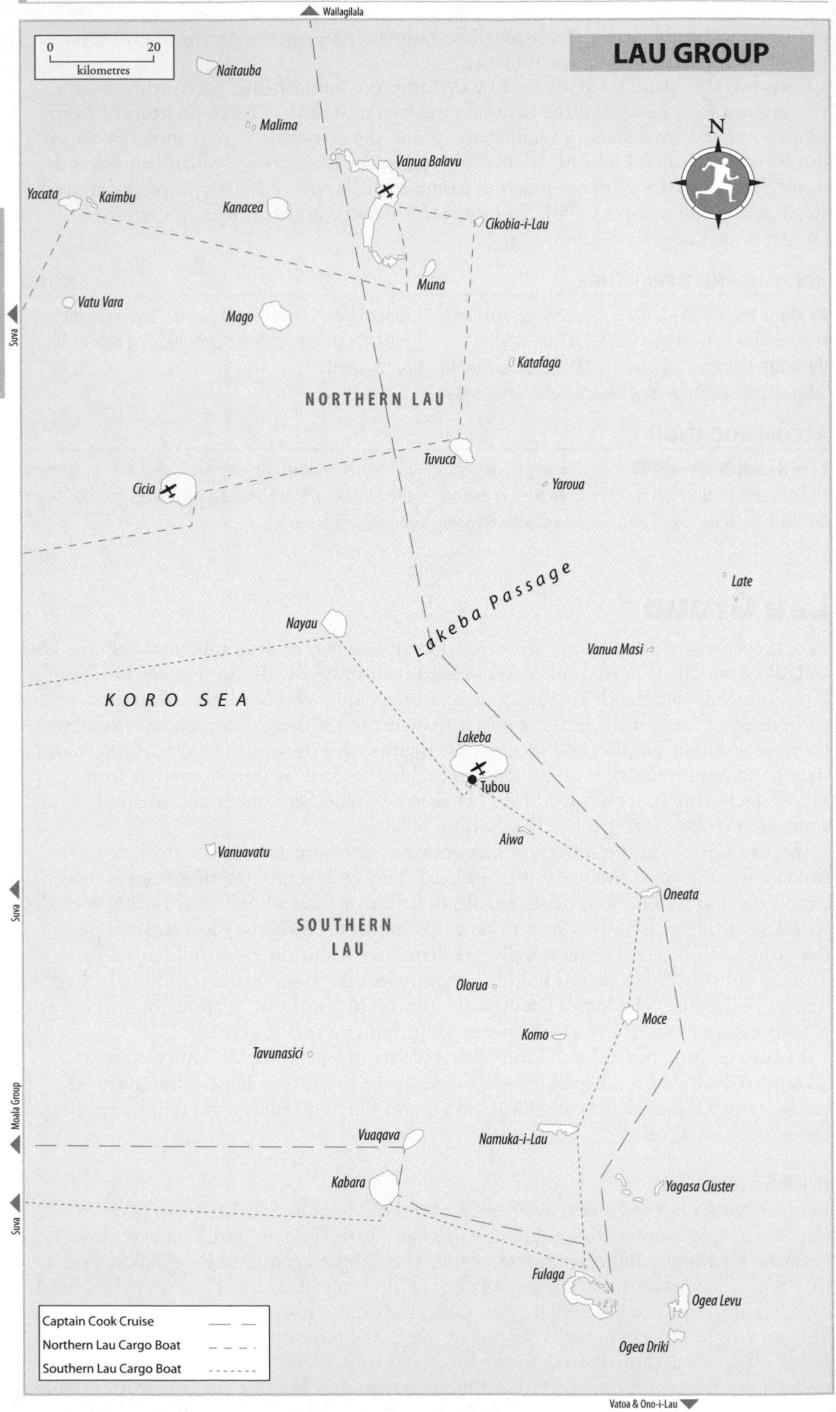

LAU GROUP

0   20
kilometres

N

Wailagilala

Naitauba

Malima

Vanua Balavu

Yacata   Kaimbu

Kanacea

Cikobia-i-Lau

Vatu Vara

Muna

Mago

Katafaga

NORTHERN LAU

Tuvuca

Yaroua

Cicia

Late

Nayau

Lakeba Passage

Vanua Masi

KORO SEA

Lakeba

Tubou

Vanuavatu

Aiwa

Oneata

SOUTHERN
LAU

Olorua

Moce

Komo

Tavunasici

Vuaqava

Namuka-i-Lau

Yagasa Cluster

Kabara

Fulaga

Ogea Levu

Ogea Driki

Captain Cook Cruise	— —
Northern Lau Cargo Boat	– – ·
Southern Lau Cargo Boat	· · · · ·

Suva

Suva

Moala Group

Suva

Vatoa & Ono-i-Lau

to live among Fijians. Items from the ship including ceramic plates and buttons moved briskly around the islands, providing much curiosity. Sadly the ship also brought with it a strain of **cholera** which caused many deaths throughout the islands.

In 1835, two Wesleyan Methodist **missionaries**, the Rev William Cross from England and Rev David Cargill from Scotland, landed at Tubou on Lakeba, becoming the first missionaries to arrive in Fiji. The pair had already worked in Tonga for several years and were accompanied by several envoys of the **Taufa'ahau**, the Christian King of Tonga. During the great **wars** of the 1840s between Bau and Rewa, fierce Tongan warriors fought for both sides in different parts of the islands. By 1848, their reputation had begun to embarrass Taufa'ahau, so he sent the headstrong **Prince Ma'afu** to Lakeba to control his people. Ma'afu excelled at his task and soon began to dominate the Lau Group. He moved his seat of power to Lakeba and by 1869 had declared himself *Tui Lau* or "**King of Lau**". With the islands pacified and a Christian ruler in place, European planters moved in, purchasing the fertile islands of Northern Lau to grow cotton, and later for coconut oil production. When the entire Fijian archipelago was ceded to Britain in 1874, Ma'afu was granted control of the Lau Group and remained here until his death in 1881.

Today, Lauans walk tall among Fijians, retaining much power in political life. Two of Fiji's most revered figureheads hailed from Tubou on Lakeba: Ratu Sir Lala Sukuna (1888–1958), who paved the way for the nation's independence; and **Ratu Sir Kamisese Mara** (1920–2004), Fiji's first Prime Minister. The latter held the title of President from 1993 to 2000 before being unceremoniously deposed by the Speight coup (see p.227).

ARRIVAL AND DEPARTURE

THE LAU GROUP

By plane Fiji Link (☎ 672 0888, ⓦ fijiairways.com) operates weekly flights from Nausori Airport direct to Cicia, Northern Lau (Tues; 1hr; F$262); Lakeba, Southern Lau (Thurs; 1hr 15min; F$273); and Vanua Balavu, Northern Lau (Wed; 1hr 10min; F$273), but no flights between the islands. Flights are often booked out months in advance, especially around Christmas and other school holidays. Northern Airways (☎ 992 2449, ⓦ www .northernairfiji.com.fj) flies from Nausori (Suva) to Moala (Thurs; 45min; F$186).

By cargo boat Cargo boats (see box below) leave several times a month from Nerain Jetty at the end of Tofua St in Suva's Walu Bay, and travel various routes around the islands: fares are around F$100 for deck passage and F$200 for a cabin. Shipping companies come and go and routes change frequently, so for the latest information enquire at the departure jetty. Currently, Goundar Shipping (☎ 330 1035, ⓦ goundarshipping.com) has two monthly routes, one visiting Northern Lau, and the other the Moala Group. Victoria Marine (☎ 330 0711, ⓔ victoriamarinelimited@gmail.com) also visits

---

CARGO BOATS

An intriguing way to explore the Lau islands is on board one of the monthly **cargo boats** that bring supplies and passengers to and from the islands. The round-trip journey from Suva on all routes takes between six and ten days, offering a wonderful opportunity to mingle with the locals and to get a feel for the vastness of the region. Although there is no fixed schedule, there's usually at least one departure a week from **Suva**, with each boat visiting between three and eight islands before heading back to the capital. Most islands don't have a jetty, so small local boats meet the ships and shuttle the supplies back and forth to the villages. It should be possible to take one of these local boats and have a quick look around the island, but things are often chaotic so make sure you don't miss the boat's departure – if you do, it could be several weeks before the next boat arrives.

Conditions on board are basic. A few boats have **cabins** with bunk beds, but these are often stuffy, stink of diesel fumes and crammed with luggage. You're better off sleeping under the stars on the open deck – bring a pillow and preferably a mat for spreading out on the floor. Simple meals of boiled cassava and tinned fish (and occasionally something better that has been caught en route) are usually provided, although sometimes only to cabin passengers, so bring plenty of drinks and convenience food yourself. Toilet paper is another necessity – and be prepared for the vile conditions of a cargo boat bathroom, especially when the seas are even a little bit rough.

Northern Lau and the Moala Group monthly, plus runs a third route to Southern Lau from Lakeba down to Kabara. Lehona Shipping (T 354 3833 or T 893 9203, E ben_cavu@yahoo.com.au) visits the remote Southern Lau islands of Kabara, Fulaga, Ogea Vatoa and Ono-i-Lau once a month.

By small-ship cruise The only organized way to visit the Lau islands in comfort is on a small-ship cruise from Nadi with Captain Cook Cruises (T 670 1823, W captaincookcruisesfiji.com). Its epic 11-night Lau trip leaves three times a year, taking in eight islands from Wailagilala in the north to Totoya in the Moala Group: highlights include Vanua Balavu's Bay of Islands, Fulaga Lagoon, a church on Oneata, a village visit on Kabara and plenty of snorkelling.

6

Northern Lau

For an offbeat adventure, exploring **Northern Lau** is an unforgettable experience. The most appealing of all the Lauan destinations, **Vanua Balavu**, lies in the heart of the region, capped by the dramatic, uplifted limestone islands of the **Bay of Islands** – a popular yachting destination. If you plan carefully, you can get to Vanua Balavu by plane, spend a few days exploring and then catch the **cargo boat** back to Suva via five other Lauan islands. Be warned, though, that boat schedules and sometimes even flights may change last-minute or become delayed due to bad weather and both are overbooked during Christmas holidays.

Vanua Balavu

On a map, the long, thin curving island of **Vanua Balavu** looks uncannily like a sea horse with Masomo Bay as its eye and the small islets of Malata and Susui forming its hooked tail. Vanua Balavu is the second most populated island of the Lau Group, with 1800 people in fourteen coastal villages, farming copra and fishing the lagoons as income. In 1855, when the Tongan prince Ma'afu invaded Vanua Balavu, it became the first of his Fijian conquests: he hid all his war canoes in the Bay of Islands and based his court in the village of **Lomaloma**, now the island's main village. The island remains heavily influenced by **Tongan customs**, with the local dialect formed mostly of Tongan words and the bures following the rounded Tongan style of architecture.

On foot you can **hike** the 5km from Lomaloma to the southern tip of the island, passing the cliffs flanking the settlement of Nakama, where you can ask around for a guide to show you the **hot springs** and burial caves in the hills. Local boatmen can take you to **Susui Island**, a quieter alternative to the Bay of Islands and a favourite local picnic spot with beautiful cove beaches, small bays for swimming and snorkelling, and an inland lake – just offshore is a deep blue hole where turtles can often be seen.

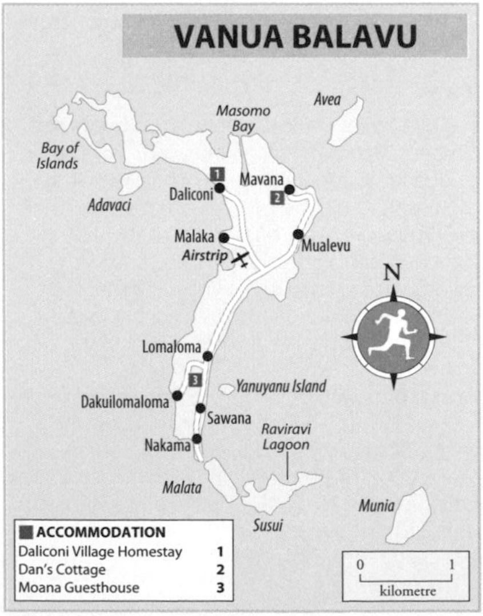
VANUA BALAVU
Masomo Bay
Avea
Bay of Islands
Adavaci
Daliconi
Mavana
Malaka
Airstrip
Mualevu
N
Lomaloma
Yanuyanu Island
Dakuilomaloma
Sawana
Raviravi Lagoon
Nakama
Malata
Munia
Susui
ACCOMMODATION
Daliconi Village Homestay 1
Dan's Cottage 2
Moana Guesthouse 3
0 1 kilometre

The northern half of Vanua Balavu, beyond the grass airstrip, is mostly rocky with sharp limestone pinnacles along the coast and mostly inaccessible except for a road leading to **Daliconi village**, home to the traditional owners of the Bay of Islands. Ask around here and you'll find someone to take you on the short 20-minute boat trip to the Bay of Islands. A small shop stocks a decent selection of provisions, including *kava* to present as a *sevusevu* before visiting the Bay of Islands.

The Bay of Islands

Off the northwestern tip of Vanua Balavu is the pretty **Bay of Islands**, known locally as Qilaqila, a collection of limestone islands and islets, deep indented bays, secluded beaches and cathedral caves, with excellent snorkelling in its brilliant turquoise lagoon. The protected bays make exceptional anchorage for visiting **yachts** between May and October, though yacht owners will need to call in at Daliconi village first to pay the F$30 anchorage fee. Be aware that in the winter months, it can get very busy here with up to fifty yachts anchored at any one time, each with a little outboard dinghy whizzing around the lagoon.

The islands themselves are mostly impenetrable – difficult to approach by boat and covered in a tangled yet velvety mass of shrubs and *vesi* trees. However, there are a couple of walking tracks worth exploring with outstanding views over the islands. Also, check out **Vale ni Bose**, "the Meeting Place of the Gods", a 40m-high cave etched into limestone cliffs full of stalactites and with several windows letting in dashes of light – access can be tricky and at high tide you'll need to duck under the water to avoid scraping your back along the sharp limestone ceiling of its narrow tunnel-like entrance.

6

ACCOMMODATION | **VANUA BALAVU**

Daliconi Village Homestay Daliconi village ☏727 3915 or ☏728 1026. Organized by the community, this homestay offers accommodation in local houses around Daliconi village. Rates include meals. **F$250**

Dan's Cottage Mavana ☏940 6926, ✉danvakacegu @yahoo.com. Located on a hilltop overlooking Mavana village on the island's northeast coast, this peaceful wooden cottage has one en-suite bedroom with cold-water shower and guests can either use the family kitchen or have meals prepared. **F$200**

Moana Guesthouse Sawana, Lomaloma ☏718 2886 or ☏822 1148. Two simple beachside bures with mosquito nets, shared toilet, cold-water shower and solar power. The owner Tevita can organize village visits, hiking trips and boat trips to Susui Island and the Bay of Islands (bring snorkelling gear); a sightseeing vehicle costs F$130 for half a day. Rates include meals, and you'll be well fed with local vegetables and fish, although there are also several small stores in Lomaloma village, a 15min walk north. **F$190**

Vatu Vara and the private islands

To explore the Northern Lau islands **beyond Vanua Balavu**, you could try hitching a ride on one of the yachts anchored in the Bay of Islands. Alternatively, with some persuasion and around F$600 in cash, a boatman from Lomaloma or Daliconi might take you on a day-trip. One of the most dramatic islands to visit is forest-covered **Vatu Vara**. Its 305m plateau is the highest point in the Lau Group and can be seen from Vanua Balavu, 60km to the east. Up close, the limestone cliffs of the plateau cascade down to a coral terrace with rich farming land and palm-fringed beaches. It's rumoured that a treasure chest of gold coins was buried on the island by Joe Thompson, an American eccentric who lived and died here in the late 1800s.

Several islands in Northern Lau have been bought by foreign millionaires as **private island retreats**. These include the most northerly of the Lau islands, **Wailagilala**, a natural coral atoll with an abundance of seabird colonies including nesting boobies, noddies and terns. Some 30km northwest of Vanua Balavu, **Naitauba** is the "spiritual hermitage" of the American religious cult of Adi Dam Samraj; while **Mago**, less than 20km off the southern tip of Vanua Balavu, was bought by Mel Gibson in 2005 for US$15 million – he seldom visits, though several of his A-list colleagues have. Fifty kilometres west of Vanua Balavu, the twin islands of **Yacata** and **Kaimbu** are owned by James Janard, owner of Oakley's sunglasses and if you have a spare US$25,000 you could spend a week here at one of its three incredibly beautiful villas.

Southern Lau

The diffuse islands of **Southern Lau** are the most remote in Fiji. The main island, **Lakeba**, administrative capital of the entire Lau Group, lies in its northern sphere, leaving all islands to the south far removed from shipping and air services. The southernmost island of Ono-i-Lau lies 200km south of Lakeba, a journey that can take several days by boat – it's so remote that half the island's twenty houses have been abandoned, and you can easily rent one for a month-long stay through Lehona Shipping, which services the island monthly (see p.180). The two most intriguing islands to visit are Lakeba, rich in history and culture, and the stunning **Fulaga**, a rugged coral atoll with unusual limestone formations.

Lakeba

Lakeba, almost circular in shape with a diameter of 8km, has the region's only **airstrip** (connected by weekly flights from Nausori; see p.142 for details) and is the main link with the Fijian mainland. Lakeba is the dominant seat of power in the group, and home to the chief of Lau, *Tui Nayau*, although the name actually originates from the island of Nayau, just to the north of Lakeba. The most recent *Tui Nayau* was former prime minister Ratu Sir Kamisese Mara, who also held the *Tui Lau* title created by Tongan prince Ma'afu.

Tubou

The island's main village is **Tubou**, located on the southwest coast. With a population of around six hundred, it forms Lakeba's heartbeat and is home to the government and provincial headquarters, hospital, post office, several stores and jetty. The village has a strong Tongan influence, with people living in rounded thatch bures and wearing *ta'avala* (woven mats) around the waist. The graveyard behind the provincial office has a small stepped platform where the Tongan prince and warrior **Ma'afu** lies buried.

The rest of the island

A well-maintained dirt road hugs much of the flat **coastline**, making it easy to get around by foot. Several impressive **caves** with stalactites and stalagmites can be explored including Delaiono, south of Tubou on the southern tip, and Oso Nabukete along the uplifted west coast. Slightly inland, close to the airstrip, are more caves, originally used as refuges in times of war or for banishment. In the centre of the island is the largest **hillfort** in Fiji. Situated on top of the 360m-high Ketekete Peak, the fort was capable of sheltering over 2500 people, although today most of its stone walls lie buried in the undergrowth. Off the east coast is a myriad of tiny islands ideal for exploring: you should be able to hire a boatman from the village of Nukunuku for around F$150.

ACCOMMODATION	LAKEBA

Lau Provincial Council Rodwell Road, Suva ☎331 6801. The Lau Provincial Council can help arrange homestay accommodation throughout the Southern Lau islands. You should present a *sevusevu* (see box, p.40) when you arrive as your traditional request for assistance. Expect to pay a round F$100 per person per night for board and meals.

Fulaga

The crescent-shaped limestone island of **Fulaga** lies in the distant southern part of the group, 100km south of Lakeba. The low-lying, three-tiered island shelters a large, almost completely enclosed lagoon opening into the sea via a series of tiny passages. Within the lagoon are a myriad of limestone islands and islets, many eroded into mushroom-shaped rocks popping out of the turquoise waters, and others peppered with white-sand cove beaches. It's a breathtaking spot, even more spectacular than Vanua Balavu, and a stunning place to kayak, snorkel or tour by small boat. Fulaga has three small villages but no accommodation, though you may be able to arrange a homestay through the Lau Provincial Council (see above). Alternatively, Captain Cook Cruises spends a day in the lagoon on its Lau trip (see p.92).

THE WOODCARVERS OF LAU

The people of Southern Lau are fine **artisans**: the women from Oneata are skilled makers of *tapa* cloth (see p.157), while the men, particularly from Kabara and Fulaga, are known as Fiji's best **woodcarvers**. You'll find examples of their work, such as *tanoa* bowls, available in the handicraft markets around Suva or in Nadi's more expensive souvenir shops. Carvings from Kabara are distinguished by their intricate patterns, while the craftsmen on Fulaga specialize in making large outrigger canoes carved from a single *vesi* tree.

As well as *tapa* cloth and woodcarving, Lau islanders produce the coarse twine known as **magimagi**. Commonly seen binding together bures, *magimagi* comes from the fibres of a coconut husk, baked in the sun, soaked in the sea and briskly rubbed together to make long threads. The threads are meticulously braided to form a strong twine, often several kilometres in length. *Magimagi* was once used to lash together the parts of a canoe, although today it is most often seen extending from a *tanoa* or *kava* bowl towards the person of highest rank, or attached to either end of a *tabua*, or whale's tooth (see box, p.232).

The Moala Group

The three islands of the **Moala Group** – Moala, Totoya and Matuku – lie in a rather isolated part of the Fijian archipelago, south of Lomaiviti, east of Kadavu and west of the main portion of the Lauan islands. Culturally linked to the Lomaiviti Group, all three islands were raided and seized by Ma'afu during the 1850s and have remained under the administrative control of the Lau Group ever since. Although there's an airstrip on Moala, there's no accommodation on any of the islands.

Moala

Covering 63 square kilometres, **Moala** is the largest and most populated of all islands in the Lau Group. It's an easy place to explore, with eleven villages all linked by walking tracks crisscrossing the hills. The government station, airstrip and jetty are at Naroi on the northeast tip.

Totoya

Forty kilometres south of Moala, the stunning collapsed volcanic crater of **Totoya** has formed a steep rim shaped like a horseshoe and is surrounded by a deep lagoon. From the air, the setting is spectacular but access into the horseshoe bay is difficult even in calm seas. There are four villages on the island; three of these are located on the bay.

Matuku

Matuku, the southernmost of the three islands, is slightly smaller than Moala. Graced with lush tropical forests rising to a peak of 388m, the rich volcanic soil on its slopes is ideal for farming and some of the finest *dalo* is grown here. Three of the island's four villages sit alongside one of several long, white-sand beaches which flank the south side of the island – you'll usually find the village women here engaged in basket weaving using spiky *voi voi* leaves (*Pandanus thurstoni*).

Vanua Levu and Taveuni

TAVEUNI SUNSET

Vanua Levu and Taveuni

Known collectively as "The Friendly North", the northern islands of Vanua Levu and Taveuni are Fiji's forgotten frontier. Once the centre of European exploration and the ensuing copra (coconut oil) trade, they are far removed from mainstream tourism yet offer accessible opportunities for adventure travel. Vanua Levu, Fiji's second-largest island at 5587 square kilometres, is dominated by rambling countryside and has just two towns, Labasa and Savusavu. The northern town of Labasa has a hilly rural hinterland worth exploring by bus, while the serene Savusavu Bay on the south coast boasts quaint drinking holes and restaurants as well as plenty of nearby hikes and snorkelling beaches. Off Vanua Levu's southeast tip is the rugged, forest-covered Taveuni, the third-largest island in Fiji, yet not even a tenth the size of its neighbour. Dubbed the "Garden Island", Taveuni is dominated by the stunning Bouma National Heritage Park, a magnet for hikers and bird-watching enthusiasts.

In recent years, however, the islands have suffered devastating **hurricanes,** floods and landslides, in particular Cyclone Winston (see box, p.26), which left thousands of people homeless. In addition, the falling prices of both sugar and copra have led to fewer opportunities for the younger generation, many of whom have moved to Viti Levu in search of a better life. **Tourism** is the region's greatest hope – and **scuba diving** in particular, with one of the world's most bountiful soft coral colonies on the **Rainbow Reef** hugging Vanua Levu's eastern tip. Further fantastic dive sites include those off the island of **Matangi** as well as the massive **Great Sea Reef** along Vanua Levu's north coast. The **snorkelling** in this region is excellent too, while **Kia Island** and the south coast of **Qamea** have begun to emerge as **surfing** hotspots. A dozen upmarket boutique beach resorts tempt honeymooners seeking seclusion, while **Matei** on Taveuni is popular with backpackers attracted by the island's lush tropical rainforests and impressive waterfalls.

ARRIVAL AND DEPARTURE   VANUA LEVU AND TAVEUNI

Vanua Levu and Taveuni are both served by passenger **ferries** and **flights** from Viti Levu. It's relatively simple to combine a trip to both islands, as most ferry routes call in at both Vanua Levu and Taveuni. A good itinerary is to fly into Labasa, travel by bus to Savusavu and then over to Taveuni by boat: from Taveuni you can either take a passenger ferry over to Suva or a flight back to Nadi – ten days should be enough time to get a feel for the islands.

BY PLANE
Flights to the islands are in small propeller planes from either Nadi or Suva. Seats can fill up quickly with dive groups and their equipment, so book as far in advance as possible. The baggage allowance is 20kg per person, so call ahead if you're bringing your own scuba gear or surf

TAVORO WATERFALL, BOUMA NATIONAL HERITAGE PARK

Highlights

❶ **Labasa countryside** Mingle with the locals on an open-sided bus ride into the pretty Labasa Hills. **See p.193**

❷ **Savusavu** Hike in the Hills, marvel at the hot springs, snorkel in the clear waters and end the day with a sundowner drink overlooking the bobbing yachts in the bay. **See p.194**

❸ **Rainbow Reef** Both snorkellers and divers can explore the soft corals and tropical fish at this world-renowned reef between Vanua Levu and Taveuni. **See p.202**

❹ **Kioa and Rabi islands** Sample two South Pacific cultures, one from Polynesia, the other from Micronesia, living on these adopted islands. **See p.202 & p.203**

❺ **Bouma National Heritage Park** Fiji's most varied national park, offering walks in lush forest, high waterfalls, historical sites and an intriguing marine reserve. **See p.208**

❻ **Des Vœux Peak** Spot the elusive orange dove or the rare tagimaucia flower on the hike to Taveuni's second highest peak. **See p.212**

HIGHLIGHTS ARE MARKED ON THE MAP ON P.188

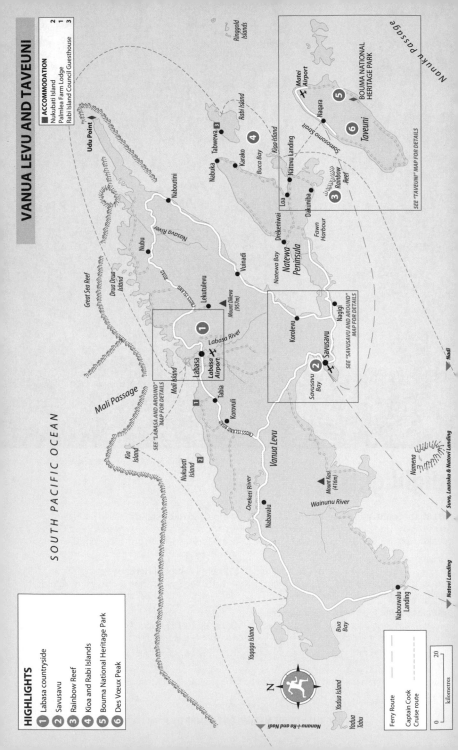

VANUA LEVU AND TAVEUNI

HIGHLIGHTS

1. Labasa countryside
2. Savusavu
3. Rainbow Reef
4. Kioa and Rabi Islands
5. Bouma National Heritage Park
6. Des Vœux Peak

ACCOMMODATION
Nukubati Island — 2
Palmlea Farm Lodge — 1
Rabi Island Council Guesthouse — 3

SOUTH PACIFIC OCEAN

Ringgold Islands

Nanuku Passage

BOUMA NATIONAL
HERITAGE PARK

Matei Airport

Taveuni

Naqara

SEE "TAVEUNI" MAP FOR DETAILS

Somosomo Strait

Natewa Landing

Kioa Island

Rabi Island

Nabuka

Tabwewa

Karako

Bucа Bay

Udu Point

Naboutini

Nubu

Great Sea Reef

Drua Drua Island

Nasorolevu River

CROSS ISLAND ROAD

Lekutulevu

Mount Dikeva (957m)

Vuinadi

Rainbow Reef

Loa

Dakumiba

Drekeniwai

Natewa Bay

Natewa Peninsula

Fawn Harbour

Korolevu

Nagigi

Savusavu

SEE "SAVUSAVU AND AROUND" MAP FOR DETAILS

Savusavu Bay

Labasa River

Labasa

Labasa Airport

SEE "LABASA AND AROUND" MAP FOR DETAILS

Mali Island

Mali Passage

Kia Island

Nukubati Island

Tabia

Korovuli

CROSS ISLAND ROAD

Dreketi River

Nabavalu

Mount Kasi (416m)

Wainunu River

Vanua Levu

Namena

Suva, Lautoka & Natovi Landing

Nabouwalu Landing

Natovi Landing

Bua Bay

Yaqaga Island

Yadua Island

Yadua Tabu

Nananu-i-Ra and Nadi

Nadi

N

Ferry Route
Captain Cook
Cruise route

0   20
kilometres

boards. There are no direct flights between Labasa or Savusavu and Taveuni.

Fiji Link ☎ 672 0888, �🌐 fijiairways.com. Flies to Labasa in a 44-seater ATR from Nadi (1 daily; 45min; F$277) and Suva (3 daily; 40min; F$256); to Savusavu in small 12-seater twin-propeller Twin Otters from Nadi (2 daily; 1hr 10min; F$322) and Suva (2 daily; 1hr; F$277); and to Taveuni, also in Twin Otters, from Nadi (2 daily; 1hr 25min; F$389) and Suva (3 weekly; 1hr; F$277).

Northern Air ☎ 347 5005, �🌐 northernair.com.fj. Flies from Suva to Labasa (2 daily; 40min; F$130), Savusavu (1 daily; 40min; F$170) and Taveuni (3 weekly; 45min; F$196).

BY BOAT

To Vanua Levu Passenger ferries to the islands depart from Suva and Natovi Landing (on the east coast of Viti Levu). The Patterson Brothers daily ferries from Natovi Landing are the fastest (4hr) although they arrive at the remote Nabouwalu Landing on the west coast of Vanua Levu with bus connections to Labasa and Savusavu.

To Taveuni Ferries from Suva arrive at the Wairiki Wharf, half-way down the west coast of Taveuni; the ferry calls in at Savusavu along the way, giving you the option of getting off and catching the next ferry to Taveuni at a later date.

FERRIES FROM VITI LEVU

Goundar Shipping ☎ 330 1020 in Suva, ☎ 881 6089 in Labasa, ☎ 7771 5472 in Savusavu; �🌐 goundarshipping .com. Operates the comfortable nine-hundred-passenger MV *Lomaiviti Princess* from Suva to Savusavu (12hr; F$49, cabin bunk F$210) on Mon & Fri at 6pm: it has a 4hr stopover at Savusavu before continuing on to Taveuni (16hr; F$67, cabin bunk F$240). Charter buses meet passengers arriving at Savusavu Wharf for connections to Labasa town. Travel between Savusavu and Taveuni costs F$29 one way and takes 4hr.

Interlink Shipping ☎ 999 2026 in Suva, ☎ 999 2031 in Savusavu; �🌐 interlinkshipping.com.fj. Its four-hundred-passenger ferry leaves Natovi for Nabouwalu (5 weekly; 7hr; from F$44) with bus connections to Savusavu and

Labasa: it also runs direct from Natovi to Savusavu (1 weekly; 9hr; from F$55).

Patterson Brothers ☎ 331 5644 in Suva, ☎ 881 2444 in Labasa; �🌐 fijisearoad.com. A charter bus leaves Suva bus stand at 5am arriving at Natovi Landing for the 7am ferry to Nabouwalu (1 daily; 4hr; F$45) on the southwest tip of Vanua Levu. A charter bus runs from Nabouwalu to Labasa (1hr 30min; F$6) and Savusavu (1hr 30min; F$6).

INTER-ISLAND FERRIES

Two ferries run between Natuvu Landing in Buca Bay on the eastern side of Vanua Levu and the old wharf in Taveuni at Lovonivonu, known as the Korean Wharf, 3km south of Naqara town on the west coast.

Goundar Shipping ☎ 330 1020 in Suva, ☎ 7771 5472 in Savusavu; ⚲ goundarshipping.com. Two daily ferries leave Natuvu at 9am & 4pm, and also depart Taveuni at 7am & 2pm; bus connections to Savusavu and Labasa (F$20 one way).

Suncity Ferries Tickets can be bought at the agent in Ravin's Shopping Centre, opposite the bus stand in Savusavu, and at Suncity Supermarket in Matei, Taveuni. The 90-seater ferry departs daily at 9am from the Korean Wharf in Taveuni, crossing to Natuvu Landing on the eastern tip of Vanua Levu (1hr 30min; F$20) with a connecting bus to Savusavu. The bus leaves Savusavu at 7.30am for Natuvu Landing in time for the daily ferry to Taveuni at 10.30am (1hr 30min; F$20).

SMALL SHIP CRUISE

Captain Cook Cruises ☎ 670 1823, ⚲ captaincook cruisesfiji.com. The seven-night "Four Cultures Discovery" cruise leaves from Port Denarau in Nadi to visit the cultural enclaves of Kioa and Rabi (see p.203), two Fijian villages on the islands of Drua Drua and Kia, as well as rural settlements around Labasa (see p.190). With 62 air-conditioned cabins, a swimming pool and spa treatments available as well as a dedicated PADI scuba diving operator offering daily dives, it's also a great way to dive the Great Sea (see p.194) and Rainbow (see p.206) reefs. From F$4920 per person including meals and activities.

Vanua Levu

VANUA LEVU is about half the size of its big brother Viti Levu, but in terms of tourist facilities it pales by comparison. There are few white sandy beaches and limited accommodation outside of Labasa and Savusavu. However, the lack of other tourists makes it a joy to explore, especially by local bus, and to meet the local islanders.

Off Vanua Levu's northern coast, the **Great Sea Reef** is the world's third-largest coral reef system, covering more than two hundred thousand square kilometres. On land, the island's dry north coast is strewn with sugarcane farms, pine forests and mangroves with the delightful Indo-Fijian-dominated **Labasa town** as its focal point. The more tropical southern side is caressed by high mountains, covered in pristine rainforest and with huge coconut plantations along its eastern coast. Midway along the south coast is **Savusavu**, a picturesque sailing town which makes a good base for hiking and watersports.

Three remarkable islands lie off Vanua Levu's coast: **Yadua Taba** to the west, home to the endemic crested iguana; and to the east, facing Taveuni, the two culturally unique islands of **Rabi** and **Kioa**, each home to a displaced South Pacific community.

Brief history

Vanua Levu was the site of the initial European rush into Fiji in the early nineteenth century, fuelled by the discovery of **sandalwood** in Bua Bay on the southwestern coast of the island. Opportunist merchants from Port Jackson (Sydney) and London first began arriving in 1804, loading up with sandalwood before sailing on to the ports of Asia, where their cargo was sold at a great profit. In return the Fijian landowners received muskets, pans, mirrors and other trinkets, until every tract of the prized resource had been cut down.

During the 1860s more Europeans began to arrive, this time in search of land for the **cotton trade**. The chief of Vanua Levu and Taveuni, Tui Cakau, sold fifty thousand acres of fertile land on Vanua Levu to European traders for just two shillings per acre. After the collapse of cotton prices at the end of the 1860s, the Europeans switched to the **copra trade**, which flourished until the 1940s. Huge areas of coconut plantations still stand tall among the coastal landscape and a few die-hard *kai loma* planters, mixed-blood descendants of the original Europeans, continue to eke out a living from the crop.

Labasa and around

The hot and dusty market centre of **LABASA** on Vanua Levu's north coast is Fiji's largest town outside of Viti Levu but receives virtually no tourists. The administrative centre of Vanua Levu, it has a purposeful bustle during the day, but by sundown,

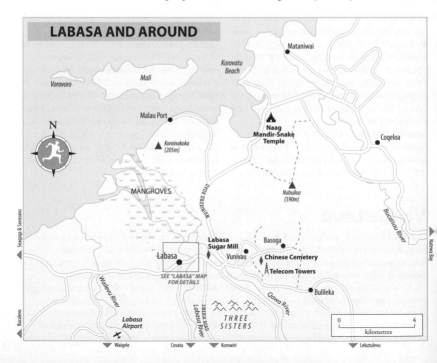

with the departure of the last local bus, the streets become deserted. On the outskirts is the town's lifeline, the Labasa Sugar Mill, which perpetually hisses, creaks and bellows out smoke during the sugar-crushing season between September and December. Labasa's surrounding hilly **countryside** is the main attraction for visitors and exploring this area by 4WD or on an open-sided local bus offers great mountain vistas. Also nearby are two resorts with diving access to the fabulous, uncharted **Great Sea Reef**.

Town centre

Labasa is a small town and most places are within walking distance. Its **town centre** is flanked on its east side by the flood-prone Labasa River, which snakes 6km north to the coast through mangrove forest, and inland for around 16km. The town's main street is the long **Nasekula Road**: its busiest area, around the main bus stand, is full of colourful Indo-Fijian shops jostling for business. A short detour south of Nasekula Road down Sangam Street will bring you to the tiny **Sangam Hindu Temple** (dawn to dusk free access). Continue beyond the temple, then turn right after the Labasa Club, and you'll come to a pleasant **riverside walk** leading to Nacula village.

The Municipal Market

Between the river and bus stand is Labasa's lively **Municipal Market** (Mon–Sat 7am–6pm), a good place to mingle with the locals. The adjacent **Handicraft Market** (Mon–Sat 7am–6pm) abutting the river, is a good place for locally made, non-touristy crafts, including the high-quality pandanus mats made by the women of Macuata Province. In a small patch of grassland across the road from the markets beside the river are six small open-sided huts where locals gather to drink *yaqona* – you can join in by offering a F$2 donation towards the grog bowl.

ARRIVAL AND DEPARTURE   **LABASA**

BY PLANE

Airport Diminutive Labasa Airport is located 10km southwest of town. Taxis into the centre of Labasa cost F$12; buses (hourly; 6am–5pm) pass along the main road near the terminal and cost F$1.10 into town.

Destinations Nadi Airport (2 daily; 45min); Nausori, Suva (2 daily; 40min).

BY BOAT

Labasa's port at Malau is 8km east of town and generally receives container ships only. Passengers arriving by ferry at Nabouwalu or Savusavu on the south coast of Vanua Levu can get a connecting charter bus to Labasa.

BY BUS

All public buses arrive at and depart from the Labasa bus stand, adjacent to the Municipal Market.

To Savusavu From Labasa, regular buses head west along the Seaqaqa Highway to Savusavu (6 daily; F$6.60; 2hr 15min). You can also reach Savusavu the long way round via Natewa Bay. This route follows the Wainikoro–Dama Road east of Labasa, then heads over the mountains to Wainigadru village and finally south along the coast to Savusavu. A daily service run by VHL Buses covers the scenic route, leaving Labasa at 9am and arriving in Savusavu at 4.30pm (7hr 30min).

To Nabouwalu Labasa to the ferry terminal at Nabouwalu (4 daily; F$12; 4hr).

Destinations Basoga (8 daily; 40min); Coqeloa (10 daily; 45min); Dreketililia, for Lekutulevu (4 daily; 45min); Nabouwalu (4 daily; 4hr); Savusavu (6 daily; 2hr 15min); Vunivau (8 daily; 30min).

GETTING AROUND

By taxi Taxis can be found adjacent to the bus stand. They cost twenty cents per 200m within the town area, plus a flag fall of F$1.70. If hiring a taxi to tour the countryside, you should negotiate a price before departing; expect to pay around F$40 for an hour's tour. A one-way trip to Savusavu will cost around F$100 and take 1hr 30min.

By car Renting a car is a good way to explore the countryside around Labasa. Northpole Rentals, on the corner of Nasekula Rd (☎881 8088, ⓦwww.northpole .com.fj), has cheap 4WD Suzuki Jimnys at F$120/day and Toyota Hilux for $210/day, while Vanua Rentals, at *Grand Eastern Hotel* on Gibson St (ⓔvanua.rental@cjsgroup.com .fj, ☎881 1060), has similar cars and prices. Budget, on Nasekula Rd opposite St Thomas Anglican Church (☎881 1999) is slightly more expensive.

7

By boat A boat trip upstream is a great way of seeing the scenery and some of the life that goes on along its riverbanks. Boats are usually tied up at the back of the Labasa market and it's easy to hire one for a few hours; alternatively, contact boatman Vilisoni (☎876 2333; F$60/2hr).

ACCOMMODATION

Labasa's **hotels** are mostly aimed at Fijians travelling on business. You shouldn't have a problem finding a room and discounted rates are usually available at weekends.

Friendly North Inn Siberia Rd ☎881 1555, ✉fni @cjsgroup.com.fj. Just beyond the hospital, 15min walk from the town centre, this is the best option if you're staying awhile as most of the sixteen duplex cottage rooms have kitchenettes. There's a pleasant garden, bar and restaurant and the Labasa swimming pool is a short walk along the road past the hospital. **F$85**

Grand Eastern Hotel Gibson St ☎881 1022, ✉grandeastern@cjsgroup.com.fj. Popular with business travellers, this is Labasa's smartest hotel. The 24 a/c rooms are a little tired but the setting is lovely, in a quiet cul-de-sac close to the busy bus stand. The hotel has a swimming pool and slightly expensive restaurant and bar. 24hr reception. 📶 **F$100**

Hotel Northpole Nasekula Rd, corner of Park St and Damanu St ☎881 8008, ⊕www.northpole.com.fj. Two separate buildings, 150 metres apart, in a central location on Labasa's main shopping street: both buildings have 24hr receptions. The 31 tidy, modern, a/c rooms are all on the second and third floors, and aimed at business travellers. 📶$ **F$90**

EATING AND DRINKING

Colonial Arms Grand Eastern Hotel, Gibson St ☎881 1022. If you're after decent European cuisine this is the only place to go, with salads (F$14.50), burgers (F$16.50) and excellent wood-fired pizzas (F$14.50–18.50). You can also get a really tasty boneless curry here, but it's surprisingly expensive at F$28.50. Daily 6.30am–10.30pm.

Oriental Bar and Restaurant Jaduram St. Labasa's best place to eat out, this a/c Chinese restaurant has pleasant decor, background music and over a hundred dishes on its menu from tasty chilli tofu (F$10) to large portions of chow mein (F$14), as well as more expensive crab curries ($35). It's also a popular bar, with beer served by the jug. Come early at lunchtime to get one of the window tables overlooking the bustling bus stand. Mon–Sat 9am–9pm, Sun 5pm–9pm.

Restaurant 786 Upstairs in the SB Khan Mall, 10 Jaduram St. The best of the town's many Indian restaurants and one of the few that doesn't serve pre-cooked canteen-style food. The menu is small and features duck, jungle rooster or vegetable thalis (F$10–15), along with *dalo* sticks (20¢), samosas (60¢) and bhajis (20¢). It's a quiet place away from the street bustle and with the added comfort of a/c. Mon–Sat 8am–6pm.

DIRECTORY

Banks ANZ, corner of Nasekula Rd and Gibson St (Mon–Fri 9am–4pm); BSP, opposite the bus stand on the corner of Nasekula Rd and Jaduram St (Mon 9.30am–4pm, Tues–Fri 9am–4pm). Both have ATMs.

Doctors Prakash Medical, 13 Sangam St (Mon–Fri 8am–7.30pm, Sat 9am–3pm & Sun 10am–3pm ; ☎ 921 7602).

Hospital Northern District Hospital, off Siberia Rd on the east side of the river, a 10-minute walk from the market (open 24hr; ☎ 881 1444).

Internet access Northwinds Plaza on Nasekula Rd has ten terminals and a/c (F$2/hr; Mon–Sat 8am–5pm).

Pharmacy My Chemist, 5 Nasekula Rd (Mon–Sat 8am–6pm; ☎ 881 4611).

Police Nadawa St (open 24hr; ☎ 881 1222).

Post office Nasekula Rd (Mon–Fri 7.30am–5pm, Sat 8am–12.30pm).

Telephone Plenty outside the post office, although you'll need a calling card.

East of Labasa

Some of the most attractive countryside around Labasa lies to the east of the sugar mill across the Qawa River. Past the river, the main Wainikoro–Dama road turns north towards the coast. Five kilometres along is the turn-off for **Malau Port**, protected by the large offshore island of Mali.

The snake temple

Parmod Buses from Labasa heading to Coqeloa pass the temple every hour (30min; F$1.10); a taxi should cost F$15

Twelve kilometres northeast of Labasa is the Hindu shrine of Naag Mandir, better known as the **snake temple**. Inside is a peculiar attraction: a cobra-shaped rock that devotees claim has grown by 3m over the space of seventy years – the roof has had to be raised four times. Visitors are welcome to visit the shrine (remove shoes first).

Korovatu Beach and beyond

Two hundred metres past the snake temple is the turn-off to palm-backed **Korovatu Beach**, the nearest sandy beach to Labasa. It's 1km from the main road to the beach: entry to the beach is F$3 per person or F$10 per car. Beyond the turn-off, the main road continues in a perfectly straight line for 3km, the longest stretch of straight road in Fiji. The surrounding **scenery** – with big mountains to the south and unusual rocky outcrops to the north – is an excellent place to **explore** by foot, with opportunities to wander along dusty roads through Indian settlements and climb hills for panoramic views.

SIGHTSEEING BY LOCAL BUS

Hopping on and off Labasa's charming **open-sided buses** is a great way to see the countryside and meet the locals. The following routes are highly recommended, each departing hourly from Labasa bus stand from 6am to 6pm, with increased services during peak hours.

Labasa to Basoga or Vunivau (20min; 70¢). Board one of the striking yellow Northern Buses to Basoga: after passing the sugar mill and turning left up Valebasoga Road, get off the bus at the brow of the hill before the Chinese Cemetery. Walk back 100 metres and head up the dirt road leading towards two telecoms towers (15min) keeping an eye out for a steep grassy trail to the top. From the lower tower, follow the ridge to the highest tower for stunning mountain views; then continue back downhill via the access road, past Indo–Fijian houses to Bulileka Road

(20min). From here, frequent buses head back into Labasa. Alternatively, for a loop bus ride, get on the Vunivau bus that meanders around these hills and settlements.

Labasa to Coqeloa (50min; F$1.60). This route passes the sugar mill and snake temple and travels through Indo–Fijian sugarcane settlements around the Bucaisau River Valley. Plenty of dirt roads branch out from the valley, making tempting walking diversions among beautiful mountain scenery.

7

FIJI CRESTED IGUANA

The seldom seen **Fiji crested iguana** (*Brachylophus* vitiensis) is one of the few large reptiles living in the South Pacific and found only on a handful of islands in Fiji. Averaging 40cm in length (split evenly between body and tail), they are distinguished from the more common and slightly smaller banded iguana by three thin white stripes around the body and a mohican-style headdress. If aroused, their skin turns from a pale green colour to jet black.

These fascinating creatures were first discovered by Australian zoologist John Gibbons in 1979 on the tiny island of **Yadua Taba**, which nuzzles its larger sister Yadua 20km off the western tip of Vanua Levu. The 170-acre uninhabited island, declared Fiji's first wildlife reserve in 1981, is home to around twelve thousand crested iguanas, which eat the leaves and flowers of the island's wild hibiscus trees. Other habitats include Monuriki in the Mamanucas and several small islands in the Yasawas, although populations at these locations are small. The only way to **visit** Yadua Taba is on a scientific research project, but you can view the iguanas without disturbing their natural habitat at Kula Eco Park on the Coral Coast (see p.114).

Lekutulevu

Buses run from Labasa to Dreketilialia (5 daily; F$1.55), some 4km from Lekutulevu – it's a 30min walk from here along a rough road or, if the road is passable, taxis or carrier vans wait for the bus (F$30)

Twelve kilometres south of Labasa, accessible along the Bulileka Road, is the remote village of **Lekutulevu**. The village offers a delightful guided one-hour hike to a **waterfall** (local guide F$20). Along the way you'll pass a natural stone *tanoa* (drinking bowl) 3m in diameter which is reputed to be used by the ancient god Dakuwaqa. A thirty-minute detour from the waterfall leads to the summit of **Mount Uluinamolo**, from where you can see Taveuni on a clear day.

West of Labasa

Fourteen kilometres west of Labasa at Tabia, a dirt road braches off towards the coast to a couple of remote resorts where you can explore the **Great Sea Reef**. This is the third longest continuous barrier reef system in the world, boasting 44 percent of Fiji's endemic marine life and 74 percent of its corals. Forty minutes by boat in the far reaches of the Great Sea Reef sits **Kia Island**, where surfers can enjoy impressive **breaks**.

ACCOMMODATION   **WEST OF LABASA**

Nukubati Island ☎ 603 0919, ⊛ www.nukubati.com. The best access to the massive Great Sea Reef is available from this private island retreat. The upmarket resort is aimed at honeymooners and divers and offers seven luxury bures, as well as game fishing, sailing and trips to the breaks around Kia Island (Nov–March). Rates include meals. 🛜 ($) F$1980

★**Palmlea Farm Lodge** Naduri–Tabia Rd, 30 minutes' drive west of Labasa ☎ 828 2220, ⊛ palmlea farms.com. On a secluded farm growing its own organic fruit and vegetables, this inviting eco-resort has three elegant bures, all overlooking the ocean. Scuba diving trips to the Great Sea Reef can be arranged. Rates include breakfast. F$295

Savusavu and around

SAVUSAVU, Vanua Levu's main tourist centre, is a small one-street town squeezed between rolling hills and a silvery bay. Although it's not really a beach destination, it's a popular anchorage for visiting **yachts** and there's good scuba diving in the nearby Namena Lagoon. With several excellent **restaurants** and bars along the waterfront, peaceful walks in the **Savusavu Hills**, fabulous snorkelling at **Lesiaceva Point** and game fishing around the bay, the town makes for a pleasant short stay.

From Savusavu, the sedate **Hibiscus Highway** travels east passing coconut plantations and small resorts, while to the north are two refreshing waterfalls surrounded by tropical rainforests, one at the village of **Vuadomo**, and the other at the **Waisali Nature Reserve**.

FESTIVALS IN SAVUSAVU

Two of the best times to visit Savusavu are during **Savusavu Festival Week** in November, when local arts, music and culture are promoted, and during the annual **Hindu Krishna Lele Festival**, which features firewalking and is held at the Khemendra School just before Christmas.

The town centre

Savusavu town consists of little more than a 1km stretch of road along the foreshore, known as Main Street and lined by low-rise shops and the occasional three-storey building. At the heart of the **town centre** is the bus stand and municipal market, with a post office, two banks, a few general stores and several small supermarkets nearby. Usually a fairly sleepy spot, the area springs to life on Fridays and Saturdays with an influx of visitors from the countryside, who come to trade at the **market** and drink beer.

Copra Shed Marina

To the west of the commercial centre is the **Copra Shed Marina**, which marks the beginning of the town's quieter quarters where Main Street hugs the foreshore. Here you'll find the **Yacht Club**, which has beautiful views overlooking the bay across to distant blue-tinted mountains. You can sip a drink at the water's edge here, eat at one of two lovely waterfront restaurants or shop in the posh boutiques nearby.

The hot springs

Nakama Rd, across from the playing field

Two hundred metres south of the marina up Nakama Road are Savusavu's **hot springs**. The three small bubbling pools are too hot to bathe in and are often full of sacks of *dalo* being slowly cooked. The boiling water trickles into a small stream below the pools where it cools sufficiently to dip a toe in – look out, too, for the steam vents escaping

7

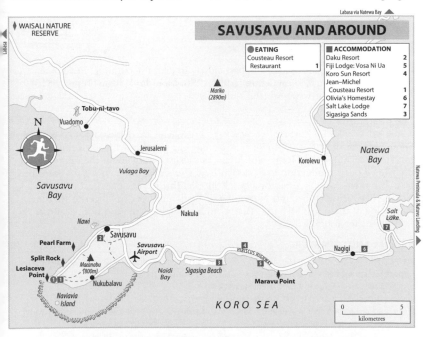

7

● EATING	
Captains Café	1
Captain's Table	2
Surf n Turf	3

■ ACCOMMODATION	
Gecko Lodge	3
Hidden Paradise	1
Hot Springs Hotel	4
Naveria Heights Lodge	5
Savusavu Budget Lodge	2

■ DRINKING AND NIGHTLIFE	
Decked Out	3
Planters Club	2
Yacht Club	1

SAVUSAVU

N

Nawi Island

Lesiaceva Point

Wharf

Waitui Marina

Steam Vents

Copra Shed Marina

Savusavu Marina

Municipal Market

Bus Stand

MAIN STREET

Customs House

J Hunter Pearls

Hot Springs

Khemendra School

LESIACEVA ROAD

NAKAMA ROAD

HIGH STREET

HIBISCUS HIGHWAY

KAWI STREET

SAVUSAVU HILLS

ACCESS ROAD

WOODWARD DRIVE

NAKANASE ROAD

Telecom Tower

Road closed (walking track only)

0   250
metres

▼ Airport   ▼ Airport

from the sand along the beachfront, particularly in the early morning. Beside the stream, the **Savusavu Medical Centre** (☏998 1786; Mon–Fri 7.30am–10pm; F$15) offers therapeutic hot-water mineral baths.

The pearl farm

Lesiaceva Point • Tours (1hr 30min) leave from J. Hunter Pearls, Main Street Mon–Fri at 9.30am • F$30 • ☏ 885 0821, ⓦ fijipearls.com

Some 3km southwest of the town centre along the gritty beachfront is the jetty for the underwater **pearl farm**, which you can visit to learn about the unique multihued pearl production in Savusavu Bay. Tours take place on a glass-bottomed boat and there's usually time for a quick snorkel (bring your own gear). If you're visiting between October and November or April and May you'll get to see the harvesting of the pearls by hand. Pearls can be bought at the end of the tour, at the J. Hunter showroom.

ARRIVAL AND DEPARTURE   SAVUSAVU

BY PLANE

Airport Fiji Link and Northern Air fly several times daily from Nadi and Suva to Savusavu Airport, which involves a dramatic descent over the hills to land at a short runway fronting the ocean. It's a 5min ride from the airport to town: buses run hourly (F$1.10) and taxis cost F$5.

Destinations Nadi Airport (2 daily; 1hr 10min); Nausori, Suva (2 daily; 1hr).

BY BOAT

Ferries Passenger and car ferries arrive at Savusavu Wharf, a 5min walk west of the town centre.

Destinations Suva, Viti Levu (3 weekly; 12hr); Wairiki Wharf, Taveuni (2 weekly; 4hr).

Private yachts If you are arriving from international waters by private yacht you should contact Customs House (Mon–Fri 8am–4.30pm; other times incur overtime charges; ☎885 0727, VHF16) on the corner of Main Street and Nakama Rd. There are three privately run marinas running east–west: Waitui Marina (☎885 3031, ✉waituimarina@gmail.com), The Copra Shed (☎885 0457, ⊚coprashed.com.fj) and Savusavu Marina (☎885 3543, ✉savumari@connect.com.fj). All offer moorings for F$12–15 per day depending on the season, with weekly and monthly rates available.

BY BUS

All buses arrive at and depart from the Savusavu bus stand.

To Labasa From Savusavu there are regular direct buses to Labasa (6 daily; 2hr 15min; F$15). Alternatively, you can reach Labasa via Natewa Bay, a rough journey with Waiqele Buses departing Savusavu daily at 9am and reaching Labasa around 4.30pm.

To Natuvu Landing Those travelling to Taveuni can catch a charter bus from Savusavu to Natuvu Landing (daily at 7.15am), which connects with the ferry across the Somosomo Straits to the west coast of Taveuni (1hr 30min). In addition, there are 3 public buses daily (2hr 30min) to Natuvu Landing, which don't connect with the Taveuni ferry, but are useful if you are going to Koia, Rabi or one of the Buca Bay resorts.

GETTING AROUND

By car The best way to explore the Hibiscus Highway and Natewa Peninsula is by renting a car. James Rentals (☎885 0455, ✉jamescarrental@yahoo.com) rent out small 4WDs for F$110 per day or larger vehicles for F$250. Otherwise try Budget (☎881 1999).

By bus Buses depart from the Savusavu bus stand on Main Street. Vishnu Buses head east past the airport and along the Hibiscus Highway every hour or so; most buses turn around at Naigini (F$1.90), 40 minutes from Savusavu; three buses continue on to Nabuka on Buca Bay (F$6.75).

For the Waisali Nature Reserve (F$1.60), catch the Labasa bus (see p.191). Buses to Lesiaceva Point leave at 7.15am, noon and 4pm returning at 7.45am, 12.30pm and 4.30pm.

By taxi It's easy to flag down taxis around town. A taxi to Lesiaceva Point costs F$8 to *Cousteau Resort* or F$4 to *Daku Resort*.

By bike Mountain bikes can be rented from *Naveria Heights Lodge* (see p.198) for F$30 per day; they also offer mountain-bike tours for experienced cyclists (from F$75 including lunch).

INFORMATION AND TOURS

Tourist information There is no official information office in Savusavu: check the Savusavu Tourism

Association (⊚facebook.com/savusavufiji) for local news and events.

7

A WALK IN THE SAVUSAVU HILLS AND LESIACEVA POINT

To marvel at the fine views over Savusavu Bay, take a **walk** around **Savusavu Hills**. The easiest **route** starts from the eastern end of town, turning right up Buca Bay Road towards the airport. After a steep fifteen-minute walk, turn right again up the imaginatively named "Access Road" – you could take a bus or taxi to the Access Road junction to save your legs – then follow the ridge westwards for beautiful **views** over the town and Nawi Island.

You can continue along the Access Road down towards the airport (20min), and from here walk for 3km along the road past small settlements to **Nukubalavu village**; then it's another 3km along the palm-fringed beach to *Cousteau Resort* at Lesiaceva Point (see below), a good 3hr walk in total. Alternatively, a shorter trail loops back to town, diverting off the Access Road towards the telecoms tower perched on the hilltop. From the far end of the clearing above the tower, a small grassy track leads down to a dirt road and winds its way through light forest, past corrugated iron lean-tos and back into the western side of town.

The coastal walk to **Lesiaceva Point** follows Lesiaceva Road along Savusavu Bay: 3km out of town the road turns to dirt. It's 7km to the *Cousteau Resort* (see p.198) at end of the road, but 1km before here is a public beach with excellent **snorkelling** at Split Rock, 500m offshore. On the way back, you can detour up to explore the hills by taking the steep driveway 350m before *Cousteau Resort*. At the top, enter the gate and turn left to follow a narrow trail along the ridge which leads up to another telecoms tower: from here you can walk back down to the coast at Korovesi village.

Alternatively, **guided hikes** and **bike tours** around the Savusavu Hills are available with Sharon from *Naveria Heights Lodge* (3–7hr; F$35–120; min 2 people; ☎936 4808).

7

WATERSPORTS AROUND SAVUSAVU

Diving Two excellent dive operators, Koro Sun Divers (☎934 1033, ⊛korosundive.com; two-tank dive F$270) and Jean-Michel Cousteau Diving (☎885 0694, ⊛jeanmichelcousteaudiving.com; two-tank dive F$390) dive the nearby reefs in the Koro Sea with daily pick-ups from the Savusavu area: they also lay on twice-weekly trips (dependent on numbers and weather conditions) to the outstanding isolated reefs around Namena Lagoon, 40 minutes to the south.

Fishing If you want to catch mahi-mahi or tuna, or simply go on a leisurely cruise, contact Savusavu Fishing (☎885 0674, ⊛jeanmichelcousteaudiving.com; F$750 for half-day private charter).

Paragliding Paragliding over the town and bay can be organized at *Fiji Lodge* (see p.200).

Sailing In the busy sailing season between May and October, visiting yachts sometimes offer day- or overnight sailing charters – ask around at the Copra Shed or Waitui marinas.

Snorkelling The best place to snorkel in Savusavu is at Split Rock close to the *Cousteau Resort*. Snorkel out towards the pearl buoys for the best coral patches. You can get a public bus or taxi here from town (see p.197), or take a wonderful organized snorkelling trip to Namena Lagoon with Cousteau Diving (F$120 per person; see above).

Rafa's Adventure Tours ☎838 0406, ⊛rafas adventuretours.weebly.com. Runs a guided four-hour nature walk along the Nakula Trail (F$95) plus a half-day village, school and snorkelling tour (F$125).

Trip N Tour In the Copra Shed Marina ☎885 3154, ✉tripntours@connect.com.fj. The helpful staff here can book game-fishing charters as well as snorkelling and diving trips. Mon–Fri 9am–4.30pm, Sat 9am–noon.

ACCOMMODATION

Accommodation in Savusavu ranges from basic guesthouses in town to the lavish *Cousteau Resort* out on Lesiaceva Point. The hotels in Savusavu town are rather dull but adequate for exploring the restaurants and sometimes rowdy bars, while the resorts along Lesiaceva Road and up in the hills are more peaceful and only a few dollars' taxi ride away from town.

SAVUSAVU TOWN

★**Gecko Lodge** Lesiaceva Rd ☎921 3181, ⊛geckolodgefiji.com; map p.196. A 10-minute walk from town, this quaint guesthouse has a communal kitchen and three comfortable en-suite rooms with a/c. The largest room at the front sleeps four and has a private balcony with ocean views. ☏($) F$135

Hidden Paradise West Main St ☎873 7845; map p.196. Just west of the Copra Shed Marina, this friendly Fijian guesthouse has the only dorm beds on Vanua Levu along with six claustrophobic a/c rooms. It's fronted by the cute shack-like *Seaview Café*. Rates include breakfast. Dorms F$25, rooms F$55

Hot Springs Hotel Off Nakama Rd ☎885 0195, ⊛savusavufiji.com; map p.196. This ugly four-storey cement block is the largest hotel in Vanua Levu, and has superb views from its top two floors. The 46 box-like rooms are uninspiring, but there's a pool, bar and 24hr reception. ☏ F$175

Naveria Heights Lodge Savusavu Hills ☎885 0348, ⊛naveriaheightsfiji.com; map p.196. This superb homestay in the hills has four rooms all with stunning views, polished wooden floors and a sun deck. The focus here is on wellness and healthy living with massage, detox and weight-loss programmes available as well as plenty of organized fitness activities. It's a steep 15min walk uphill from the town but the owner will happily pick up guests. A healthy, home-made breakfast is included in the rate. ☏($) F$250

Savusavu Budget Lodge West Main St ☎885 3127, ✉ssvbudgetlodge@connect.com.fj; map p.196. Located at the quiet west end of town, this affordable lodge has 14 simple rooms on the first floor, most with tiny TVs and small en-suite hot water shower rooms, plus a communal veranda overlooking the street. Non-a/c rooms F$65, a/c rooms F$95

LESIACEVA POINT

Daku Resort Lesiaceva Rd ☎885 0046, ⊛dakuresort .com; map p.195. Set in spacious landscaped gardens, this plantation-style resort has eight bures sleeping 2 and four 3- or 4-bed villas for families or groups. There's a restaurant, spa and swimming pool as well as decent swimming and snorkelling in the lagoon across the road. ☏ Bures F$360, villas F$445

★**Jean-Michel Cousteau Resort** Lesiaceva Point ☎885 0188, ⊛fijiresort.com; map p.195. Owned by the son of Jacques Cousteau, this luxurious and environmentally sensitive resort boasts 25 beautifully hand-crafted thatch bures plus a fabulously opulent villa. As you'd expect, the scuba diving is brilliantly managed and there also are well-organized kayaking and waterfall trips – they even lay on private picnics on an uninhabited island with a gorgeous beach. There's also an ocean-view spa plus organized activities, personalized carers and a swimming pool for the kids. Rates include meals, activities and most excursions. ☏ Bures F$2175, villa F$5990

EATING AND DRINKING

Savusavu is a wonderful place for dining out with several good **restaurants** and **bars** on the water's edge. Although the town has a genteel feel by day, don't be surprised to see drunks staggering around on Friday and Saturday nights – one notorious place to avoid is the *Tavern Bar* next door to the *Planters Club*. After 9pm it's probably best to take a **taxi** back to your accommodation.

RESTAURANTS AND CAFÉS

Captains Café Copra Shed Marina ☎ 885 0511; map p.196. Shakes, cakes and coffees with views over the water. Light meals include Caesar salad and curry of the day for F$12 or pizzas from F$18. Daily 7am–9.30pm.

Captain's Table Copra Shed Marina ☎ 885 0511; map p.196. A tad expensive, but the fish and seafood dishes such as firecracker tiger prawns (F$40) and spicy wahoo (F$18.50) are superbly cooked. The glamorous setting on the water's edge is outstanding. Daily 10.30am–3pm & 5.30–9.30pm.

Cousteau Resort Restaurant Lesiaceva Point ☎ 885 0188; map p.195. Exquisitely presented food served in the elaborate setting of a 20m-high thatch bure. The set lunch (F$85) and dinner (F$100) menus include three courses, with a choice of around five mains. Advance bookings required. Daily lunch and dinner only.

★**Surf n Turf** East Main St ☎ 885 3033; map p.196. Trendy café-restaurant with a cute wooden veranda on the foreshore. Fish is caught from its own boats, so you know it's fresh – try the superb mud crabs or flipper lobsters when they're on the menu; if not, go for the sweet & sour tempura snapper (F$15) or one of the excellent Indian curries (F$15). It closes early, so arrive in time. Mon–Fri 11am–2pm & 5–8pm, Sat 11am–4pm.

BARS AND CLUBS

Decked Out Central Main Street ☎ 885 2929; map p.196. A popular local hangout, this is a good spot to grab a beer and a burger, sit on the decked area overlooking the bus stand and watch the world go by. Live music at the weekends gets the place really rocking. Happy hour daily 5–7pm. Sun–Thurs 8am–10pm, Fri & Sat 8am–midnight.

Planters Club West Main St ☎ 885 0233; map p.196. Old-boys' hangout where you can sit in peace with a draught beer. The lounge displays interesting memorabilia recounting the bygone copra days. Mon–Sat 10am–10pm, Sun 8am–8pm.

★**Yacht Club** Copra Shed Marina ☎ 885 0457, ⓦ savusavuyachtclub.com; map p.196. Refined watering hole with lawns beside the bay and a small deck overlooking the marina: there's beer on draught, sunset views and live reggae music on Sat at 5pm. Happy hour daily 5–7pm. Daily 10am–10pm.

DIRECTORY

Banks ANZ and Westpac are both on Main St, opposite and either side of the bus stand.

Doctors Savusavu Medical Centre, Nakama Rd (Mon–Fri 8am–12.30pm & 2–4.30pm, Sat 9am–noon; ☎ 885 0721).

Hospital Savusavu District Hospital is 2km east of Savusavu on the road to Labasa (Mon–Fri 8am–1pm & 2–4.30pm; outside these times on-call for emergencies only; ☎ 885 0444).

Internet access Savusavu Computers, Planters House at east end of town (Mon–Fri 8.30am–5pm, Sat 9am–1pm; F$2 per hr); also serves delicious coffee and cake.

Pharmacy Savusavu Pharmacy, opposite bus stand on Main St (Mon–Sat 8am–4.30pm).

Police There's a multicoloured painted Tourist Police Unit inconveniently located 2km east of town on the road to Labasa (☎ 855 0222).

Post office East Main St, almost on the corner of Buca Bay Rd (Mon–Fri 8am–4.30pm, Sat 8am–noon).

Telephone Opposite Copra Shed Marina and in front of the post office.

Tobu-ni-tavo Waterfall

18km north of Savusavu, off the Labasa Rd • Mon–Sat 9am–4pm • F$10 • Buses from Savusavu to Labasa drop you at the turn-off to Vuadomo, from where it's a 20-minute walk down the hill to the village; a taxi from Savusavu will cost F$20

North of Savusavu, the attractive **Tobu-ni-tavo Waterfall** makes a pleasant day-trip. Head north on the road to Labasa, past the pretty village of Jerusalemi, keeping an eye out for Vuadomo Road on the left, 16km from Savusavu. A steep 2km dirt track leads down to **Vuadomo village** on the coast, where you pay a small entrance fee to visit the waterfall, an easy twenty-minute hike up the valley.

Waisali Nature Reserve

31km north of Savusavu, off the Labasa Rd • Mon–Sat 9am–2pm • F$8 • Call ☎ 828 0267 to check the guide is here to open the Reserve gate, or to book an optional guided tour (F$15) • Buses from Savusavu to Labasa can drop you at the Reserve (F$1.60); a taxi costs F$40

Just over 25km north of Savusavu, the refreshingly natural **Waisali Nature Reserve** is administered by the National Trust. From the car park, a thirty-minute **trail** leads down through lush tropical rainforest to the waterfall. One of the last remaining habitats of the endangered Fiji ground frog, the reserve is also home to around thirty species of orchid – look out for them en route to the waterfall.

The Hibiscus Highway

Heading south from Savusavu, past the airport, the Hibiscus Highway hugs the southern coastline of Vanua Levu before heading across the Natewa Peninsula to the eastern tip of the island at Buca Bay. The first 20km passes old copra plantations, colonial-style homesteads and a handful of quiet **resorts** along the coast. A decent **sandy beach** backed by massively tall coconut palms is accessed from *Sigasiga Sands* (see below), and there's excellent snorkelling along an inner reef some 600 metres from the beach. From Sigasiga Sands, it's 10km to **Nagigi village** with a small beach, beautiful turquoise lagoon and a humble village homestay (see below). Twenty-five kilometres east of Savusavu, the Hibiscus Highway turns inland to cross the Qaloqalo River. Just before the bridge is the turn-off to **Salt Lake**, a brackish lake fed by the mangrove-lined Qaloqalo River, which boasts excellent **fishing** and birdwatching.

GETTING AROUND   **THE HIBISCUS HIGHWAY**

By bus The Hibiscus Highway is served by hourly buses   travelling between Savusavu and Nagigi village.

ACCOMMODATION

Fiji Lodge: Vosa Ni Ua ☎ 929 8437, ⊛ flyseastay.com; map p.195. With two self-contained bures and a beach house sleeping eight, this hidden gem is a great centre for activities. Kitesurfing equipment and lessons are available, you can paraglide over Savusavu and mountain bikes are free to use for exploring the region's dirt trails. There's no restaurant but a cook is available for a small extra charge. 📶 ($) Bures **F$170**, beach house **F$280**

Koro Sun Resort ☎ 885 3247, ⊛ korosunresort.com; map p.195. This elegant resort has two very different types of accommodation divided by the Hibiscus Highway. The glitzy coastal side is aimed at romantic couples, with oceanfront villas lining an enclosed harbour and bures floating over the lagoon; across the road is the more serene plantation- and rainforest-style accommodation set around a nine-hole golf course, which is better suited to families and nature lovers. 📶($) Plantation bures **F$755**, Lagoon bures **F$1350**

Olivia's Homestay Nagigi village; map p.195. A classic village homestay experience, run by Olivia and involving interaction with her relatives. The rooms are basic and cold-water showers are shared by all. The only way to contact Olivia is to visit her stall at Savusavu market (Wed–Sun 8.30am–3pm), or write in advance to PO Box 138, Savusavu. Rates are per person, and meals can be provided for F$25 a day. **F$50**

Salt Lake Lodge Qaloqalo River, ☎ 828 3005, ⊛ saltlakelodgefiji.com; map p.195. Inland from the coast, the riverside lodge is surrounded by lowland forests with lots of birdlife and has just three cabins. There's fishing from the pontoon and kayaks are available for drifting up and down the river. **F$365**

★**Sigasiga Sands** ☎ 885 0413, ⊛ theultimate paradise.com; map p.195. Set beside a beach among towering coconut trees, this peaceful retreat has two pretty thatch-roof bures and a two-bedroom holiday villa, each with kitchen facilities and expansive views from their verandas. The Indo–Fijian caretaker can prepare meals on request. 📶 Bures **F$125**, villa **F$365**

The Natewa Peninsula

The **Natewa Peninsula** is almost severed from the main chunk of Vanua Levu, connected only by a kilometre-wide sliver of land east of Savusavu. To the north of the peninsula is Natewa Bay, while to the south is the Somosomo Strait separating Vanua Levu from Taveuni. East of Salt Lake, the peninsula broadens and features increasingly dense rainforest teeming with endemic birdlife – it's one of the few places in Fiji to spot the rare **silktail**, a tiny black bird with a speckled blue head. A 4WD vehicle is needed to explore the region as, once you are off the main highway, the roads here are terrible,

VIEW FROM *MATANGI ISLAND RESORT* (P.208) >

especially during the rainy season. Two side-roads branch off the Hibiscus Highway to the fishing villages of Drekeniwai and Vusasivo on **Natewa Bay**; ask around at either village to hire a boat and guide to search for **spinner dolphins**, commonly sighted in the bay – expect to pay around F$120 for an hour.

Buca Bay

At the eastern end of the Natewa Peninsula, the Hibiscus Highway finally hits **Buca Bay** at Loa, from where dirt roads branch off north and south along the coast. The road north heads past several small fishing villages to **Nabuka** at the tip of Natewa Bay, facing Rabi Island. Two kilometres south of Loa is **Natuvu Landing**, departure point for ferries to Taveuni. Twelve kilometres south of Natuvu you can see **petroglyphs** etched into stone boulders alongside the creek bed at the village of Dakuniba (ask to see them). A couple of **dive resorts** are hidden in the heavily indented southeastern tip of the peninsula, which has the closest access to the stunning **Rainbow Reef**, just ten minutes by boat.

ARRIVAL AND DEPARTURE	BUCA BAY

By bus Private buses between Savusavu and Natuvu Landing (3 daily; 4hr) connect with the ferry to Taveuni. Otherwise, a local bus runs from Savusavu to Nabuka three times a day.

By boat Ferries to and from Taveuni dock 2km south of Loa at Natuvu Landing (3 daily; 1hr 30min). Both *Dolphin Bay Divers Retreat* and *Sau Bay Fiji Retreat* (see below) are set in remote bays, inaccessible by road, and send boats to pick up guests from Natuvu or across the straits from Taveuni.

ACCOMMODATION

★**Dolphin Bay Divers Retreat** Viani Bay ☏ 999 9995, ⓦ dolphinbaydivers.com. Here, simple but appealing bamboo bures and jungle tents sit beside the beach. The dive instructors are adept, and the coral reef just offshore is a paradise for snorkellers. Excellent meals are available communally at a central bure. ☏($) Tents F$90, bures F$190

Rasalala Lodge 400 metres north of Natuvu Landing ☏ 805 8813. The only place to stay along the coastal road is this very basic lodge: it's exceptionally cheap with just two rooms, a dorm and five outdoor bathrooms. Dorm F$18, rooms F$36

★**Sau Bay Fiji Retreat** ☏ 992 0046, ⓦ saubayfiji .com. Dominated by an ancient rainforest tree which twists around the beachside restaurant, this intimate resort has four neat a/c wooden cottages, plus a deluxe safari tent with polished wooden floors, surrounded by more rainforest trees. There's excellent diving and snorkelling on the Rainbow Reef just 15 minutes by boat as well as good snorkelling off the beach, plus kayaking in the mangroves, fishing, massages and village visits to Kioa. ☏($) Cottages F$468, safari tent F$978

Kioa Island

Just offshore from Buca Bay, the small, hilly island of **Kioa** is home to four hundred Tuvaluans, who came here in the 1940s from the island of Vaitupu, in Tuvalu. Faced with overcrowding on their own island, in 1947 the people of Vaitupu paid £3000 for the freehold of Kioa, 1000km to the south in Fiji. The initial migration of 37 people was followed by five similar migrations, the last being in 1963, and in 1970 the settlers were formally granted Fijian citizenship. Today, the islanders live in Kioa's only village, **Salia** on the south coast, and are renowned for weaving beautiful mats and for collecting todi, the sap of the coconut tree, to make jams and alcohol. They are also skilled fishermen, often seen handline fishing from beautifully carved outrigger canoes way out to sea.

ARRIVAL AND ACCOMMODATION	KIOA ISLAND

By boat Boat charters (F$60) pick up from Valeasia near Vunikoro village, and can be arranged through the Kioa Council.

Kioa Council Homestay ☏ 850 6194, ⓔ kioacouncil @gmail.com. There is no official accommodation on Kioa but you can arrange a homestay visit through the Kioa Island Council. F$30

Rabi Island

Rabi Island, 66 square kilometres in size, is home to the displaced **Banaban Islanders** from Kiribati in Micronesia. Their original homeland, tiny Banaba, was stripped of its **phosphate** deposits by British mining interests for forty years until 1942, when it was captured by the Japanese who slaughtered many of the islanders. At the end of the war the British Government relocated the remaining Banabans to Rabi Island, which it had purchased shortly before the Japanese occupation. The islanders received formal Fijian citizenship in 2005, and today almost five thousand Banabans live on Rabi. **Tabwewa**, halfway along the north coast, is the largest of the island's four untidy villages; it's home to the government headquarters, a guesthouse and a wharf where you can often see manta rays swimming in the lagoon.

ARRIVAL AND ACCOMMODATION — RABI ISLAND

By plane The seldom-used airstrip is at Tabiang village on the southern tip of the island.

By boat Catch the daily Nabuka bus from Savusavu at 10.30am: get off at Karoko village, 2km south of Nabuka, where you should be able to charter a boat over to the island for F$80.

Rabi Island Council Guesthouse Tabwewa ☎ 330 3653 (in Suva). Used mostly by visiting government workers, but it also accepts tourists by prior arrangement. Beds are in plain four-bed rooms, and the villagers provide food. **F$50**

7

Taveuni

Across the Somosomo Strait from Vanua Levu, the smaller island of **TAVEUNI** is a stunning combination of luxuriant forest, soaring mountains and colourful coral reefs. Much of the island's pristine rainforest is protected within the **Bouma National Heritage Park**, which covers a third of the island, making Taveuni one of the best places to sample Fiji's varied **wildlife**.

Most visitors arrive at the small settlement of **Matei** on Taveuni's northern tip, which is home to the airstrip, plenty of accommodation and a series of pretty beaches. East of here are several small **offshore islands** surrounded by beautiful coral reefs and with an excellent surfing break. Covering most of the rugged east coast of Taveuni is the huge **Bouma National Heritage Park**, which features world-class birdwatching and hikes through a series of waterfalls. Just offshore are the thriving coral reefs of the **Waitabu Marine Park**. Across the knife-edge ridge, splitting the 42km-long island, lies the smoothly sloping **west coast**, where most of the island's eleven thousand inhabitants live. Here, **Somosomo**, head village of the powerful Cakaudrove Province, merges into the modern trade centre of **Naqara**. The peaceful Catholic Mission at Wairiki lies to the south, with **Des Vœux Peak**, another great spot for birdwatching and hiking, towering high above. Close by, in the heart of the island, is the remote **Lake Tagimaucia**. The west coast also has several dive resorts with easy access to the phenomenal **Rainbow Reef**.

Brief history

Archeological evidence indicates that Taveuni was first inhabited around 250 BC and that ring ditches and **hillforts** around the volcanic cones were built around 1200 AD. In 1643 **Abel Tasman** was the first European to record sighting the island, though he made no attempt to land. This is probably fortunate as the Taveunians were renowned as fierce warriors. In the early nineteenth century they sent great **war canoes** to help the alliance of Bau in its struggle with the Rewans. By the 1840s, they faced a battle on home turf as the Tongan Prince **Ma'afu** threatened to take over the island. Allegiances were split, with some Taveunians supporting the prince and the remainder sticking with the **Tui Cakau**, high chief of the island. In 1862, after much wrangling, Tui Cakau's army defeated Ma'afu in a bloody sea battle off the coast near Somosomo.

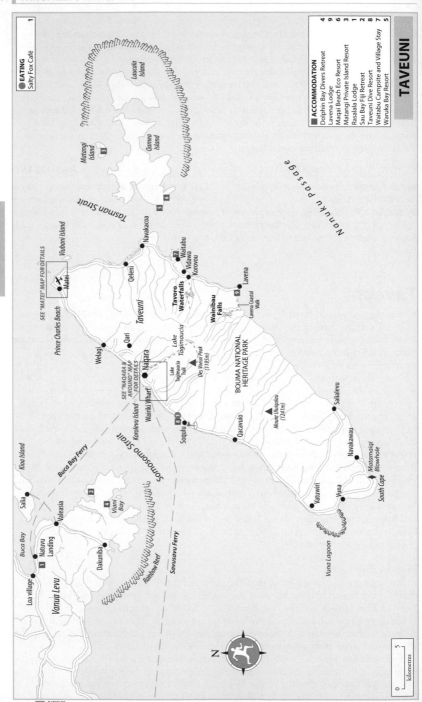

TAVEUNI

● EATING
Salty Fox Café 1

■ ACCOMMODATION
Dolphin Bay Divers Retreat 4
Lavena Lodge 9
Maqai Beach Eco Resort 6
Matangi Private Island Resort 3
Rasalala Lodge 1
Sau Bay Fiji Retreat 2
Taveuni Dive Resort 8
Waitabu Campsite and Village Stay 7
Waruka Bay Resort 5

Nanuku Passage

Tasman Strait

Laucala Island

Qamea Island

Matangi Island

Viubani Island

SEE "MATEI" MAP FOR DETAILS

Prince Charles Beach

Matei

Navakacoa

Qeleni

Waitabu
Vidawa
Korovou

Tavoro Waterfalls

Taveuni

Qari

Welagi

Lake Tagimaucia

Lavena
Lavena Coastal Walk

Wainibau Falls

Des Voeux Peak
(1195m)

Lake Tagimaucia Trail

SEE "NAQARA & AROUND" MAP FOR DETAILS

Naqara

Waitiki Wharf

Korovou Island

BOUMA NATIONAL HERITAGE PARK

Soqulu

Qacavulo

Mount Uluigalau
(1241m)

Salialevu

Somosomo Strait

Buca Bay Ferry

Kioa Island

Salia

Valesia

Viani Bay

Natuvu Landing

Buca Bay

Dakuniba

Loa village

Vanua Levu

Rainbow Reef

Savusavu Ferry

Navakawau

Matamaiqi Blowhole

Vatuwiri

Vuna

South Cape

Vuna Lagoon

N

0 ——— 5
kilometres

Savusavu

7

Lured by the rich soils and gentle slopes ideal for growing **cotton**, Europeans soon began buying up large tracts of Taveuni's west coast. After the collapse in cotton prices following the American Civil War, copra took over as the most viable cash crop and the organized lines of coconut palms still loom high on the west- and south-coast plantations. Some of the original **colonial families** remain on the island and have moved tentatively into the tourism industry; this in turn has attracted a growing number of expats.

GETTING AROUND   TAVEUNI

Bear in mind that **getting around** Taveuni can be unpredictable. There's only one road following the coast, but heavy downpours cause frequent **flooding**, particularly at the bridge at Qeleni, which separates the two tourist hubs of Matei and the Bouma National Heritage Park. Floods generally subside within a few hours and seldom last for more than a day, although **landslides** along the steep and muddy roadside may cause longer delays. The only section of **sealed road** extends for 20km along the northwest coast from Matei to Wairiki. Potholes, stray cattle and fallen coconuts on the dirt coastal road are notorious hazards.

By taxi or carrier van Taxis are based at Naqara, Waiyevo and occasionally at Matei Airport. With luck, you might be able to wave down a taxi or carrier van on the roadside. The fare from Matei to Bouma is F$50. Carrier vans are based at the larger villages including Bouma and Lavena and charge much the same as taxis.

By bus Pacific Transport (☏ 888 0278), based at Naqara, runs the island's limited bus service. Buses run from Naqara to Navakawau in the south (Mon–Sat 9am, 11.30am & 4.30pm, Sun 9am & 11.30am; 2hr; F$4.55) and from Wairiki to Lavena on the northeast coast via Matei and Bouma (Mon–Sat 8.30am, 11.30am & 4.30pm, Sun 8.30am & 11.30am; F$5). The last bus from Wairiki spends

the night at Lavena and departs the following morning at 6am – useful for those who want to spend a lazy afternoon on the beautiful Lavena Coastal Walk and overnight in the village.

Car rental Ruz Rentals in Waiyevo (Mon–Fri 8am–4pm; ☏ 888 0894, ✉ ruzrentals@gmail.com; 4WD only, F$210 per day) is the only car rental company on the island.

Sightseeing tours Most hotels and resorts on Taveuni offer private sightseeing tours, usually with a minimum of four guests and on a fixed route. It's often cheaper to hire a local taxi or carrier van driver for sightseeing: contact Bula Taxis & Tours (☏ 932 9931 or ☏ 888 0230; F$85 for 4hr, F$150 for 7hr), which also has 4WDs.

Matei

MATEI, jutting out on the northernmost tip of Taveuni, is the ideal base for exploring the island: lying midway between the Bouma National Heritage Park and Rainbow Reef, it offers plenty of water-based activities (see box, p.206), pleasant **beaches** and a couple of restaurants. This modern settlement of around five hundred people is a mix of old colonial families, Indo–Fijian entrepreneurs and a new wave of foreigners living in luxury oceanfront villas. It's a thirty-minute walk from one end of Matei to the other around a small bluff known as **Naselesele Point**, which marks the divide between east and west Matei.

Fronted by local houses, Matei's northeast coast runs parallel to the airstrip, with the Suncity supermarket at its eastern boundary and pretty Naselesele village beyond. A few kilometres southwest of Naselesele Point, the deep, sandy **Beverley Beach** is home to most of Matei's accommodation. The coral reef here lies close to shore and offers great **snorkelling** along a 30m-deep drop-off, with reef sharks occasionally paying a visit. There's another quieter beach just to the south at **Vacala Bay**, backed by lush hardwood trees and with a small **surfing** break around its northern point.

ARRIVAL AND DEPARTURE   MATEI

By plane Regular flights from Nadi and Nausori, Suva, arrive at Matei Airport, where a small, much photographed wooden hut welcomes visitors. A taxi usually waits for incoming flights (F$4 to the Matei area) although hosts generally meet guests with pre-booked accommodation.

Destinations Nadi Airport (2 daily; 1hr 25min); Nausori, Suva (Mon–Sat 1–2 daily; 1hr); Savusavu (1 weekly; 20min).

By bus A bus service links Matei with locations to the west and east; you can flag down the bus anywhere along the road.

Destinations Lavena (3 daily; 1hr 15min); Naqara (3 daily; 30min).

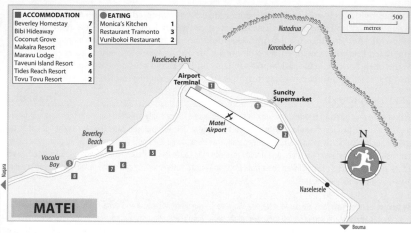

ACCOMMODATION

■ ACCOMMODATION	
Beverley Homestay	7
Bibi Hideaway	5
Coconut Grove	1
Makaira Resort	8
Maravu Lodge	6
Taveuni Island Resort	3
Tides Reach Resort	4
Tovu Tovu Resort	2

● EATING	
Monica's Kitchen	1
Restaurant Tramonto	3
Vunibokoi Restaurant	2

7

MATEI

ACCOMMODATION

Beverley Homestay West Matei ☎ 888 0684, ✉ madden.annie@outlook.com. Tila, the warm-hearted Fijian owner, rents out two double rooms in her simple tin-roof home up the hill. Cold-water bathrooms are shared and meals can be prepared on request. **F$60**

★ **Bibi Hideaway** West Matei ☎ 888 0443, ✉ paulina bibi@yahoo.com. Two cottages with basic kitchens, one for couples and the other with two bedrooms, both very reasonably priced and delightfully rustic. This is a family property set in a large hillside plantation full of flowering shrubs and fruit trees (the fruit is free to guests) with a campsite too. The beach is just a 3min walk away. Camping **F$20**, cottages **F$130**

Coconut Grove East Matei ☎ 888 0000, ⊕ coconut grovefiji.com. Three well-kept cottages on a hillside overlooking a narrow beach, with nice views over the lagoon. The restaurant serves some of the best food on Taveuni. ☞ **F$505**

Makaira Resort Vacala Bay ☎ 888 0680, ⊕ fijibeach frontatmakaira.com. Owned by a lovely Hawaiian couple with a passion for deep-sea fishing, this two-acre hilltop property has two bungalows with stunning sea views plus access to Beverley Beach across the road. Both cottages have quality furnishings with decorative artwork. There's a massage bure and sundeck. **F$490**

Maravu Lodge West Matei ☎ 888 0005, ⊕ maravu lodge. This stylish backpacker lodge was once an upmarket resort and retains some of its plush trimmings including a pretty reception, open-plan restaurant and bar and a landscaped pool. It's set on a 90-acre coconut plantation and offers daily activities including village visits, snorkelling, surfing and copious *kava* drinking in the evenings. The 21 bures have a warm, colonial feel, with dark wood furnishings and thatch roofs. ☞ Dorms **F$35**, rooms **F$120**, bures **F$200**

★ **Taveuni Island Resort** West Matei ☎ 888 0441, ⊕ taveuniislandresort.com. Exclusive adult-only resort set on a landscaped hilltop with views across the straits to

---

WATERSPORTS AROUND MATEI

From Matei it takes roughly forty minutes by boat to reach the superb dive sites along the **Rainbow Reef**, off the south coast of Vanua Levu. The rich current-fed waters off Matei are also fantastic for big **game fishing**, with plentiful marlin, swordfish and yellowfin tuna. As well as the operators below, *Makaira Resort* (see above) can organize game-fishing trips in a 24ft aluminium boat (F$1170 per half-day).

OPERATORS

Sailing Fiji Vacala Bay ☎ 906 8600, ⊕ sailfarnorthfiji .com. Runs day- and overnight yacht charters to the Ringgold Islands (F$3890 for up to six people).

Taveuni Dive Waiyevo ☎ 828 1063, ⊕ taveunidive .com. Diving and snorkelling trips to the Great White Wall on Rainbow Reef. Two-tank dive F$280.

Taveuni Ocean Sports Beverley Beach ☎ 867 7513, ⊕ taveunioceansports.com. Rents out bikes (F$35/day), snorkel gear ($25/day), kayaks (F$50/day), surfboards (F$50/day) and runs surf trips to Qamea (F$315). Half-day rates also available.

Vanua Levu. The twelve plantation villas are spacious and come with luxury fittings and private rainforest showers. Steps lead from the beautiful infinity pool down to a small sandy beach. Rates include meals. ☎ **F$1430**
Tides Reach Resort West Matei ☎ 888 2080, ⓦ tides reachresort.com. Four stylish, spacious villas with stone floors and African-inspired decor sit right alongside the beach, albeit a bit too close together. There are plenty of activities too, including horseriding and boat trips to the

remote Ringgold Islands. Rates include meals. ☎ **F$1800**
Tovu Tovu Resort East Matei ☎ 888 0560, ⓔ tovutovu @connect.com.fj. This locally owned budget retreat with an excellent-value restaurant is just beyond the supermarket at the eastern end of Matei. The five bamboo cottages come with old-fashioned furniture and tiny bathrooms but are clean and comfortable – three have small kitchens. There's no beach, although the lagoon across the road is good for kayaking. **F$115**

EATING AND DRINKING

There are several **grocery stores** along the roadside in east Matei, the most comprehensive being Suncity Supermarket which also sells alcohol. There are also a couple of good independent **restaurants**, but no nightclubs or bars – the only place to drink is at a resort bar or licensed restaurant.

Monica's Kitchen ☎ 804 4150. Delicious home-style chicken or lamb curries (on the bone F$15, boneless F$25) served from the wooden veranda beside Monica Prawan's secondhand clothes shop. Her friend Ashwin (☎ 837 40304) delivers dinner to your accommodation for the same price if you call a few hours in advance. Mon–Sat 11am–5pm.
★**Restaurant Tramonto** ☎ 888 2224. Perched on a hilltop, this pizza restaurant offers the most spectacular waterside dining in Fiji from a wooden veranda overlooking

the placid waters of the Somosomo Straits. The pizzas are thin crust and delicious (from F$30) and there's a bar serving cocktails. Daily 10am–9pm.
★**Vunibokoi Restaurant** Tovu Tovu Resort ☎ 888 0560. Resort restaurant specializing in delicious Fijian food, with mains starting at F$15. The creamy *rourou* (vegetable leaf) soup is divine, and there's usually fresh *qari* (crab) and *kari* (prawns) cooked in *lolo* (coconut cream). They also serve home-made burgers for the less adventurous. Mon–Sat noon–2pm & 6–9pm.

The offshore islands

The three offshore islands of **Qamea**, **Matangi** and **Laucala**, scattered across the deep Tasman Straits from Matei, possess some of the best private island resorts in Fiji. Almost 30km north of Taveuni, the remote **Ringgold Islands** (see box, p.208) pop out of the horizon, just about visible from Matei on a clear day.

Qamea

Just over 2km offshore, **Qamea** is the closest and largest of the islands, with a rugged coastline and white sandy beaches backed by lush forests and hilly peaks. There are six fishing villages on the island, though no roads connect them. There's fantastic **surfing** off the south coast, with the year-round barrelling breaks Maqai Right and Bula Bowls: both are generally most popular with the cleaner conditions from October to May.

Matangi

The 240-acre, private **Matangi Island** was bought in the 1880s by the Mitchell family, who ran it as a coconut plantation for over a century. The Mitchells' fifth-generation descendants have turned Matangi into one of Fiji's finest resorts and declared the lagoon surrounding the island a marine reserve. **Horseshoe Bay** has one of the prettiest

---

THE AMERICAN IGUANA: A NATIONAL PEST

Qamea, and to a lesser extent Taveuni, has been cursed by the introduction of the giant American iguana. In 2000, a mating pair was released illegally from an American yacht and they have since flourished on Qamea where its offspring are often spotted feasting in local vegetable gardens. Capable of swimming, the iguana has crossed to and spread around the northern end of Taveuni ,where it has caused similar damage to the local flora. It has been declared a National Pest by the authorities who are struggling to eradicate the pesky beast.

beaches and snorkelling lagoons in Fiji, and a walking trail following the crater ridge offers stunning views and birdlife.

Laucala

At the northern tip of Qamea, **Laucala** was once owned by publishing tycoon Malcolm Forbes, then sold for US$11million in 2003 to Dietrich Mateschitz, founder of Red Bull energy drinks. He has built a new multimillion-dollar **private resort** (ⓦlaucala.com), where visiting celebs fork out US$7000 per night.

ARRIVAL AND DEPARTURE   THE OFFSHORE ISLANDS

By boat Boats for the islands leave from either Qeleni, 9km south of Matei, or the black-sand beach at Navakacoa village, 12km south of Matei: both are served by three daily buses between Lavena and Matei.

ACCOMMODATION

★**Maqai Beach Eco Resort** Qamea ☎990 7761, ⓦmaqai.com. The eight simple wooden huts strung out along the beach are comfortable, if nothing fancy. The centrepiece of the resort is its stunning sand-floor restaurant with a large curved wooden bar. Two renowned surfing breaks, Maqai Right and Bula Bowls, are right offshore making this the top choice for surfers, but it's good too for snorkelling and walking. Dorm F$85, huts F$195
★**Matangi Private Island Resort** Matangi ☎888 0260, ⓦmatangiisland.com. This superb private island resort is managed by Fijian owners whose jovial staff make you feel part of the family, and its beautiful treehouse

bures are set in forest that is home to orange doves and parrot finches. The bures, both treehouse and beachside, mix traditional Fijian elements with contemporary design and have outdoor rainforest showers. There's a pool and delightful restaurant and the scuba diving nearby is first-class. ᯤ F$1310
Waruka Bay Resort Qamea ☎999 5167, ⓦwaruka .com. This secluded retreat is the kind of place you dream of, set alongside a beautiful white-sand beach backed by ancient rainforest trees and with fantastic views across to Taveuni. There are just three thatch bures, none closer than 50 metres apart, and two can take families. F$330

Bouma National Heritage Park

Fifteen kilometres southeast of Matei is the northern boundary of the **Bouma National Heritage Park**, an important wildlife reserve, protecting forty thousand acres of ancient **rainforest** laced with waterfalls and home to rare birds and plants.

Within the park are four villages, each running a specific eco-attraction: **Waitabu**, the first of the villages encountered along the road from Matei, has a protected **marine park**; 4km further into the park, **Vidawa** offers a rewarding rainforest hike to ancient ruins in the hills; neighbouring **Korovou** (also known as Bouma) maintains the spectacular Tavoro Waterfall Trail through three sets of falls; and the last of the four villages, **Lavena**, 15km to the south and at the end of the road, has a beautiful coastal walk with kayaking and another refreshing waterfall at its end. Also within the park are **Lake Tagimaucia** and **Des Vœux Peak**, although these are most easily accessed from the west coast.

Waitabu Marine Park

Park entry F$30 • Guided snorkelling and bamboo raft trip F$20 • Bookings ☎820 1999, ⓦwaitabu.org

Waitabu Marine Park is set in a secluded bay off the main road. There's no sign to Waitabu village, so look out for the access road heading towards the coast from the brow of a steep hill, about fifteen minutes' drive south of Navakacoa. Waitabu

---

THE RINGGOLD ISLANDS

Almost 30km northwest from Taveuni, the remote **Ringgold Islands** are a collection of small islands supporting thousands of breeding **seabirds**, including the red-footed booby and black noddy on Vetaua Island. The only inhabitants live on rolling Yanuca Island where farming is viable. **Nuku**, an atoll surrounded by tiny coral islets, has some of the finest white sand in Fiji, where hundreds of sea turtles lay their eggs between September and January.

translates as "sacred waters", and in 1998 the seven Fijian communities here signed an agreement to neither fish nor anchor in a one-kilometre stretch of coastline up to the fringing reef. Consequently, the coral and fish here are thriving – to view them, you can either head off with your own snorkelling gear, or book a **guided snorkelling trip** at the visitor centre: it's best to book in advance, to make sure there's someone around.

Vidawa Rainforest Hike

Guided hike (6–7hr) F$60 • Bookings essential on ☎ 820 4709

A kilometre beyond the Waitabu turn-off, the road passes through the smallest of the four villages, Vidawa. Here, the community has organized the **Vidawa Rainforest Hike**, a full-day trek to the pristine upper forests. The guided hike departs from the small **visitor centre** in the village. The earlier you start, the more chance you have of spotting the **native birds** which forage in the fruit trees of the lower slopes before heading back to the cover of the high forest – golden whistlers, silktails, red shining parrots and blue-crested broadbills are commonly sighted. After trudging through the sweaty and often muddy rainforest, the hike emerges in the lower forests at the first Tavoro waterfall (see below) where you can take a refreshing swim.

Tavoro Waterfall Trail

Daily 8am–5pm • Trail access F$30

The most popular of the park's adventures is the **Tavoro Waterfall Trail**. The self-guided walk starts from a roadside **visitor centre** in Korovou, which has toilets and sells cold drinks.

To the first waterfall

From the visitor centre, an easy ten-minute stroll through gardens leads to the first of the three **waterfalls**, arguably the most picturesque and with the best pool for swimming. Boulders on the left side of the pool lead to a 5m-high rock ledge which cuts in behind the cascading water – if you summon up the courage, you can throw yourself through the falls and into the deep pool beneath.

To the second waterfall

The section of trail between the first and **second falls** is the prettiest, starting with a steep ten-minute climb, helped along by wooden steps and a crushed-coral path to the ridge above the first set of falls. From the top there's a covered platform with a view over Thurston Point towards Qamea Island. The track then heads into light forest and crosses the Tavoro River, where there are large boulders to hop across and a rope for hanging onto. Another ten minutes brings you to the photogenic 30m-high second falls, which cascade over numerous ledges into a natural pool.

To the third waterfall

The trail to the least-visited **third falls** offers the most demanding hiking and can be extremely slippery after heavy rain. It starts 30m downstream from the second falls, and climbs a steep bank on the far side of the stream into thick forest. It takes another thirty minutes to reach the falls. At only 10m high, they are the smallest of the three, but the wide pool below is great for swimming and deep enough to jump into. Allow yourself an hour to return from the third falls to the roadside.

Lavena Coastal Walk

Trail access F$25 • Guide F$20 • ☎ 729 0154 or ☎ 820 3639

The pretty beach at **Lavena**, 6km south of Tavoro, marks the start of a scenic **coastal walk** to another set of waterfalls hidden in forest. Accommodation is available at *Lavena Lodge* (see below), at the entrance to the village where the coastal road from Matei ends; the lodge also doubles as the **visitor centre** where you pay your entrance fee

> ### LAVENA BY BOAT AND KAYAK
>
> A great way to explore the coast around Lavena is on a **guided kayak tour** (4hr; F$120, including lunch), which you can arrange at *Lavena Lodge* (see below). Experienced guides from the village will accompany you on a one-hour paddle south from Lavena before trekking inland to Wainibau Falls for lunch. The guides will then tow your kayak back to the village, allowing you to return along the **Lavena Coastal Walk** (see above). You can also reach the falls on a village **boat trip** (F$120; 4hr), with the option of continuing further south along the coast to **Savu Le Vea Vonu** waterfall, that tumbles into the sea (F$300; 5hr).

for the coastal trail (3hr return) and can arrange guides, kayak tours and boat trips (see box above).

The first forty-minute section of the trail is a flat amble through light coastal forest with wonderful views along the coast and passing several beaches. Once you reach the tiny settlement of **Naba**, you'll have to wade across a river that can be impassable after heavy rains. The other side of the river, the trail gets steeper and narrower and passes through denser forest until, after about twenty minutes, it reaches another river. Here, you'll need to wade upstream for ten minutes to reach **Wainibau Falls**, where you can jump from the top into a deep pool.

ARRIVAL AND DEPARTURE

By car The only road access to the park's four main attractions is from the north, along the winding dirt coastal road from Matei via Qeleni. The majority of people visit on a day-trip organized by their accommodation.

By bus You can get to the park by public bus on the Pacific Transport service (3 daily) running between Lavena and

BOUMA NATIONAL HERITAGE PARK

Naqara (1hr 45min) via Matei (1hr 15min). The last bus back towards Matei leaves at 2pm so if you are departing later than this you will have to order a taxi back from the park; note that this 2pm bus doesn't always start out at Lavena, so it's worth checking, and wait at the Korovou village bus stop rather than the waterfall one.

INFORMATION

Entry General access to the park is free. However, to participate in the four village enterprises, a small fee is paid at each village visitor centre.

Information For more information enquire at the visitor

centres at Waitabu Marine Park (☎820 1999), Vidawa (☎820 4709), or Lavena (☎729 0154), though phone reception at all the visitor centres can be erratic.

ACCOMMODATION

Lavena Lodge Lavena village ☎820 3639. On the beachfront at Lavena, the three very basic twin rooms here are screened and have mosquito nets, but the shared bathroom is rather dingy. However, it's worth staying here to make an early morning start on the Lavena Coastal Walk (guests get free access). Meals (F$10/plate) can be arranged with one of the villagers or you can use the

lodge's kitchen facilities. **F$30**
Waitabu Campsite and Village Stay ☎820 1999. The marine park campsite provides a great opportunity for a remote night under the stars. There are toilets and showers, and you can pre-order simple Fijian meals. Alternatively, you can stay with a family in the village. Camping (with own tent) **F$20**, homestay **F$60**

The west coast

Looking over the Somosomo Straits towards Vanua Levu, Taveuni's **west coast** is mostly rocky with few beaches. Much of the land was cleared of its hardwood trees by colonial farmers and planted instead with neat rows of **coconut palms**. Today, the 6km stretch of road between the chiefly coastal village of **Somosomo** and the Catholic mission at **Wairiki** is the population centre of the island, home to the only town, **Naqara**, and the hospital and police headquarters at Waiyevo. To the north of Somosomo, the large sprawling inland settlement of **Qari** is where most of the island's Indo-Fijians live on small farm holdings.

The bulk of travellers visit the region solely for its close access to the **Rainbow Reef** (see box, p.206). However there are also a few land-based attractions nearby including

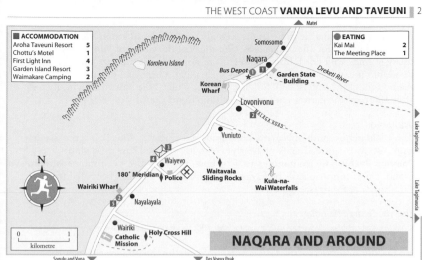

■ ACCOMMODATION	
Aroha Taveuni Resort	5
Chottu's Motel	1
First Light Inn	4
Garden Island Resort	3
Waimakare Camping	2

● EATING	
Kai Mai	2
The Meeting Place	1

NAQARA AND AROUND

the hair-raising **natural waterslide** at Waitavala and the **180 Degree Meridian** line which passes through Taveuni here. Also nearby is the access road to **De Vœux Peak**, the island's second-highest mountain, and **Lake Tagimaucia.**

Somosomo

Eighteen kilometres south of Matei is the chiefly village of **SOMOSOMO**, traditional home of the **Tui Cakau**, high chief of the whole of Taveuni and much of Vanua Levu. The current chief no longer lives here, having moved up into the hills, but the village remains home to a community of indigenous people and is symbolically important as the chiefly village of a traditionally powerful province. There's little to see here today, save a tiny limestone-walled church, and the only reason for visitors to stop is to stock up at the Morris Hedstrom store (Mon–Fri 8am–6pm, Sat 8am–noon), Taveuni's largest **supermarket**.

Naqara

Separated from Somosomo by a bridge over a small river, **NAQARA** is a rather disorganized collection of wooden shacks and corrugated-iron buildings that passes for the island's main town. Looking completely out of place in the centre of town is the four-storey Garden State building, site of several handy services including a bank, ATM and internet shop, while several street-side shacks nearby sell food.

Waitavala Sliding Rocks

The west coast's main attraction is **Waitavala Sliding Rocks**, a fun 200m-long natural waterslide where you chute down the rapids of a narrow stream on your backside. Old clothes are recommended, and if the water is foaming in the lower pool at the bottom

CAKOBAU'S WAR CANOE

Ra Marama, the last great double-hulled **Fijian war canoe** to grace the South Seas, was built at Somosomo during the 1830s to 1840s. The canoe, measuring 30m long and 6m wide, took seven years to build and could carry over 130 warriors. At the keel-laying ceremony, several young warriors were clubbed to death to increase the canoe's *mana*, or spiritual power; missionaries intervened at the canoe's launch when more warriors were due to be sacrificed. The canoe was presented as a gift to **Cakobau** of Bau who used it as a powerful symbol of strength in his wars against Rewa which eventually crowned him King of Fiji. After Cakobau's death in 1882, the canoe was returned to Somosomo where, beached, it perished to the wind and sea.

it means the currents are fast – in these conditions it's wise to watch a local slide down before giving it a go. The water slide, 1km south of the village of **Vuniuto**, is a little tricky to find: walk north from *Garden Island Resort* for five minutes and turn up Sand Road into the hills beside a wooden bus shelter. From here it's a twenty-minute walk to the bottom of the waterslide – fork left just past a metal shed on your right, then right after 100m on the narrow path which leads up to the pools.

Waiyevo

Three kilometres south of Naqara, the hillside settlement of **WAIYEVO** is the island's administrative centre. There's no beach here, but it's a good base for **diving** – access to **Rainbow Reef** is only ten minutes away by boat, and non-divers can snorkel at **Korolevu Island**, a five-minute paddle by kayak from the coast; kayaks can be rented from the *Garden Island Resort* (see opposite).

The 180 Degree Meridian

Off Hospital Road, which leads from central Waiyevo up to the hospital. The meridian board is on the far right side of the rugby field opposite the fire station

At Taveuni's quirkiest attraction, a small information board covered by a tin roof marks the exact location of the **180 Degree Meridian**. Fiji is one of only two places in the world where this line of longitude crosses land, the other being at the far eastern tip of Russia. The meridian theoretically marks the beginning and end of each day, although for the sake of convenience the International Date Line kinks eastwards to avoid splitting Fiji into two time zones and two different days. In colonial times, unscrupulous planters justified working their labourers on Sunday by claiming they were actually working on Monday's side of the dateline.

Wairiki

A ten-minute stroll south of Waiyevo, the pretty settlement of **WAIRIKI** revolves around the imposing **Catholic Mission**, where a two-hour Mass is celebrated every Sunday at 10am with such enthusiasm that cracks have appeared in the windows. Located on a hill, the Mission overlooks the ocean where the island's warriors once fought off thousands of invading Tongans in a **sea battle**. The Taveunians won the day, promptly ate their adversaries and halted the Tongan invasion of Fiji. You can get great views over the bay from **Holy Cross Hill** above the Mission: it's a 25min walk along a track that starts from the dirt road beside the secondary school.

Des Vœux Peak and Lake Tagimaucia

From Wairiki, the 6km-long Tuvaki Road, little more than a dirt track, heads to the telecoms tower at **Des Vœux Peak** (1195m). If you're fit, you can walk to the top from the turning off the coast road, just north of the Catholic Mission, in under two hours. You'll have to pay a F$5 fee at the gate just beyond Tuvaki village, about a 50-minute walk from the Catholic Mission. Beyond the gate, the road becomes steeper and the walk to the **summit** can take a further hour. On a clear day the view over Taveuni, Vanua Levu and south to Gau and Koro is incredible. Be warned, though, clouds often obscure the peak and even when it's sunny by the coast, rain can easily be falling on the mountain. The **birdwatching** up here is excellent, with regular sightings of silktails and orange doves, especially in the nesting season (Aug & Sept) and you may spot **tagimaucia flowers** growing among the trees, too. If the walk is too daunting, you can hire a 4WD and driver from Bula Taxis & Tours in Naqara town (see p.205) to take you to the summit and back for F$150: note that the Tuvaki gate is sometimes closed to vehicles, though you can still walk to the summit.

From the summit, it's possible to continue for another two hours, hacking through bush along the northern ridge to **Lake Tagimaucia** (see box opposite), a crater lake

THE WEEPING TAGIMAUCIA FLOWER

The only place in the world where the beautiful **tagimaucia flower** (*Medinilla waterhousei*) grows is at high altitude on Taveuni – most famously around the shores of Lake Tagimaucia – and at a couple of locations on eastern Vanua Levu. The beautiful flowers bloom between September and December, and hang in bright clusters from a liana vine, with two red waxy outer petals and four white inner petals resembling a bell. This being Fiji, there is a romantic legend attached: the tumbling flowers represent the tears of a maiden forbidden to marry her true love.

823m above sea level where the endemic tagimaucia flower blooms in profusion. A relatively well-maintained but arduous trail leads direct to the lake from Naqara (7hr return), though the shortest route leads up from the village of Lovonivonu, 1km south of Naqara (6hr return) – either way, a guide is essential and can be arranged through most west-coast resorts for F$60–100.

ARRIVAL AND INFORMATION

THE WEST COAST

7

By boat Ferries from Suva arrive at Wairiki Wharf between Wairiki and Waiyevo. Small boats crossing Buca Bay from Vanua Levu arrive at the old wharf in Lovonivonu (known as the Korean Wharf), between Waiyevo and Naqara.
Destinations Natuvu Landing (3 daily; 1hr 30min); Suva (2 weekly; 16hr).
By bus Pacific Transport (☎ 888 0278) head north and south from Naqara: expect delayed services on rainy days.

Destinations Lavena (Mon–Sat 3 daily, Sun 2 daily; 1hr 45min); Matei (Mon–Sat 3 daily, Sun 2 daily; 30min); Navakawau (Mon–Sat 3 daily, Sun 2 daily; 2hr).
Services There's a branch of Colonial Bank, with an ATM machine, on the ground floor of the Garden State building in Naqara (Mon 9.30am–4pm, Tues–Fri 9am–4pm). Waiyevo has a hospital and police station, on a small hill 200m from the main road; there's also a post office in the centre of town.

ACCOMMODATION AND EATING

NAQARA AND AROUND

Chottu's Motel Naqara ☎ 888 0233, ✉ chottusmotel @connect.com.fj; map p.211. In the centre of town, this long-standing place has the cheapest hotel rooms on Taveuni, with shared bathrooms. Larger self-contained units have basic kitchen facilities, fridge and en-suite bathrooms. Rooms F$50, units F$75

The Meeting Place On the Main Street, Naqara ☎ 888 0000; map p.211. A favourite with the Taveuni locals, this restaurant is a good place to eat cheap curries (F$8) or pizzas (F$15), have a beer and play a game of pool (F$1). Mon–Sat 8am–10pm, Sun 3pm–10pm.

Waimakare Camping Lovonivonu Rd, Lovonivonu ☎ 888 0051 or ☎ 716 0105; map p.211. A ten-minute walk south of the Korean Wharf, this secluded campsite is set in light forest within the grounds of a Fijian family home. There's a plain wooden dormitory with a kitchen: beds consist of a mat and mattress laid on the floor. The family will cook for you, and are generous with the abundant fruit from their garden – pawpaws, bananas, pineapples and avocados. Guided walks to Lake Tagimaucia and Des Vœux Peak can be arranged. Camping (with own tent) F$10, dorms F$25

WAIYEVO

First Light Inn Above the post office ☎ 888 0339, ✉ firstlight@connect.com.fj; map p.211. The sixteen

pastel-coloured motel rooms with a/c and satellite TV are clean and simple, and there's an Indian restaurant downstairs. F$80

Garden Island Resort ☎ 888 0286, ⓦ gardenisland resort.com; map p.211. The oceanfront setting of this resort is pleasant enough with modern, attractive rooms (some have sea views). Six Pacific almond trees along the foreshore host thousands of fruit bats. F$415

WAIRIKI AND AROUND

★**Aroha Taveuni Resort** Wairiki ☎ 888 1882, ⓦ arohataveuni.com; map p.211. Owned by New Zealanders, this efficiently run resort, with a small beachfront, has a comfortable and relaxed vibe. The five rooms with outdoor showers are housed in two bures, and guests can use the owner's infinity pool. Diving trips can be arranged and the excellent on-site *Kai Mai* restaurant is also open to the public. ☎ F$315

Salty Fox Café Taveuni Dive Resort, Soqulu ☎ 891 1083. Sitting on a hillside with pleasant views over the coast, this resort restaurant serves up a good selection of lunchtime burgers ($35). The two-course dinner menu ($45) offers a choice of three dishes, usually including steak sourced from nearby farms and fish from the lagoon. Bookings essential at dinner. Daily 6am–8pm.

★**Taveuni Dive Resort** 4km south of Wairiki in Soqulu ☎ 888 0125, ⓦ taveunidiveresort.com. Located on the

ROTUMA

The most remote of the Fijian islands, 43-square-kilometre **Rotuma** lies over 600km north of Suva in a lonely stretch of ocean south of Tuvalu. Its Polynesian culture and language are significantly different from that of the Micronesian Fijians, and the island is only part of Fiji at all thanks to an accident of history.

In 1881, tired of internal friction, the seven chiefs of Rotuma decided to cede their island to Britain. However, the island was deemed too isolated to justify its own British governor and, instead, it was decided that Rotuma should politically become part of Fiji, its remote neighbour to the south. So, on May 13, 1881, at a spot in Motusa marked by a stone wall embedded with a brass plaque, Rotuma relinquished its sovereignty to Fiji.

Today, just under 2000 people live a subsistence lifestyle on the island, while a further 6000 Rotumans live permanently in Suva and other towns around Fiji, many holding good positions in society such as doctors, lawyers and teachers. In 2016, a prominent Rotuman, Major General Konrote, became the first non-iTaukei President of Fiji.

AROUND THE ISLAND

The government headquarters for Rotuma have been stationed at **'Ahau** since 1902. Colonial-style buildings house the hospital, police and judiciary as well as a small cement jail with two tiny cells. The island's post office is also located here.

Rotuma is enclosed by a lagoon fringed by a reef and is almost completely surrounded by stunning white sandy **beaches** set off by jet-black volcanic rock. Two of the best are **Oinafa Beach** on the northeastern point of the island, which is also a good spot for bodysurfing and snorkelling in the turquoise lagoon around the twin islands of Haua; and isolated **Vai'oa Beach**, one of the prettiest in the South Pacific, and usually deserted, with towering palm trees and fabulous snorkelling.

A handful of impressive **archeological sites** can be found inland – including the ancient **burial site** of the kings of Rotuma on top of **Sisilo Hill** and an ancient stone tomb near **Islepi village** – as well as over a dozen **volcanic cones**. The highest of these rises to 256m, protruding from the gently rolling hills which are extensively planted with *taro*, yams, *kava* and numerous varieties of fruit tree, particularly oranges.

FARA

The liveliest time to visit is over Christmas, during the singing and dancing festivities of **Fara**. The party begins on December 1 (Dec 24 for the Catholic districts of Juju and Pepjei) and lasts until mid-January. Each evening children wander around their villages singing *fara* songs and clapping their hands. When they stop at a house, the family comes out and rewards them with gifts of perfume, talc and fruit, usually watermelon. If the singing is poor, water is thrown to chase the group away. As the evening progresses, the rest of the villagers join in, grabbing guitars, ukuleles and perhaps a bucket of orange wine. If you visit Rotuma during *fara* you will certainly be invited to take part.

ARRIVAL AND DEPARTURE

By plane The gravel airstrip at Malhaha on the north coast of Rotuma is served by Fiji Link from Nadi (departs Wed; 2hr 30min; F$610 one way) and Suva (departs Fri; 2hr 30min; F$630 one way). There are always plenty of small trucks meeting incoming flights at the airstrip and you should be able to negotiate a ride.

By boat Goundar Shipping runs a cargo boat between Suva and Oinafa wharf on the northeast coast of Rotuma (monthly, usually on Sat; 2-day journey; deck F$118, cabin F$180).

INFORMATION AND ACCOMMODATION

The Rotumans want to keep the island free from mass tourism – indeed, in 1985, 85 percent voted to keep tourist development at bay – making the island hard to visit without a **personal invitation**. One option is to post a message on the Rotuman community Facebook page ⓦ facebook.com/groups/rotumans, and someone locally may be willing to organize a **homestay** for you. Otherwise, try asking around in Suva to locate expatriate Rotumans who may put you in contact with a relative back home.

mountain side of the pretty coastal road in Taveuni Estates, with a nine-hole golf-course, this purpose-built dive resort has eight Fijian-styled bures beside an infinity pool. The diving facilities are excellent with three dive boats, and it runs daily dive trips to the Rainbow Reef, just 15min away. There's a great restaurant here too (see p.213). 🛜 **F$750**

Southern Taveuni

Rarely visited by tourists, **Southern Taveuni** is dominated by a few huge coconut plantations growing on the rich volcanic soil. Inland, a series of volcanic cones pop out from the gentle slopes rising to the island's highest point, the inaccessible Mount Uluiqalau (1241m). At the southwestern tip of the island, **Vuna Lagoon** has good snorkelling, with the picturesque Namoli Beach a short walk to the north. Southern Taveuni was one of the regions worst affected by Cyclone Winston in 2016 (see box, p.26), and most of the houses in the village of Vuna were destroyed, along with the surrounding farms. The government was slow to provide aid to the area, with many of its people still living in temporary tents a year later.

The Matamaiqi Blowhole

Buses from Naqara to Navakawau village pass the blowhole, but head back to Naqara via the inland road

From Navakawau village, it's a fifteen-minute walk south along a coastal track to the promontory known as the **South Cape**, littered with jet-black rocks, where Taveuni's last volcanic eruption spilled into the sea around five hundred years ago. The highlight of the area is the **Matamaiqi Blowhole**, an unpredictable beast which occasionally spouts jets of seawater 15m or more into the air – it's most likely to perform on the turn of the low tide. Watch to see what the seas are doing for at least five minutes before getting too close to the blowhole.

7

DETAIL OF TRADITIONAL FAN

Contexts

History

Feared for its cannibal tendencies and avoided by mariners for its treacherous reefs, Fiji was one of the last island groups in the world to be encroached upon by the West. When the *kaivalagi*, "the people from far away", finally arrived in 1803 they found a deeply hierarchical tribal culture characterized by allegiance to village chiefs, fierce warfare and pagan religion. Europeans exploited the Fijians' natural resources, particularly sandalwood, coconuts and bêche de mer (sea cucumber), and brought with them firearms and alcohol with which to pay off the local chiefs.

The arrival of firearms intensified tribal wars particularly between the quarrelling clans from Rewa and Bau on eastern Viti Levu. This turbulent state of affairs eased in 1874 after **Cakobau**, the self-proclaimed "King of Fiji", converted to Christianity and renounced cannibalism, events which would lead to Fiji becoming a **British colony**. The Fijians, however, proved a reluctant workforce for the new authorities and so indentured labourers from India were shipped in to work the land and make profitable this curious outpost of the empire. This situation continued for almost a hundred years until the country secured its independence in 1970 and was faced with the challenging task of forming a harmonious national identity, a struggle that continues today.

The first Fijians

With no written record, the movement and lifestyles of the first Fijian peoples have been revealed only with the advent of accurate archeological research, particularly the discovery of **Lapita pottery**. Many Fijians, however, give credence to the legend of **Lutunasobasoba** as the first settler of the islands.

Lapita migration

Scientific findings place **Bourewa**, north of Natadola Beach on the west coast of Viti Levu, as the earliest site of human habitation in Fiji, dating back to 1220 BC. Distinctive **Lapita pottery** (see box, p.111) found all around the Melanesian archipelago, suggests that the settlers originated from Southeast Asia, most probably Taiwan or the Philippines. Thought to be lighter skinned than modern Fijians, they inhabited Papua New Guinea, then the Solomon Islands before settling on Vanuatu, New Caledonia, Fiji and Tonga. This migration was followed by a more dynamic flow of people, likely to be darker-skinned Melanesians who reached Fiji between 1000 and 500 BC. The Melanesians continued east to Tonga, the remote islands of Rarotonga and Tahiti, before eventually reaching Aotearoa (New Zealand) and Hawaii, all part of present-day Polynesia, around 800 AD.

Date unknown	1220 BC	1000–500 BC
The Fijian myths of Degree, the snake god, and Lutunasobasoba, the first settler, are born.	Settlers from Southeast Asia arrive on western Viti Levu.	Melanesians arrive in Fiji, on a migration that would take them on to Hawaii.

Lutunasobasoba and Degei

Many Fijians recognize **Lutunasobasoba** as the first person to settle the islands and as founder of the tribal system. Supposedly the great chief Lutunasobasoba landed on the west coast of Viti Levu at Vuda, arriving by canoe from Tanzania in East Africa. However, the story of his discovery of Fiji only entered the national consciousness in 1892 after a competition in a local newspaper to find the best explanation for Fijian evolution.

The people from Ra disagree with this legend, believing instead that their descendants, including **Degei**, arrived earlier from Egypt, while others believe the first settlers came from the Biblical tribes of ancient Israel. By all accounts Degei, who lived in a cave in the sacred Nakauvadra Mountains of northern Viti Levu in the form of a **snake**, was the supreme god of all Fiji. Today, it's common for iTaukei Fijians to claim an impressive genealogical network of around twelve generations tracing their tribe (*yavusa*) back to either Lutunasobasoba or Degei.

Tribal culture

Very little is known about the indigenous Fijian people in the centuries before European contact, although it's clear that they built extensive hill fortifications and stone fish traps around the coastline. They also created beautiful **woodcarvings** including war clubs, *yaqona* bowls and head rests, wove *tapa* cloth to adorn the body and made jewellery. **Tattooing** or *qai* was commonplace, often around the mouth and in patterns leading to the genitals, painfully etched with a chipped *kai* shell to form a raised scar.

Warlike in nature, particularly on the larger islands, tribes seldom ventured beyond their territorial boundaries unless to hunt or pay homage to their superior neighbouring chiefs. Consequently, a variety of distinct tribes evolved in relative isolation, each with their identifying customs, mekes, gods and dialects (see box opposite).

European encounters

Bypassed by the early Spanish explorers who had headed north to the Philippines, Fiji had to wait until the seventeenth century before European ships reached Fijian waters. In 1643, Dutch navigator **Abel Tasman**, who had discovered New Zealand and Tasmania the previous year, sailed past the Fijian island of Taveuni on his way back to Jakarta in Indonesia. He narrowly avoided shipwreck off the Nanuku Reef east of Vanua Levu and quickly made a northward passage away from the islands. Another 130 years were to pass before European explorers returned.

William Bligh and the Bounty, 1789

During his celebrated voyage of 1774, **Captain James Cook** made a note of the remote Vatoa Island in the southern Lau Group. Although he didn't explore the region further he later met Fijians while in Tonga. Greater recognition goes to **William Bligh**, who in 1789 found himself passing through the heart of the Fijian archipelago aboard a small wooden launch along with seventeen men and just six rowing oars. Having captained his ship, **HMS Bounty**, to Tahiti, Bligh was famously the victim of a mutiny led by

1000 AD	1643	1774	1789
As Tongans and Samoans attack the islands, the Fijians become a warrior people.	Dutch navigator Abel Tasman sails past Taveuni.	Captain Cook writes of the existence of Vatoa Island.	Cast onto a small rowing boat by mutineers, William Bligh successfully navigates to Fiji.

EARLY RELIGION AND CUSTOMS

Two tiers of **gods** ruled the living: the highest-ranked gods, the *kalou-vu*, were universally venerated immortals. For everyday affairs, the people sought blessings from a collection of localized gods known as the *kalou-yalo*. These were ancestral spirits who in the living world had been respected chiefs or triumphant warriors. These gods commanded the weather, had powers over war and sickness and were called upon to bless the people with abundant fish and fruits, but were otherwise not invoked. Contact with these gods was conducted through the **high priest** (*bete*), a member of the priestly clan or *bete mataqali*. The *bete* sat in a high-roofed temple known as the *bure kalou* and, possessed with *yaqona*, would call the spirits to descend down the *masi* cloth hanging from the temple roof and speak through his body.

MANA

Blood spilling was an integral part of Fijian custom and imbued items with what was known as **mana**, or spirituality. *Mana* was especially important for warriors and chiefs; their personal war clubs were anointed in human blood in order to bring them mystical powers. War canoes were launched over the bodies of sacrificial victims and the building of temples and chiefly houses required people to be buried alive with the foundations. **Cannibalism** (see box, p.221) was the apotheosis of such blood lust, with war parties constantly scouting for unsuspecting victims. Direct tribal confrontations were less frequent, though when they occurred they tended to take the form of the sacking of entire villages by uprooting crops and burning houses, usually once the survivors had surrendered and moved on to new land.

POLYGAMY AND WIDOW STRANGULATION

Polygamy was commonplace among the early Fijians. On a man's **death**, his spirit was believed to linger in the village for four days to haunt his enemies, during which period it was also customary for the widows to be strangled to death in order to accompany the husband's spirit to the afterlife or *bulu*.

WITCHCRAFT AND SUPERSTITION

Witchcraft and superstition were similarly deeply ingrained in Fijian culture. Certain people had the power to invoke malevolent spirits (*tevoro*) to taunt their enemies, most notably through illness, in which case the village **sorcerer** would perform an elaborate *yaqona* ceremony (see box, p.31) to chase the spirit away and reveal the perpetrator.

Fletcher Christian on April 28 just off Tofua in Tonga. Mindful of the dreadful stories of the warlike, cannibalistic people from Tonga, Bligh and his small crew anxiously paddled for five days past Gau and between Vanua Levu and Viti Levu. On the sixth day, in the Yasawas, two war canoes set out in pursuit of their vessel but, thanks to a timely squall, Bligh escaped and eventually made it to the Dutch settlement at Coupang on Timor forty days later. Bligh had managed to successfully chart 39 Fijian islands and the section of sea where he made good his escape is known as Bligh Waters.

The Argo and the arrival of beachcombers 1800–1810

The first white people to land on Fijian soil were probably the crew of the schooner **Argo**, who were shipwrecked off Oneata in Lau in 1800. They brought with them Asian cholera which promptly annihilated much of the local population. A few years later, a steady stream of merchant ships from Sydney Harbour began to arrive, attracted

1800	1804	1813
The schooner *Argo* is shipwrecked and the first white people arrive in Fiji.	Europeans discover – and decimate – Fiji's sandalwood trees.	Swedish mercenary Charlie Savage is eaten on Vanua Levu.

by the fragrant **sandalwood** newly discovered at Bua Bay on the remote southwestern coast of Vanua Levu.

A few Europeans, mostly escaped convicts or mercenaries, chose to settle on the islands. Known as "**beachcombers**", they aligned themselves with local chiefs and acted as go-betweens for the merchants and Fijians. One particular beachcomber, a Swede named **Charlie Savage** (see box opposite) had a strong influence on the tribal balance of power in Fiji. Shipwrecked aboard the *Eliza* in 1808, he was presented as a hostage to the chief of **Bau**, a tiny island off the east coast of Viti Levu. Over the following years his unscrupulous demeanour and knowledge of muskets soon saw the island's opportunist chiefs – Naulivou and later Cakobau (see below) – with whom Savage had aligned himself, begin to dominate the region. The possession of **firearms** soon became a matter of survival for rival villages. With gun in hand and mercenaries by their sides, they turned the previous petty marauding style of warfare into full-blown genocidal campaigns with entire villages being laid waste and their inhabitants shot, cooked and eaten.

The arrival of the missionaries, 1835

In 1835, after a lull in visiting European merchant ships, Cross and Cargill of the Wesleyan London Missionary Society arrived on Lakeba in the Lau Group and established the first mission in Fiji. Though they found little resistance to their efforts they managed to convert only a few Tongans living on the island. Other **missionaries** soon followed and set up base around **Levuka**, where a few hardened European merchants had huddled together in a small trading outpost. Appalled at the entrenched traditions of cannibalism and widow strangulation, the missionaries soon realized that the spread of Christianity would depend on the powerful pagan chief of Bau.

Cakobau's war with Rewa

Bau's ruling chief, **Cakobau**, was a particularly ruthless warrior and received homage from many islands in Fiji, from Kadavu in the south to Taveuni in the north. But having waged an unsuccessful war with Qaraniqio, chief of bitter neighbour **Rewa** since 1840, Cakobau had overstretched his domain and accrued too many dangerous enemies. He had also lost the support of the white traders of Levuka and had to endure a trade and ammunition blockade.

In 1853, several disaffected chiefs and five hundred warriors rebelled at Kaba Point, a few kilometres south of Bau, and stole the sails of Cakobau's prized 72-tonne **gunboat** which he'd recently acquired from the Americans. In retaliation Cakobau led a raid on Kaba, but the heavily fortified stronghold proved resilient. In March the following year Cakobau's status was further eroded by a devastating fire which destroyed many houses on Bau as well as his sacred war temple. The chief took this as a sign that his gods had abandoned him.

On April 30, Cakobau received a letter from his old adversary, King George of Tonga, encouraging him to accept **Christianity**. After a long conversation with Joseph Waterhouse, the resident Methodist missionary on Bau, he decided to *lotu*, or convert. There were so many subsequent conversions throughout the islands that there were not enough missionaries to baptize all the newly faithful, let alone instruct them in the scriptures. Such mass conversion was a seismic social shift,

1822	1835	1840	1853
Levuka town becomes a trading port for European whalers and merchants.	Wesleyan missionaries arrive on Lakeba.	The US navy arrives in Fiji, with violent results – 70 Fijians die at Malolo.	Cakobau, the powerful chief of Bau, converts to Christianity.

THE CANNIBAL ISLES

And now the drums beat pat, pat, pat, pat, pat. What is the signal? It means that a man is about to be cut up and prepared for food, as is a bullock in our own country. See the commotion! The majority of the population, old and young, run to gaze upon the intended victim. He is stripped naked, struck down with the club, his body ignominiously dashed against a stone in front of a temple, and then cut up and divided amongst a chosen few, ere the vital spark is extinct.

Rev Joseph Waterhouse, *The King and People of Fiji*, Pasifika Press, 1886

Cannibalism in Fiji wasn't something that happened every so often, it was a routine part of life. In crudely pragmatic terms, human flesh served as a much-needed source of protein, especially among the hill people, for Fiji was almost devoid of meat-bearing animals. But its real power lay in **intimidation** – by eating the flesh of an enemy, a Fijian was consuming the *mana* or strength of their foe. **Warfare** was usually a tit-for-tat process. Small bands of marauding warriors would prowl the countryside looking for easy prey. If a stand-off between two warring parties ensued, taunts would be cast but seldom was there a full confrontation – securing just one victim was enough for a wild orgy back home.

With the procurement of a **bokola**, or uncooked human, men performed a *cibi* or war dance and unmarried girls responded in an erotic *wate* dance around the captive. The humiliation of the victim didn't usually end there. Young boys were given sharpened sticks and encouraged to taunt and torture the captive, a practice echoed today when a pig is brought down from the plantation for eating. In some severe accounts recorded by missionaries living among the Fijians in the 1800s, the tongue was cut out while the victim was still alive and eaten while his blood was drained and drunk. Eventually, the *bokola* was placed at the **killing stone** and the head smashed using a war club. The body was cleaned and cooked. The heart and tongue were considered the choicest parts and given to the chief, who would consume the flesh using a specially carved cannibal fork with four prongs, while other body parts were distributed among the villagers.

Understandably, in the early days of encounter, Europeans were afraid of the "Cannibal Isles" although most often, visitors, however strange looking, were treated gracefully and generously. A few did end up in the pot: Charlie Savage met his end on the island of Vanua Levu in 1813. It is said his bones were later made into sail needles. The most notorious case of cannibalism in the islands, though, rests with the unfortunate **Reverend Thomas Baker** who was killed and eaten by the Colo hill people of Viti Levu (see box, p.127) in 1867.

By the mid-1800s, with the introduction of firearms and the ensuing power struggle of Cakobau over his Rewan enemies, cannibalism hit its peak. Some first-hand accounts of missionaries stationed at Bau claimed that as many as three hundred people were brought back as the spoils of a single war and body parts hung off every house waiting for consumption. By the 1870s, Cakobau had converted to **Christianity** and ceased to practise cannibalism; following his lead, so did the majority of the Fiji islanders.

necessitating not just the widespread acceptance of the Christian God and the rejection of all other gods, but also the destruction of the temples and the cessation of cannibalism and widow strangulation.

In early 1855, Qaraniqio, chief of Rewa, died. Weary of war, the Rewans sued for peace. Cakobau's other enemies, however, hearing of his abandonment of Fijian traditions, now rallied at **Kaba Point** to wage war not only on Bau, but on Christianity.

1855	**1860s**	**1867**
Cakobau defeats his tribal enemy, Rewa, and declares himself King of Fiji.	Ma'afu, a Tongan prince, is declared King of Lau	The Reverend Thomas Baker is attacked and eaten by hill tribes in Viti Levu.

King George of Tonga came to Cakobau's assistance with two thousand Tongan warriors led in part by **Ma'afu**, ruler over the Lau Group. Their intervention proved decisive, with the Tongans leading the main assault and Bauan warriors holding back any retreat. After victory was assured, Cakobau, keeping faith with his new religion, forbade celebratory feasting on his enemies. With Rewa and Verata finally subdued, he arrogantly declared himself *Tui Viti* or **King of Fiji** although it was to be years before the title was formally recognized.

The path to colonialism

It soon became apparent that King George's assistance in the Kaba victory had come at a price – the control of northern Fiji. The Tongan prince **Ma'afu** had already established his seat of power on Vanua Balavu in the Lau Group and was making steady inroads into the province of Cakaudrove, hitherto home of Cakobau's strongest allies. Ma'afu, full of confidence after his leading role in the assault on Kaba, now became a serious threat to Cakobau's kingdom and over the nineteen years leading up to cession, the two chiefs **battled** indirectly for absolute control over Fiji, with Ma'afu steadily gaining the upper hand.

The American claims

While dealing with the Tongans, Cakobau faced a new problem – a **debt** to the US government. Back in 1849 on Nukulau Island off Suva, the house of **John Williams**, the US commercial agent, had accidentally burned to the ground during US Independence Day celebrations. What remained of his stockpile of supplies was subsequently ransacked by locals. Ever since the fire, Williams had been pressing the US government to claim compensation from the Fijians. In 1851 he had asked the captain of a US warship to demand US$5000, but the claim was dismissed as unfounded. However, the next time a US Navy ship visited in 1855, Williams was successful in gaining the support of its captain for his and a number of other American claims for compensation.

Cakobau, now the most powerful local chief, was held accountable to the impossible tune of US$42,000. Taken aboard the warship, he was bullied into signing acceptance of these claims and forced to promise payment within a year. Afraid of being taken prisoner to the US, Cakobau appealed to Pritchard, the British consul in Levuka, and promised **sovereignty of Fiji** to the British along with thousands of acres of land if the debt to the US was paid off and Ma'afu could be persuaded to relinquish his pursuit of power. Pritchard, hopeful of cession, managed to stall the American demands, and at a gathering of chiefs in Levuka in 1859, he persuaded Ma'afu to cease his war with Bau. Despite his efforts, cession was initially rejected by Britain in 1862 on the grounds that Cakobau, despite claiming kingly Status, did not represent the united peoples of Fiji. There were also concerns that the colony would prove unprofitable and a hindrance in times of war.

The second wave of European migration

Although Britain had rejected taking on Fiji as a colony, the following decade saw a new **rush** of Europeans to the islands, fuelled by rumours of imminent cession. A further one hundred thousand acres of land were sold to white traders usually by rogue

1871	1872	1874
Cakobau declares his government in Levuka.	Blackbirding, the importation of slave labourers into Fiji, is outlawed.	Heavily in debt, Cakobau cedes Fijian sovereignty to Britain.

BLACKBIRDING

Blackbirding, the recruitment of slave labourers through trickery, flourished in Fiji during the 1860s, driven by labour shortages in the cotton plantations. European merchants would drop anchor at remote islands, particularly Vanuatu and the Solomon Islands, and persuade the illiterate locals into signing papers which legitimized a work contract to take them off to far-away islands as labourers. The locals usually knew nothing of what they had signed and were lured onto the merchant ships by trinkets and locked in the hold to prevent them jumping overboard.

As trade in this "black ivory" flourished, merchants became more unscrupulous, succumbing to blatant kidnapping, rape and murder along the way before selling their human cargo in Levuka for £10 per head. By 1872, when the trade was stopped by the presence of British warships, roughly four thousand overseas labourers were working in Fiji's plantations, each man being paid £6 a year under a three-year contract. Most of the labourers were eventually **freed**, some returning to their homelands, but many stayed on, establishing new settlements on Ovalau and Viti Levu, or being adopted into nearby Fijian villages.

chiefs in return for firearms and alcohol. Plantations of **cotton** were established on Taveuni, Vanua Levu and the Lau Group, and **blackbirding ships** (see box above) began to bring in captives from the Melanesian Islands to fill the labour shortage. As more traders arrived, the central whaling port of Levuka began to take on the role of Fiji's capital. Beyond the control of the authorities, it soon developed into a debauched frontier-like town characterized by vice and alcoholism.

Meanwhile, Ma'afu continued his advances on Bau and the Americans again pursued their claim with Cakobau. In 1867, with an American warship threatening to bombard Levuka, Cakobau turned to the newly formed Australian-owned **Polynesian Company**, which guaranteed payment of the claim by instalments in return for land around Suva.

The deed of cession, October 10, 1874

With the Americans off his back, Cakobau declared the formation of a **government** in Levuka in 1871 with the backing of a few regional chiefs, and gained formal recognition of his claim to be **king**. Of the many bills passed, most concerned regulations in the sale of land, alcohol and firearms, and a poll and land tax was introduced to raise funds. These laws didn't go down well with some parts of the lawless society in Levuka, who immediately incited riots. Meanwhile, the local Fijians, unable to pay their land taxes, were coerced to work on plantations as their penalty. After two years of government, Cakobau had lost the trust of his people, divided the Levuka traders and accrued a **financial deficit** of £87,000. If that wasn't enough, Ma'afu and his allies in the north had refused to pay their land taxes and the wild Colo hill people of Viti Levu had begun to attack Christian villages.

With the situation looking bleak, Cakobau once again offered to cede Fiji to Britain. This time, anxious that the Americans, Prussians and French were all keen to annex the islands themselves, the new consul, James Goodenough, reported favourably and the British government agreed. On **October 10, 1874**, in a pompous ceremony in Levuka, Cakobau, Ma'afu, other high chiefs and representatives of Queen Victoria signed the deed ceding sovereignty to Britain.

1875	1876	1879	1881
Measles kills a third of the population.	The Great Council of Chiefs is established.	Indian indentured labourers arrive in Levuka.	Rotuma cedes to Fiji to become a British colony.

One of the first and most significant acts to be passed by the first Governor General, Sir Arthur Gordon, was the indefinite **suspension of land sales** in order to protect the Fijian system of *vanua* or ancestral land ownership. The British were keen to preserve the Fijian tribal system in order to rule more efficiently. In 1876 the **Great Council of Chiefs**, or *Bose Levu Vakaturaga*, was established to advise the colonial government on Fijian matters, with Queen Victoria recognized as the most powerful chief.

Indenture and development

Immediately after cession Cakobau and his two sons made a stately visit to Sydney. They returned carrying **measles**, and swiftly passed it on to chiefs from all around Fiji who had come to learn about their adventures overseas. Within two months almost a third of the Fijian population had died from the outbreak. Faced with this crisis, those opposed to cession and Christianity reverted to their heathen ways. A longer-lasting effect of the outbreak was a decimated workforce, and one unwilling to toil in the plantations to add to the coffers of empire. In response Sir Arthur Gordon proposed to bring in **indentured labourers** from India – a move that would have lasting consequences for the evolution of Fijian society.

The first shipment of Indian labourers arrived aboard the *Leonadis* in Levuka in 1879. Between then and 1920 when the scheme was abolished, 60,553 Indians, mostly men, arrived in Fiji. Their working contract or "**girmit**" (from the word "agreement") was to last for five years, after which time the labourer could return home. Although life was harsh on the sugar and copra plantations, the majority opted to stay on in Fiji working as farm hands or clerks and eventually setting up trading stores or leasing small tracts of farmland with the savings they had made; many had also broken caste rules by intermarrying, making life back in India impossible. Word of these new opportunities soon reached India and by 1904, **Indian merchants**, mostly Gujarats and Punjabis of all castes and religions, began to arrive.

The largest employer and backbone of the Fijian economy was the Australian-owned **Colonial Sugar Refining Company (CSR)**, established in 1880. But once the indenture programme ceased in 1920, a series of strikes for better living and working conditions eventually forced CSR to transform its huge plantations into smallholdings, to be leased by Indian farmers. By the 1930s indigenous Fijians were becoming resentful of the wealth and status accrued by the Indians and began to refuse to renew their leases. Pressure was exerted by CSR but it was **Ratu Sir Lala Sukuna**, high chief and Oxford graduate, who persuaded his people to work with the Indians. To protect indigenous interests, the Native Land Trust Ordinance (later to become the present-day iTaukei Land Trust Board) was established to negotiate land tenure leases on behalf of Fijian landowners.

World War II

During World War II, Fiji's strategic position saw it being used as a base by Allied forces. With the British occupied in Singapore and Burma, Fiji's defence was initially placed under the control of **New Zealand**. Three airfields were built at Nadi and a series of gun batteries were erected overlooking Nadi Bay and Suva Harbour. After the Japanese attack on Pearl Harbor in December 1941, the **US Navy** was given control of Nadi Bay.

1882	1904	1920
Suva becomes capital of Fiji.	Indian merchants come to seek their fortunes in Fiji.	Indentured labour is abolished: 60,553 Indians have been brought to Fiji.

With the Japanese encroaching into Papua New Guinea and the Solomons, Fijian soldiers volunteered for combat duty. The Americans immediately recognized their aptitude for **jungle warfare** and sent Fijians to assist in the Solomons, notably at Guadalcanal and Bougainville, where they served with distinction. Indo-Fijians were not encouraged to enlist under the orders of the British who were fearful of giving them military training in light of the independence movement in India.

Independence

As the war ended, politics in Fiji split along ethnic lines. The majority of indigenous Fijians, **iTaukei**, remained content with the colonial administration, ruled in essence by their village chiefs and with both their land and chiefly system protected. **Indo-Fijians** had always wielded economic clout, as demonstrated through sporadic trade union strikes against the CSR, but as their population increased, so too did their political power. Disenchanted with low sugar pay-outs, their inability to buy freehold land, and growing antagonism fuelled by India's independence from Britain in 1947, they became more vocal and determined to oust the colonial government. The British, too, wanted to move on from their control of the islands, but were reluctant to let the Indo-Fijians take their place.

An initial move towards **self-government** occurred in 1953, with the expansion of powers of the Legislative Council. Half its members were elected, a third of whom were iTaukei, a third European and a third Indo-Fijian. By 1963, the Legislative Council became an entirely elected council, except for two members appointed by the Great Council of Chiefs to ensure iTaukei political dominance. But this was not enough for dissident Indo-Fijians. At the forefront of this group was A.D. Patel, founder of the National Federation Party. He demanded independence for Fiji with a government elected by universal suffrage.

The iTaukei became increasingly wary of the Indo-Fijian influence, and fearing loss of land they lobbied Britain for support. As a compromise, the British introduced a form of self-government in 1967, with **Ratu Kamisese Mara** appointed the first Chief Minister and seats allocated ethnically. In April 1970, the Legislative Council was replaced by a parliament with a 52-member House of Representatives. Indo-Fijians and iTaukei were each allocated 22 seats, with the rest elected by "general voters", Europeans, Rotumans and other minority groups. The general voters tended to vote for iTaukei candidates, so Indo-Fijian dominance was held in check.

Full **independence** from Britain was granted on October 10, 1970, ending 96 years of colonial rule. The Alliance Party, headed by **Ratu Sir Kamisese Mara** of the Lau Group, ruled the nation for the first seventeen years of independence and set in motion policies to prioritize **iTaukei affairs** over those of the Indo–Fijian population. The most contentious policy of the era was to restrict land leases to a maximum thirty-year tenure.

The four coups

Simmering ethnic tension, a large, well-funded military and a relatively recent transition to democracy have seen Fiji experience **four coups** since independence. Although all were relatively peaceful in nature, they have permanently altered the political landscape and caused immense damage to Fiji's international reputation.

1930s	1940s	1953
Ratu Sir Lala Sukuna attempts to resolve growing conflicts between ethnic Fijians and Indians.	Fiji used as an Allied base during World War II.	Limited moves towards Fijian self-government, with the establishment of the Legislative Council.

COUP CAST LIST

Ratu Sir Kamisese Mara iTaukei high chief of Lau and leader of the Alliance Party, which ruled Fiji from 1970 to 1987. Accused of being behind the first coup of 1987.

Dr Timoci Bavadra iTaukei from western Viti Levu and founder of the multiracial Fiji Labour Party. Served as prime minister for one month before being ousted by the Rabuka coup.

Sitiveni Rabuka iTaukei of common blood from Cakaudrove in Vanua Levu and colonel in the Fiji Military Force. Carried out Fiji's first military-led coup in May 1987 and was suspiciously silent during the 2000 coup events.

Mahendra Chaudhry Indo-Fijian leader of the Fiji Labour Party, which defeated Rabuka in the 1999 general elections. Appointed as minister of finance in 2007.

George Speight iTaukei civilian who stormed parliament with rebel militants on May 19, 2000, holding Chaudhry and 35 government officials hostage for almost two months.

Laisenia Qarase iTaukei chief from Lau and banker appointed by Bainimarama as interim prime minister in 2000. Introduced contentious ethnically-biased parliamentary bills favouring the iTaukei. Removed from power in a coup led by Bainimarama on Dec 5, 2006, after a year of continuous political tension.

Commodore Frank Bainimarama iTaukei from Tailevu, Commander of the Fiji Military Force and traditional enemy of the Bauan and Lauan aristocracy. He is currently prime minister following his coup of 2006.

Rabuka and the first two coups, 1987

Ratu Mara's Alliance Party dominated Fijian politics in the post-independence years. However, in 1987 a **coalition** of the Indo-Fijian-supported Labour Party and the Fijian breakaway National Federation Party won a historic victory in the April elections. Headed by **Dr Timoci Bavadra**, a chief from the west of Viti Levu, this new-look government seemed to promise a bright and harmonious future. Unfortunately, this hope proved premature, and the government was dogged by the insecurities of the Fijian chiefly system, which not only opposed the political power of the Indo-Fijians but also battled against its own historical factions that placed Western Fiji as a minor authority. Influenced by the racist Taukei Movement, which sanctioned a "Fiji for Fijians only" policy, and encouraged by the authoritarian Methodist Church, **Sitiveni Rabuka**, a little-known military commander from Cakaudrove, stormed parliament on May 14, 1987, and took over the country in a **bloodless coup**. He handed power to the Governor General, **Ratu Penaia Ganilau**, high chief of Cakaudrove.

To Rabuka's surprise, Ratu Ganilau, a strong supporter of parliamentary democracy, ruled the military takeover unconstitutional and attempted to form a government of national unity comprising both parties. In response Rabuka staged a **second coup** on September 23, 1987. He proclaimed Fiji a **republic**, with the intention to serve only the interests of the Fijian people and to sever all links with the Commonwealth. Under a new **constitution** legalized in 1990 government seats were allocated solely along racial lines and heavily weighted towards indigenous Fijians. Rabuka won the nominally democratic elections which followed in 1992. Flushed with victory, he now set himself above the chiefly hierarchal system that he had initially intended to uphold.

Internal conflict led to Josefata Kamikamica walking out of Rabuka's government with his five seats, causing Rabuka to lose his majority. Elections were forced in 1994 and this time, failing to homogenize the Fijian voters, Rabuka made a

1958	1960s	1970
Death of popular statesman and founder of the Native Land Trust Ordinance, Ratu Sir Lala Sukuna.	Indo-Fijians ramp up their opposition to British rule.	Full independence is granted: Ratu Kamisese Mara becomes Fiji's first Prime Minister.

coalition with the independent General Voters Party, promising a new constitution removing the ethnically biased voting system. Subsequently, Fiji was **readmitted to the Commonwealth** in 1997.

Speight and the third coup, 2000

While Fijian politicians bickered over provincial power struggles, **Mahendra Chaudhry**, the grandson of an indentured labourer, rallied the Indians into a combined force under the Fiji Labour Party and won a resounding victory in the 1999 elections. Aware of the ethnic tension that could result, Chaudhry appointed eleven of the eighteen cabinet posts to indigenous Fijians. Unfortunately, even this was not enough to appease the extreme right.

On May 19, 2000, **George Speight**, a failed indigenous businessman, stormed parliament with a gang of armed thugs and took Chaudhry and his government hostage for 56 days. Whether Speight worked alone in the coup remains uncertain, but it is unlikely. Ratu Mara, at that time president, tried to assume control over the country in a coup within a coup, but was removed by the army commander, **Frank Bainimarama**, on the advice of his colleague and 1987 coup perpetrator Sitiveni Rabuka. A public spat ensued, with Ratu Mara and Rabuka both accusing each other of being behind Speight. Bainimarama, caught in the middle, declared martial law and appointed **Laisenia Qarase**, an ethnic Fijian, as the interim prime minister. Speight was arrested, having been assured sanctuary by Bainimarama, and found guilty of treason – he remains locked up at the Naboro Maximum Security Prison.

On September 2, 2000, an attempted **mutiny** within Bainimarama's army was quashed with the loss of eight lives – again Rabuka was accused of being its instigator. Afraid peace wouldn't last, Qarase resigned as prime minister to ensure the dissolution of parliament and force a general election. Five months later, campaigning under a newly formed SDL party, **Qarase** was returned legally as prime minister. The country regained economic stability but the government introduced several extremely controversial policies, including the **Reconciliation, Tolerance and Unity Bill** (2005) which would pardon all preceding coup perpetrators, and the **Qoliqoli Bill** (2006), which entrusted all beaches, lagoons and reefs to indigenous landowners with strong implications for the tourism industry.

Bainimarama and the fourth coup, 2006

Commodore Frank Bainimarama, head of Fiji's oversized military forces, had publicly disapproved of Qarase's contention of the 2001 elections, claiming that it had been a condition of his appointment as interim prime minister after the 2000 coup that he would not stand for re-election. Bainimarama was hell-bent on prosecuting all those involved in the previous coups, regardless of chiefly status, and on undertaking the even greater task of weeding out the **corruption** and nepotism rife among Qarase's highly paid and bumbling senior civil servants. Despite a very public war of words between the two, Qarase and his SDL party were returned to power in the general elections of May 2006.

By October, Bainimarama had issued a number of demands to the Qarase government relating to corruption and bringing the 2000 coup perpetrators to justice. A three-month deadline was set and when it came and went he announced that the

1987	1988–1996	1992	1999
Army colonel Sitiveni Rabuka leads two coups against the rising threat of Indo-Fijians.	Indo-Fijians emigrate in their droves, mostly to New Zealand and Canada.	Democratic elections won by Rabuka.	Mahendra Chaudhry becomes the first Indo-Fijian prime minister.

Fijian military was taking control of the country in a televised address on **December 5, 2006**. Qarase was flown to his home island of Vanua Balavu in Lau. The coup, Fiji's fourth, had been widely expected and there was little disruption to daily life apart from army roadblocks. Foreign governments, particularly **Australia** and **New Zealand**, condemned the coup as illegal and issued stern advisories against all travel to Fiji, paralyzing the country's tourist industry.

Post-coup Fiji

In order to appease the international community, Bainimarama promised **democratic elections** for March 2009 and established a multiracial interim government that included Mahendra Chaudhry as minister of finance, with Bainimarama acting as interim prime minister. However, a major constitutional crisis and the ensuing disagreement over the proposed **People's Charter for Change, Peace and Progress** prevented elections from taking place. A two-year period of **Public Emergency Regulations** followed, clamping down on the media and curtailing freedom of speech and assembly.

In 2013, Fiji's **Fourth Constitution** was signed into law, effectively putting an end to race-based electoral rolls and formally dissolving both the Senate and Great Council of Chiefs. In 2014, Bainimarama's FijiFirst government was endorsed by the majority of Fijians when it won **free elections** with almost sixty percent of the general vote. In recognition of this, Fiji was reinstated as a member of the Commonwealth for the second time in its short history.

Bainimarama has received widespread praise for his work in reducing the power of the archaic chiefdoms, cleaning up corruption and nepotism and making the country democratic for all races. However, human rights advocates, including Amnesty International, have been critical of the sometimes brutal methods used to achieve these goals. The **media** remains parochial and bland, much of it owned (FBC) or influenced by the government: staff working in independent and local media have suffered intimidation, and several expat publishers have been expelled from the country for innocuous reasons. It's rare to hear criticism of the government in any form except from overseas blogs; see ⓦtruthforfiji.com or ⓦfijileaks.com for further information.

There's no doubt that Bainimarama's FijiFirst party has improved the lives of many Fijians, building roads, schools, village health centres and, of course, national unity. However, opposition parties are critical of his resolute support for Attorney General **Aiyaz Sayed-Khaiyum**: many traditional iTaukei suspect that Sayed-Khaiyum is the real power behind the throne, possibly in some sort of Islamic conspiracy, and that Bainimarama simply benefits financially from the arrangement. Anti-Muslim sentiment came to the fore in 2015 when sixty iTaukei were arrested on sedition charges after plotting a separatist Christian State for Ra in northern Viti Levu; sixteen remain on trial.

Ground-roots condemnation of Bainimarama surfaced again in 2016 when the government failed to act quickly in the aftermath of **Cyclone Winston**, waiting instead for international aid agencies to take responsibility. There is also real concern among economists that **government borrowing** for its nation-building projects will become a burden to the country's future development. Despite these

2000	2000	2006	2010
George Speight stages a third coup, holding Prime Minister Chaudhry hostage.	Army commander Frank Bainimarama intervenes and removes Speight.	Bainimarama stages a fourth coup in attempt to prosecute previous insurgents.	All citizens are officially known as Fijian: indigenous Fijians are officially called iTaukei.

WHAT'S IN A NAME?

Under Fiji's former constitution only the indigenous people were known as "Fijian" and those of Indian heritage were called "Indians". One of Frank Bainimarama's most important acts was to make Fiji a non-racist, all-encompassing country. In 2010, Bainimarama introduced laws allowing any citizen of Fiji to call themselves **Fijian**, not just the indigenous people – and this was written into the Constitution in 2013. The name **iTaukei**, meaning indigenous in the Bauan language, is used to identify the ethnic people, those Fijians that form part of the Native Land Registrar and can claim ancestral land through a *mataqali*. Those who claim descent from the Indian subcontinent are identified as **Indo-Fijians**, although the pre-2010 term of Fiji-Indian is still widely used.

failings, the **2017 general election** is expected to be a comfortable victory for Bainimarama over his old adversary, Rabuka, leader of SODELPA, the iTaukei traditionalist opposition party.

Tourism and the economy

Fiji's great economic hope lies in **tourism** and, fickle though the industry can be, visitor numbers have bounced back after each coup. However, with the proliferation of overseas investors in the industry, and the domination of large international brands, it is increasingly difficult to ensure that tourist profits are reinvested in Fiji. The imposition of a sixteen percent tourist tax, on top of the mandatory nine percent VAT, has gone some way to address this.

Tourism aside, the future of industry on the islands looks bleak. The country's dependence on imported produce has crippled Fiji's balance of trade. **Sugar**, once the mainstay of foreign income has slipped desperately in price, although preferential price agreements from the EU are in place until 2023. **Fishing** rights within Fiji's huge Exclusive Economic Zone offer some hope, but without a policing unit to rid its waters of illegal longline Taiwanese fishing vessels, there is real concern about the rapid depletion of fish stocks. Fiji's greatest success in recent years has been the export of bottled drinking **water** – several brands, especially Fiji Water, now compete successfully in global markets – and the establishment of international **call centres** in Suva harnessing the Fijians' beautifully spoken English and friendly nature.

2014	2016	2017
Bainimarama, having resigned from the military, wins democratic elections.	Tropical Cyclone Winston rips through Fiji causing 44 deaths and widespread damage.	General elections pit past coup leaders: Bainimarama's FijiFirst party versus Rabuka's SODELPA.

Society and culture

Fijian society is essentially split into two groups: indigenous or iTaukei Fijians, and the "Indo-Fijian" minority. iTaukei culture is a unique blend of Melanesian and Polynesian tradition influenced by rigid Methodist Christianity introduced in the nineteenth century. Indo-Fijians maintain Hindu, Sikh and Muslim customs that were brought to the islands by indentured labourers from the Indian subcontinent. Other smaller minority groups include the Chinese, as well as other Pacific Islanders such as the Rotumans and Banabans.

iTaukei

Indigenous Fijians, the **iTaukei**, are bound in a strict hierarchal order based on a loyalty to their home village and tribe, an attachment which connects them in a broader sense to the land or *vanua*. At the pinnacle of this hierarchy sit the **chiefs** or *ratu*, whose titles are inherited through the paternal lineage.

The tribal structure

Fiji is split into three **confederacies** or tribal unions: Burebasaga (southern and western Viti Levu, Rewa and Kadavu); Tovata (northern Fiji and the Lau Group); and Kubuna (eastern Viti Levu, excluding Rewa, and Lomaiviti). Kubuna is traditionally considered the most powerful, and was once ruled by Cakobau (see p.223), who became King of Fiji in 1871. Tovata is the smallest but has been the most politically successful in recent times, contributing two post-independence prime ministers (Ratu Sir Kamisese Mara and Laisenia Qarase). Burebasaga is the largest union, incorporating Suva, Lautoka and Nadi, and is the only one permitting a woman to be its paramount chief.

Each confederacy is made up of a collection of **yavusa** or tribes. Each tribe usually lives in one village and is subdivided into **mataqali** or clans. There are usually between three and six *mataqali* in a tribe. Each has a prescribed role within the village – the chiefly *mataqali* is known as the *turaga* and it is from here that the *yavusa*'s high chief is selected. The final order in the hierarchy is the **tokatoka**, or extended household, which binds closely related families. Within the *tokatoka* are individual households known as *vuvale*, and these are presided over by the senior male. All iTaukei can thus define their position in society by declaring their family name, *tokatoka*, *mataqali* and *yavusa*.

Administration and village law

For administrative purposes, the colonial government divided Fiji into four geographic areas – Western, Central, Eastern and Northern – made up of fourteen **provinces**, or *yasana*. These divisions still apply today. Within each province are a number of districts known as *tikina* which share a common pool of amenities such as health centres and schools. Villages are each expected to elect an administrator or **turaga ni koro** to enforce government rules. It is the *turaga ni koro* whom visitors should address when first entering a village, and not the chief, who is considered above such matters.

In most instances, **village law** takes precedence over the law of the land. For example, if a theft takes place, the suspect's family is advised and expected to punish the wrongdoer and seek forgiveness for the crime, usually by presenting food to the victim. Should this fail to resolve the matter, the *tokatoka* are gathered at a formal *yaqona* ceremony at which the individual is shamed and held accountable. Persistent offenders are dealt with by the leader of the *mataqali*, who in extreme cases may insist on a

VANUA – THE LAND, SPIRITS AND PEOPLE

The concept of **vanua** has always been incredibly important to the iTaukei. While the meaning of the word relates directly to the land, the concept includes the godly spirits imbued in the land (usually living in a pool, banyan tree, cave or unusual rock feature); the ancestral spirits living in sacred, often taboo sites; and the group of people or clan who lived off the land and passed down mana or power through the male lineage. Each clan had sacred totems, usually three, including a tree, an animal or fish, and a plant or root crop. It was forbidden to harm, eat or even talk about the totems, as to do so caused sickness and sometimes death to the culprits. In such cases, massage was performed to rid the body of the sickness. Today, massage is the first cure used for healing sickness and a surprising number of iTaukei still recognize and respect their sacred totems.

public flogging. For serious crimes, for example drug dealing, murder or rape, the *turaga ni koro* steps in to enforce government law. The proposed **Village By-Laws Act**, if passed in parliament, will act as a guideline for the enforcement of these laws.

Land rights

The issue of **land rights** is central to ethnic Fijian culture and identity (see box above). Eighty-seven percent of the country is "native land", owned communally by the *mataqali* and protected by a tenure system introduced by the British to prevent the sale of land to Europeans. Clan chiefs distribute land among their members for building homes or planting gardens for personal use. Should an individual wish to make a profit from the land, or establish a business on it, an official **government lease** must be obtained through the iTaukei Land Trust Board (TLTB). It is from these land leases that the majority of rural Fijians receive an income to support their traditional lifestyles.

Traditional customs

One of Fiji's great achievements has been the retention of **traditional customs** in everyday life, not only within the village community but also throughout the business and political world. The most visible of these traditions is **yaqona drinking** (see box, p.31). The drink, known as *kava* across the rest of the South Pacific, is obtained by pouring water through pounded roots of the *Piper methysticum* plant. It was once a tradition reserved only for high priests and chiefs as a means of communicating with the ancient spirits. In times gone by, the *yaqona* roots were chewed by young maidens to make them soft and then grated and squeezed through hibiscus fibres into a wooden or clay bowl known as the *tanoa*. By the late 1800s, *yaqona* drinking had become the social event it is today and it remains very much at the heart of village culture.

Traditional *yaqona* ceremonies are performed when hosting important visitors or visiting chiefs, or to mark the most important **life celebrations**: the first birthday, marriage and death. Each features elaborate feasts and gift presentations, followed by a **meke** performed by the host. Money for hosting such elaborate events is usually raised by a **soli**, a community fundraising event such as dance exhibitions or selling handicrafts in a nearby town.

Indo-Fijians

First brought to Fiji as indentured labourers, **Indo-Fijians** today make up just over a third of the population. They have integrated well into Fijian society with many in mixed marriages and speaking fluent Bauan in rural areas. Their Indian influence can be seen throughout the islands, especially in the towns and cities of Viti Levu and Vanua Levu, where you'll find colourful temples, mosques and home-made shrines flying red flags. Most of Fiji's small shops, taxis and independent businesses are run by

TABUA

The **tabua**, the tooth of a sperm whale, is a much prized possession in Fijian culture. Usually fashioned into a necklace with coconut fibre, *tabua* were traditionally given for atonement or as a gift between chiefs to request a bonding relationship. Before the whaling days of the 1820s, whales' teeth were extremely rare and other items such as the barb of a stingray or the shell known as *cava* were used as the *tabua*. But with the slaughter of thousands of whales during the mid-nineteenth century, whales' teeth began to circulate around the islands and their symbolic status was established as the norm. Today, *tabua* are still used to settle disputes between villages and are often presented at wedding ceremonies.

Indo-Fijians, many of whom also grow sugarcane on smallholding farms to supplement their income. During the postwar period Indo-Fijians outnumbered indigenous Fijians, though over the last couple of decades, this number has decreased as many of the educated Indo-Fijians have emigrated to Canada, Australia and New Zealand in response to Fiji's repeated coups and lack of prosperity.

When Indian labourers first arrived from the subcontinent under the *girmit* contract, the **caste system** which regulated life back home was instantly shed. Those of different castes were forced to live and work together and inter-caste marriage was common. In time, a form of pidgin Hindi became the universal language of both Hindus and Muslims, with words, phrases and accents borrowed from both English and Fijian. The resulting language, now known as **Fiji-Hindi**, is today almost unintelligible to Indians from the subcontinent.

Fiji's Hindu and Muslim populations share the same **religion** as their forefathers and celebrate all the major festivals. There are noisy celebrations at Diwali (October), face-painting at Holi (March), enthralling firewalking ceremonies (April and September), and feasting at Eid (dates vary with Muslim calendar).

Women in Fiji

Unless born of chiefly status, **women in Fiji** hold few positions of authority and the general attitude among both iTaukei and Indo-Fijians is that a woman's place is at home or as a menial worker. Women received the right to vote in 1963 but appreciation of women's rights and equal opportunities is mostly overlooked by politicians. The nongovernmental Fiji Women's Rights Movement (Ⓦfwrm.org.fj) has aimed to redress this balance since its establishment in 1986 and has set up programmes to encourage women in leadership. By far the greatest concern to women of Fiji is **domestic violence**, accounting for sixty percent of cases reported to the Fiji Women's Crisis Centre (Ⓦfijiwomen.com).

Modern culture

Modern Fijian culture preserves aspects of traditional Fijian and Indian life, but is very strongly influenced by globalization. Brought up with the internet, satellite TV and a strong tourism industry encouraging engagement, young Fijians tend to mimic the trends in modern music and fashion of the West, especially Australia and New Zealand.

Music

A few **Fijian musicians** have established themselves over the past two decades, including female singer Laisa Vulakoro, who blends Fijian folk with R&B in a style of music known locally as vude; and Rotuman/Irish Daniel Rae Costello, who has released over thirty albums and created a fusion style of calypso, Latin and reggae. The most successful Fijian band of recent years is **Rosiloa** (formerly Black Rose), who started out performing covers at tourist resorts in Nadi and ended up selling out gigs across the

South Pacific. Their biggest hit, *Raude*, a blend of traditional meke music mixed with high-tempo dance beats, can be heard on their debut album *Voices of Nature* (2000). More recent bands and musicians that have made a name for themselves playing Fiji's resorts include InsideOut and Makare, vude artists Inoke Kalounisiga and Suliasi Uluilakeba, and hip-hop artists J-Deuce and the Taki Mai Squad. The current music trend in Fiji is **DJ mixes** with a reggae influence, though the soundtrack blasting from buses and cars tends towards cheesy **pop**.

Film

Fiji's first and most celebrated native **film**, *The Land Has Eyes*, premiered at the Sundance Film Festival in 2004. Directed by Vilsoni Hereniko and filmed mostly on Rotuma, the film is a fabulous low-budget depiction of the islanders' conflicting attitudes to change. Focusing on the struggle of a young Rotuman girl caught between two worlds – the traditional life on Rotuma and a possible scholarship to the Fijian mainland – the film shares parallels with the internationally successful Maori film *Whale Rider*. Fiji has also proved a popular location for **Hollywood films** including *Blue Lagoon* (1979), *Return to the Blue Lagoon* (1991*)* and *Castaway* (2001), as well as the forgettable sequel to snake horror *Anaconda* (2004) and the suspense thriller *Boot Camp* (2008). More recently, several of Fiji's stunning islands have served as locations for American and Australian **reality TV shows**: the most prominent is *Survivor*, which filmed US seasons 33–36 on Mana Island in the Mamanucas in 2016 and 2017.

Art and craft

Contemporary Fijian **art and craft** reflects tradition, with paintings made upon *tapa* cloth and the wooden designs of war clubs, priest dishes and *tanoa* bowls providing inspiration. You can view displays and sometimes performing arts at the Oceania Centre for Arts and Culture (☎323 2832), part of the University of the South Pacific in Suva.

Sport

For a tiny nation, Fiji has had a significant impact in the world of sport. **Rugby Union** is a particular obsession and fills the back (and often front) pages of all the daily newspapers. The Fijian team first won the prestigious Hong Kong Sevens in 1997, with the flamboyant Waisale Serevi, then won again in 1998 and 1999. The national team was crowned champions of the World Rugby Sevens Series in 2006, with Serevi as player-coach, then went on to win the series title again in 2015 and 2016. The Sevens team's greatest triumph, however, was to bring home Fiji's first ever Olympic medal – gold, no less – from Rio in 2016: the country celebrated with four days of public holiday.

The full **fifteen-a-side** team has also excelled on the global stage, though it never quite matches the high expectations of its people – the national team reached the last eight of the 2007 Rugby World Cup, and were prevented from reaching the quarter finals in 2011 by a thumping Welsh victory. Fiji was crowned champions of the Pacific Nations Cup in 2013 and 2015, leading to high hopes for the 2015 Rugby World Cup – sadly, these weren't fulfilled, though the team received great credit for its dogged performances against hosts England, Australia and Wales. In 2016, Fiji again won the Pacific Nations Cup in a tri-tournament with Samoa and Tonga. A handful of **Fiji-born players**, including Lote Tuqiri and Tevita Kuridrani, have represented Australia, while youngster Waisake Naholo made his All Blacks debut in 2015.

Fiji's top international **golfer** is **Vijay Singh** who claimed the World Number One title from Tiger Woods between 2004 and 2005. He won three major championships (The Masters, 2000; PGA Championship, 1998 and 2004), and still plays today in seniors tournaments – not bad considering he used to practise with palm nuts on the beach as a child in Nadi. Other sports Fiji has excelled at on the world stage include netball, lawn bowls and judo.

Wildlife

The most obvious natural wonders of Fiji are to be found in its vast ocean habitats, littered with diverse coral reefs and bursting with over four thousand species of fish. Equally fascinating are the islands' steamy rainforests and mangroves, thick in vegetation and home to an elusive and vivid collection of native birds, though, with the exception of bats, devoid of any native mammals.

As with many isolated island groups, Fiji's terrestrial and freshwater ecosystems are particularly rich in **endemic species** (unique occurrences of species within a limited geographic area). Almost a thousand have been documented and over half of the country's plant species are unique to the islands.

Coral reefs and marine life

Fiji has some of the most accessible **coral reefs** in the world, often starting just metres from the beach and extending along veins or passages to the steep drop-offs of the fringing reefs where **reef sharks** or spinner dolphins can often be spotted. Deep, rich currents support large pelagic fish including tuna and trevally as well as bull, tiger and hammerhead sharks. Humpback **whales**, once frequent visitors between May and October, are now seldom encountered, with only a handful of sightings each year mostly around Lomaiviti, though smaller **pilot whales** can be seen year-round.

Extensive **barrier reefs** flank most of the larger volcanic islands. The longest is the Great Sea Reef off Vanua Levu, which has been ranked as globally significant owing to its unique diversity and exceptional level of endemic species. Other globally important **reef system**s include the Lomaiviti Triangle in the Koro Sea as well as the isolated reefs of Rotuma which support unique coral species. Smaller **patch reefs** can be found within the huge lagoon system of the Mamanucas Group and make popular snorkelling and diving spots. In the shallow lagoons of Viti Levu, those reefs not damaged by fishing are increasingly becoming bleached as a result of rising sea temperatures.

The reef

The building block of all coral reefs is the **coral polyp**, a small spineless animal similar to an anemone with a series of six or eight tentacles. In **hard corals**, the polyp uses calcium carbonate from seawater to build itself a tough, cup-shaped skeleton. Polyps grow

---

THE RISING OF THE BALOLO

This fascinating annual natural event occurs at various locations around the Pacific, but most prolifically in Fiji. The **balolo** (*Eunice viridis*) is a long spaghetti worm that lives deep in the coral reef. On two nights each year the male and female worms release their tails, containing sperm or eggs, to the surface in a perfectly synchronized spawning event. Among Fijians the worm's tail is a delicacy. Villagers head out to the reefs to gather the tails before the sun rises when they melt into a gooey mess. The worm is eaten raw or fried and said to taste like caviar. The larger of the two risings is known as the *Vula i Balolo Levu*, and occurs at high tide at the last quarter of the moon in either October or November.

On Vanua Levu, the appearance of the *balolo* coincides with the arrival of a deep-water fish called **deu** which swims up the mangrove estuaries to lay its eggs. Fijian women from villages along the southeast coast gather in the rivers to catch the deu with nets – if a lady doesn't catch one she's believed to have committed adultery and may be banished from the village for a year.

together in colonies of thousands, gradually constructing the reefs we see today. **Soft corals**, particularly common in Fiji, do not build skeletons and are soft or leathery in texture. They are found only in rich nutrient-fed currents and at lower light intensities.

Coral reefs are extremely sensitive to climatic conditions, partly due to their symbiotic relationship with a type of algae known as **zooxanthellae**. These algae live within the coral polyp and convert ocean nutrients through photosynthesis into food. Zooxanthellae also produce a range of pigments which give the otherwise clear, white coral its beautiful colour. Zooxanthellae depend on **light** for photosynthesis which is why corals can only thrive in clear waters less than 50m deep. Ideal water temperatures range between 24°C and 29°C, hence the large profusion of reefs in Fiji. If water temperatures change, the polyps stop growing and may expel the zooxanthellae, leading to the effect known as **coral bleaching**.

Like most of the world's coral reefs, sustained stress is causing concern for the **future of Fiji's reefs**, with damage from bleaching increasing as seawater temperatures frequently rise above 30°C between December and March. In addition, long-term harm is caused by the proliferation of the crown of thorns starfish which eats the coral; invasive algal blooms which prevent the coral from obtaining light; long-line fishing which significantly reduces fish stocks; and tourists' sunscreens containing the common chemical oxybenzone. Furthermore, 2016's Cyclone Winston caused significant damage to several of Fiji's reefs, with those around the Lomaiviti and Lau groups suffering the worst effects.

Reef fish

In almost every lagoon you'll find a huge range of small **reef fish**, some darting in and out of the coral, others coalescing in great schools.

Perhaps the most iconic reef fish is the orange and white **clown anemonefish**. Clownfish are found weaving through the tentacles of stinging sea anemones with which they form a symbiotic relationship. Although they live in pairs as lifetime partners, you may notice a third, smaller clown fish hanging around. This is a non-mating male who functions as a kind of insurance policy. If the female clown fish dies, the dominant male changes sex and the smaller fish takes over as the male. Surprisingly feisty, clown fish will rush up to your mask if you get too close.

Closely related to the clownfish is the ubiquitous **damselfish**. Only around 5cm from nose to tail, damselfish come in a huge range of colours, the most vivid being the golden and black-and-white striped versions. Larger but just as colourful are the elegant **butterflyfish** and **angelfish**. Difficult to tell apart, these species both whizz around the reef in pairs. If you can get up close you may notice a small spine by the gills that indicates an angelfish rather than a butterflyfish. Also possessing a sharp spine is the aptly named **surgeonfish**, a streamlined version of the angelfish often found in large schools.

One of the few fish you can hear underwater is the **parrotfish**, who munch away at the reef making a distinctive scraping sound with their sharp, beaked mouth. Larger reef fish found in lagoons include the thick-lipped, grumpy-looking **grouper** and the long, streamlined **barracuda**, who often file past in squadrons.

Sharks

Of the dozens of shark species found in Fijian waters, by far the most common are the smaller **reef sharks** (blacktips, whitetips and, to a lesser extent, grey reef). These elegant shallow-water predators seldom reach over 2m in length and feed on small reef fish, squid and crustaceans. Of the **big sharks**, bulls, tigers and hammerheads are present in Fiji but rarely enter the lagoons, preferring the deep current-fed passages along the outer edges of the reefs, or, as is the case with bull sharks, lurking in the murky coastal waters and mangrove estuaries. **Shark attacks** in Fiji are incredibly rare and it's commonly believed among Fijians that Dakuwaqa, the shark god, protects them.

DO NOT DISTURB!

Triggerfish Fiercely territorial, the brightly coloured triggerfish has an unnerving habit of rushing full speed towards divers encroaching on its space. It has small but sharp teeth and can give a nasty nip.

Lionfish Named after its large mane of feathers, this beautiful fish is often seen hovering at reef walls. Between the feathers is a set of sharp, venomous spines that can deliver a painful sting.

Moray eel Growing up to 3m in length, moray eels are nocturnal predators with sharp teeth and large, gaping jaws. By day they rest in crevices and holes in the reef, occasionally poking their heads out to have a look around. They will only bite humans if provoked.

Pufferfish The most poisonous marine animal in the world, pufferfish blow themselves up into a ball when threatened – an obvious sign to leave well alone.

Rays

Three types of ray are found in Fiji. The largest is the bat-like **manta ray** that can grow to over 4m in width and can be seen in numbers feeding in passages around Drawaqa, in the Yasawa Islands, and Vuro, off Kadavu. The smaller **stingray** is more widespread but harder to spot, preferring to bury itself in the sandy bottom of lagoons. Armed with a razor-sharp venomous barb, stingrays only present a danger when stood upon – always look before settling on a patch of sand. The rarest type of ray in Fiji is the beautiful **spotted eagle ray**. This species, which features numerous white spots on an inky blue body, hunts in the open ocean.

Turtles

Five species of **sea turtle** – loggerhead, leatherback, green, hawksbill and Olive Ridley – lay their eggs deep in the sand of Fiji's beaches, particularly on the coral cays of the Mamanucas and the secluded beaches of Kadavu, the Yasawa Islands and Lau Group. Hawksbill and green turtles are the most common, and can be found in Fiji's oceans year-round while the giant leatherbacks and the rare Olive Ridley only visit during the nesting season (Nov–Feb). It's estimated that there are between 300 and 500 nesting sites in Fiji, with each nest holding between 80 and 200 eggs – the baby turtles emerge en masse after two months.

In Fijian culture, vonu or turtles, were once considered a delicacy and were an important ceremonial meat for chiefs. Today, they are legally protected as an endangered species and most Fijians refrain from eating them, though they are still illegally harvested for chiefly ceremonial functions.

Invertebrates

Marine **invertebrates** include crustaceans, molluscs and starfish as well as sponges and sea anemones. One of the most fascinating is the colourful **nudibranch** or "sea slug". Tiny creatures, barely the width of a fingernail, nudibranchs come in over three thousand varieties. Their Latin name means "naked gills" and refers to the feather-like appendages above their bodies. Also found crawling across the reef are tiny **coral shrimps**. Certain species of shrimp creep into the mouths of reef fish to clear away parasites. Found on the bottom of shallow lagoons is the leathery **sea cucumber**, the vacuum cleaner of the seabed: also known as "bêche de mer", it's considered a delicacy in China.

The islands' seagrass beds and coral reefs also provide habitats for three species of **sea snakes** including the distinctive black-and-white banded sea snake. **Hermit crabs** in stolen shells can be seen crawling around most beaches leaving curious trails in their wake, while massive **coconut crabs**, whose claws are so powerful that they can rip through the husk of a coconut, make a tasty meal if caught – a tin strip is often wrapped around the trunk of coconut palms to stop the crab from climbing up to scavenge the nuts.

Seabirds

Nineteen species of endemic **seabird** are found in Fiji's lagoons, most nesting on tiny coral and limestone islands or on cliff edges along the larger islands. The stately **frigate bird** is the largest of this group and its distinctive split tail outline is often seen high in the sky and near the coastline when stormy weather is approaching. Strikingly white **tropicbirds** with long tail feathers are also prolific, as are clumsy-looking oversized **boobies**, along with the smaller terns and noddies which follow each other around on fishing expeditions and dive bomb the lagoons in spectacular fashion. Shearwaters and **reef herons** can be spotted island-wide, cautiously prancing along the beach edge in search of fish.

Mangrove forest

Fiji's eighteen thousand hectares of **mangrove forest** buffer much of the coastline along Viti Levu and Vanua Levu and provide important breeding grounds for many of Fiji's reef fish. They also perform an invaluable role in protecting the coastline from hurricanes and wave erosion. With thick tentacle roots draping from the forest canopy and stumps thrusting upwards from the murky blend of fresh and salt water, these forests are unforgiving environments but incredibly productive. **Birdlife** abounds, with mangrove herons, kingfishers, lories and orange-breasted honey-eaters the most commonly found species. For the Fijians living around the river deltas, the *tiri* (mangrove) offer a plethora of foodstuffs, with an abundance of **small fish** caught in reed traps, shrimps and, most delicious of all, **mud crabs** scooped up in fishing nets.

Rainforests and terrestrial wildlife

Fiji's tropical **rainforests** are incredibly dense, with tall, thin trees entangled with vines and creepers crowding upwards towards the elusive light. Below the canopy, impressive prehistoric-looking **tree ferns** grow in profusion while several beautiful species of **wild orchid** can be found on the forest floor. Of the 1600 known plants found in Fiji, 56 percent are endemic, most found only within the rainforest.

More than forty percent of the forest cover of the islands remains intact, and some islands, such as Taveuni, still have contiguous forest stretching from the high-altitude cloud forest all the way to the coast. The largest tract of virgin primary forest is the Sovi Basin on Viti Levu, which has become an important area for sustaining birdlife. The remainder of Fiji's rainforest has usually been influenced by people, either through logging or farming. On the wet **windward** sides of the islands, Fijian hardwood species such as *kauvula* and *kadamu* are common as well as *dakua*, a softer conifer from the kauri family used locally for furniture making. The heavier hardwoods of *damanu*, *vesi* and *rosawa* have been cut extensively for timber export and craft. Perhaps the most

---

COCONUT – A LIFELINE

The **coconut palm** (*Cocos nucifera*) is a symbol of paradise and lines the shores of most Fijian beaches. For the islanders, it's a symbol of life and once accompanied the early Polynesians on their epic journeys across the Pacific. Its practical uses are considerable: the **leaves** are woven to make hats and baskets and used to thatch roofs, while the rigid discarded midrib of the leaf is gathered to make *sasa* brooms. **Milk** from the young nuts is drunk while the meaty **flesh** is eaten or scraped to make coconut cream. The mature nut has a hard flesh which is dried and cut to make **copra**, from which commercial-grade coconut oil is produced. The hard inner **shell** of the coconut makes a handy bowl traditionally used for *yaqona* drinking (see box, p.31) and to make earrings and other jewellery. The dry stringy fibres of the outer husk are rolled to make *magimagi* (see box, p.183), a coil used for binding bures and for decorative art. Coconut fibres are also perfect for use as kindling and the husks often fuel the village kitchen stove.

beautiful of trees found in the forest is the **banyan**, a member of the fig family. The banyan initially grows as a vine on a host tree before its aerial prop roots descend and embed themselves in the ground, creating huge buttress roots which meander along the forest floor.

The dry **leeward** sides of Fiji's islands were once home to large tracts of casuarinas, ironwood and sandalwood forests. Most of the land is now covered in **grassland** or planted with imported Caribbean pine. The most fertile soil is found along the river valleys, particularly on the larger islands, and this is almost always converted to **sugarcane farmland**.

Several rogue species are beginning to dominate Fiji's native forests, notably the soft-wooded and fast-growing **African tulip** found along riverbeds and the **mahogany tree** introduced over forty years ago. Over forty thousand acres of mahogany plantation are now ready for cultivation, the largest supply of the lucrative hardwood outside Brazil.

Terrestrial birds and animals

Of Fiji's 57 native breeding terrestrial **birds**, the most impressive is the crimson **Kadavu shining parrot**, unique to Kadavu. Other large parrots can be found on Taveuni, Gau and Koro, along with fruit doves, fantails, white-eyes and golden doves which are commonly found throughout Fiji's forests. The **velvet-black silktail** is the most elusive of Fiji's birds and listed as critically endangered, while the vivid **orange dove** is highly sought after by photographers; both are found around Taveuni and parts of Vanua Levu. Almost flightless, **banded rails** can be seen foraging along the beaches of the Mamanucas and Yasawas. The dry grasslands are the preferred hunting grounds for Fiji's **birds of prey**, which include the Fiji goshawk, Pacific harrier and peregrine falcon. Collared lories, parrot finches and honey-eaters can be spotted in urban gardens. The best islands for **birdwatching** are Kadavu and Taveuni, which remain free of the mongoose (see below).

The only terrestrial **mammals** native to Fiji are **bats**, of which there are two endemic species – the Fijian flying fox and the small Fiji blossom bat. Otherwise the islands' largest land-based species are comprised solely of reptiles and amphibians. These include the crested iguana (see box, p.194), two snakes – the Pacific boa and the mildly poisonous but seldom seen Fijian burrowing snake – two frogs and a variety of tiny geckos or skinks. Fiji's forests support a huge range of **insects** including 44 recorded varieties of **butterfly**; most have simple brown and black colourings in order to blend in with the dark foliage. Much more vivid are the **dragonflies**, commonly seen at streams within the forest.

Non-native invasive species

The **mongoose**, often caught scuttling across roads between cane fields, was introduced from India in the 1880s to control rats that were damaging sugar plantations. Without a natural predator they thrived and along with the **mynah**, an aggressive and chatty black-and-white bird introduced at the same time, they have been responsible for chasing much of Fiji's native birdlife away from the coastal areas and into the deep forest. The introduction of the exceptionally ugly **cane toad** from South America in the 1930s to check the spread of cane beetles was similarly short-sighted. When threatened, the cane toad and its tadpoles excrete a milky poison from glands on the back which can kill native wildlife. Unfortunately, the toad is now prolific around Fiji's countryside. In 2000, a pair of **American iguana** were released illegally on Qamea off Taveuni: its offspring have since flourished and crossed over to Taveuni, threatening the flora there (see box, p.207).

Books

Fijian literature has focused mostly on political analysis, with numerous critical writings confronting the country's ethnic problems and military coups. Fiction makes for slim pickings and Fijian books can be hard to find outside of the country. The most reliable source is the USP Book Shop at the University of the South Pacific (☎323 2521, ⓦusp.ac.fj) which will ship books internationally. Other bookshops are listed in the Guide.

HISTORY

R.A. Derrick *A History of Fiji* (Government Press, Fiji). Originally written in 1942, this classic of early Fijian history up to cession in 1874 is arranged thematically, which makes it much more interesting than the usual trawl through dates.

Kim Gravelle *Fiji's Heritage – A History of Fiji* (Tiara Enterprises, Fiji). Thoroughly readable history highlighting fifty important events that have shaped the destiny of the country.

★**Baron Anatole von Hügel** *Fiji Journals 1875–1877* (Fiji Museum Press). Wonderful diary of a young half-British, half-Austrian rogue who tramped around Fiji in the late nineteenth century. Von Hügel made several expeditions into the interior of Viti Levu, collecting many artefacts and drinking vast quantities of *yaqona* along the way. A lively insight into Fijian life during early colonial times.

Rajendra Prasad *Tears in Paradise* (Glade, New Zealand). Documenting the Indian struggle for acceptance and identity, this book is the best of a collection of contemporary writings giving the Indian perspective on the last 125 years.

David Routledge *The struggle for power in early Fiji* (Institute of Pacific Studies, Fiji). An academic perspective tracing events from early Fijian history to independence in 1970 – historical photos and engravings keep things lively.

CULTURE AND SOCIETY

Mensah Adinkrah *Crime, Deviance and Delinquency in Fiji* (Fiji Council of Social Services). If you can't quite believe Fiji has a dark side, this thought-provoking collection of essays, balanced with sociological reasoning, makes for essential reading.

Solomoni Biturogoiwasa *My Village, My World: Everyday Life in Nadoria, Fiji* (University of the South Pacific). Refreshingly simple insight into everyday village life, packed with colourful detail.

★**Winston Halapua** *Tradition, Lotu & Militarism in Fiji.* An insider's view of local politics and ethnicity, revealing the deceptive world of self-interest and fascism amongst Fiji's elite.

Asesela Ravuvu *The Facade of Democracy: Fijian Struggles for Political Control* (Reader Publishing, Fiji). An insight into the mind of a Fijian nationalist, critical of both European and Indian involvement in Fijian society.

Sir Vijay R. Singh *Speaking Out* (Knightsbrook, Australia). Not to be confused with the golfer of the same name, the author of this bold collection of thought-provoking articles is one of Fiji's most prominent Indo-Fijian politicians. Focusing on the events of the 1987 and 2000 coups, the book ruffled quite a few feathers, prompting several nationalist politicians to call for it to be banned.

★**Peter Thomson** *Kava in the Blood* (Tandem Press, UK). A recollection of life growing up in Fiji, of serving in the government administration and of confronting and ultimately accepting the hard realities of the coups.

NATURE AND THE ENVIRONMENT

Clare Morrison *Herpetofauna of Fiji* (University of the South Pacific). A little book covering a pretty slim subject in scientific detail, with colour photos of Fiji's reptiles and amphibians.

Dick Watling *A Guide to the Birds of Fiji & Western Polynesia* (Environmental Consultants, Fiji). The birdies' bible, with colour plates and detailed accounts of 173 species found throughout the region.

Dr Michael A. Weiner *Secrets of Fijian Medicine* (University of California Press, US). Records some of Fiji's dying knowledge of traditional medicine. Arranged by type of illness and listing Fijian and English plant names.

TRAVELLERS' TALES

★**Kim Gravelle** *Romancing the Islands* (Graphics Pacific, Fiji). Written by one of the South Pacific's leading photojournalists, Gravelle recounts 44 of his liveliest tales of adventure, all featuring a refreshing hint of humour.

Paul Theroux *Happy Isles of Oceania* (Penguin, US & UK). A good read from one of the few big-name travel writers to have written about the South Pacific. His account of Fiji, one of several island nations covered, portrays some of the less-than-democratic aspects of Fijian society and was felt by many to have cut a little too close to the bone.

J. Maarten Troost *Getting Stoned with Savages* (Broadway Books, US). A witty tale of misadventure that begins in Vanuatu and ends with a candid view of Fiji in the modern world.

FICTION

Robert Campbell *Tradewinds & Treachery* (Steele Roberts, New Zealand). A clash of cultures and ideologies haunts this tale of love in the turbulent years leading up to colonial rule.

Allan Carson *Pacific Intrigue* (Durban House, US). A fast-paced American detective story of Islamic terrorist activity set between Seattle and Suva, touching on the simmering tensions between Fijians and Indians.

★**Daryl Tarte** *Fiji: a Bloody and Lustful Story of Fiji's History* (Pascoe Publishing, Australia). Renowned local writer Tarte permits himself a little bit of fantasy entwined with the facts to produce this fine tale of intrigue in grand Michener-style proportions.

Joseph C. Veramu *Moving through the Streets* (Mana Publications, Fiji). This Suva-set novel by a lecturer at the University of the South Pacific provides a realistic account of the pressures and temptations facing Fiji's urban youth.

DICTIONARIES AND LANGUAGE

A. Capell *The Fijian Dictionary.* Comprehensive dictionary with Fijian/English and English/Fijian.

A.J. Schütz *Say It in Fijian.* Well-written guide to Fijian; includes a small dictionary.

G.B. Milner *Fijian Grammar.* Detailed text covering all grammatical aspects of Fijian.

Language

English is the official language of Fiji, taught and spoken in schools and used in parliament and in business. Throughout the upper strata of Fijian society the language is spoken with great fluency, with an accent not dissimilar to British Received Pronunciation or "Queen's English". Young people speak their own casual blend of English, spoken with a hint of a South African accent, and with words and phrases borrowed from both Bauan and Fiji Hindi.

At home, indigenous Fijians speak one of nine local dialects along with Bauan, the unified Fijian language; Rotumans speak **Rotuman;** and Indo-Fijians speak **Fiji Hindi**, a unique form of Hindustani. Many Indo-Fijians, especially in the rural areas around northern Viti Levu, Vanua Levu and Taveuni, speak Bauan as a third language and some iTaukei speak Fiji Hindi, though the two ethnic groups tend to converse in English. Learning a few basic phrases in either language will raise a smile among the locals.

Fijian

Fijian is part of the Malayo-Polynesian branch of the huge Austronesian family of languages, which stretches from Madagascar to Easter Island, and from Taiwan to New Zealand. Within Fiji, regional isolation has led to the formation of nine distinct dialects, with almost 300 variations within these. For example, the commonly used word "*vinaka*", which in its simplest form means "good", has many variations: "*vinaduriki*" in the Yasawas, "*vina'a*" in Taveuni and "*malo*" in Lau. In the 1840s, the dialect known as **Bauan** was the first version of Fijian to be transcribed into the roman alphabet (by Scottish missionary David Cargill). This has led Bauan to become the most universally accepted type of Fijian, and it is the version taught in schools and used at formal occasions.

The two most difficult aspects of Fijian to a foreign ear are the pronunciation of consonants and the difficulty in differentiating words. Fijian sentences sound as if they are spoken as one long jumbled word with syllables rolling into each other. It is common for Fijians to speak in a **monotone**, with one person talking uninterrupted before the second person speaks – bouncing conversations back and forth is considered impolite. See opposite for details of Fijian **dictionaries** and language textbooks.

Pronunciation

The majority of letters are pronounced as in spoken English, although the first **vowel** in a word is usually emphasized. Some vowels are drawn out, in which case they are marked with a macron (ā). More awkward to pronounce are the **consonants**:

b is pronounced "mb" with a soft m as in number   g has a soft "ng" sound as in singer

c is pronounced as a "th" sound as in mother   q has a harder "ngg" as in finger

d sounds like the "nd" in sandy   r is usually rolled

Once the above system is mastered, **place names** begin to make sense. For example, Lakeba is pronounced "Lakemba", Nadi becomes "Nandi" and Beqa is pronounced "Mbenga".

GREETINGS

The versatile, and ubiquitous, greeting **bula** literally means "live" but is used as a casual "hello" or "how are you" – the reply is "*bula vinaka*". Among Indo-Fijians, **kaise** is the casual greeting to use, but make sure you don't say the iTaukei word *kaisi*, by mistake – it's a derogatory term for a person of the lowest rank.

BASIC PHRASES

hello (polite)	(nī sā) bula	when?	naica?
yes	io	how many?	vica?
no	sega	it's ok	sa vinaka
please	yalo vinaka, mada	no problem	sega na leqa
thank you (very much)	vinaka (vakalevu)	excuse me	tulou
good morning (polite)	(nī sā) yadra	I'm sorry	lomana
what is your name? (polite)	o cei na yacamu (nī)?	go away	lako tani
my name is …	na yacaqu o …	stop!	kua!
where are you from?	o nī lako mai vei?	slow down!	malua!
I'm from …	au lako mai …	one more	dua tale
who?	cei?	see you again	sota tale
where?	vei?	see you tomorrow	sota ni mataka
what?	cawa?	goodbye (polite)	(nī sā) moce

NUMBERS

1	dua	13	tini ka tolu
2	rua	14	tini ka vā
3	tolu	15	tini ka lima
4	vā	16	tini ka ono
5	lima	17	tini ka vitu
6	ono	18	tini ka walu
7	vitu	19	tini ka ciwa
8	walu	20	ruasagavulu
9	ciwa	21	ruasagavulu ka dua
10	tini	30	tolusagavulu
11	tini ka dua	100	dua na drau
12	tini ka rua	1000	dua na udolu

GETTING AROUND

where is the …?	e vai (beka) na …?	farm, garden	teitei
where are you going? (also used as how are you?)	o lai vei?	forest	veikau
		house	vale
nowhere particular (general response)	sega, gāde gā	island	yanuyanu
		mountain	qulunivanua
near	vōleka	road, path	sala
far	yawa	school	koronivuli
let's go	daru lako	shop	sitoa
I am going to …	au lai na …	sleeping house	bure
beach	matāsawa	village	koro

TIMINGS

today	ni kua	late	bera
tomorrow	ni mataka	night	bogi
yesterday	nanoa	ready	vaka rau

USEFUL VOCABULARY

beautiful	totoka	diarrhoea	coka
big, many	levu	difficult	drēdrē
busy, full	osooso	dirty	duka
clean	savata	fishing	siwa
cold	batabatā	hot	katakata
cup	bilo	knife	isele
delicious	maleka	money	ilavo

old	makawa	strong	kaukaua
perhaps	beka	sunny	siga
photo	taba	swim	qalo
possible	rawa	tired	oca
rain	uca	toilet	vale lailai
request	kerekere	too much	rui
sanitary towel	qamuqamu	turtle	vonu
shark	qio	walk	gādē
single, alone	taudua	wind	cagi
small, little	lailai		

FOOD AND DRINK

bele	green vegetable	qari	cooked crab
bulumakau	beef	rourou	spinach
dalo	taro, a root crop	saqa	boiled
ika	fish (general)	tapioca	cassava, root crop
jaina	banana	ura	cooked prawn
kokoda	fish marinated in lime juice	uvi	yam
		vakalolo	pudding made from *dalo* and coconut cream
lolo	coconut cream		
lovo	underground oven		
mai kana!	come and eat!	vua	fruit
niu	coconut	wai	water
ota	seaweed	weleti	papaya/pawpaw

Fiji Hindi

Fiji Hindi, spoken by all Indo-Fijians, is a unique blend of several Hindustani dialects with a smattering of Arabic, English and Fijian words and phrases thrown in. In religious worship, classical Sanskrit written in Devanagari is used and Devanagari is taught in Indian schools. Gujaratis and Sikhs retain closer ties with their traditional languages when speaking among each other.

BASICS

hello (casual, how are you?)	kaise?	please	thoraa
hello (religious greeting)	ram ram, hare krishna	thank you, goodbye	dhanyewaad
hello (Muslim)	salaam walekum	good, I see	achaa
good	achchaa	bad	kharaab
fine, all right (in reply)	thik hae	ok	ha or rite
what is your name?	**tumhar** ke naam konchi he?	come and eat	aao khana khao
		drink, smoke	pio
my name is …	hamar naam hai …	tea	cha
what's this?	honchi he?	warm, hot	garam
how much?	kitna?	wait	sabur karo
yes	ha	sit	baitho
no	nai or na	perhaps	**saait or** shayad
too much	bahut	photograph	chaapaa
I don't want it	nahi magta	see you again	phir milenge
excuse me, sorry	maaf karo		

NUMBERS

1	ek	4	chaar
2	dui	5	paanch
3	tiin	6	chhe

7	saat	10	das
8	aath	100	sao
9	nau	1000	hazaar

INDO-FIJIAN FOOD

archaar	pickles		baked in a tandoor
baigan	eggplant		oven
bhaath	cooked rice	pilau	rice, gently fried with
bhindii	okra		spices
biryani	rice dish of meat or	puri	puffed-up bread,
	vegetables baked		deep-fried and crispy
	with turmeric and	roti	round unleavened
	whole spices		flat-bread, cooked on
chapatti	unleavened		a hot plate
	flat-bread	samosa	stuffed pastry cooked
dhal	lentils, often cooked		in oil
	in soup	thali	combination of
ghee	clarified butter		vegetarian and
gulgula	pancake		sometimes meat
halwa	Indian sweet		dishes with chutney,
korma	meat braised in		pickles, rice, roti and
	yoghurt		dhal; served as a
	sauce (mild)		single meal
masala	curry powder	vindaloo	meat, usually pork,
murga	chicken		seasoned in vinegar
naan	white leavened bread		(hot)

Rotuman

Rotuman is spoken exclusively by the people of Rotuma, a Polynesian island in the far north of Fiji. It has a distinctive word structure featuring metathesis (two vowels following each other but creating two separate quite abrupt sounds) and an extensive use of diphthongs (vowel clusters). To confuse matters further, many words have been borrowed or adapted from Samoan and Tongan. The apostrophe is used between vowels to indicate a glottal stop while the macron (ā) indicates extended vowels as in Fijian. The use of diaeresis (ä) means that a vowel should be pronounced apart from the letter which precedes it.

If you're interested in **studying Rotuman** it's worth getting hold of Elizabeth Inia's *A New Rotuman Dictionary* available from ⓦpacificislandbooks.com. Alternatively, the excellent Rotuman website ⓦrotuma.net has links to sound files of spoken Rotuman.

BASICS

hello	faiäksia noa'ia	please	figalelei
where are you going?	'äe la'se tei?	thank you	faiäksia
what is your name?	sei ta 'ou asa?	yes	'i
my name is ...	'otou asa le ...	no	'igka
what's this?	ka tese te?	goodbye	nonoam

USEFUL WORDS

dance	mak	rest	au'ua se
drink	īom	sea	sasi
eat	äte	sit down	päe se lopo
fishing	hagoat	sleep	mös
hurry up	rue la mij	slow down	ariri'se
plantation	vekaogta	swim, shower	kakou

ROTUMAN DISHES

fekei	sticky, starchy sweet	**tähroro**	fermented coconut milk
porasam	*taro* leaf cooked in		flavoured with chili
	coconut cream		

Glossary

Adi female chiefly title

balabala the trunk of a tree fern, used decoratively in villages and gardens

balolo marine worm living in coral reefs and considered a delicacy

bati warrior

bete priest

bilibili bamboo raft

bilo coconut shell used for drinking *yaqona*

boso slang for "boss"

bure bose meeting hall

bure kalou traditional Fijian temple

chautaal traditional songs sung at the Hindu Holi festival

cobo clapping with cupped hands

copra the dried, oil-yielding kernel of the coconut

dakua popular wood for carving

Daquwaqa Fijian shark god

Degei most revered of the Fijian gods

Diwali Hindu celebration, festival of lights

drua war canoe

Eid Muslim holiday marking the end of Ramadan

Fara Rotuman Christmas festival

girmit labour contract given to Indian indentured labourers

Holi Hindu celebration, festival of colours

ivi Tahitian chestnut tree believed to have spiritual connotations and found in ancient villages

kai colo hill people from the interior of Viti Levu

kai loma people of part Fijian, part European descent

kai viti people of Fiji

kai vulagi people from overseas

kava Polynesian word for *yaqona*

kerekere communal borrowing

lali slit drum hollowed from a hardwood tree

Lapita ancient Pacific Ocean culture named after their distinct style of pottery

loloma affectionate greeting

lotu in broad terms, Christianity or the Church

lovo traditional food cooked in an underground oven

magimagi plaited coconut fibre

mana spiritual power

manumanu the three totems of a clan, usually a fish, an animal and a fruit or tree

masi *tapa* cloth decorated with stencilled designs

masu prayer said before meal

mataqali land-owning clan

meke traditional song and dance performance

qai tattoo

qoliqoli area from high tide mark to the reef edge, perceived by some as public access and others as *mataqali*-owned

Ramadan the Islamic holy month of fasting

rara village green

Ratu male chiefly title

reguregu sniff to the cheeks, used as a greeting between clan members

Ro chiefly title of Rewa, Naitasiri, Namosi and Serua provinces

Roko chiefly title of the Lau Group

salwar kameez traditional dress worn by Muslims

sari traditional Indian dress

sere chant at a *yaqona* ceremony

sevusevu ceremonial offering of *yaqona*

solevu large ceremonial gathering

soli fundraising event

sulu Fijian sarong

suluka home-made, rolled tobacco leaf

tabu forbidden, sometimes sacred

tabua traditional gift, usually a whale's tooth, given in return for a favour or to ask for atonement

tanoa wooden bowl with four or more legs used for preparing *yaqona*

tapa paper cloth made from the mulberry tree, used as traditional dress

taukei original inhabitant; movement for indigenous rights

tauvu tribes sharing the same totemic god

tiri mangrove forests

tokatoka extended household

tualeita ancient pathway connecting villages

Turaga ni vuvale head of the house

Turanga ni koro head of the village

Turanga respected title donating the head of a group of people; old-fashioned address similar to "gentleman"

vanua land to which Fijians are spiritually bound

vasu the concept of a nephew or niece having privileges over an uncle

vesi popular wood for carving

voivoi leaf of the pandanus plant used for weaving

vude Fijian music blending folk and R&B

waqa *yaqona* roots in powder form

yaqona mildly narcotic ceremonial and social drink strained from the root of the *Piper methysticum* plant

yavusa tribe

Small print and index

Rough Guide credits

Editor: Amanda Tomlin
Layout: Ankur Guha
Cartography: Rajesh Chhibber
Picture editor: Michelle Bhatia
Proofreader: Diane Margolis
Managing editor: Andy Turner
Assistant editor: Divya Grace Mathew

Production: Jimmy Lao
Cover photo research: Marta Bescos
Photographer: Chris Christoforo
Editorial assistant: Aimee White
Senior DTP coordinator: Dan May
Programme manager: Gareth Lowe
Publishing director: Georgina Dee

Publishing information

This third edition published November 2017 by
Rough Guides Ltd,
80 Strand, London WC2R 0RL
11, Community Centre, Panchsheel Park,
New Delhi 110017, India
Distributed by Penguin Random House
Penguin Books Ltd, 80 Strand, London WC2R 0RL
Penguin Group (USA), 345 Hudson Street, NY 10014, USA
Penguin Group (Australia), 250 Camberwell Road,
Camberwell, Victoria 3124, Australia
Penguin Group (NZ), 67 Apollo Drive, Mairangi Bay,
Auckland 1310, New Zealand
Penguin Group (South Africa), Block D, Rosebank Office
Park, 181 Jan Smuts Avenue, Parktown North, Gauteng,
South Africa 2193
Rough Guides is represented in Canada by DK Canada, 320
Front Street West, Suite 1400, Toronto, Ontario M5V 3B6
Printed in Singapore
© Rough Guides 2017
Maps © Rough Guides

Help us update

We've gone to a lot of effort to ensure that the third
edition of **The Rough Guide to Fiji** is accurate and up-to-date. However, things change – places get "discovered",
opening hours are notoriously fickle, restaurants and
rooms raise prices or lower standards. If you feel we've got
it wrong or left something out, we'd like to know, and if
you can remember the address, the price, the hours, the
phone number, so much the better.

Please send your comments with the subject line
"**Rough Guide Fiji Update**" to mail@uk.roughguides.com.
We'll credit all contributions and send a copy of the next
edition (or any other Rough Guide if you prefer) for the
very best emails.

A ROUGH GUIDE TO ROUGH GUIDES

Published in 1982, the first Rough Guide – to Greece – was a student scheme that became a
publishing phenomenon. Mark Ellingham, a recent graduate in English from Bristol University,
had been travelling in Greece the previous summer and couldn't find the right guidebook.
With a small group of friends he wrote his own guide, combining a contemporary, journalistic
style with a thoroughly practical approach to travellers' needs.

The immediate success of the book spawned a series that rapidly covered dozens of
destinations. And, in addition to impecunious backpackers, Rough Guides soon acquired a
much broader readership that relished the guides' wit and inquisitiveness as much as their
enthusiastic, critical approach and value-for-money ethos. These days, Rough Guides include
recommendations from budget to luxury and cover more than 120 destinations around the
globe, from Amsterdam to Zanzibar, all regularly updated by our team of roaming writers.

Browse all our latest guides, read inspirational features and book your trip at **roughguides.com**.

ABOUT THE AUTHORS

Since his mid twenties, **Ian Osborn** has lived around the South Pacific with his Rotuman wife, Sia, focusing on photography, travel writing and their tourism business, Beautiful Pacific. Today he splits his time between friends and family in his homeland England, with his student children in Brisbane, and living amongst the community around Wailoaloa in Nadi.

Martin Zatko has written or contributed to almost thirty Rough Guides, including those to Fiji, Korea, China, Japan, Vietnam, Myanmar, Turkey, Morocco and Europe. When not travelling for work he's usually doing much the same for pleasure, but thanks to a fondness for raw fish and coconut milk, his tastebuds would like to stay in the South Pacific indefinitely.

Acknowledgements

Ian Osborn gives special thanks to old friends the Douglas Family, Flo & Noel and also Nigel along with Robbie Rickman of Vuda. Thanks, too, to Sala and Christene McCann in Savusavu and David Patterson for valuable insights into Ovalau as well as John and Marilyn for their hospitality; to Jackie from Captain Cook Cruises for my first glimpses of the remote Lau islands; to Filo, Mere and Lani for the latest gossip in the Yasawas, and to Lailanie who made getting there easy, despite the awful weather. Thanks always to my beautiful wife Sia and our children who gave me the freedom to enjoy my travels around the islands; to Geraldine and little Samurai who made Taveuni even more enjoyable to visit; to Andy and Mandy, book editors, who made this task a lot simpler with their support and efficiency. And lastly, thanks to Fiji

and the people I met in markets, on buses and travelling in small boats for being the beautiful place it is.

Martin Zatko would like to thank the great number of people he met and received assistance from on his way around Fiji, including Charles Hadrill in Korogoto; Andrew Brown on the Coral Coast; Alana Bentley and the team in Pacific Harbour; Sunny and Jenny on the road; Suzie in Suva; Brian Riches in Colo-i-Suva; Adrian and the team in Kadavu; Sofie Kastrup Nissen in Mana; and any number of backpackers by Wailoaloa Beach. He would also like to thank co-author Ian Osborn for his Fiji know-how, Amanda Tomlin for her typically excellent editing work, and Andy Turner at Rough Guides HQ for allowing him to be part of such an enjoyable project.

Readers' updates

Thanks to all the readers who have taken the time to write in with comments and suggestions (and apologies if we've inadvertently omitted or misspelt anyone's name):

John Carlson; Dennis Murphy; Jamie Ragg.

Index

Maps are marked in grey

Map symbols

The symbols below are used on maps throughout the book

✈	International airport	↑	Wind farm	$	Bank
✈	Domestic airport/airstrip	🗼	Lighthouse	🚤	Boat
♦	Place of interest	▯	Tower	— —	Ferry
✉	Post office	⚶	Viewpoint	- - - -	Footpath
ⓘ	Information office	⛰	Mountain range	═══	Road
⊞	Hospital	▲	Mountain peak	•═•═•	Unpaved road
★	Transport stand	⧄	Volcano	▬▬▬	Pedestrian road
⚓	Anchorage	⩗	Spring	▬▬▬	Railway
⛽	Fuel station	ᙏᙏ	Reef	▪	Building
⊥	Gardens	⌒	Cave	⊞	Church (town)
⚲	Swimming pool	⚉	Waterfall	▢	Market
⚐	Golf course	🏰	Mosque	⬭	Stadium
⊙	War memorial	⚜	Temple	⬧ ▢	National Reserve/park
⊠	Gate	ⴕ	Church (regional)	▢	Beach
✎	Dam	🏛	Monument	▢	Mangrove

Listings key

■ Accommodation
● Eating
■ Drinking/nightlife/bar/club
● Shopping

ROUGH GUIDES

Long bus journey?
Phone run out of juice?

👉 **TEST YOUR KNOWLEDGE** WITH OUR ROUGH GUIDES TRAVEL QUIZ

1 Denim, the pencil, the stethoscope and the hot-air balloon were all invented in which country?

a. Italy
b. France
c. Germany
d. Switzerland

2 What is the currency of Vietnam?

a. Dong
b. Yuan
c. Baht
d. Kip

3 In which city would you find the Majorelle Garden?

a. Marseille
b. Marrakesh
c. Tunis
d. Malaga

4 What is the busiest airport in the world?

a. London Heathrow
b. Tokyo International
c. Chicago O'Hare
d. Hartsfield-Jackson Atlanta International

5 Which of these countries does not have the equator running through it?

a. Brazil
b. Tanzania
c. Indonesia
d. Colombia

6 Which country has the most UNESCO World Heritage Sites?

a. Mexico
b. France
c. Italy
d. India

7 What is the principal religion of Japan?

a. Confucianism
b. Buddhism
c. Jainism
d. Shinto

8 Every July in Sonkajärvi, central Finland, contestants gather for the World Championships of which sport?

a. Zorbing
b. Wife-carrying
c. Chess-boxing
d. Extreme ironing

9 What colour are post boxes in Germany?

a. Red
b. Green
c. Blue
d. Yellow

10 For three days each April during Songkran festival in Thailand, people take to the streets to throw what at each other?

a. Water
b. Oranges
c. Tomatoes
d. Underwear

💡 For more quizzes, competitions and inspirational features go to **roughguides.com**

1:b / 2:a / 3:b / 4:d / 5:b / 6:c / 7:d / 8:b / 9:d / 10:a